ISBN 978-1-332-03460-4
PIBN 10273145

This book is a reproduction of an important historical work. Forgotten Books uses
state-of-the-art technology to digitally reconstruct the work, preserving the original format
whilst repairing imperfections present in the aged copy. In rare cases, an imperfection in
the original, such as a blemish or missing page, may be replicated in our edition. We do,
however, repair the vast majority of imperfections successfully; any imperfections that
remain are intentionally left to preserve the state of such historical works.

1 MONTH OF
FREE
READING

at

www.ForgottenBooks.com

By purchasing this book you are eligible for one month membership to ForgottenBooks.com, giving you unlimited access to our entire collection of over 700,000 titles via our web site and mobile apps.

To claim your free month visit:

www.forgottenbooks.com/free273145

How to Handle and Educate Vicious Horses
Together With Hints on the Training and Health of Dogs, by Oscar R. Gleason

Pheasants in Covert and Aviary
by Frank Townend Barton

Pets and How to Care for Them
by Lee S. Crandall

Studies in Horse Breeding
Illustrated Treatise on the Science and Practice of the Breeding of Horses, by G. L. Carlson

Pets for Pleasure and Profit
by Alpheus Hyatt Verrill

Some Pekingese Pets
by M. N. Daniel

Manual of Farm Animals
by Merritt W. Harper

The Aquarium
by Unknown Author

Pets
Their History and Care, by Lee S. Crandall

Man's Best Friend, the Dog
A Treatise Upon the Dog, by George B. Taylor

Concerning Cats
My Own and Some Others, by Helen Maria Winslow

Rabbit and Cat Diseases
by Charles Greatley Saunders

Things Worth Knowing About Horses
by Harry Hieover

The Angora Cat
How to Breed Train and Keep It, by Robert Kent James

Notes on Pet Monkeys and How to Manage Them
by Arthur Henry Patterson

Care and Management of Rabbits
by Chesla Clella Sherlock

Training the Dog
by Robert S. Lemmon

Garden and Aviary Birds of India
by Frank Finn

Biggle Pet Book
by Jacob Biggle

Pets of the Household
Their Care in Health and Disease, by Thomas M. Earl

TOHO.

London. Pannoned from a sketch by his Brother Edwin.

Pub.d Oct.1 1828 by S.rwood Jones & C.o

THE

Shooter's Companion;

OR,

A description of POINTERS and
SETTERS, &c. as well as of
those Birds which are the objects
of pursuit.
Of the Breeding of Pointers and Setters, the Diseases to which they
are liable, and the modes of cure.
Of Training Dogs for the Gun.
Of Scent; and the reason why one
Dog's Sense of Smell is superior to another's.
The Fowling Piece fully considered,
particularly as it relates to the
use of Percussion Powder.

Of Percussion Powder, and the best
method of making it.
Of Gunpowder.
Shooting illustrated, and the Art of
Shooting Flying simplified and
clearly laid down.
The Game Laws familiarly explained, and illustrated by a variety
of cases.
Of Wild Fowl and Fen Shooting;
as well as every information connected with the use of the Fowling Piece.

BY T. B. JOHNSON.

SECOND EDITION,

IMPROVED, AND VERY CONSIDERABLY ENLARGED.

With Plates.

LONDON
Printed for SHERWOOD, JONES, & Co.
PATERNOSTER ROW.

1823

JOHNSON, PRINTER, LIVERPOOL.

VALUABLE SPORTING BOOKS,

Printed for Sherwood, Jones, & Co. Paternoster Row, London.

1.—SCOTT'S HORSES AND DOGS.

Beautifully printed in Quarto, and embellished with *Forty* highly-finished Copper-plate Engravings and numerous Wood Cuts, price Three Guineas in boards,

THE SPORTSMAN'S REPOSITORY; comprising a Series of highly-finished Engravings, representing the HORSE and the DOG in all their varieties, executed in the Line Manner, by Mr. JOHN SCOTT, from original Paintings by *Marshall, Reinagle, Gilpin, Stubbs,* and *Cooper ;*—accompanied with a comprehensive historical and systematic Description of the different Species of each, their appropriate Uses, Management, and Improvement; interspersed with Anecdotes of the most celebrated Horses and Dogs, and their Proprietors; also, a Variety of practical Information on Training and the Amusements of the Field.

By the Author of "BRITISH FIELD SPORTS."

.*. It may be had in *Six Parts,* price 10s. 6d. each.

2. THOUGHTS on FOX and HARE HUNTING: in a series of Letters to a Friend. By PETER BECKFORD, Esq. With numerous Cuts. 14s.

3. AN ESSAY on HUNTING ; in which a great variety of most important Information is communicated under the Heads, *Hunting, Lawfulness, Benefits, Pleasure, Pastime, Game, Scent, Hounds, the Horse, Huntsman, Sagacity, &c.* In 8vo. 7s.—In 4to, 12.

4. BRITISH FIELD SPORTS; embracing Practical Instructions in *Shooting, Hunting, Coursing, Racing, Fishing, &c.;* with Observations on the Breaking and Training of Dogs and Horses; also, on the Management of Fowling Pieces, and all other Sporting Implements. By W. H. SCOTT. *Second Edition ;* with upwards of *Sixty* highly-finished Engravings. £1. 18s. demy 8vo. or, on royal paper, with *Proof Plates,* £3. 3s.

5. A PRACTICAL ESSAY on BREAKING and TRAINING the ENGLISH SPANIEL and POINTER: with Instructions for SHOOTING FLYING. By V. DOBSON, Esq. *Second Edition.* 10s. 6d.

6. THE SPORTSMAN'S PROGRESS; a Poem, descriptive of the Pleasures derived from FIELD SPORTS : with Thirteen Wood Cuts. 1s.

7. SOMERVILE'S celebrated Poem of the CHASE ; to which is annexed, his Poem of FIELD SPORTS: with Memoirs of the Author, and an Essay on the Chase, by EDWARD TOPHAM, Esq. The Engravings, by Mr. John Scott. 6s.

8. THE ANGLER; a Poem, in Ten Cantos; comprising proper Instructions in the Art, with Rules to choose Fishing Rods, Lines, Hooks, Floats, Baits, and to make Artificial Flies; Receipts for Pastes, &c. By T. P. LATHY, Esq. With upwards of 20 Wood Cuts. 10s. 6d.

9. SPORTING ANECDOTES, Original and Selected; forming a complete Delineation of the *Sporting World.* By PIERCE EGAN, 9s.

10. THE SPORTSMAN'S VOCAL LIBRARY; containing nearly 400 Songs relating to Hunting, Racing, Shooting, Angling, Hawking, Archery, &c. 9s.

A New Work on SPORTING SUBJECTS, *published Monthly, entitled*

THE ANNALS of SPORTING, and FANCY GA-ZETTE; a *Magazine* entirely appropriated to *Sporting Subjects* and *Fancy Pursuits :* containing every thing worthy of. Remark on *Hunting, Shooting, Coursing, Racing, Fishing, Cocking, Archery, Pugilism, Wrestling, Single Stick, Pedestrianism, Cricket, Billiards, Rowing, Sailing, &c.;* accompanied with striking *Representations* of the various Subjects.

This interesting work is regularly published on the first day of every month, price 2s. 6d.; and, it is intended, by a decided superiority in *Paper, Printing,* and *Illustration,* to continue to place the ANNALS of SPORTING far above the reach of competition, and to render it an appropriate ornament for the Library of the *Country Gentleman* and the *Man of Fashion.* The Drawings are made from *life* by the most esteemed Artists; and, from their superior style of execution, have the effect of so many " Animated Pictures;" the work is further illustrated with numerous Engravings on *Wood.* The Subjects will include the best breeds of Horses and Dogs used in the Field: also every species of known Game in the habitable world.

.*. Three Volumes of this interesting work, price 17s. each, neatly half bound, are now before the Public; and they record every thing connected with FIELD SPORTS since Jan. 2, 1822.

A Volume is completed every six months, and will be found a most valuable present to Friends abroad—as comprising a complete register of Sporting Subjects.

DEDICATION.

To Hans Francis, Earl of Huntingdon.

My Lord,

I am perfectly aware that Dedications are but too frequently prefixed to a volume for the purpose of ushering it into the world under the sanction of exalted rank, in order to obtain that patronage which generally results from high birth and pre-eminent distinction. Under the present circumstances, my Lord, when we are separated by an immense expanse of ocean, it is not possible that such motives could have influenced my conduct on this occasion. Accept, therefore, this tribute of sincere regard for that candour and generosity which have always distinguished your Lordship, from your old Schoolfellow and

Obedient Servant,

T. B. JOHNSON.

Liverpool,
Aug. 1, 1823.

PREFACE.

As custom seems to demand a Preface, so I shall comply with the imperious mandate; but the reader need be under no alarm, as I shall not exhaust his patience by the length, nor excite his disgust by the prolixity, of my prefatory observations.

In the first place, I acknowledge the obligations I feel for the very handsome manner in which several Reviews noticed the first edition of the present work, particularly the Literary Chronicle, a publication, as much distinguished for the independence and candour of its criticisms, as for the ability with which it is conducted.

To the present edition (the second) very considerable additions have been added. The first edition, in fact, was, in its observations, confined to *Game*, strictly speaking, and the accompaniments indispensible for its pursuit; in the present volume, it will be found, that, in addition to every possible information on this subject, all those birds which come under the general denomination of *Wild Fowl,* and which, during the winter season, occasionally occupy the Sportsman's attention, have also been duly noticed, and the diversion of Wild Fowl Shooting considered in all its varieties : indeed, every attention has been bestowed, in order to render " the Shooter's Companion" as clear and as complete as possible.

CONTENTS.

Shooting.

LIKE most other sciences, shooting has experienced the effect of the superiority of modern knowledge; and, since the application of percussion powder, has perhaps attained the acme of perfection: but, though great attention has been paid to the breeding of setting dogs, it is, nevertheless, doubtful whether our present variety of these animals is superior to the dog which was formerly used for the net. At all events, the pursuit of feathered game has assumed a very different character; and the old diversion of hawking and netting has been superseded by the fowling-piece, and almost forgotten. However, while we admit the progressive improvement in the pursuit of the feathered tribe, the same remark appears by no means so applicable to another fascinating department of British field sports :—I allude to hunting. I believe (and much regret the circumstance) that the old English talbot is no where to be found: the modern fox-chase is rapid and dashing, and partakes more of the character of the steeple-race, than of real hunting: the exquisite scent, steady pace, and delightful music, which distinguished the deep-flewed hound are no longer to be met with: the noble talbot has been superseded by a fleet, unsteady, yelping mongrel, with olfactory organs immeasurably inferior to his predecessor, and utterly inadequate to the pursuit of the fox without almost constant assistance from the huntsman.

That a passion also existed for extraordinary speed in the setting dog must be admitted; but the experiments for this purpose have been generally attended with such ill success, that the idea seems, in some degree, to be abandoned. However, before a

A

particular description of the various setting dogs is given, I will just sketch the general history of the dog principally from the celebrated Buffon:—

THE DOG.

The dog, independent of the beauty of his form, his vivacity, force, and swiftness, is possessed of all those internal qualifications that can conciliate the affections of man, and make the tyrant a protector. A natural share of courage, an angry and ferocious disposition, render the dog, in its savage state, a formidable enemy to all other animals: but these readily give way to very different qualities in the domestic dog, whose only ambition seems the desire to please; he is seen to come crouching along to lay his force, his courage, and all his useful talents, at the feet of his master; he waits his orders, to which he pays implicit obedience: he consults his looks, and a single glance is sufficient to put him in motion; he is more faithful even than the most boasted among men; he is constant in his affections, friendly without interest, and grateful for the slightest favours; much more mindful of benefits received than injuries offered; he is not driven off by unkindness; he still continues humble, submissive, and imploring; his only hope to be serviceable, his only terror to displease; he licks the hand that has been just lifted to strike him, and at last disarms resentment by submissive perseverance.

More docile than man, more obedient than any other animal, he is not only instructed in a short time, but he also conforms to the dispositions and manners of those who command him. He takes his tone from the house he inhabits; like the rest of the domestics, he is disdainful among the great, and churlish among clowns. Always assiduous in serving his master; and, only a friend to his friends, he is indifferent to all the rest, and declares himself openly against such as seem to be dependent like himself. He knows a beggar by his clothes, by his voice, or by his gestures, and forbids his approach. When at night the guard of the house is committed to his care, he seems proud of the charge : he continues a watchful sentinel, he goes his rounds, scents strangers at a distance, and gives them warning of his being upon duty. If they attempt to break in upon his territories, he becomes more fierce, flies at them, threatens, fights, and either conquers alone, or alarms those who have most interest in coming to his assistance ; however, when he has conquered, he quietly reposes upon the spoil, and abstains from what he has deterred others from abusing ; giving thus at once a lesson of courage, temperance, and fidelity.

The dog, thus useful in himself, taken into participation of empire, exerts a degree of superiority over all animals that require human protection. The flock and the herd obey his voice more readily even than that of the shepherd or the herdsman ; he conducts them, guards them, keeps them from capriciously seeking danger, and their enemies he considers as his own. Nor is he less useful in the pursuit ; when the sound of the horn, or the voice of the huntsman, calls him to the field, he testifies his pleasure by every little art, and pursues with perseverance, those animals, which, when taken, he must not expect to divide. The desire of hunting is indeed natural to him, as well as to his master, since war and the chase are the only employments of savages. All animals that live upon flesh, hunt by nature ; the lion and the tiger, whose force is so great that they are sure to conquer, hunt alone and without art ; the wolf, the fox, and the wild dog, hunt in packs, assist each other, and partake the spoil. But when education has perfected this talent in the domestic dog ; when he has been taught by man to repress his ardour, to measure his motions, and not to exhaust his force by too sudden an exertion of it, he then hunts with method, and always with success.

" As the dog is of the most complying disposition, so also it is the most susceptible of change in its form; the varieties of this animal being too many for even the most careful describer to mention. Climate, food, and education, all make strong impressions upon the animal, and produce alterations in its shape, its colour, its hair, its size, and in every thing but its nature. The same dog, taken from one climate and brought to another, seems to become another animal; but different breeds are as much separated, to all appearance, as any two animals the most distinct in nature. Nothing appears to continue constant with them, but their internal conformation; different in the figure of the body, in the length of the nose, in the shape of the head, in the length and direction of the ears and tail, in the colour, the quality, and the quantity of the hair; in short, different in every thing but that make of the parts which serves to continue the species, and keeps the animal distinct from all others. It is this peculiar conformation, this power of producing an animal that can reproduce, that marks the kind, and approxmiates forms, that at first sight appear in no degree calculated for conjunction.

From this single consideration, therefore, we may at once pronounce all dogs to be of one kind; but which of them is the original of all the rest, which of them is the savage dog from whence such a variety of descendants have come down, is no easy matter to determine. We may easily indeed, observe, that all those animals which are under the influence of man, are subject to great variations. Such as have been sufficiently independent, so as to choose their own climate, their own nourishment, and to pursue their own habitudes, preserve their original marks of nature, without much deviation; and it is probable, that the first of these is even at this day very well represented in their descendants. But such as man has subdued, transported from one climate to another, controlled in their manner of living, and

their food, have most probably been changed also in their forms ;
particularly the dog has felt these alterations more strongly than
any other of the domestic kinds ; for, living more like man, he
may be thus said to live more irregularly also, and, consequently,
must have felt all those changes that such variety would naturally
produce. Some other causes also may be assigned for this
variety in the species of the dog ; as he is perpetually under the
eye of his master, when accident has produced any singularity
in his productions, man uses all his art to continue this peculiarity unchanged ; either by breeding from such as had those
singularities, or by destroying such as happened to want them;
besides, as the dog produces much more frequently than some
other animals, and lives a shorter time, so the chance for its
varieties will be offered in greater proportion.

But which is the original animal, and which is the artificial or
accidental variety, is a question which, as was said, is not easily
resolved. If the internal structure of dogs of different sorts, be
compared with each other, it will be found, except in point of
size, that in this respect they are exactly the same. This, therefore, affords no criterion. If other animals be compared with
the dog internally, the wolf and the fox will be found to have
the most perfect resemblance ; in fact, there is no perceptible
difference : it is probable, therefore, that the dog which most
nearly resembles the wolf or the fox externally, is the original
animal of its kind : for it is natural to suppose, that as the dog
exactly resembles them internally, so he may be near them in external resemblance also, except where art or accident has altered
his form. This being supposed, if we look among the number
of varieties to be found in the dog, we shall not find one so like
the wolf or the fox, as that which is called the *shepherd's dog*.
This is that dog with long, coarse hair on all parts except the
nose, pricked ears, and a long nose, which is common enough
among us, and receives his name from being principally used in

A 3

guarding and attending on sheep. This seems to be the primitive animal of his kind: and we shall be still more confirmed in this opinion, if we attend to the different characters which climate produces in the animal, and the different races of dogs which are propagated in every country; and, in the first place, if we examine those countries which are still savage, or but half civilized, where it is most probable the dog, like his master, has received but few impressions from art, we shall find the shepherd's dog, or one very like him, still prevailing amongst them. The dogs that have run wild in America, and in Congo, approach this form. The dog of Siberia, Lapland, and Iceland, of the Cape of Good Hope, of Madagascar, Madura, Calicut, and Malabar, have all a long nose, pricked ears, and resemble the shepherd's dog very nearly. In Guinea, the dog very speedily takes this form; for at the second or third generation, the animal forgets to bark, his ears and his tail become pointed, and his hair drops off, while a coarser, thinner kind comes in the place. This sort of dog is likewise to be found in the temperate climates in great abundance, particularly among those who, preferring usefulness to beauty, employ an animal that requires very little instruction to be serviceable. Notwithstanding this creature's deformity, his melancholy and savage air, he is superior to all the rest of his kind in instinct; and, without any teaching, naturally takes to tending flocks, with an assiduity and vigilance that at once astonishes, and, at the same time, relieves, his master.

In more polished and civilized places, the dog seems to partake of the universal refinement; and, like man, becomes more beautiful, more majestic, and more capable of assuming an education foreign to his nature. The dogs of Albany, of Greece, of Denmark, and of Ireland, are larger and stronger than those of any other country. In France, Germany, Spain, and Italy, the dogs are of various kinds, like the men; and this variety seems formed by crossing the breed of such as are imported from various climes.

The shepherd's dog may, therefore, be considered as the primitive stock from whence these varieties are all derived. He makes the stem of that genealogical tree which has been branched out into every part of the world. This animal still continues pretty nearly in its original state among the poor in temperate climates; in the colder regions, he grows less and more ugly among the Laplanders; but becomes more perfect in Iceland, Russia, and Siberia, where the climate is less rigorous, and the people more civilized. Whatever differences there may be among the dogs of these countries, they are not very considerable, as they have all straight ears, long and thick hair, a savage aspect, and do not bark either so often or so loud as dogs of the more cultivated kind

The shepherd's dog transported into the temperate climates, and among people entirely civilized, such as England, France, and Germany, will be divested of his savage air, his pricked ears, his rough, long and thick hair, and from the single influence of climate and food alone, will become either a matin, a mastiff, or a hound. These three seem the immediate descendants of the former; and from them the other varieties are produced."

How far this last assertion of Buffon, that the shepherd's dog, "from the single influence of climate and food alone, will become either a matin, a mastiff, or a hound," may be founded on fact, I am unable to decide; but I am much inclined to doubt it. All animals feel the influence of climate; and we have abundant proof that the very same species, even in latitudes not very widely dissimilar, exhibit marks of the difference of their situation: the lion, for instance, which is never found so high as the temperate latitudes (unless in a state of captivity) to whose very existence a burning sun, or a great degree of heat, seems indispensable, and whose form and manner appear little susceptible of change, is nevertheless, marked like a graduated scale, with the varied effect of latitude. The lion of Mount Atlas is a small, dark tawney-coloured animal, and, as he approaches the torrid zone, his colour not only becomes much lighter, but he increases in size, strength, and fierceness. The difference is still more manifest between the Esquimaux and the inhabitant of more southern latitudes. On this principle of reasoning, therefore, it requires no great strength of imagination to suppose, that the wild dog assumes various forms and colours according to situation; and that " the influence of climate and food alone," were not sufficient to produce those varieties above-mentioned, but that the natives of remote countries were also resorted to for this purpose.

It is a generally received opinion, that the wolf and the dog, as well as the fox and the dog, will engender, and, that the offspring of such a conjunction is capable of procreation ; which, if true, would clearly prove that these animals are merely accidental ramifications of the same stock : but I am almost equally inclined to doubt on this head ; nor would any thing short of ocular demonstration remove my infidelity upon a subject, which, however first appearances may seem to favor it, I am perfectly convinced has in general been inconsiderately asserted, and handed from one to another without experiment or reflection.

All the endeavours of M. Buffon to make them engender, as he assures us, were ineffectual. For this purpose, he bred up a young wolf, taken in the woods, at two months old, with a matin dog of the same age. They were shut up together, without any other, in a large yard, where they had a shelter for retiring. They neither of them knew any other individual of their kind, nor even any other man but he who had the charge of feeding them. In this manner they were kept for three years; still with the same attention, and without constraining or tying them up. During the first year the young animals played with each other continually, and seemed to love each other very much. In the second year, they began to dispute about their victuals, although they were given more than they could use. The quarrel always began on the wolf's side. They were always brought their food, which consisted of flesh and bones, upon a large wooden platter, which was laid on the ground. Just as it was put down, the wolf, instead of falling on the meat, began by driving off the dog; and took the platter in its teeth so expertly, that it let nothing of what it contained fall upon the ground, and in this manner carried it off; but as the wolf could not entirely escape, it was frequently seen to run with the platter round the yard five or six times, still carrying it in a position that none of its contents could fall. In this manner it would continue running, only now and then stopping to take breath, until the dog came up, when the wolf would leave the victuals to attack him. The dog, however, was the stronger of the two, but as it was more gentle, in order to secure him from the wolf's attack, he had a collar put round his neck. In the third year, the quarrels of these ill-paired associates were more vehement, and their combats more frequent ; the wolf, therefore, had a collar put about its neck, as well as the dog, which began to be more fierce and unmerciful. During the two first years, neither seemed to testify the least tendency towards engendering; and it was not till the end of the third, that the wolf, which was the female, shewed the natural desire, but without abating either in its fierceness or obstinancy. This appetite rather increased than repressed their mutual animosity ; they became every day more untractable and ferocious, and nothing was heard between them but the sounds of rage and resentment. They both, in less than three weeks, became remarkably lean, without ever approaching each other, but to combat. At length, their quarrels became so desperate, that the dog killed the wolf, which was become more weak and feeble; and he was soon after himself obliged to be killed, for, upon being set at liberty, he instantly flew upon every animal he met, fowls, dogs, and even men themselves, not escaping his savage fury.

The same experiment was tried upon foxes, taken young, but with no better success, they were never found to engender with dogs; and our learned naturalist seems to be of opinion, that their natures are too opposite ever to provoke mutual desire.

A young dog shudders at the sight of a wolf; he even shuns his scent, which, though unknown, is so repugnant to his nature, that he comes trembling to seek protection near his master. A dog that is stronger, and knows his strength, bristles up at the sight, testifies his animosity, attacks him with courage, endeavours to put him to flight, and does all in his power to rid himself of a presence that is hateful to him. They never meet without either flying or fighting; fighting for life and death, and without mercy on either side. If the wolf is the stronger, he tears and devours his prey: the dog, on the contrary, is more generous, and contents himself with his victory; he does not seem to think that *the body of a dead enemy smells well;* he leaves him where he falls, to serve as food for birds of prey, or for other wolves, since they devour each other; and when one wolf happens to be desperately wounded, the rest track him by his blood, and are sure to shew him no mercy.

The dog, even in his savage state, is not cruel; he is easily tamed, and continues firmly attached to his master. The wolf, when taken young, becomes tame, but never has any attachment: nature is stronger in him than education; he resumes with age, his natural dispositions, and returns as soon as he can to the woods from whence he was taken. Dogs, even of the dullest kinds, seek the company of other animals; they are naturally disposed to follow and accompany other creatures besides themselves; and even by instinct, without any education, take to the care of flocks and herds. The wolf, on the contrary, is the enemy of all society; he does not even keep much company with those of his kind. When they are seen in packs together, it is not to be considered as a peaceful society, but a combination for war; they testify their hostile intentions by their loud howlings, and, by their fierceness, discover a project for attacking some great animal, such as a stag or a bull, or to destroy some more redoubtable watch dog. The instant their military expedition is completed, their society is at an end; they then part, and each returns in silence to his solitary retreat. There is not even any strong attachment between the male and female: they seek each other only once a year, and remain but a few days together; they always couple in winter; at which time several males are seen following one female, and this association is still more bloody than the former: they dispute most cruelly, growl, bark, fight, and tear each other; and it sometimes happens, that the majority kill the wolf, which has been chiefly preferred by the female. It is usual for the she wolf to fly from them all with him she has chosen; and watches this opportunity when the rest are asleep.

In a state of nature, I am of opinion, the different species of quadrupeds continue faithful to their own particular tribe, and that various kinds never approach each other for the sake of conjunction; nor were the mare and the ass ever known to produce in a wild state, though in a state of domestication nothing is more common. Were it possible to reduce the wolf or the fox to that degree of subordination or civilization which so superlatively distinguishes the domestic dog, a race of mongrels might in all probability be obtained. But to accomplish such an object, infinite trouble would be indispensable, as well as perhaps ages of time; for wolves and foxes must be bred in a tame or domestic state before they could be expected to couple with the dog: and, should the tedious experiment eventually be crowned with success, it is very doubtful whether the mongrel race thus produced, would repay a thousandth part of the trouble.

" With regard to the dogs of our country in particular, the varieties are very great, and the number every day increasing. And this must happen in a country so open, by commerce, to all others, and where wealth is apt to produce capricious predilection. Here the ugliest and most useless of their kinds will be entertained merely for their singularity; and, being imported only to be looked at, they will lose even that small degree of sagacity which they possessed in their natural climates. From this importation of foreign, useless dogs, our own native breed is, perhaps, degenerated, and the varieties now to be found in England are much more numerous than they were in the times of Queen Elizabeth, when Doctor Caius attempted their natural history. Some of those he mentions are no longer to be found among us, although many have since been introduced, by no means so serviceable as those which have been suffered to decay.

He divides the whole race into three kinds. The first is the generous kind, which consists of the terrier, the harrier, and the blood hound; the gaze-hound, the grey-hound, the leymmer, and the tumbler; all these are used for hunting. Then the spaniel, the setter, and the water-spaniel, or finder, were used for fowling; and the spaniel gentle or lap dog, for amusement. The second is the farm kind; consisting of the shepherd's dog and the mastiff. And the third is the mongrel kind; consisting of the wappe, the turnspit, and the dancer. To these varieties we may add at present, the bull dog, the Dutch mastiff, the harlequin, the pointer, and the Dane, with a variety of lap-dogs, which, as they are perfectly useless, may be considered as unworthy of a name.

" The blood-hound was a dog of great use, and in high

esteem among our ancestors. Its employ was to recover any game that had escaped from the hunter, or had been killed and stolen out of the forest. But it was still more employed in hunting thieves and robbers by their footsteps.

" The land spaniel, which probably had its name from Spain, where it might have acquired the softness of its hair, is well known at present."

———

THE SETTER.

The Setter is the handsomest and perhaps the most generous of the canine race ; but by what peculiar cross he originated, is not well known ; and all conjectures on this head, though very interesting to the sportsman, are too much involved in uncertainty, to be much depended on. An ingenious friend is of opinion, that the setter was produced by crossing the talbot or blood hound with the small land spaniel or springer ; and certainly the appearance of some of these animals seem to warrant such an idea ; while others, equally good or superior, seem altogether at variance with such a conjecture. Even if we admit this position, we are still unable to trace the primeval stock precisely, as the springer exhibits an almost endless variety, while its origin appears to be buried in oblivion.

It may be safely asserted that the setter or large land spaniel was known in this country long before the introduction of the present more fashionable dog, known by the appellation of the Spanish Pointer. The large land spaniel or English setter is not more eminently distinguished for the beauty of his form, than for his vivacity, unwearied perseverance, and sagacity, as well as for his generous and ardent attachment to man. His body is formed much like that of the greyhound, his countenance is very expressive, he has large pendant ears, a long, brushy, handsome tail, and covered all over with long wavy hair: his speed is very great ; and as his feet are small, and much protected with hair, he has thus a decided advantage over his more delicate rival, and will run with indifference on hard ground, whether produced by frost or otherwise, when the Spanish pointer cannot be induced to move from the sportsman's heels. Also, while the latter, from the tenderness of the skin, manifests the utmost reluctance to enter a thicket, the setter will rush through the brambles with dauntless impetuosity.

At the commencement of the shooting season, when the weather is excessively hot, the setter is supposed to suffer more from thirst than the pointer ; this is undoubtedly the case, and arises from the long warm coat of the former ; and on the grouse mountains, where water is seldom met with, exposes this generous animal to great inconvenience ; not that the pointer is by any means exempt from that excessive thirst which is uniformly produced by great exertion under a burning sun ; but, as he is more thinly clad, and generally moves much slower, so he is consequently less in want of water.

Another supposition, which generally obtains belief, respecting the comparative merits of these two animals, is neither so reasonably nor so justly .founded, namely, that the olfactory organs of the setter are inferior to those of his foreign rival. On this subject, it seems necessary, in the first place to observe, that the *best nosed* pointers are those which still retain much of the blood of the old English talbot or blood-hound (as no doubt, I think, can exist, that the Spanish pointer when first brought to this country was crossed with the talbot) ; and almost all those pointers of the present day, which have the best noses, are found to approximate in form and appearance the old English blood hound, whose olfactory organs were no doubt superior to those of any other race of dogs which was ever known in these islands. The old English setter, which many years ago, existed perhaps in the greatest possible perfection, has since undergone various crosses, which have not only injured the beauty of his appearance, but diminished that exquisite sense of smell, which is so essential to the delightful recreation of shoot ing: Dogs, *called setters*, are now to be met with of all forms, miserably deficient in the most prominent quality, *setting*, and generally very inferior to the modern pointer in every respect. Not one in a hundred of these mongrels are worth the notice of the sportsman; many of them it is utterly impossible to *break* or train, and even of those which are in some measure forced into subordination, very few become sufficiently steady to be fully depended on, or to render their services satisfactory. It is true, sometimes one is met with of approved worth; but the instances were so few which had come within my knowledge, that I despised what was called the setter altogether.

Speaking, however, on this subject to a friend, he remarked that he was no sportsman himself, but that his father had a breed of setters, which he believed would alter my opinion; and that he would procure me a specimen for that purpose. I paid but little attention, aware that promises of this sort are very often neglected; but I did my friend injustice; for in the course of a few weeks, I received a whelp about six weeks old. In the course of a short time afterwards, I happened to be walking across some fields near my residence, accompanied by a favourite pointer bitch; the whelp followed and kept close to my heels. As I had not gone out for the purpose of finding game, I devoted but little attention to my canine companions; nevertheless, after walking a few minutes, I missed the whelp, and on looking round, was much surprised and delighted at seeing him abreast of my favourite bitch, pointing, as well as she, with all the steadiness of a veteran. I walked to the spot and was astonished at the earnestness of the whelp's countenance; and had it not been for his whelpish appearance, from his manner no person would have doubted that he had gone through all the requisite degrees of education, and had become a perfect master of the science. I sprung the birds and permitted my whelp to enjoy the scent. He followed me the next day on a shooting excursion ; I lifted him over the ditches, and though he was not able to *gallop*, whenever the bitch came to a point, he also set as steadily as possible : nor was this all—happening to pass a small bush, with the whelp close to me (for he could not run) when the bitch was at a distance, he made a dead set, I regarded him for some time—I never saw a handsomer or a steadier point : and when I had satisfied myself with looking at what appeared to me little less than a phenomenon, I kicked the bush and up rose a pheasant. Thenceforward the whelp constantly accompanied me, whenever I went out for the purpose of shooting ; as soon as he acquired sufficient strength, he began to run, set, and *backed* without the least teaching ; he has uniformly manifested an acuteness of olfactory nerve quite astonishing ; but, I am sorry to add, that it is only by incessant hard labour he can be kept steady.

He was bred by a Mr. Harley, who resides near Dumfries. He is liver coloured, about the middle size, and extremely handsome: I am inclined to think that this is the true bred English setter, the dog so celebrated when the net was as much in fashion, as the fowling-piece is at the present day.

Dogs the most distinguished for acute sense of smell have large broad heads.

THE POINTER.

The dog which is distinguished by the appellation of the Pointer is of foreign origin, and is known not only in Spain, but in Portugal, and also in France, with but slight difference of form. Those pointers which I have seen direct from Spain are heavy and clumsily formed; those from Portugal are somewhat lighter; while the French breed is remarkable for a wide furrow which runs between the nostrils, and which gives to the animal's countenance a very grotesque appearance. They all, however, exhibit a very different form and character to the setter; they are thick and heavy creatures, with large chubby heads, long pendant ears, and covered with short smooth hair; nor do they possess that generosity of disposition, which is so distinguishing a trait in the character of the setter; on the contrary, they are often ill-tempered and snappish ; and, in fact, are good for little in this country till they have been crossed with the more generous blood of these islands. Yet the conjunction of the setter and the pointer is by no means advisable, since the production generally unites the worst qualities of the two without any of those requisites perhaps for which the two breeds are most highly prized. Dogs thus produced, are for the most part head-strong and turbulent, require excessive correction, and are rarely brought to that steadiness which marks the distinct breeds. It is true, sometimes a first-rate dog is produced between a setter and a pointer; but it rarely happens: the cross at best is never to be depended on, and for one good dog thus obtained, there will be found twenty very indifferent or bad ones

on an average ; while not the least dependance can be placed on
the offspring of the very best dogs thus propagated. Excellent
pointers have been produced by the fox-hound and the Spaniard ; and in all probability the fox-hound had much of the talbot blood ; nor have I the least hesitation in supposing, that the
best pointers would be those bred from the talbot and the Spaniard ; but since the former is nearly, if not altogether, extinct,
and as all hounds have been produced from him, and still retain
more or less of his blood, the nearer we can approach him the
better : therefore the deep-flewed hound is to be preferred ; the
kibble, and even lighter kinds of hounds, may answer the purpose ; but what is thus gained in speed is not a sufficient com-
pensation for unsteadiness and an inferior nose. The Spaniard,
however, from having been judiciously crossed, has arrived at a
degree of perfection so as to leave little to be desired on this
head ; and excellent pointers are to be met with in most parts
of England. They differ from the setter inasmuch as when
they have approached sufficiently near the game, they stand
erect ; whereas the true bred setter will either sit upon his
haunches, or lie close to the ground—generally the latter. It
may be also very justly remarked, that though a particular strain
of either the pointer or setter may have arrived at a great degree
of perfection ; yet, if continued on the same strain for a length
of time, it will degenerate ; in order, therefore, to prevent that
dwindling or falling off which would inevitably take place, recourse must occasionally be had to other strains ; that is, to
dogs of the same kind, but bred in different parts of the kingdom, taking care to choose animals of undoubted merit from
which to breed ; and in order to avoid the possibility of being
misunderstood, I must observe, that in thus giving directions for
preserving the requisite qualities in perfection, I do not mean in
this case, that recourse should be had to the talbot, fox-hound,
or any other kind of dog used for a distinct purpose, but merely

to procure a pointer (either sire or dam) from a distant part of the country, if pointers are the object; and the same in respect to setters.

Pointers often suffer much from sore feet; considerable dif·ference, however, will be found amongst them in respect to their feet. I have generally found white footed dogs much more tender in this respect than those whose feet are of a dark colour.—Black, brown, or any dark-coloured pointers have generally better feet than white or light-coloured dogs; though the latter, if their legs are brown or dark-coloured towards the feet, are. unobjectionable.

THE RUSSIAN POINTER.

Within a few years, a rough-coated dog, of the water-spaniel breed, has been introduced to the notice of the sportsmen of this country, under the denomination of the *Russian Pointer*. Whether he be originally Russian is very doubtful; but he is evidently the ugliest strain of the water-spaniel species; and, like all dogs of this kind, is remarkable for penetrating thickets and bramble bushes, runs very awkwardly, his nose close to the ground (if not muzzle-pegged), and frequently springs his game. He may be taught to *set*, and so may a terrier, or any dog that will run and hunt, and even pigs, if we are to believe the story of Sir Henry Mildmay's black sow; but to compare him with the animals which have formed the subjects of the two preceding chapters, would be outrageous: nevertheless, I am not prepared to say, that out of a hundred of these animals, one tolerable could not be found; but I should think it madness to recommend the *Russian pointer* to sportsmen, unless for the purpose of pursuing the coot or the water-hen.

THE SPRINGER.

This beautiful little animal, is too well known to need description. There is a great variety of this species, all remarkable, however, for their cheerful activity. They are not calculated for an extensive range ; and are therefore of no use either for grouse or partridge shooting: but are very serviceable in strong covers in the pursuit of the pheasant or wood cock, and give notice of their approach to the object by a sort of *whimper*, which increases to a bark as the game springs. They are affectionate and docile, and easily broken or trained : in fact, their whole system of education consists of nothing more than merely to keep them tolerably close to the sportsman ; since, if they are suffered to ramble out of gun-shot, the game rises at too great a distance, the object is thus defeated which they were intended to promote, and a mortification, much better felt than described, must inevitably ensue. They are evidently of the spaniel species, and frequently called the small land spaniel. Their beauty and affectionate disposition will always excite attention ; but they are, after all, perhaps better calculated for coursing, than the fowling-piece, as they may be usefully employed in driving a hare from a copse or a thicket, while a pointer, or particularly a setter, will answer all the purposes of pheasant and woodcock shooting. However, if sporting on a grand scale, and the utmost pinnacle of perfection, are the objects to be attained, let relays of dogs be kept for the moors or grouse alone, others for the partridge, and the pheasant and woodcock consigned to the small land spaniel or springer.

THE GROUSE.

It has been already shewn to what an endless variety the breed of the dog may be extended, and the same remark will apply, in a greater or less degree, to all animals reclaimed from a state of nature and domesticated by man ; a pigeon, for instance, may be bred to assume any shape or any colour; but the case is widely different with all other animals which preserve their native freedom, and thus we find a grouse, a partridge, or a hare, always the same, or at least the deviations are so extremely rare, that they are regarded as phenomena, and are either the effect of disease, or appear as a fantastic whim of nature. Yet, if we are to believe Cowper, hares, when reduced to a state of familiar captivity, are easily recognised by the varied aspect or countenance, which each individually offers to minute and constant observation ; but, at all events, nature when left to herself seems to proceed in one regular course, and wild animals uniformly exhibit the same general appearance, whatever nice distinctions may be discovered by that minute and repeated observation which can only be obtained by familiar acquaintance.

The Grouse and its Affinities.—" The cock of the wood, the black cock, the grouse, and the ptarmigan—these are all birds of a similar nature, and chiefly found in heathy mountains and piny forests, at a distance from mankind. They might once indeed have been common enough all over England, when a great part of the country was covered with heath ; but at present their numbers are thinned.

The cock of the wood is sometimes of the size of a turkey, and often weighs near fourteen pounds; the black cock, of which the male is all over black, though the female is of the colour of the partridge, is about the size of a hen; the grouse is about half as large again as a partridge, and its colour much like that of a woodcock, but redder; the ptarmigan is still somewhat less, and is of a pale brown or ash-colour. They are all distinguishable from other birds of the poultry kind by a naked skin of a scarlet colour, above the eyes, in the place and of the figure of eye-brows.

It seems to be something extraordinary, that all the larger wild animals of every species choose the darkest and the inmost recesses of the woods for their residence, while the smaller kinds come more into the open and cultivated parts, where there are more food and more danger. It is thus with the birds I am describing: while the cock of the wood is seldom seen, except on the inaccessible parts of heathy mountains, or in the midst of piny forests, the grouse is found in great numbers in the neighbourhood of corn fields, where there is heath to afford retreat and shelter. Their food too somewhat differs; while the smaller kinds live upon heath blossoms, cranberries, and corn, the larger feeds upon the cones of the pine tree; and will sometimes entirely strip one tree, before it offers to touch those of another, though just beside him. In other respects, the manners of these birds are the same; being both equally simple in their diet and licentious in their amours.

The cock of the wood is, as was said, chiefly fond of a mountainous and woody situation. In winter he resides in the darkest and inmost part of the woods; in summer he ventures down from his retreats, to make short depredations on the farmer's corn. The delicacy of his flesh, in some measure, sets a high price upon his head; and as he is greatly sought after, so he continues, when he comes down from the hills, always on his guard. Upon these occasions he is seldom surprised; and those who would take him, must venture up to find him in his native retreats.

The cock of the wood, when in the forests, attaches himself principally to the oak and the pine tree; the cones of the latter serving for his food, and the thick boughs for a habitation. He even makes a choice of what cones he shall feed upon; for he sometimes will strip one tree bare before he will deign to touch the cones of another. He feeds also upon ants' eggs, which seem a high delicacy to all birds of the poultry kind; cranberries are likewise often found in his crop; and his gizzard, like that of domestic fowls, contains a quantity of gravel, for the purpose of assisting his powers of digestion.

At the earliest return of spring, this bird begins to feel the genial influence of the season. During the month of March, the approaches of courtship are continued, and do not desist till the trees have all their leaves, and the forest is in full bloom. During this whole season, the cock of the wood is seen at sunrise and setting, extremely active, upon one of the largest branches of the pine tree. With his tail raised and expanded like a fan, and the wings drooping, he is seen walking backward and forward, his neck stretched out, his head swollen and red, and making a thousand ridiculous postures: his cry upon that occasion is a kind of loud explosion, which is instantly followed by a noise like the whetting of a scythe, which ceases and commences alternately for about an hour, and is then terminated by the same explosion.

During the time this singular cry continues, the bird seems entirely deaf and insensible of every danger; whatever noise may be made near him, or even though fired at, he still continues his call. Upon all other occasions, he is the most timorous and watchful bird in nature; but now he appears entirely absorbed in his instincts; and seldom leaves the place where he first

c

begins to feel the accesses of desire. This extraordinary cry, which is accompanied by a clapping of the wings, is no sooner finished, than the female, hearing it, replies, approaches, and places herself under the tree, from whence the cock descends to impregnate her. The number of females that, on this occasion, resort to his call is uncertain; but one male generally suffices for all.

The female is much less than her mate, and entirely unlike him in plumage, so that she might be mistaken for a bird of another species : she seldom lays more that six or seven eggs, which are white and marked with yellow, of the size of a hen's egg ; she generally lays them in a dry place, and a mossy ground, and hatches them without the company of the cock. When she is obliged, during the time of incubation, to leave her eggs in quest of food, she covers them up so artfully, with moss or dry leaves, that it is extremely difficult to discover them. On this occasion, she is extremely tame and tranquil, however wild and timorous in ordinary. She often keeps to her nest, though strangers attempt to drag her away.

As soon as the young ones are hatched, they are seen running with extreme agility after the mother, though sometimes they are not entirely disengaged from the shell. The hen leads them forward, for the first time, into the woods, and shews them ants' eggs, and the wild mountain-berries, which, while young, are their only food. As they grow older, their appetites grow stronger, and they then feed upon the tops of the heath and the cones of the pine tree. In this manner they soon come to perfection : they are a hardy bird, their food lies every where before them, and it would seem that they should increase in great abundance. But this is not the case ; their numbers are thinned by rapacious birds and beasts of all kinds ; and still more by their own salacious contests.

As soon as the clutching is over, which the female performs

in the manner of a hen, the whole brood follows the mother for about a month or two; at the end of which the young males entirely forsake her, and continue in great harmony together till the beginning of spring. At this season they begin, for the first time, to feel the genial access; and then adieu to all their former friendship! They begin to consider each other as rivals; and the rage of concupiscence quite extinguishes the spirit of society. They fight each other like game cocks; and at that time are so inattentive to their own safety, that it often happens that two or three are killed at a shot. It is probable, that in these contests, the bird which comes off victorious, takes possession of the female seraglio, as it is certain they have no faithful attachment."

The above account is copied from Goldsmith, nor will I pledge myself for its accuracy. What he calls the cock of the wood is certainly unknown in England: the bird to which he alludes is occasionally met with, I believe, in some parts of Scotland; but whether so large as to weigh fourteen pounds is doubtful. It is a lamentable circumstance that little dependence can be placed upon our natural histories, as the historians themselves appear to have no more knowledge of the subject than what they gained in their study from the perusal of anterior works upon the same subject; therefore, their descriptions can only be relied on, where they happen to be corroborated by practical knowledge; while, strange as it may appear, some of the most important subjects (to the sportsman at least) are noticed in so slight and confused a manner as to afford little or no information upon the matter. Such is precisely the case with that beautiful bird, the black cock, or black grouse, also frequently distinguished by the appellation of black game. The black cock is one of the finest birds offered to the attention of the sportsman: he is the first of the game species known in this kingdom, and is to be met with only in a few places in England,

and not in great abundance. The male bird generally weighs about four pounds, of a beautiful black colour, with the tail forked in a peculiar manner. The female is much less than the male, and altogether different in plumage ; her colour is brown, and from her appearance she might be easily mistaken for a bird of a different species. These birds are found in tolerable abundance in some parts of the Highlands of Scotland, as well as on the borders of that country ; and are also to be met with on the hilly parts of Derbyshire and Staffordshire, in Devonshire, and also in the New Forest, in Hampshire. They breed on the heathy moors : but are generally found in the vicinity of woods and corn fields, where they frequently feed. The shooting season for black game commences on the 20th August. They *lie* remarkably well at the beginning of the season, but soon become very wild, and will often fly to a great height.

Their food is various, but principally consists of mountain fruits and berries, and in winter the tops of heath, as well as the cones of the pine tree, and corn where they can procure it. It is somewhat remarkable that cherries and pease are fatal to these birds. They perch and roost in the same manner as the pheasant.

The *red grouse*, or *moor game*, is found in most of the mountainous districts of the united kingdom : I will state a few particulars respecting them :—

The grouse is a bird which is found in different parts of the globe, and of which there are various kinds. However, as this volume is intended not for the naturalist, but the sportsman, it will be necessary to describe only those which breed in Great Britain, and that kind in particular, which is the general object of pursuit, and which is known by the name of *red grouse*, or *moor game.*

These birds are larger than the partridge ; the male weighing about nineteen to twenty four ounces. The bill is black, the

iris orange-coloured, the throat red, the plumage on the head
and neck a light tawny red, each feather being marked with
several transverse bars of black; the back and scapulars are a
deeper red, and on the middle of each feather is a large black
spot; the breast and belly are of a dull purplish-brown colour,
crossed with narrow dusky lines; the quill feathers are dusky;
the tail consists of sixteen black feathers, the four middlemost
of which are barred with red; the thighs are a pale red, ob-
scurely barred with black; the legs and feet are clothed down
to the claws with thick, soft, white and brown feathers; the
outer and inner toes are connected to the first joint by a small
membrane. The female is considerably less than the male,
weighing only about fifteen ounces. Her colours in general are
less vivid, and she has more of the white and less of the red feathers than the male.

The heathy and mountainous parts of the northern counties
of England, are in general stocked with these birds; but they
abound in the Highlands of Scotland, and are very common in
Wales and Ireland. They feed on mountain berries and the
tender tops of the heath.

Grouse pair very early in the spring, and the female lays from
eight to twelve or thirteen eggs, in a very simple nest, formed
on the ground. The young leave the nest almost as soon as
hatched, and continue to follow the hen till the severity of the
winter sets in, when they unite in packs of twenty or thirty
brace. They continue together in the greatest harmony till the
approach of spring, when they feel the access of genial desire;
the old females then, contrary to what is generally supposed,
drive off the young cocks, and a general dispersion takes place:
the males view each other with a jealous eye, and furious battles
are the consequence.

Grouse are very difficult to be netted, owing to the straggling manner in which they lie, and their scattering on the approach of the sportsman, or the least noise.

The care and stratagem of the hen for the security of the young is wonderful, and similar to those of the partridge, to which we refer the reader.

THE PTARMIGAN.

————

The Ptarmigan is somewhat larger than a pigeon. Its bill is black; and its plumage, in summer, is of a pale brown colour, elegantly mottled with small bars and dusky spots. The head and neck are marked with broad bars of black, rust colour, and white. The wings and belly are white.

These birds moult in the winter months, and change their summer dress for one more warm; and, instead of having their feathers of many colours, they then become white. By a wonderful provision every feather also, except those of the wings and tail, becomes double, a downy one shooting out of the base of each; which gives an additional protection against the cold. In the latter end of February, a new plumage begins to appear, first about the rump, in brown stumps: the first rudiments of the coat they assume in the warm season, when each feather is single. In answer to enquiries made by Sir Joseph Banks, Dr. Solander, and some other naturalists, from Captain George Cartwright, who resided many years on the coast of Labrador, on the subject of the grouse changing their colour, he says, "I took particular notice of those I killed, and can aver, for a fact, that they get at this time of the year (September) a very large addition of feathers, all of which are white; and that the coloured feathers at the same time change to white. In spring, most of the white feathers drop off, and are succeeded by coloured ones; or, I rather believe, all the white ones drop off, and they get an entirely new set. At the two seasons they change very differently: in the spring beginning at the neck, and spreading from thence; now they begin on the belly and end on th neck."

Their feet, by being feathered entirely to the toes, are protected from the cold of the northern regions. Every morning they take a flight directly upwards into the air, apparently to shake the snow from their wings and bodies. They feed in the mornings and evenings, and in the middle of the day they bask in the sun.

About the beginning of October they assemble in flocks of a hundred and fifty or two hundred, and live much among the willows, the tops of which they eat. In December they retire from the flats about Hudson's-bay to the mountains, where in that month the snow is less deep than in the low lands, to feed on the mountain berries.

Some of the Greenlanders believe that the ptarmigans, to provide a subsistence through the winter, collect a store of mountain berries into some cranny of a rock near their retreat. It is, however, generally supposed, that by means of their long, broad, and hollow nails, they form lodges under the snow, where they lie in heaps to protect themselves from the cold. During winter they are often seen flying in great numbers among the rocks.

Though sometimes found in the mountains of the north of Scotland, the ptarmigans are chiefly inhabitants of that part of the globe which lies about the Arctic Circle. Their food consists of the buds of trees, young shoots of pine, heath, and fruits and berries which grow on the mountains. They are so stupid and so silly, as often to suffer themselves, without any difficulty, to be knocked on the head, or to be driven into any snare that is set for them. When frightened they fly off; but immediately alight, and stand staring at their foe. When the hen bird is killed, it is said that the male will not forsake her, but may then also be killed with great ease. So little alarmed are they at the presence of mankind, as even to bear driving like poultry: yet, notwithstanding this apparent gentleness of disposition, it is impossible to domesticate them ; for, when caught, they refuse to eat, and always die soon afterwards.

Their voice is very extraordinary ; and they do not often exert it but in the night. It is very rarely that they are found in Denmark : but by some accident one of these birds, some years ago, happened to stray within a hundred miles of Stockholm, which very much alarmed the common people of the neighbourhood ; for from its nightly noise a report very soon arose, that the wood where it took up its residence, was haunted by a ghost. So much were the people terrified, that nothing could tempt the post boys to pass the wood after dusk. The spirit was, however, at last happily removed, by some gentlemen sending their gamekeepers into the wood by moonlight, who soon discovered and killed the harmless ptarmigan.

Ptarmigans form their nests on the ground, in dry ridges ; and lay from six to ten dusky eggs with reddish-brown spots.

The usual method of taking these birds is in nets made or twine, twenty feet square, connected to four poles, and propped with sticks in front. A long line is fastened to these, the end of which is held by a person who lies concealed at a distance. Several people drive the birds within reach of the net ; which is then pulled down, and is found to cover fifty or sixty of them. They are in such plenty in the northern parts of America, that upwards of ten thousand are frequently caught for the use of the Hudson's-bay Settlement, between November and May.

They are taken by the Laplanders by means of a hedge formed with the branches of birch trees, and having small openings at certain intervals with a snare in each. The birds are tempted to feed on the buds and catkins of the birch ; and whenever they endeavour to pass through the openings, they are caught.

They are excellent food ; being said to taste so like the common grouse, as to be scarcely distinguishable from it.

THE PARTRIDGE.

The partridge is an inhabitant of all the temperate parts of Europe. The extremes of heat and cold are unfavourable to its propagation ; and it flourishes best in cultivated countries, living principally on the labours of the husbandman. In Sweden these birds burrow beneath the snow ; and the whole covey crowd together under this shelter to guard against the intense cold. In Greenland the partridge is brown during summer; but as soon as winter sets in, it becomes clothed with a thick and warm down, and its exterior assumes the colour of the snows. Near the mouth of the river Ol, in Russia, the partridges are in such quantities, that the adjacent mountains are crowded with them.—These birds have been seen variegated with white, and sometimes entirely white, where the climate could not be supposed to have any influence in this variation, and even among those whose plumage was of the usual colour.

Partridges have ever held a distinguished place at the tables of the luxurious, both in this country and in France. We have an old distich,

> If the partridge had the woodcock's thigh,
> 'Twould be the best bird that e'er did fly.

They generally pair early in February ; and sometimes after pairing, if the weather be very severe, they collect together again, and form into packs. The female lays her eggs, usually from fifteen to eighteen in number, in a rude nest of dry leaves and grass, formed upon the ground : these are of a greenish-grey colour. The period of incubation is about three weeks. So closely do these birds sit on their eggs when near hatching, that a partridge with her nest has been carried in a hat to some distance, and in confinement she has continued her incubation, and there produced young ones. The great hatch is about the middle of June; and the earliest birds begin to fly towards the latter end of that month. The young brood are able to run about as soon as they are hatched, and they are even sometimes seen incumbered with a piece of a shell sticking to them. The parents immediately lead them to ant hills, on the grubs of which they at first principally feed.

At the season when the partridge is produced, the various species of ants loosen the earth about their habitations. The young birds therefore have only to scrape away the earth, and they can satisfy their hunger without difficulty. A covey that some years ago excited the attention of the Rev. Mr. Gould, gave him an opportunity of remarking the great delight they take in this kind of food. On his turning up a colony of ants, and withdrawing to some distance, the parent birds conducted their young to the hill, and fed very heartily. After a few days, they grew more bold, and ventured to eat within twelve or fourteen yards of him. The surrounding grass was high; by which means they could, on the least disturbance, immediately run out of sight, and conceal themselves. The excellence of this food for partridges may be ascertained from those that are bred up under a domestic hen, if constantly supplied with ants' grubs and fresh water, seldom failing to arrive at maturity. Along with the grubs it is recommended to give them, at intervals, a mixture of millepedes, or wood lice, and earwigs, to prevent their surfeiting on one luxurious diet; fresh curds mixed with lettuce, chickweed, or groundsel, should also be given them.

The affection of partridges for their young is peculiarly interesting. Both the parents lead them out to feed; they point out to them the proper places for their food, and assist them in finding it by scratching the ground with their feet. They frequently sit close together, covering their young ones with their wings; and from this situation they are not easily roused. If, however, they are disturbed, most persons acquainted with rural affairs know the confusion that ensues. The male gives the first signal of alarm, by a peculiar cry of distress; throwing himself at the same moment more immediately into the way of danger, in order to mislead the enemy. He flutters along the ground, hanging his wings, and exhibiting every symptom of debility. By this stratagem he seldom fails of so far attracting the attention of the intruder, as to allow the female to conduct the helpless, unfledged brood into some place of security.— " A partridge (says Mr. White, who gives an instance of this instinctive sagacity) came out of a ditch, and ran along shivering with her wings, and crying out as if wounded and unable to get from us. While the dam feigned this distress, a boy who attended me, saw the brood, which was small and unable to fly, run for shelter into an old fox's hole, under the bank."—Mr. Markwick relates, that " as he was once hunting with a young pointer, the dog ran on a brood of very small partridges. The old bird cried, fluttered, and ran tumbling along just before the dog's nose, till she had drawn him to a considerable distance; when she took wing and flew farther off, but not out of the field. On this the dog returned nearly to the place where the young ones lay concealed in the grass; which the old bird no sooner perceived, than she flew back again, settled just before the dog's nose, and a second time acted the same part, rolling and tumbling about till she drew off his attention from her brood, and thus succeeded in preserving them."

The eggs of the partridge are frequently destroyed by weasels, stoats, crows, magpies, and other animals. When this has been the case, the female frequently makes another nest and lays afresh. The produce of these second hatchings is always a puny, sickly race; and the individuals seldom outlive the rigours of the winter.

It is said that those partridges which are hatched under a domestic hen, retain through life the habit of *calling* when they hear the clucking of hens.

The partridge, even when reared by the hand, soon neglects those who have the care of it; and shortly after its full growth, always estranges itself from the house where it was bred. This will almost invariably be its conduct, however intimately it may have connected itself with the place and inhabitants in the early part of its existence. Among the very few instances of the partridge's remaining tame, was that of one reared by the Rev. Mr. Bird. This, long after its full growth, attended the parlour at breakfast and other times, received food from any hand that gave it, and stretched itself before the fire and seemed much to enjoy the warmth. At length, it fell a victim to the decided foe of all favourite birds, a cat.

On the farm of Lion Hall, in Essex, belonging to Colonel Hawker, a partridge, in the year 1788, formed her nest, and hatched sixteen eggs *on the top of a pollard oak tree.* What renders this circumstance more remarkable is, that the tree had fastened to it the bars of a stile, where there was a footpath; and the passengers in going over, discovered and disturbed her before she sat close. When the brood was hatched, they scrambled down the short and rough boughs, which grew out all around from the trunk of the tree, and reached the ground in safety.

In the year 1798, the following occurrence took place at East Dean, in Sussex, which will tend to prove that partridges have no powers of migration.—A covey of sixteen partridges being routed by some men at plough, directed their flight across the cliff to the sea, over which they continued their course about three hundred yards. Either intimidated or otherwise affected

D

by that element, the whole were then observed to drop into the water.

It has long been a received opinion among sportsmen as well as naturalists, that the female partridge has none of the bay feathers on the breast (forming a kind of horse shoe) like the male. This, however, on dissection, has proved to be a mistake; for Mr. Montagu happening to kill nine birds in one day, with very little variation as to the bay mark on the breast, he was led to open them all, and discovered that five of them were females. On carefully examining the plumage, he found that the males could only be known by the superior brightness of colour about the head; which alone, after the first or second year, seems to be the mark of distinction.

THE QUAIL.

The Quail is an inhabitant of nearly all the countries of the world, and in all is esteemed excellent food. In appearance it is so like the partridge, as sometimes to be called the *dwarf partridge;* and in the manners of the two species there is a great resemblance. They feed, form their nest, and rear their young, nearly in the same way. They are, however, in many respects very different. Quails migrate to other countries; they are always smaller; and have not a bare space between the eyes, nor the figure of a horse shoe on their breasts. The eggs too are less than those of the partridge, and very different in colour. Their voices are unlike. Quails seldom live in covies; except when their wants unite the feeble family to their mother, or some powerful cause urges at once the whole species to assemble, and traverse together the extent of the ocean, holding their course to the same distant lands. They are much less cunning than the partridge; and more easily ensnared, especially when young.

The females lay about ten eggs, in the incubation of which they are occupied three weeks. The eggs are whitish; but marked with ragged, rust-coloured spots.

These birds usually sleep during the day, concealed in the tallest grass, lying on their sides, with their legs extended, in the same spot, even for hours together. So very indolent are they, that a dog must absolutely run upon them before they are sprung; and when they are forced upon wing, they seldom fly far. Quails are easily drawn within reach of a net, by a call imitating their cry, which is not unlike the words *whit, whit, whit :* this is done with an instrument called a quail pipe.

They are found in some parts of Great Britain, but no where in any great quantity.— They are supposed to winter in Africa, and return early in the spring. If to the circumstance of their generally sleeping in the day, is added that of their being seldom known to make their first annual appearance in the day time, it may be inferred that they perform their *journey by night*, and that they direct their course to those countries where the harvest is preparing, and thus change their abode to obtain a subsistence. On their arrival at Alexandria, such multitudes are exposed in the markets for sale, that three or four may be bought for a medina (less than three farthings). Crews of merchant vessels have been fed upon them; and complaints have been laid at the consul's office by mariners against their captains, for giving them nothing but quails to eat.

With wind and weather in their favour, they have been known to perform a flight of fifty leagues across the Black Sea in the course of a night; a wonderful distance for so short-winged a bird.

Such prodigious quantities have appeared on the western coasts of the kingdom of Naples, in the vicinity of Nettuno, that a hundred thousand have been caught within the space of three or four miles. Most of these are taken to Rome, where they are in great request, and are sold at extremely high prices. Clouds of quails also alight, in spring, along the coasts of Provence; especially in the lands belonging to the Bishop of Frejus, which border on the sea. Here they are sometimes found so exhausted, that for a few of the first days they may be caught with the hand.—In some parts of the south of Russia they abound so greatly, that at the time of their migration they are caught by thousands, and sent in casks to Moscow and Petersburgh.

Quails are birds of undaunted courage; and their quarrels often terminate in mutual destruction. This irascible disposition induced the ancient Greeks and Romans to fight them with each other, as the moderns do game cocks. And such favourites were the conquerors, that, in one instance, Augustus punished a prefect of Egypt with death, for bringing to his table one of these birds which had acquired celebrity for its victories.

THE PHEASANT.

The characters of the pheasant tribe are a short, convex, and strong bill; the head more or less covered with carunculated bare flesh on the sides, which, in some species, is continued upwards to the crown, and beneath so as to hang pendant under each jaw; and the legs, for the most part, furnished with spurs.

The females produce many young ones at a brood; which they take care of for some time, leading them abroad and pointing out food for them. These are at first clad with a thick, soft down. The nests of the whole tribe are formed on the ground.

————◄◆►————

THE PHEASANT.

———

This beautiful bird is very common in almost all the southern parts of the old continent, whence it was originally imported into our country. In America it is not known.

Pheasants are much attached to the shelter of thickets and woods where the grass is very long; but, like the partridges, they often breed also in clover fields. They form their nests on the ground: and the females lay from twelve to fifteen eggs, which are smaller than those of the domestic hen. In the mowing of clover near the woods frequented by pheasants, the destruction of their eggs is sometimes very great. Poultry hens are often kept ready for sitting on any eggs that may be exposed by the scythe; and with care, numbers are thus rescued from destruction. The nest is usually composed of a few dry vegetables put carelessly together; and the young follow the mother like chickens, as soon as they break the shell.—The pheasants and their brood remain in the stubbles and hedge-rows, if undisturbed, for some time after the corn is ripe. If disturbed, they seek the woods, and only issue thence in the mornings and evenings to feed in the stubbles.—They are very fond of corn: they can, however, procure a subsistence without it; since they often feed on the wild berries of the woods and on acorns.

In confinement the female neither lays so many eggs, nor hatches and rears her brood with so much care and vigilance, as in the fields out of the immediate observation of man. In a mew she will very rarely dispose them in a nest or sit upon them at all. Indeed, in the business of incubation and rearing the young, the domestic hen is generally made a substitute for the hen pheasant.

The wings of these birds are very short, and ill adapted for considerable flights. On this account, the pheasants on the island called *Isola Madre* in the *Lago Maggiore*, at Turin, as they cannot fly over the lake, are altogether imprisoned. When they attempt to cross the lake, unless picked up by the boatmen, they are always drowned.

The pheasant is in some respects a very stupid bird. On being roused, it will often perch on a neighbouring tree; where its attention will be so fixed on the dogs, as to suffer any person to approach very near. It has been asserted, that the pheasant imagines itself out of danger whenever its head only is concealed. Sportsmen, however, who will recount the stratagems that they have known old cock pheasants adopt in thick and extensive coverts, when they have found themselves pursued, before they could be compelled to take wing, will convince us that this bird is by no means deficient in at least some of the contrivances ne‑ cessary for its own preservation.

As the cold weather draws on, the pheasants begin to fly at sunset into the branches of the oak trees, for roosting during the night. This they do more frequently as the winter advances, and the trees lose their foliage. The male birds, at these times, make a noise, which they repeat three or four times, called by sportsmen, *cocketing*. The hens, on flying up, utter one *shrill whistle*, and then are silent. Foxes destroy great numbers of pheasants.

The males begin to *crow* the first week in March. This noise can be heard at a considerable distance.—They will occa‑ sionally come into farm yards in the vicinity of coverts where they abound, and sometimes produce a cross breed with the common fowls.

It has been contended that pheasants are so shy as not to be tamed without great difficulty. Where, however, their natural fear of man has been counteracted from their having been bred under his protection; and where he has almost constantly ap‑ peared before their eyes in their coverts, they will come to feed immediately on hearing the keeper's whistle. They will follow him in flocks; and scarcely allow the pease to run from his bag into the troughs placed for the purpose, before they begin to eat. Those that cannot find room at one trough, follow him with the same familiarity to others.

Pheasants are found in most parts of England; but are sel‑ dom seen in Scotland; while in Ireland, I am not certain that there are any in a state of freedom. Wood and corn lands seem necessary to their existence.

The general weight of male pheasants is from two pounds and twelve ounces, to three pounds and four ounces. That of the hens, is usually about ten ounces less.

The female birds have sometimes been known to assume the

elegant plumage of the male. But with pheasants in a state of confinement, those that take this new plumage always become barren, and are spurned and buffeted by the rest. From what took place in a hen pheasant, in the possession of a lady, a friend of Sir Joseph Banks, it would seem probable that this change arises from some alteration of temperament at a late period in the animal's life. This lady had paid particular attention to the breeding of pheasants. One of the hens, after having produced several broods, moulted, and the succeeding feathers were exactly those of a cock. This animal never afterwards had young ones.—Similar observations have been made respecting the *pea hen*. Lady Tynte had a favourite pied peahen, which at eight several times produced chicks. Having moulted when about eleven years old, the lady and her family were astonished by her displaying the feathers peculiar to the other sex, and appearing like a pied peacock. In this process the tail, which was like that of the cock, first appeared. In the following year she moulted again, and produced similar feathers. In the third year she did the same, and then had also spurs resembling those of the cock. The hen never bred after this change of her plumage. She is now preserved in the Leverian Museum.

THE BUSTARD.

The bustards have a somewhat convex bill, with open and oblong nostrils. The legs are long, and naked above the knees. The feet have only three toes, all placed forward.

There are about twelve different species, all of which are confined to the old continent.

THE GREAT BUSTARD.

This is the largest land fowl produced in our island, the male often weighing twenty-five pounds and upwards. The length is near four feet, and the breadth nine. The head and neck are ash-coloured. The back is transversely barred with black, and bright rust colour. The belly is white; and the tail, consisting of twenty feathers, is barred with red and black. The legs are dusky. On each side of the lower mandible of the bill, there is a tuft of feathers about nine inches long.

The female is not much more than half the size of the male. The top of her head is of a deep orange, and the rest of the head brown. Her colours are not so bright as those of the male, and she wants the tuft on each side of the head. There is likewise another very essential difference between the male and the female: the former being furnished with a sack, or pouch, situated in the fore part of the neck, and capable of containing

above two quarts of water; the entrance of which is immediately under the tongue. This singular reservoir was first discovered by Dr. Douglas, who supposes that the bird fills it with
water to supply its thirst in the midst of those extensive plains
where it is accustomed to wander: it likewise makes a further
use of it in defending itself against the attacks of birds of prey;
on these occasions it throws out the water with such violence, as
not unfrequently to baffle the pursuit of its enemy.

This bird makes no nest; but the female lays her eggs in
some hole in the ground, in a dry corn-field; these are two in
number, as big as those of a goose, and of a pale olive brown,
marked with spots of a deeper colour. If, during her absence
from the nest, any one handles or even breathes upon the eggs,
she immediately abandons them. The young follow the dam
soon after they are excluded from the egg, but are not capable
for some time of flying.

Bustards are, I believe, confined to the old continent, and a
few of its adjacent islands; and feed on green corn, the tops of
turnips, and various other vegetables, as well as on worms; but
they have been known to eat frogs, mice, and young birds of
the smaller kind, which they swallow whole. They are remarkable for their great timidity; carefully avoiding mankind, and
being easily driven away in whole herds by the smallest dog.

In England they are now and then met with in flocks of fifty
or more: they frequent the open countries of the south and
east parts, from Dorsetshire as far as the wolds in Yorkshire,
and are often seen on Salisbury plain. They are slow in taking
wing, but run with great rapidity; and the young ones are even
sometimes coursed and taken by greyhounds.

THE WOODCOCK.

This bird has a long, slender, straight bill. The nostrils are linear, and lodged in a furrow. The head is intirely covered with feathers. The feet have four toes, the hind one of which is very short, and consists of several joints. The female woodcock may be distinguished from the male by a narrow stripe of white along the lower part of the exterior veil of the outermost feather of the wing. The same part in the outermost feather of the male is elegantly and regularly spotted with black and reddish white. In the bastard wing of both is a small-pointed, narrow feather, very elastic, and much sought after by painters, as it makes a good pencil.

The woodcock, during summer, is an inhabitant of Norway, Sweden, Lapland, and other northern countries, where it breeds. But when winter approaches, the severe frosts of those northern latitudes, by depriving it of food, force it southwards to milder climates. These birds arrive in Great Britain in flocks; sometimes as early as September, but not in great numbers till November and December. They generally take advantage of the night, being seldom seen to come before sun·set. The time of their arrival depends much upon the prevailing winds; for, as they are unable to struggle with the boisterous gales of the northern ocean, they wait for the advantage of a favourable wind. When they have had bad weather to encounter on their passage, they are frequently so much exhausted on their arrival as to remain on the same spot many hours, almost helpless, and much reduced in fiesh, by the fatigue of their voyage. In very stormy weather, we are told, they occasionally take refuge in the rigging of vessels at sea, and that numbers are frequently lost in their passage.

They feed on worms and insects, which they search for with their long bills, in soft ground and moist woods, flying and feeding principally in the night. They go out in the evening, and generally return in the same direction, or through the same glades, to their day retreat.

The greater part of them leave this country about the latter end of February, or the beginning of March. They retire to the coast; and, if the wind be favourable, set out immediately; but if contrary, they are often detained for some time, and thus afford good diversion to those sportsmen who reside near the sea.

Very few of them remain in England during the summer; though instances of this kind occasionally happen, and the female has been known to make a nest and lay eggs. But even these instances have most likely arisen from the birds having been so wounded by the sportsman in the winter, as to be disabled from taking their long journey in spring. They build their nests on the ground, generally at the foot of some tree, and lay four or five eggs, the size of those of a pigeon, of a rusty colour, and marked with brown spots. A single bird was observed to remain in a coppice, belonging to a gentleman in Dorsetshire, through the summer. The place, from its shady and moist situation, was well calculated to maintain it; yet, by degrees, it lost almost all its feathers, so that for some time it was unable to fly, and was often caught; but in the autumn it recovered its strength and feathers, and flew away.

Woodcocks generally weigh from twelve to fourteen ounces, and are chiefly found in covers, particularly those with wet bottoms, and underneath holly bushes; they are not, however, fond of covers where there is long grass growing in the bottom, and

E

at the roots of the trees. In mild weather they are to be met
with chiefly in the open country, in hedge-rows, &c. but a severe
frost forces them to the thickest covers, and to springs and small
running streams that are sheltered with trees or underwood.

The sight of the woodcock is very indifferent in the day time,
but he sees better in the dusk of the evening and by moonlight;
and it may also be remarked, that woodcocks will lie much better
the day following a moonlight night, than when it has been preceded by a very dark one: the reason is obvious—the bird has
been enabled, by the light of the moon, to make a plentiful repast, and the next day is lazy and unwilling to fly ; whereas,
when the darkness of the night has rendered it impossible for
him to satisfy the calls of hunger, he is constantly uneasy, and
on the alert in search of food, which he never attempts to seek
but when necessity compels him.

Shooting woodcocks is a very pleasant amusement in woods
which are not too thick ; and, if they are cut through in several
places, it renders it more easy to shoot this bird in his passage
when he rises, and also to mark him with greater certainty ; and
woodcocks will generally be found near the openings or roads
through the woods, if there are any. In this diversion a good
marker is of essential service ; for with his assistance it will be
difficult for a woodcock to escape, as he will generally suffer
himself to be shot at three or four times, before he takes a long
flight.

The woodcock is a clumsy walker, and rises heavily from the
ground, which, I believe, is the case with most birds that have
long wings, and short legs. When a woodcock is found in an
open field, in a hedge-row, in the pass of a wood, or an unfrequented lane, he skims the ground slowly, and is very easily
shot ; but it is occasionally otherwise, particularly when he is
flushed in a tall wood, where he is obliged to clear the tops o.
trees before he can take a horizontal direction; at which time

he frequently rises very high, and with great rapidity, a nd it becomes very difficult to seize the moment of shooting, by reason of the turnings and twistings which he is obliged to make, in order to pass between the trees.

In this diversion a person is often employed as a beater, which is highly necessary, and may be very useful at the same time in marking.

THE SNIPE.

THE WOODCOCK.

Having given a particular description of the woodcock, it will only be necessary to observe, that the plumage and shape of the snipe are much the same; and indeed its habits and manners bear a great analogy. But there are three different sizes of snipes, the largest of which, however, is much smaller than the woodcock. The common snipe weighs about four ounces, the jack snipe is not much bigger than a lark; the large snipe weighs about eight ounces, but is seldom met with. Some have supposed that the common snipe is the jack's female; however, the contrary is now too well known to need a refutation in this place.

Snipes are to be found all the winter in wet and marshy grounds, particularly where there are rushes; they are frequently to be found on mountains and moors among the heath, but a severe frost forces them to the springs and running streams. Numbers of these birds remain with us all the year, and breed in our marshes, laying generally six eggs the latter end of May. In saying this, I wish to be understood as meaning the common snipe; for I am of opinion the jack snipe, like the woodcock, goes to a more southern latitude to breed; though he is sometimes seen here in the summer, which may arise from similar causes to those which have induced the occasional stay of the woodcock. But numbers of the common snipe are found to stay and breed from choice, though by far the greater part migrate for this purpose.

The snipe is generally regarded as a difficult shot; and it must be allowed that it requires practice to surmount this difficulty, which arises from the zig-zag manner in which the bird flies immediately after rising. The best method to pursue in this diversion, is to walk down the wind, as snipes generally fly against it; and if a snipe rise before the sportsman, it will not fly far before it turns, and describes a sort of semi-circle, which will afford more time to take aim, by thus remaining longer within gun-shot. If, however, the bird should fly straight forward, it will be highly proper to let it get some little distance, as its flight will become much steadier. The slightest wound is sufficient to bring these birds to the ground.

An old pointer is the best in snipe shooting. To accustom a young dog to snipes, slackens his mettle, and renders him of little use for partridge or grouse, owing to getting a number of points with little exertion. However, when these birds are plentiful, a dog is unnecessary, as walking them up will answer equally well.

THE HARE.

Strictly speaking, this animal is an improper object for the *shooting* sportsman; in fact, there is an act of parliament which subjects any person to a penalty for shooting a hare; but this act is superseded by a posterior one, and the practice of shooting these animals has become very general.

The hare is one of the most timid animals in nature; fearful of every danger, and attentive to every alarm, it is continually upon the watch; and being provided with very long ears, which are moveable at pleasure, and easily directed to any quarter, it is warned of the distant approach of its enemies. As the hare is destitute of the means of defence, nature has endowed it with powers of evasion in a superior degree: every part and member of this animal seems peculiarly formed for celerity, and it is consequently one of the swiftest quadrupeds in the world. Its hind legs are much longer than the fore ones, and are furnished with strong muscles, which give it a singular advantage in running up a hill; and of this it appears very sensible, as it is generally observed to fly towards rising ground when first started.

The colour of this animal is another great means of preservation, as it often so much resembles the ground on which it sits, as not to be easily distinguished. In cold countries, near the pole, where the ground is covered the greatest part of the year with snow, the hare becomes white, which consequently renders it less conspicuous in those frigid regions.

Thus formed for escape, it might be supposed the hare would enjoy a state of tolerable security; but, although harmless and inoffensive in itself, it has no friend. Dogs of all kinds, as well as foxes, pursue it, seemingly by instinct; wild cats, weasels, &c. catch and destroy it; birds of prey are still more dangerous enemies; while man, more powerful than all, makes use of every artifice to obtain a creature, which constitutes one of the numerous delicacies of his table.

According to naturalists, the hare lives six or seven years, and attains its full growth in one. It engenders frequently before it is a year old. The buck seeks the doe principally from the month of December to the month of April. The female goes with young thirty or thirty-one days, and brings forth generally two young ones, though they have been known to produce three or four, and deposits them in a tuft of grass or heath, or in a little bush, without any apparent preparation.

The ridiculous assertions which some writers on natural history have made, viz. of hares being generally hermaphrodites, or of their changing their sex every month, as well as of possessing the power of superfetation, are too glaringly absurd to need a detailed refutation in this place. The circumstance which seems to have given rise to the first of these notions is the formation of the genital parts of the male hare, whose testicles do not obviously appear, especially when he is young, being contained in the same cover with the intestines. Another reason is, that on the side of the penis, which is scarcely to be distinguished, there is an oblong and deep slit; the orifice of which, in some measure, resembles the vulva of the female. The male and female are known to the sportsman by the following distinctions: the head of the male is more short and round, the whiskers long, the shoulders more ruddy, and the ears shorter and broader than those of the female; whose head is long and narrow, the ears long and sharp at the tip, the fur on the back of a grey colour, inclining to black, and in point of size she is frequently found smaller than the male. There is also considerable difference in the feet. In the male, the feet are small and pointed, and the nails short; whereas, in the female, they are much larger and more spread; the nails also are much longer.

Two species of hares may be distinguished: those of the wood, and those of the plain. The hares of the wood are in general much larger than those of the open ground: the fur is not of so dark a colour, and they are better covered with it; they are also swifter in the chase, and their flesh has a better flavour. Among the hares of the plain, those may be distinguished which inhabit marshes: they are not so swift of foot, are less covered with fur, and their flesh is not so fine flavoured and delicate.

A young hare, that has attained the full growth, may be known from an old one by feeling the knee joints of the fore legs with the thumb nail. When the heads of the two bones, which form the joints, are so close, that little or no space is to be perceived between them, the hare is old. If, on the contrary, there is a perceptible separation, the hare is young; and is more or less so, in proportion to the separation of the bones. It may also be known whether a hare is old or young, but without pretending to ascertain the precise age, by compressing the under jaw-bones: if they break at the point immediately under the fore-teeth, upon a slight degree of pressure, the hare is certainly a young one; but if considerable force is required, the contrary may be inferred.

The hare is very prolific, and I believe the female will sometimes take the buck the latter end of the same season the early part of which gave it birth. In fact, were it not for its surprising fecundity, the species (in England at least) would soon become extinct. To say nothing of its other numerous enemies this animal appears the peculiar object of the poacher. Ther are various methods of taking them, and so little skill is required that any bungler is able to execute his purpose. The wir snare is most commonly employed by poachers; though I believe it is not generally known, that hares may be covered on their seats in the day time with a net, much easier than a covey of partridges.

Those who are desirous of having hares very numerous in their parks, or warrens, should destroy some of the buck hares before the rutting season; as, if the latter are left in great numbers, they will prevent the does breeding properly, by their incessant teazing.

THE WILD DUCK.

Wild ducks are very artful birds. They do not always build their nest close to the water; but often at a good distance from it; in which case, the female will take the young in her beak, or between her legs, to the water. They have been known sometimes to lay their eggs in a high tree, in a deserted magpie or crow's nest; and an instance has likewise been recorded of one being found at Etchingham, in Sussex, sitting upon nine eggs, in an oak, at the height of twenty-five feet from the ground: the eggs were supported by some small twigs, laid crossways.

Wild-duck-shooting appears to be a diversion by no means calculated to promote health, since these fowls are chiefly to be found in marshes and other wet places.

The dog best calculated for this diversion is a water-spaniel, which ought to be taught to fetch a duck out of the water. As to a dog setting this kind of game, it is quite out of the question. The places where the ducks are known to resort, should be beat with as little noise as possible, and the sportsman must take his chance of their rising within gun-shot.

These birds may be shot in winter at the dawn of day, and also at the dusk of the evening, when they fly in search of food. In very severe frosts, they are compelled to seek those springs and running streams that do not freeze, in order to find aquatic herbs, which, at this period are their only food. The shooter should then follow the course of these streams at any time of the day. Coracles or small boats are useful on large pieces of water.

Wigeon and Teal are found in the marshes. The former is nearly as large as a duck, the latter much smaller; both resemble the duck in form and manners.

BREEDING POINTERS & SETTERS.

This subject has been already noticed under the head *Setter*, as well as under that of *Pointer*, but in what may be called the outline only : it will therefore be necessary, in this place, to descend to those particulars, without which, I should regard the present volume as incomplete.

In the first place, I would wish it to be fully impressed upon the mind of the sportsman, that, whenever, by judicious crosses or otherwise, he has obtained a breed of first-rate excellence, he must, nevertheless, in order to preserve such excellence, call in the assistance of other breeds of repute ; since, if he confine the propagation to the same family, the *strain* will degenerate, and in the third or fourth generation become literally good for nothing.—Relationship should be as much as possible avoided in breeding, nor can any better plan be adopted than procuring either the dog or bitch from a distant part of the country. Thus by crossing the Norfolk and the Yorkshire blood, the two best greyhounds (Snowball and Major) ever known, were produced.

The ill consequences of breeding *in and in*, to use a sportsman's phrase, are now tolerably well known, and the remark is not confined to dogs only, but would seem to apply equally perhaps to the whole circle of nature. The judicious farmer, aware of the evil, spares neither expense nor pains in crossing his horses, cows, and sheep ; his pigs and poultry. Even the human species, by the intermarriages of families strikingly exemplifies these observations—degeneracy of mind as of body is thus produced; scrofulous diseases are the certain result; and hence scrofula is less frequent in large towns; but is uniformly found to prevail in all secluded villages, where the continued inter-course of the same families has existed for a few generations.

If, therefore, the object of the sportsman be to procure and maintain a good breed of pointers or setters, let him have re-course to other breeds of pointers or setters of undisputed merit, if from a distant part the better perhaps; but if his neighbour's dogs stand in no degree of affinity, he need not be at the trouble of seeking for greater strangers.

The foregoing remarks are not exclusively applicable to ani-mated nature, but may be very justly extended to the vegetable world: hence the farmer never sows corn on the land where it was produced; and hence seed potatoes grown in Scotland are imported into Lancashire, where this useful vegetable attains the utmost possible perfection.   :

The best modes of crossing have been already pointed out under the articles *setter* and *pointer* in a great degree; but I will take the liberty further to observe, in addition to the remarks made in the last paragraph, that a pointer from Spain, Portugal, or France, crossed with a deep-flewed hound (I believe the true talbot is no longer to be found in Great Britain or Ireland) will produce excellent dogs; or they may be crossed with a pointer already naturalized as it were in this country, and the result an-ticipated with confidence. But there cannot be a worse cross than the pointer and setter—see the article *Pointer*, page 18.

If the opinion be correct, that the setter was originally pro-duced by the conjunction of the talbot or blood-hound and the springer (and I have no objection to believe it), for want of the former a reproduction of this sort seems out of the question, unless recourse be had to Denmark or Norway, where I am told the talbot is still to be found.—The blood-hound of Cuba and the West Indies is a very different animal, and no way calculated to improve the breed of dogs in this country, however it may be admired by the Spaniards : it is employed for a horrible purpose, and is extremely fierce and courageous—its master, is still more ferocious.

However, there are, I believe, to be met with, particularly in Scotland, setters of first-rate excellence, probably superior to the best breed of pointers. At all events, if setters be the object of the sportsman, let him select the sire and dam from families of repute, and let the individuals, if possible, be remarkable, not only for goodness of nose, but beauty of form, good temper and the middle size. No better rule can be adopted in breeding pointers, or indeed any other kind of dogs.

A bitch will become *proud* very frequently before she is twelve months old, the first symptoms of which are the red appearance and swelling of the *vulva;* but she will not, for some days suffer the dog to *ward* her : however, as the heat advances, she will play and dally with him, and manifest every inclination to copulate. But as these animals grow generally till they are nearly two years old, they ought not to be suffered to breed before that period.

To breed from either an old dog or bitch is improper. However, when two animals are chosen for this purpose, they should remain together for some time, one night, for instance, is sufficient ; but where the dog is only once admitted, the bitch will sometimes prove barren. Nor is it a little remarkable, that, if you suffer a bitch to receive several dogs, such as a terrier, a greyhound, a bulldog, &c. she will produce puppies of all the different kinds.

Young dogs should be tied up or confined as little as possible, as it spreads their feet, and they become *out at the elbows,* and bandy legged. The same effects will be produced in a full grown dog, but in a much less degree. Dogs of all ages should have free access to good clean water, a clear stream if possible.

The period of gestation in the bitch is about sixty-three days, and she produces from four to ten at a litter. The young are brought forth blind: the two eye-lids are not merely glued together, but shut up with a membrane, which is torn off as soon as the muscles of the upper eye-lids acquire sufficient strength to overcome this obstacle to vision, which generally happens about the tenth day. At this period the young animals are extremely clumsy and awkward. The bones of the head are not completed; the body and muzzle are bloated, and the whole figure appears ill-designed. Their growth, however, is rapid; and in about six weeks they acquire the use of all their senses. When four months old, they lose their teeth, which are quickly replaced, and are never afterwards changed.

A dog's age may be tolerably well ascertained by the appearance of his teeth. A young dog's teeth generally look clean and white;—at an early period of his existence, his front teeth are serrated, and as he increases in age, this saw-like appearance gradually wears out. At four years old, or perhaps sooner, it is no longer observable: the teeth turn yellow, fade, and drop out as the animal grows old; and if he be fed principally on bones his teeth become short and blunt at an early period. A dog, if worked hard, will turn grey at eight or nine years of age, and exhibit every symptom of decay—such as bad sight, loss of hearing, &c. Fourteen years is the general period allotted for the life of a dog; but if he be kept to hard labour each season, he will seldom live so long.

The best time for a bitch to take the dog is the month of March, when the whelps will have all the advantages of the summer, and will have become sufficiently strong to endure the rigour of the hardest winter.

There are various methods recommended to prevent a bitch from taking the dog, if she happens to become *proud* at an improper period, most of which are ridiculous enough : I know of but two effectual remedies, the first is to keep the bitch under lock and key; where this is inconvenient, if her *shape* be touched with a red hot iron, so as to make it sufficiently sore, without seriously injuring the animal, she will not suffer the conjunction of the dog : the reason is obvious, the pain caused, under these circumstances, by his approaches, will induce the bitch to resist, and drive him off.

Dogs, and young ones in particular, should be kept in the country. If when a whelp be taken from its dam, it is fed upon light food, such as potatoes and buttermilk, with a little oatmeal, &c. and seldom or never indulged with carrion, or flesh of any kind, it will scarcely ever be attacked with the *distemper*, a disease which has been long known in this country, and which makes frightful havoc among dogs bred in towns, highly fed, and which have little exercise:—exercise in particular is a very essential requisite to the health of young dogs.

In selecting whelps for the purpose of rearing, the sportsman will of course consult his own judgment, and will no doubt choose the most vigorous. Whelps may be taken from the dam at five or six weeks old, or so soon as they will lap sufficiently. If the sportsman is desirous of rearing more whelps than the dam can conveniently suckle, he must procure a foster-mother. If another bitch happens to pup about the same time, she will adopt strangers, if her own are taken away, particularly if they are rubbed with her own whelps, or her own milk :—indeed a bitch will frequently suffer strangers and her own to suck at the same time. It is a bad plan to keep whelps in a stable, as they are very liable to be trod upon; indeed grown dogs are best out of the stable for the same reason.

When puppies leave the bitch, her teats should be anointed or washed several times, with warm vinegar and brandy.

My whelps are always reared in the country, and sleep in kennels in the open air, and I have never had a whelp (thus

treated) even injured by the distemper. I feed them in the manner above described, and if they happen to be costive, I give
them a table spoonful of syrup of buckthorn.   However, with
a view to ascertain the effect of a different mode of treatment, I
took a whelp into the house, fed him plentifully with bones and
flesh, and suffered him to lie before the fire and to take but little
exercise.   He was attacked with the distemper when he was
nearly five months old, and died after lingering several weeks ;
but for a week before his dissolution, he became so exceedingly
offensive that it was impossible to keep him in the house.   In
another similar experiment, the animal, by good nursing and
medicine, lived through the distemper apparently, but never
enjoyed health ; it was incapable of much exertion, and was at
length attacked with convulsions, the violence of which encreased
to such a degree, that I was under the necessity of destroying
it, at the age of fifteen months.

Spaying bitches or castrating dogs is a diabolical practice.
The animals, shortly after the operation, grow extremely fat, and
very soon become useless.

Worming puppies is a ridiculous operation ;—it will not have
the effect, which is erroneously attributed to it, namely, of
rendering the animal incapable of biting when labouring under paroxysms of hydrophobia.   How it ever could be supposed
that extracting a sinew which runs longitudinally under a dog's
tongue would have the above effect, is a matter of surprise ;
and I blush at my own thoughtlessness in adopting in several
instances the foolish idea, the offspring of ignorance, and putting
an animal to pain, where no possible benefit could ever be reasonably expected.

I have known cantharides given to a bitch, in order to induce
her to take the dog.   It is an injurious, and consequently a bad,
method ; and such as I should not recommend under any circumstances.

Diseases of Dogs.

It has been shewn, in the early part of this volume, that wild animals reclaimed from a state of nature and domesticated, are susceptible of great change and variety in form, colour, and character; and owing no doubt to being thus compelled to assume in some degree, an artificial mode of life, they are rendered more liable to disorders. Animals in a state of nature are little subject to disease : and though the wild dog subsists on flesh and carrion, it is more than probable he is never troubled with what is distinguished by the appellation of the *distemper*, or any of that long catalogue of disorders, to which the dog is rendered obnoxious after having become the companion of man. However, thus much may be very truly observed, that if a dog be properly fed and exercised, has plenty of good clean water, and his bed kept clean, he will not in general be much troubled with disease ; and this rule will be found to obtain more particularly if he be kept in the country.

THE DISTEMPER.

The distemper generally attacks a dog before he has attained his first year. As a preliminary observation, it may be remarked, that the same membrane which lines the nostrils extends down the wind pipe into the lungs ; and the distemper, in the first instance, may be regarded as an inflammation of this membrane; which, if not timely removed extends down to the lungs, where suppuration will soon be produced ; when the animal's eye will become dull, accompanied shortly after by a mucous discharge, a cough, and loss of appetite. As the disease advances it presents various appearances, but is frequently attended with twitchings about the head, while the animal becomes excessively weak in the loins and hinder extremities; indeed he appears completely emaciated, and smells intolerably. At length, the twitchings assume the appearance of convulsive fits, accompanied with giddiness, which cause the dog to turn round: he has a constant disposition to dung, with obstinate costiveness, or incessant purging.

On the first appearance of the symptoms which I have described, I should recommend the dog to be bled,* and his body opened with a little castor oil: this will sometimes remove the disease altogether, if applied the moment the first symptoms appear. If, however, this treatment should not have the desired effect and a cough ensues, accompanied with a discharge at the nose, give him from two grains to eight of tartar emetic (according to the age and size of the dog) every other day. Also a seton or blister on the side will be serviceable, if adopted prior to suppuration of the lungs taking place. When the nervous symptoms ensue, which I have already described, external stimulants (such as sal-ammoniac and oil, equal parts) should be rubbed along the course of the spinal marrow, and tonics given internally, such as bark, &c.

There are few game-keepers, who will not tell you, that they can cure the distemper; and assume an air of mysterious secrecy if questioned as to the remedy; but they so frequently experience the inefficacy of their own receipt, as to place its infalli-

* The quantity of blood taken to be regulated by the age and size of the dog.

bility out of question, and even to induce doubt as to its most remote propriety. Of the various remedies, the following was given with success to a dog, so afflicted as to be scarcely able to stand :—

Turbeth's mineral, six grains,

mixed with sulphur, and divided into three doses, one given every other morning. Let a few days elapse, and repeat the course.

Another :—

Calomel, one grain and a half

rhubarb, five grains

given every other day for a week.

Another :—

Antimonial powder, sixteen grains

powdered fox-glove, one grain

made into four bolusses with conserve of roses, and one given at night, and another the next morning for two days.

I have known whitening administered for the distemper, a table spoonful every morning, with a little opening physic occasionally.

I am not aware of any other remedies worth notice, though a great number might be added, if we could give credit to the stories retailed by dealers in dogs as well as game-keepers. Of the recipes given, I prefer the last but one; but much will be found to depend on good nursing, and particularly to prevent the animal from taking cold.—From what I have witnessed of Blaine's medicine I should not recommend it.

It is very adviseable to inoculate for the distemper. If you can meet with a dog already afflicted, take a little muscous from his nose, and insert it up the nostrils of your whelp, after having prepared him by a dose or two of syrup of buckthorn; if the animal does not take the disease, repeat the operation. By inoculating for the distemper, the disease will be as much less severe, as the inoculated small pox compared to what is called the natural mode of taking it.

A dog never has the distemper twice, nor does it ever attack him after he has attained the age of two years; but generally makes its appearance before the animal is twelve months old. A notion became prevalent a few years back, that by inoculating a dog with the cow pock, the distemper would be prevented.

The Cow Pock.—Dr. Jenner has asserted that by inoculating dogs for the cow-pock, a " disease similar to that which is called the dog's distemper is produced, but in a very slight degree. What is most remarkable (adds Dr. Jenner) this inoculation renders them afterwards unsusceptible of that affection." Dr. Jenner is certainly no mean authority; but, having tried the experiment a number of times, from what I have witnessed, I can assert, that unless much more than ordinary pains are taken in the operation, no disease whatever whatever will be produced ; and when at length, pustules have been raised, they have not been attended with symptoms any way resembling what is called the distemper.

The catalogue of dog diseases is extended in some publications to a puzzling length, where the various ramifications or different stages of each disease receive a new name, in direct violation of that clearness and perspicuity so preferable, indeed so essentially requisite, in a statement of cases, many of which are frequently doubtful even to the skilful and experienced. Young dogs are very subject to worms, and appearances thus produced are too often mistaken for other disorders, receive various appellations, and are treated in the most injudicious manner. I shall finish this article by mentioning what I have been informed will cure the distemper; but I have never tried it; and am rather sceptical as to the fact :—

One clove of garlic given every or every other day, or according to the violence of the disorder.

WORMS.

Dogs, like human beings, are subject to worm diseases of various kinds. A disorder, generally distinguished by the appellation of *lank madness* is produced by short thick worms, which occasionally breed in prodigious quantities in the animal's stomach and intestines. This, and what is denominated *sleeping madness*, appear to be merely two names for the same disease. When a dog is thus afflicted he will become lean, though he will feed voraciously; as the disorder increases, his appetite in a great degree forsakes him; his eyes appear dull and drowsy, and he will manifest an almost continual inclination for slumber, without being able, however, to sleep soundly:—

> Take of calomel, six grains
> common soap, two scruples

made into two bolusses, one of which to be given at night, and the other the following morning: after two days, the same to be repeated, and in four days more, give the following:—

> Extract of coloquintida, two scruples

made into three bolusses and one given every morning; on the fourth morning, give the animal a table spoonful of syrup of buckthorn. If the worms should not be entirely destroyed in a little time, repeat the course.

Dogs are often troubled with large worms, which, without medicine, are occasionally voided singly or in clusters. Their existence may be known by the dog's voracity and leanness.

The best remedy is the preceding, though the following may probably answer the purpose :—

    Calomel, three grains

    jalap, twenty grains

    golden sulphur of antimony, four grains

mixed up with butter or lard into one dose. Three of these doses to be given—one every other morning.

A table spoonful or two of linseed oil given the first thing in a morning, will frequently bring away a quantity of worms : but it can never be depended on as an effectual remedy for the following reason :—upon the linseed oil being swallowed, those worms with which it comes in contact, that are not fastened on the intestines, but loose as it were, in expectation of food, will be brought away ; but such as are fast to the intestines (and many will be always found so situated) stick like leeches, and thus prevent the effects of the oil. There is nothing so effectual as calomel. Calomel administered externally, in tolerable plenty, upon the human subject, will destroy worms in the stomach.—If the worms are situated near the anus, the calomel may be so completely absorbed, when taken inwardly, as to lose its effect before it reaches that part ; some tobacco smoke blown up the anus (which may be easily done by inserting the thin end of a pipe) will most completely destroy these noxious vermin, and they will be voided most likely, in prodigious numbers.

The remark which was made on the last article would equally apply in this place, respecting the numerous remedies prescribed for the same disease. What are mentioned throughout are such as will be found to answer the purpose ; and to give a number of doubtful and ineffectual recipes, for the sake of making a long list, or giving a false air of importance to the subject, would be as perplexing to the reader, as it would be contemptible and even dishonest, in the writer.

However, for worms, generally speaking, the following may

be regarded as a sovereign remedy, and there are few cases
which it will not effectually cure—take

Linseed oil, half a pint

oil of turpentine, two drachms*

repeat the dose, if necessary.

The leaves of the walnut tree, General Hanger informs us are
an effectual remedy for worms. " In summer, when the leaves
are green, they must be dried and baked on a plate before the
fire, then rubbed to a fine powder with the hands. In winter,
when dry, you must buy them at the medical herb shop, Covent
Garden. I gave my dog two largish tea-spoons full, heaped
up; first boiling half a pint of milk, letting it cool, and putting
the powdered leaves into it : the dog will take it well ; but he
will not take it in grease, for the leaves have a very strong
taste and smell. · By the bye, I caution all sportsmen never to
give dogs milk, which has not been boiled, for it will purge them
as much as a dose of physic. I gave my dog, eight days following, one dose; after which, for above two months, he *never
voided one single worm.*

There is a peculiar excellence in these leaves; they never, in
the least, purged my dog: his body was in the same state, as
if I never had given him any thing. This is a vast benefit ;
for, as it does not purge the dog, it may be given him even
when he hunts. I am told by medical men, who have studied
botany, that walnut leaves are a positive poison to worms, but
by no means detrimental to man or beast.

You may observe, in the autumn, when the caterpillars and
grubs eat the leaves of trees, and destroy the garden stuff, you
will never see the leaves of walnut trees eaten by them : no
caterpillar nor grub will approach a walnut tree. Besides, I
will give you another proof of their abhorrence of walnut leaves :

---

* I am supposing a full grown dog.

in summer, when the ground is so dry that you cannot dig for worms to go fishing with, fill a pail, about one-third full, of walnut tree leaves, and pour a large kettle of boiling water on them ; cover the pail over with a thick cloth, and let them stand till cold; then go to a bowling green, where you observe many worm casts ; spread the water over the grass, and the worms will immediately come up above the ground.— *This I have tried.*"

CONVULSIONS or FITS.

Complaints of this nature are sometimes caused by an accumulation of worms in the stomach, which in the first stage create giddiness, and end in violent convulsive paroxysms. When the complaint is to be attributed to worms, the animal will have an itching at the nose and fundament, and will sneeze frequently. In this case, the best treatment is what has been already prescribed for worms. When convulsions proceed from other causes, which will be generally known by a wild appearance in the animal's eyes, frothing at the mouth, when labouring under the most violent paroxysm of convulsion, the dog may be recovered by being thrown into the water, perhaps a bucket of water thrown over him might answer the purpose : but this is merely a temporary relief; and to eradicate the disease, recourse must be had to something more effectual. In the first place, the animal should lose a few ounces of blood (from three to six ounces, according to his size and strength) when the following should be administered :—

> Jalap, one scruple
> cream of tartar, half a dram
> water, one ounce,

mixed ; half taken the morning after the dog has been bled ; the other half in two hours after, well shaken :— a rowel should afterwards be put in the neck, and kept open for a considerable time : the following should then be given :—

> Peruvian bark, half an ounce
> water, half a pint

boiled for a few minutes and strained ; then add, sweet spirit of nitre, one dram : a table spoonful to be given every two hours, the animal afterwards to be kept on a mild nourishing diet.

When convulsions arise from indigestion, the following has been generally found efficacious :—from two to eight grains of tartar emetic (according to the age and size of the dog) and in two days after, give the following :—

> Calomel, six grains
> Barbadoes aloes, half a dram.

Divide into six doses, and administer one every or perhaps every other morning, as you may judge the patient can bear it : when you may give tonics, as recommended under the head *Distemper.*

What is called the *megrim* or giddiness in the head is a species of fit, and may be removed by bleeding. The same disease is, by some, denominated *falling madness* (a ridiculous name certainly) from, I suppose, the animal occasionally falling from giddiness. When thus afflicted, the dog will frequently rub his feet against the sides of his mouth, and appear as if he had a bone in his throat. Any of these symptoms will give way to the treatment just described : and where the disorder is not very violent, it may generally be removed by bleeding; which, as it has formed a principal feature for the last few pages, it may not be amiss to say a word or two on the best mode of performing the operation, under a distinct head.

———

BLEEDING.

In speaking on this subject, I am not supposing that the sportsman is a member of the medical profession in any of its branches, but sufficiently skilled in anatomy to know a vein from an artery, which is all the knowledge requisite for performing the operation of bleeding a dog. A vein* may be distinguished from an artery by its having no pulsation; if an artery of any consequence should be divided, the blood will flow in irregular gushes, it will be difficult to stop (for I know of no other method than sewing it up) and may cause the death of the dog. However, there is little danger of such an unpleasant circumstance happening, and an ordinary degree of attention is quite sufficient to obviate it. The most convenient, and the best place to bleed a dog, is to open a vein (the jugular vein) in the side of the neck, round which a cord should be tied; and if the sportsman is not expert at handling a lancet, he may purchase a fleam at any of the shops where surgical instruments are sold, which, by means of springs, is so contrived that the greatest

* A vein carries back the blood to the heart; an artery brings the blood from the heart.

bungler need be under no apprehension. Those who sell this instrument will describe the method of using it, which indeed is so obvious at first view as to render elucidation superfluous in this place.

If, after the vein is opened, the animal should not bleed freely, pressure a little below the orifice will cause the blood to flow. Where sufficient blood has been taken, the bleeding will generally subside; should this not be the case, a little fur from a hat will stop it; or, if the sportsman be very anxious, he may draw the lips of the orifice together with a needle and thread.

———

COLD and COUGH.

A cough arises from an irritation of the lungs, and may be produced by a cold or otherwise; it is generally the effect of cold, and may be removed by

Antimonial powder, five grains
calomel, four grains

made with honey into two bolusses, and given in the evening for two nights successively.

If a dog should be afflicted with a cough, in the first place, examine his throat, in order to ascertain if any pieces of bone are lodged there, as such a circumstance will cause a dog to cough for weeks. If the cough arises from cold, administer a dose* or two of syrup of buckthorn. Should the cough still continue, give tartar emetic as described under the head *Distemper.*

* A table spoonful is a dose for a common sized dog.

SCAB IN THE EARS.

A little mercurial ointment rubbed upon the affected parts every two or three days will very soon effect a cure.

CANKER IN THE LIPS.

Rub the affected parts with alum-water two or three times a day.

Or, rub with bole ammoniac and burnt alum two or three times a day.

SWELLINGS IN GENERAL.

See *Inflammation,* page 81.

FILMS IN THE EYE.

Bathe the affected part twice a day with water in which a little vitriol has been dissolved (the size of a large horse bean to a pint of spring water) and in a minute or two wash it in clear water.

Or bathe with the following lotion twice a day :—

> Sulphate of copper, one scruple,
> water, four ounces

———

SPRAINS.

Sprains are painful swellings of the ligaments and tendons of the joints, and are caused by too great exertion of the limbs, of which the tendons become relaxed. They should be well rubbed with the following twice a day :—

> Camphor, two drams
> brandy, one ounce

when the camphor is well dissolved, add one ounce of sweet oil, and shake them well together. Should not this have the desired effect, try the following :—

> Spirit of hartshorn, two drams
> sweet oil, six drams

well shaken, and applied as the other. Give a spoonful or two of syrup of buckthorn.

N. B. As sprains are attended with inflammation,* which should be got rid of in the first place by fomenting with warm water four or five times a day, and the following lotion applied:

> Extract of lead, two ounces
> water, one pint.

Should any stiffness remain after the inflammation has totally subsided, apply a blister.

, AND TO STOP AN EFFUSION OF BLOOD.

If an artery is wounded, it may be known (as before observed) by the blood gushing out (not flowing regularly) and assuming a florid appearance. If a vein is wounded, the blood will be darker coloured and flow regularly.

Wounds may be divided into two classes—*incised*, or those cut with a sharp instrument; and *contused*, or those inflicted with any thing blunt or heavy.

Slight wounds require little or no attention; but supposing a serious incised wound, the first opperation should be cutting, or rather shaving, the hair from around the wound, when, if the blood continues to flow, it should be stopped by filling the wound with bits of sponge or dry lint; if the wound be in the limbs, a bandage tied very tight just above the wound will materially assist in stopping the flow of blood, should not the

* See also the article "Inflammation," page 81.

sponge or lint be found sufficient. The edges or lips of the wound should afterwards be ,stitched, or drawn close together with adhesive plaister cut into slips long enough to extend three or four inches on each side—the number of slips must of course be regulated by the size of the wound : plenty of lint or soft rag should be laid on, over which a roller or bandage must be applied to confine the dressing, which should not be removed for four or five days. The wound should afterwards be dressed with *Turner's cerate* sparingly spread on rag, and the bandage as before, and great caution used not to remove the adhesive plaister till the third or fourth dressing. A table spoonful of syrup of buckthorn may be occasionally given to keep the animal's bowels open : and he must be muzzled or otherwise so secured as to prevent his tearing away or disturbing the bandage.

Contused wounds are more painful than incised ; always swelled, ragged, and not attended with much hæmorrhage or flow of blood : no attempt should be made to bring the edges together, but a cold poultice applied, made with oatmeal and the following lotion :—

> Goulard's extract of lead, one dram
> vinegar, two ounces
> water, one pint

the poultice should extend over the swelled parts surrounding the wound, and be renewed three of four times during the day. When the wound begins to suppurate or discharge, unaccompanied with blood, the cold poultice should be changed for a warm one, consisting of oatmeal and water in which there is a little grease, and renewed three times a day as warm as the dog can bear it. In a few days the matter will be completely discharged, when the wound should be dressed daily with yellow basilicon spread on rag, and a long roller applied tightly over.

N. B. Whenever *fungus* or proud flesh appears, it should be touched with blue stone.

INFLAMMATION.

Inflammation arises from various causes; but is distinguished by the part affected becoming swoln, dry, and hot. A slight degree of inflammation will generally subside without the aid either of medicine or external application. Bleeding in the neck will frequently remove an inflammation; or the application of leeches to the affected part, having previously shaved the hair off. If the swelling or tumour becomes larger, soft, and shining, matter is forming, when warm poultices should be applied as described under *contused wounds*, and the same treatment adopted. When the matter is completely formed (which may be known by the fluctuation of the fluid upon a slight pressure) if the skin is very thin, a deep opening or incision should be made with a lancet on the prominent part; but if hardness is felt the tumour must remain till it breaks itself.—After the tumour is emptied care should be taken that the air does not penetrate, or the wound will be much more difficult to heal.

When a dog's eyes become inflamed and assume a red and fiery appearance, bleeding will generally relieve him.

Dogs, however, are not very subject to inflammation; and, generally speaking, will be troubled with few diseases if properly dietted and exercised. Dogs kept in towns are much more subject to disorders, than such as are kept in the country. Confinement is always injurious to dogs.

FOR THE BITE OF ANOTHER DOG.

See the article *Wounds*, &c. page 79.

INFLAMMATION.

WHEN WOUNDED WITH SHOT.

Extract the shot if possible, and rub with a little mercurial ointment. At all events, use the mercurial ointment.

SORE FEET.

Styptic tincture ; or, if this cannot be procured, salt and water.*

———

FOR EXTRACTING THORNS.

Thorns may be generally extracted with the thumb and fore finger nails ; or recourse may be had to the assistance of the pen-knife in the same way as the sportsman would extract a thorn from his own finger. The dog will frequently perform the operation with his mouth. If the wound festers, the thorn may be squeezed out.

* It will be necessary here to observe, that what is recommended above is generally for sore feet; but the matter requires elucidation :— In the heat of summer, when after a hard day's shooting the dog is foot sore, his feet should be well washed with soap and water, for which warm water is perhaps preferable to cold : if the skin is rubbed off, or the foot lacerated, styptic tincture or salt and water should be applied.

TO BRING HAIR UPON A SCALDED PART.

Fresh hog's lard rubbed frequently upon the affected part, will reproduce hair; indeed, I am inclined to think that animal fat in general will have the desired effect. Fresh goose grease, or the fat of fowls, unmixed with salt, will answer the purpose equally well. Vegetable oils are of too dry a nature, and their effects, as applied to the growth of hair, pernicious. Yet there are not wanting quacks who daily advertise the sale of oil for the growth of hair on the human head; and by way of the strongest possible recommendation, specifically state, that it is extracted from vegetables! This is lamentable, but it is still more so, that such numbers of the unthinking become the dupes of these ignorant pretenders, whose existence is a stigma on the liberality of the public.

TO DESTROY FLEAS, LICE, &c.

Take of white arsenic, one dram
    water, one gallon
    soft soap, one quarter of a pound

boil for ten minutes; then take it off the fire and let it stand to settle, then pour it off into another vessel, leaving about half a pint at the bottom, which throw away, and dress with the water. —A certain remedy.

Linseed oil, or Scotch snuff, rubbed well all over the body is a temporary remedy. A good washing with common soap and water will perhaps answer the purpose. In hot weather, dogs are much troubled with fleas; and if the sportsman is anxious for the comfort of the animal, he will find it necessary to use the above several times during the summer. Clean beds and cleanliness in general act as preventives.

TO RECOVER THE SENSE OF SMELL.

When the dog's olfactory organs become affected, it will frequently be found to arise from colds, costiveness, or other causes, which a dose or two of opening physic seldom fails to remove. A little sulphur or syrup of buckthorn will have the desired effect.

FOR DOGS THAT HAVE TAKEN POISON.

For all vegetable poisons, vinegar has been supposed to be a specific. At all events, whether vegetable or mineral poison has been swallowed, the sooner it is discharged from the stomach the better.

Take of sulphate of copper, half a drachm
water, six ounces

Give two table spoonfuls every five minutes till effectual

vomiting has taken place; when a strong dose of castor oil should be administered, followed by nourishing diet.

Whatever will cause instantaneous vomiting may have the desired effect. If a dog has swallowed poison, and no better remedy happen to be at hand, almost any kind of oil, (rancid or otherwise) poured down the throat is adviseable. The poison will most likely be either nox vomica, arsenic, or corrosive sublimate; however, let the poison be what it will, the best remedy is the following:—

> Ipecacuanha, fifteen grains
> water, two tablespoonfuls, mixed

Should it not operate in fifteen minutes, repeat the dose: After the operation

> Take of prepared kali, three drams
> water, one ounce

give a table spoonful every fifteen minutes, which will most likely produce vomiting and purging. Afterwards nourishing diet.

" *Antidote for vegetable poisons.*—M. Drapiez has ascertained, by numerous experiments, that the fruit of the fewillea cordifolia is a powerful antidote against vegetable poisons. He poisoned dogs with the rhus toxicodendron, hemlock, and nox vomica. All those that were left to the effects of the poison died, but those to whom the fruit of the fewillea cordifolia was administered, recovered completely, after a short illness. M. Drapiez also took two arrows which had been dipt in the juice of manchinelle, and slightly wounded with them two young cats. To the one of these he applied a poultice, composed of the fruit of the fewillea cordifolia, while the other was left without any application. The wound of the former speedily healed; while the other, in a short time, fell into convulsions, and died."

It is very difficult however to save the life of a dog that has taken poison. Nox vomica is what the base minded generally

H

use for the purpose. If recourse can be had to the process before described the moment the animal has swallowed the baneful drug, I should have no doubt of success ; but if only a few minutes elapse, the cure is extremely doubtful. I have witnessed several instances, in all of which the animals died, though every exertion was used for their preservation.

SICKNESS, or A FOUL STOMACH.

Dogs are very liable to a foul stomach ; but this is more particularly the case with such as are tied up or confined. If you tie a dog to a kennel for a few days, the moment you loose him, he will run in search of grass to eat, the broad blades of which he prefers ; this will frequently cause him to vomit: whenever the animal is troubled with sickness or a foul stomach, he will uniformly have recourse to eating grass, though vomiting does not always follow.

A foul stomach proceeds from indigestion ; therefore eight or ten grains of tartar emetic may be very beneficially given, followed, in a day or two, by a purge of syrup of buckthorn.

A dog never perspires ; but whenever he is unwell, his eyes very strongly exhibit the change, are a certain index of the state of his health, and assume a languid, a dull, or a fiery appearance, according to the nature of the disorder with which he is afflicted. The powers of digestion in a dog do not appear to be promoted by exercise. If you take a dog into the field to hunt with a full stomach, he will throw up the contents of it in a few minutes, or at least in a short period. If you suffer him to sleep after a hearty meal, the digestion is rapid and healthy. Give a dog a good supper on the evening prior to hunting, and the next morning, he will require little or nothing. I generally give my dogs a crust of bread in the morning when going out, which, however, they will not always stop to eat, so great is their anxiety for the expected diversion. Little food and that of a light nature will be found to answer best upon violent exercise—hence a man walks or labours much better after a breakfast, composed principally of tea or coffee, than after a heavy dinner. Cows, horses, and animals in general retire to rest after filling their bellies ; a full stomach, I have no doubt, is the best to sleep upon ; and I therefore differ very widely with those physicians who represent a good supper as injurious to repose.

THE COMMON MANGE.

This disorder is very infectious, and originally proceeds from dirty beds, bad food, and filth in general. It has a loathsome, scabby, dirty appearance, somewhat similar to the itch in human beings ; and, like that disease, contains animalcula in each of the pustules. It may be cured with the following :—

> Oil of tar
> sulphur vivum
> train oil, of each an equal quantity,

with which the dog should be well rubbed several times, a day or

two elapsing between each rubbing.   Sulphur given internally
will be of service.

Another :—

> Flowers of sulphur, half an ounce
> hog's lard or butter, one ounce

well mixed and rubbed completely over the animal twice a day,
giving a tea spoonful of the flowers of sulphur every evening in
a little molasses.   Keep the animal confined alone, and the
moment the cure is effected, give him a clean bed.—As the
disease is very infectious, without great care, all your dogs will
become disordered.

Mercurial ointment rubbed on the parts affected will remove
this disease; but it is rather a dangerous remedy, and will kill a
weak animal, if not carefully administered :—muzzle the dog.

An infusion of fox-glove leaves, I have reason to believe, will
answer the purpose: it is the cleanest remedy; and though I
have not had sufficient experience to pronounce its infallibility, I
have no hesitation in recommending it:—put a handful of fox-
glove leaves into a quart or three-pint jug, pour boiling water
upon them; and, when cold, rub the dog every day for three or
four days.   The dog need not be muzzled—as soon as dressed
he will attempt to lick, but will not take a second taste.

The following I have seen successfully used ·

> Sulphur, two ounces
> mercurial ointment, two drams
> hog's lard, four ounces

well mixed; with which rub the dog every other day—three or
four dressings will generally be sufficient.   Two drams of aloes,
mixed up with the above, will not injure the composition, and will
probably prevent the animal licking himself—otherwise, muzzle
him.

THE RED MANGE.

The disorder called the RED MANGE does not appear to be nearly allied to what is so well known by the common appellation of MANGE, but to be a species of disease within itself, seated in the skin, and not always infectious amongst dogs lying together, but almost invariably communicated by a bitch to her litter of whelps, particularly if she had it upon her during the time she was in pup. This disorder is most malignant in its effect; the incessant and severe itching, which, from all observation, seems accompanied by a burning heat, and this too increased by the perpetual biting and scratching of the tortured animal, gives such parts of the frame as are severely affected, the appearance of having been scalded by some boiling liquor, with a consequent loss of hair. It is this distinct kind of mange that so constantly baffles dog-doctors and dog-mongers of every description, and reduces them to their *ne plus ultra*, where the fertility of invention can go no further. It is, perhaps, the most deceptive disorder to which any part of the animal world can become unluckily subject; for when it has (seemingly and repeatedly) submitted to, and been subdued by, some of the combination of combustibles before described, it has as suddenly, as repeatedly, and as unexpectedly, made its re-appearance with all its former virulence. Great care, nice attention, and long experience, can discover but one infallible mode of perfect eradication. Let half an ounce of *corrosive sublimate* be reduced in a glass mortar to an impalpable powder; to this, by a very small quantity at a time, add two ounces (half a gill) of spirits of wine; and, lastly, one pint of rain or river water, and, with a sponge dipt in the solution, let every part palpably affected be well washed, every third day, till thrice performed ; then leave three clear days, and repeat the former ceremony of thrice as before ; letting three *mercurial purging balls* be given at the equal distances of three or four days, and not the least doubt of cure need be entertained, if the mode prescribed is properly and judiciously attended to.

Of the red mange General Hanger thus speaks :—" My dog had the mange ; not very bad, but something much worse with it ; he had eight or ten large blotches on his body, as big as large hazle nuts. I sent for an old man who made a livelihood by curing dogs : he took a bottle out of his pocket, and first dabbed the blotches with a bit of tow, each two or three times. He then stopped about five minutes, for that to dry in and penetrate ; after which he took a pot of ointment, and rubbed the dog in well, for at least ten minutes, under the fore legs, and on the belly, but *particularly on the back bone.* He then desired me not to wash the dog, or let him go into the water ; telling me, that he would call in about five days. When he called, the dog was apparently well : so much so, that he said he did not think it necessary to rub the dog again : however, I made him dab the blotches again, and rub once more in.—When he called to be paid, I told him that, upon my honour, if he would discover how the liquid and ointment were made, I would give him two guineas, and never discover it till after his death. He consented. The liquid is thus made :—Half an ounce of quicksilver is put into a bottle, with half an ounce of oil of turpentine, for about eight hours before using it : shake the bottle frequently, and shake it always when you use it, for there will be a sediment at the bottom. The ointment is thus made :— Take half an ounce of quicksilver ; put it into a bottle, with half an ounce of oil of turpentine ; let it stand for eight hours, shaking the bottle frequently : then take four ounces of hog's lard, and by degrees, mix both together, a little of each at a time, till the whole be incorporated.—He told me, that he always carried two pots of ointment with him, one stronger than the other, in case of a dog being very bad with the mange. The strongest ointment was made with *only three ounces* of hog's lard, but with the same quantity of the quicksilver and turpen-tine."

————

For the BITE of the ADDER, &c.

The adder is not uncommon in some parts of England, and is occasionally met with, in the heat of summer, among sedges and in marshy places. It differs from the snake in not being so long, the latter being found from three-quarters to a yard long; the former seldom, or never, reaching three-quarters of a yard: there is an appearance of malignity in the countenance of the adder, which does not obtain in that of the snake, the head of which is not so blunt as that of the adder; while the tail of the latter tapers more abruptly, and is generally found of a more dusky colour. There is, however, another very essential diffe-rence :—the snake is destitute of teeth; while the adder is not only prepared in this respect, but has one particular tooth, in the side of the jaw, which has a communication with a sort of alembic, situated in the reptile's head, and which contains the venom: in this tooth, there is a slit; and when the creature be-comes irritated and bites, the pressure thus occasioned upon the tooth, causes the venom to ooze through the slit, and it is thus injected into the blood.

I have heard of a reptile, called the *slow worm*, the bite of which is said to be venomous; but I never saw one.   The snake is perfectly harmless; the bite of the adder or viper will be attended with serious consequences, if a remedy is not speedily applied.   The remedy, however, is simple— the immediate application of a little sweet oil rubbed upon the affected part, counteracts the effect of the venom most surprisingly : as I have witnessed it, I speak with confidence.   Indeed, I am of opinion, that any vegetable oil (or animal either, perhaps) will answer the purpose; and have little doubt, that what will cure the bite of the adder will cure the bite of the slow worm also.   Yet, for a further illustration of this subject, I will borrow the account of a favourite author.   I am aware the same account has already appeared in various publications; but, from a conviction that much good may result from its becoming generally known, I shall transcribe it without hesitation :—

"One William Oliver, a viper catcher, of Bath, was the first who discovered this admirable remedy.   On the first of June, 1735, in the presence of a great number of persons, he suffered himself to be bit by an old black viper (brought by one of the company) upon the wrist and joint of the thumb, so that drops of blood came out of the wound; he immediately felt a violent pain both at the top of his thumb and up his arm, even before the viper was loosened from his hand : soon after he felt a pain, resembling that of burning, trickle up his arm; in a few minutes, his eyes began to look red and fiery, and to water much; in less than an hour, he perceived the venom seize his heart, with a pricking pain, which was attended with faintness, shortness of breath, and cold sweats; in a few minutes after this, his belly began to swell, with great gripings and pains in his back, which were attended with vomitings and purgings; during the violence of these symptons, his sight was gone for several minutes, but he could hear all the while. He said, that in former experiments he had never deferred making use of his remedy longer than he perceived the effects of the venom reaching his heart; but this time, being willing to satisfy the company thoroughly, and trusting to the speedy effects of his remedy, which was nothing more than olive oil, he forbore to apply anything, till he found himself exceedingly ill and quite giddy. About an hour and a quarter after the first of his being bit, a chaffing dish of glowing charcoal was brought in, and his naked arm held over it as long as he could bear, while his wife rubbed in the oil with her hand, turning his arm continually round. as if she would have roasted it over the coals : he said the poison soon abated, but the swelling did not diminish much. Most violent purgings and vomitings soon ensued ; and his pulse became so low, and so often interrupted, that it was thought proper to order him a repetition of cordial potions : he said he was not sensible of any great relief from these ; but that a glass or two of olive oil drank down, seemed to give him ease. Continuing in this dangerous condition, he was put to bed, where his arm was again bathed over a pan of charcoal, and rubbed with olive oil heated in a ladle over the charcoal, by Dr. Mortimer's direction, who was the physician that drew up the account. From this last operation he declared, that he found immediate ease, as though by some charm; he soon after fell into a profound sleep, and after nine hours' sound rest, awaked, about six the next morning, and found himself very well ; but, in the afternoon, on drinking some rum and strong beer, so as to be almost intoxicated, the swelling returned, with much pain and cold sweats, which abated soon, on bathing the arm, as before, and wrapping it up in brown paper soaked in the oil."

BURNS AND SCALDS

Assume a very different appearance according to the degree of heat or violence by which they are occasioned; if slight, and the skin only irritated, they are easily cured by instantly dashing the part affected in cold water, or constantly applying it till the pain and irritation have ceased; if slight blisters rise they should not be opened at first, as is generally recommended; for if the air penetrates it frequently produces an ulcer or sore. When a burn or scald is more severe, it must be constantly kept wet with rag dipped in the following lotion :—

> Goulard's extract of lead, two drams
> water, half a pint

and the part kept as quiet as possible. Strong spirits, or oil of turpentine is also serviceable when immediately applied, but the lotion is the most successful treatment either in scalds or burns. After the third or fourth day the blisters should be opened, but the skin not removed, and then dressed with the following ointment :—

> Olive oil, half an ounce
> Goulard's extract of lead, one ounce

well mixed together, and spread on lint or soft rag with a bandage over moderately tight.

When burns or scalds are so severe as to destroy the flesh from the bone, warm poultices of oatmeal and water should be applied, and then treated as *suppuration*.—See the article *Wounds*, &c. page 79.

THE HYDROPHOBIA.

This is a dreadful disease, and has received a very appropriate name, as not only dogs, but human beings, when afflicted with this little understood malady, uniformly testify an abhorrence of water, and, I believe, of fluids in general.

The hydrophobia affords a striking instance of successful quackery in the avidity with which the *Ormskirk Medicine* was purchased, till within these few years that the imposture has been exposed. This compound of calcined oyster shells, elecampane, roach alum, and bole ammoniac, was originally administered gratis; but no sooner was it discovered, that the medicine was eagerly sought after, than the sale of it was advertised; agents were appointed in different parts; and many hundreds purchased and took the medicine who had been bitten, but not by *mad dogs*. A dog accustomed to the country, is generally alarmed when he approaches a town or village—the shaking of a cobler's apron, or some such thing, is frequently resorted to, by the lower orders— the terrified animal takes to his heels, and will most likely snap at any person who attempts to impede his progress. Nothing is heard but the cry of mad dog! and many who have been bitten under such circumstances, have called in the assistance of the Ormskirk medicine, and have thus been willing to suppose a disorder prevented, which did not exist in the dog, and which, of course, could not be communicated.

The venders of the Ormskirk medicine, however, made the most of the matter—its infallibility was *puffed* upon the public in the most barefaced manner; and it was even publicly stated, that such was the virtue of the medicine, that even after the

hydrophobia had made its appearance, the disease could be removed by taking it.   Cases, with fictitious names, were stated,
and the grossest falsehood resorted to, in order to levy contri-
butions with more plausibility upon the credulity of the unthinking.   I believe, at present, no person who wishes to preserve
even an appearance of character, will attempt to palm the medicine upon the world ; but it has still its supporters, and a number of old women, in various parts of Lancashire, still practice
the deception ; and shew considerable dexterity in propping its
falling reputation.

The recipe was obtained by the late Mr. Hill's father, who
resided near Ormskirk, from an itinerant tinker, in the year
1704 ; the medicine is thus prepared :—take one tea spoonful
of prepared (calcined) oyster shells, one knife point full of roach
alum, as much elecampane, in powder, and half a tea spoonful
of bole ammoniac ; all to be powdered finely, and given to the
patient in the morning fasting, in a little wine and water, or
small beer : at the same time the wound is to be dressed with a
preparation, varying from that just described, only in a greater
portion of roach alum.

Not one dog in twenty, reputed mad, is so in reality—the
cure, or rather the prevention, therefore, is certain in many instances ; and where it happens otherwise, and the dog was
labouring under the hydrophobia, the result is most melancholy :
but then it is immediately and unblushingly asserted, that the
medicine had not operated in a proper manner—it had not remained upon the stomach, or been taken in sufficient quantity ;
and thus the cheat continues, though on a much more circumscribed scale.

The fact is, that the only certain remedy hitherto discovered
for this dreadful disease, is the application of the knife :—the
blood becomes infected by the saliva from the dog's teeth ; and
unless the bitten part can be immediately cut out, death will

most likely be the result, though the precise time will be very uncertain ; for so capricious is this malady, that, after infection, it sometimes lies dormant, as it were, in the system for months, sometimes for weeks ; while instances, I believe, are not wanting, where it has appeared, in all its terrible symptoms, in the course of a few days.

It is possible that a person might be bitten by a mad dog, and yet escape the hydrophobia : if, in the act of biting, the animal's teeth pass through a thick woollen coat, or other garment, so that his teeth in passing through are wiped dry, he might inflict a wound without any of the infectious saliva or fluid reaching it.

Respecting the bite of a mad dog Dr. Vandeburgh very judiciously observes :—" not a moment should be lost to destroy the poison from the wound (even if only on supposition of the animal being mad) ; many remedies are recommended but should not be trusted to ; the only effectual method is to destroy the foundation of the poison and give the following course of medicine :—the part bitten must be entirely cut out with a sharp instrument, and the edges of the wound seared with a red hot iron, to prevent the smallest particle of poison remaining ; afterwards, warm poultices of oatmeal and water to be applied as warm as the patient can possibly bear, to produce a quick and copious discharge of matter or suppuration : the following pills should be given :—

Calomel, one scruple
opium, half a scruple

well mixed and divided into ten pills of equal size, one pill to be taken every four hours ; two drams of strong ointment of quicksilver to be well rubbed in on the thighs and arms morning and evening, which, with the medicine, must be continued till the mouth becomes sore and spitting is produced : when matter discharges from the sore, it should also be dressed with strong oint-

I

ment of quicksilver thickly spread on lint and the poultice continued over it : this treatment must be pursued for the space of
one month, then the wound healed with *Turner's cerate* spread
on lint, but the mouth kept sore and slight spitting prolonged
for at least two months, as hydrophobia has been known to make
its appearance five and six months after the bite of the animal :
sea bathing is strongly advised, but I would always recommend
the foregoing treatment in preference, a trial of which should not
be omitted, if the poison was destroyed at first by cutting, neither
if the bite has happened some time, nor even when the following
symptoms have taken place : the part bitten becoming tender
and inflamed, uneasiness and stupidity, frightful dreams, convulsions, eyes red and watery, pain all over the body, difficulty in
swallowing, great thirst, and when liquid is only brought before
the patient he appears choaked, accompanied with trembling
and shivering over the whole body ; vomiting bile frequently
occurs, attended with great thirst and fever : the last symptoms
are raging and foaming at the mouth, spitting at the bystanders,
and strong convulsions, as if drawn double ;—no patient should
be given over till the last moment : the mercurial friction should
be tried, and the prescribed medicine given while he exists, as
there is hope of recovery by perseverance in the foregoing
method.

The patient should be kept on very low diet, and no spirits or
wine be used."

The following are the progressive symptoms of hydrophobia :
when a dog becomes melancholy, droops his head, forbears eating, seems to forget his former habits, and as he runs snatches
at every thing : if he often looks upwards, and that his tail at
its setting on be rather erect, and the rest of it hanging down ;
if his eyes be red, his breath strong, his voice hoarse, and that
he drivels and foams at the mouth, you may be satisfied of the
approaches of hydrophobia ; and the only thing that should be

done is instantly to despatch him, however great a favourite he may be. If at this period he should remain at liberty, he will certainly leave his home: he goes as fast as he can; and the mischief that may happen, owing thus to a mad dog breaking away, and running over an extent of country, is incalculable, as he spares no living creature.

There is another still very distinguishing feature by which this disease may be known, which is the animal's aversion to water and liquids in general. At the sight of water, not only a mad dog, but a human being who has the hydrophobia, will shudder and turn from it with abhorrence; and this, undoubtedly, is the most certain sign that a dog is mad. These animals are liable to other diseases, the symptoms of which, in some degree, resemble those of madness, and are frequently mistaken for them; but in no other disorder will the dog manifest that utter aversion to water; as, in other cases, if he will not drink, he will in general smell of it; and uniformly appears no way alarmed; on the contrary, a mad dog seems agitated, and will be almost convulsed, at the very sight.

In the very last stage of the disorder, when the animal is nearly exhausted, he has been known to fall into the water, or even to cross a brook.

When the human species become unhappily the subjects of this calamity, though in particular instances some variation may be observed, yet the first symptoms are generally the same; these are a torpid disquietude in the wound (or seat of injury), attended with slight intervening itchings, ultimately amounting to pain, and much resembling rheumatic affection. It continues to extend itself to the surrounding parts; and, at length, from the extremities it expands its poisonous power to the viscera; the cicatrice, if there has been a wound, begins to swell, inflammation hourly increases, till, at length, a serous bloody ichor is discharged, and this alone may be considered the primary and invariable prognostic of certain hydrophobia. These leading symptoms soon become progressively general, bearing with them every appearance of confirmed rheumatism; they are fluctuating, quick, acute, and of the spasmodic, convulsive kind; they suddenly attack the patient, severely affecting the head, neck, and principal joints; a dull, drowsy pain often seizes the head, neck, breast, abdomen, and even vibrates along the back bone. The patient is gloomy and inclined to solitude, murmurs much, seems lost in reflection, is forgetful, inattentive, and prone to sleep; at times agitating starts denote the mind to be disordered; by turns he is attentively watchful; his slumbers become disturbed, and suddenly awaking from those, convulsive appearances soon follow.

A deafness is sometimes complained of, the eyes are watery; the aspect sorrowful; the countenance pale, and the face contracted; sweat breaks out about the temples; an unusual flow of saliva, slimy and viscid, at length comes on with a dryness of the fauces, a foulness of the tongue, and a disagreeable smell (or rather fetid effluvia) from the breath. As the symptoms already recited increase, the second stage advances: a fever commences, which, at first is mild, but makes with gigantic strides the most rapid advances to extremity; it is accompanied with hourly increasing horrors, and all the alarming concomitants of mental derangement. Wakefulness becomes perpetual; violent periodical agitations ensue; the mind is evidently more and more disturbed; a delirium follows, at which critical moment an invincible aversion to *fluid, glass,* or any polished or shining body is plainly perceived. A constriction of the gullet takes place, and an incredible difficulty of swallowing ensues; liquids are offered, and are attempted to be taken, but the disgust and loathing become so predominant, they are most violently declined: and this symptomatic dread and aversion so wonderfully increases, that, upon the very appearance of any watery fluid, the greatest horror comes on, and the most shocking muscular distortions ensue; if the liquor is attempted to be forcibly pressed upon them, the experiment is rejected by an instantaneous succession of the most horrid gesticulations, and convulsive distortions, in which every ray of reason seems to be absorbed. Upon a temporary cessation of so serious and distressing a paroxysm, the poor unhappy patient now murmurs, groans, and mourns most miserably; loses, by degrees, all knowledge of his dearest friends and most familiar acquaintance: and their presenting themselves before him, is the very critical moment when all of this description give proof of their desire to bite, which, in the attempt, bears no ill affinity to the similar snappings of a village cur.

Awful to relate, reason returns at intervals, and he feelingly laments his own calamity, and deplores his own incapacity. A consciousness of an approaching dissolution is perceptible even to himself, and he seems truly resigned to the singularity of his fate. Severe pain and consequent heat producing thirst, a desire to drink is displayed, but nature shrinks from her office; in vain the patient raises his hand to touch the vessel, it almost magically produces instant tremor—the hand recedes, and the patient sinks into the most afflicting despondency. Conscious, likewise, of his constantly increasing inclination to bite, he in his rational moments, makes signals to warn his friends of the danger, and keep themselves at a distance. Towards the conclusion of this dreadful and most melancholy scene, the fever and parching thirst increase, the tongue becomes swelled and protruded, foam issues from the mouth, strength fails, cold sweats come on, the stricture upon the breast increases, as well as the other predominant symptoms, until, in a long succession of convulsive struggles, all-powerful death closes the scene.

The cause of the hydrophobia is utterly unknown; and its effects hitherto appear to have baffled every remedy which has been tried for its removal. Copious and repeated venesection was, a few years back, announced to the world as a cure for the hydrophobia, and instances were given in order to confirm it: it is true, they came in a questionable shape on account of the distance which they had to travel, being chiefly from the East Indies :—however, the method just mentioned has been tried in this country and found unavailing, as the following will show :

Henry, son of G. Rix, a waterman. of Southsea, was bitten in the cheek, and over the eye, by a mad dog, on the 25th of March, 1813. He continued very well until Friday morning, the 13th of the following month, when he complained of being indisposed. His friends gave him a cordial, with the hope of relieving his pain ; but he grew worse, and complained of great thirst. It was with great difficulty he was prevailed on to take medicine. He complained exceedingly of violent pains in the chest and throat ; and, on his seeing water that was brought into the room, his agony greatly increased. He foamed at the mouth sufficiently to wet many cloths, and would frequently exclaim, "O, Father! is that from the dog?" He was copiously bled, but without any good effect. He retained his senses until within a few hours of his death, when the effects of this disorder were extremely violent; but the paroxysms abated an hour before he expired.

James Sharp, glassman, son of Alexander Sharp, Queen-street, Newcastle, on Wednesday morning last, when he returned home from the Northumberland glasshouse, complained of being unwell, and told his parents that he had been vomiting throughout the night, while at work. On Thursday he was much worse, when an emetic was procured for him, but he could not bear the sight of it when made into a liquid. On Friday a medical man was brought to see him, who, after examining the youth, and trying the effect the sight of water produced on him, gave it as his opinion that it was a case of hydrophobia. Enquiry was then made whether he had ever been bitten by a dog; the young man said that a pup of his had bit his thumb three weeks ago last Sunday, and that the dog died soon after. A powder was now given him, which he swallowed with the greatest agitation, not being able to bear the sight of the water in which it was mixed. In the afternoon of Friday, he was bled in both arms, and in the temple, not to hasten his death, as the ignorant are currently reporting, but as the only means likely to lead to a recovery. It had not, however, the desired effect; for from that time he continued excessively ill till about half-past three o'clock on Saturday morning, having only about ten minutes' respite between each paroxysm. A few minutes before expiring, he expressed a wish for a drink of *warm* water—about two tea-cupsful, were given him, when he appeared something easier. Shortly after, he had a desire to rise up for some purpose, but no sooner did his feet touch the ground, than he threw himself back into his father's arms, and expired without a groan.— *Newcastle Paper, Dec 7th,* 1814.

The *alisma plantago* was also introduced as a remedy; but, on repeated trial, has proved ineffectual.

" HYDROPHOBIA.—*Alisma Plantago ineffectual.*— We last week announced the death of Matthew Laycock, a common carrier of Bradley, near Skipton, of the above calamitous malady. He was bitten by a dog of his own, about two months previous to his dissolution. He went to the sea, as directed by those whom he consulted, and took the usual medicines administered on such occasions: after which, he rested in perfect security, apprehending no future danger. On Monday the fifth instant, he was at Bury, following his occupation of carrier; and having got exceedingly wet by driving in the rain, he complained of very unpleasant sensations, and symptoms of the above complaint manifested themselves.—Having been conveyed to his residence at Bradley, every possible attention was paid him by Mr. Abbot-

son, surgeon, Skipton; and among other medicines the pulverized *alisma plantago* was repeatedly given him on bread and
butter, to the amount of five drams at a dose; but all to no purpose. On the ninth he died, leaving a widow and three small
children to deplore his melancholy and premature death.—*Leeds
Mercury, Oct.* 31, 1818.

Another remedy has been introduced. This new remedy
comes from a distance; but let us not reject it merely on that
score. The account has appeared in several medical works,
and was first published, it seems, by *Dr. Muller*, of Vienna, a
scientific physician, now resident at Paris. The German physician says, he received the particulars from M. Marochetti, a
Russian surgeon, who informed him, that, during his residence
in the Ukraine, in the year 1813, he was called on to attend
fifteen persons who had been bitten by a mad dog, when some
old men requested him to treat the unfortunate people according
to the directions of a neighbouring peasant, who had acquired
a great reputation for curing the hydrophobia. M. Marochetti
allowed the peasant to attend *fourteen*, reserving one to himself,
a female of sixteen, who was cauterized and treated in the usual
way, and expired *eight days after the attack !* The peasant gave
to the fourteen persons placed under his care a strong decoction
of the tops of the flowers of the *yellow broom* (a pound and a
half a day). He examined twice a day the under part of the
tongue, where he had generally discovered little pimples, containing, as believed, the hydrophobia poison: these pimples
really followed, and were observed by Marochetti himself. As
they formed, the peasant opened them, and cauterized the parts
with a red hot needle; after which, the patients gargled with the
decoction mentioned above. The result of this treatment was,
that the fourteen patients were cured, having only drank the
decoction for six weeks. Marochetti then states, that, five
years afterwards, he himself had an opportunity of giving this

treatment another trial. Twenty-six persons who had been bit by a mad dog, were put under his care, viz. nine men, eleven women, and six children: he ordered the decoction of the tops of the flowers of yellow broom to be given to them as soon as possible; and upon an attentive examination of their tongues, he discovered pimples on five men, three children, and all the women. Those who were most wounded were afflicted on the third day; the others on the fifth, seventh or ninth. One of the women who had been slightly bitten on the leg had no appearance till the twenty-first day. The seven who were free from pimples took the decoction of broom for six weeks, with success. M. Marochetti thinks that the hydrophobia poison, after having remained in the wound, fixes itself under the tongue, in the orifices of the ducts of the submaxillary gland, which are situated on the sides of the frænum. The inflammation, of which the little pimples are the result, has a peculiar appearance. The time in which these pimples appear, is generally between the third and ninth day after the bite. If they are not opened before twenty-four hours after their appearance, the venom is absorbed and the patient is lost.

I shall be extremely anxious, to hear of the success of this mode of treatment nearer home: for I must confess I cannot place implicit confidence in the narrative. Medical men, will, however, I trust, soon be able to submit this mode of treatment to the test of experiment, till which time I shall suspend my further judgement upon this Russian statement.

The following account of the progressive stages of hydrophobia is too interesting to be omitted in this place: with it, therefore, I will close this long chapter:—

Thomas Mason, aged 36, a porter of muscular frame and sanguine temperament, on *Thursday* evening, 2d of August, 1794, after much fatiguing work, complained of pain in his arms and shoulders, but chiefly in his left arm: the pain was of a rheumatic kind, with a feeling of tension; and he passed the night without sleeping, and at times he was observed slightly incoherent. On *Friday*, added to the pains in his arms, shoulders, and chest, he complained of violent pain in his head. On Friday night he continued restless, walked about the house all night, but was rather more composed; but it was in the course of this night that he first complained of difficulty in swallowing, and expressed his abhorrence at the sight of every sort of fluid. Although extremely ill with the pain, his restlessness carried him out on *Saturday*, but he was very irritable and uneasy; he thought he saw objects double; and the same spasmodic motions which were produced by the attempt to swallow, were also occasioned by an acquaintance accosting him suddenly, by a gust of wind upon turning a corner, or any similar impulses. On Saturday night he still continued equally restless and uneasy; his other sufferings were lost in the severity of a throbbing pain in his temples: he was again more incoherent, and the throbbing pain at both temples impressed him strongly with a notion, which he could not banish, that he had two heads: the hydrophobia was dreadful. On *Sunday* he again went out, but he was so confused, and at times vertiginous, that as he walked upon the quay, he would have fallen over, had it not been for a friend's assistance.

Monday, August 6th, 11 o'Clock, Forenoon.

The pulse was 100, breathing 32, tongue white, and heat of skin rather increased; his pain severe in his arms, chiefly in his left arm and in his shoulders; intense throbbing pain in his temples, and painful tightness in the upper part of his chest and neck; his hearing rather less acute than usual, and thinks that he often hears discordant sounds as if from a bagpipe: his vision rather impaired; and when looking at a fixed object, it often appears to move; and small specks on the wall or floor appear like insects moving: his left arm is numb, and the feeling very imperfect; the right arm and hand, as to feeling, are in their natural state, excepting that when put into water, there is this in common to them with the rest of the body, that the dreadful convulsion immediately takes place. He is quite collected in answering any question, but his sentences are uttered in a rapid and ardent manner: he has no unaccountable sensation of anxiety, his uneasiness is entirely respecting his family should he die. When he has to look about, he turns his whole body, his neck being constantly stiff from the pain and straitness deep seated in the larynx and upper part of the chest and shoulders: he thinks that his illness arises from a glass of spirits of bad quality which he drank on the first of August. I now ordered his wife to bring in some water; he had scarcely caught a glance of it, when, with a slight spasm of his mouth, he was thrown back on the bed upon which he was sitting, violently convulsed; he then started up and staggered to the door, and then back to the bed, his breast heaving violently all the time, his eyes and countenance wild and infuriate; and when he returned, he grasped the bed post in his arms, stood for some time loudly panting, and then, exhausted by the violence of the exertion, he again sunk upon the bed. When a little composed, I asked him if he had seen the water; he said he had just caught a glance of the tumbler, but that he would have been as ill had he not seen the water, from knowing that his wife had it in her hand; and he said, that when I was talking about bringing in the water, he had with the utmost uneasiness been struggling to keep down the fit: I had indeed seen a spasm pulling down the angles of his mouth, at the same time that he drew a convulsive inspiration, but I did not know that this was the beginning of the convulsion. Immediately after a violent fit, he can look at the water without much dislike, and even swallow it, although with pain and difficulty. The spasm of his lips and the convulsive breathing are produced by any one suddenly entering the room, or taking hold of him rudely, but, unless he has been long without a fit, he seems immediately to subdue hese threatenings.

If now ordered him to bare his left hand and arm, and while I was examining with great earnestness, I found a scar on the back of the hand between the root of the thumb and fore finger, ound which I thought I saw a slight blush of inflammation: he cknowledged that he had been bitten by a *mad dog* in December ast, while he was assisting to kill it ; but he said that the bite as of no consequence, his hand having soon healed; he even wished me to believe that it was in December 1792, instead of ast December, and was extremely displeased that his wife should contradict him in this statement ; and on Sunday evening, when e was interrogated by Mr. Cheyne upon this subject, he de-ied that he had *ever* been bitten by a dog. The manner in which he addressed Mr. Cheyne, shewed how little his imagina-tion had to do in this disease.

The subject seemed irksome to him, and therefore I got his fe out of the room and questioned her. She said that he was called to assist in killing a mad dog on the 9th of December, and that the dog bit him as he attempted to seize it hy the neck; the dog kept its hold till another man stabbed it; that he went to an apothecary, who dressed the bite, which was deep and lacerated, with traumatic balsam. She said he came home in very bad spirits; when she asked what had hurt his hand, he said the splinter of a log of wood had tore it up ; next day, how-ever, he told her how it happened ; he continued very unhappy, and anxious about the issue of the bite, but when in a fortnight he found the wound healed, he recovered his cheerfulness.

3 o'Clock.

He has had only one severe convulsion since I saw him at eleven ; he was sitting on the side of the bed with his elbows resting on his thighs, yet he was under restraint, was restless, and, unless asked to sit, had a perpetual desire of traversing the room : he was neither pale nor flushed, yet his face was glazed with perspiration : this appeared symptomatic of the state of circulation, and not from the unceasing motion, as he himself explained it : he says he is very feeble, but that a pain in his loins and back is the cause of his unwillingness to sit.

It was simply asked, if he thought he could now admit a little *water* into the room ; but, quick as *electricity,* he was again thrown back, and immediately after he flung himself to the other side of the room, and clung to a chest of drawers ; then he returned with the same velocity to the bed post, to which he clung with both his hands, sobbing all the while loudly. To soothe him, he was assured that the *water* should not be brought ; but this, by recalling the idea, renewed his suffering : he begged, nay, he commanded, in an agonizing, hurried manner, not to speak of it ; to address him on another subject was to give him relief. He said that he was glad to grasp at any thing near him, lest he should hurt us, for he was not himself during these fits.

His hand is hot, his pulse quicker than it was in the forenoon ; he passes his urine in very small quantities, white and turbid.

Half past 7

There were several messages for me, saying, that he was outrageously mad. I found him lying on the bed delirious, sometimes praying earnestly, sometimes crying that he was the cause of his own death. He frequently started up to spit out the saliva ; and when I wished him to lie quiet, he said he could not, if he did he would be choaked : he said that some one was blowing chaff upon him, and suffocating him. His speech was now more than ever hurried, and often quite unconnected. His pulse was 112, and very full. Immediately after one of the convulsions, he had swallowed two cupsful of tea.

K

10 o'Clock.

I found him standing at a corner of the room quite delirious ; but his delirium was not of a mischievous kind, not that of fierceness or passion, it was rather of alarm and trepidation : it was much of that kind which we see in the worst kinds of continued fevers, where there has been constant watching with severe pain in the head : he was jealous of every one, and said that I had joined the combination to kill him ; however, when I desired him to put out his tongue, he obeyed me ; it was white and I thought rather swelled, and covered with a slime or very *viscid saliva ;* this he was spitting, or rather hawking, incessantly and with great violence, and this *hawking* might easily be thought, by a warm imagination, to be a kind of barking. I had a strait jacket put on before I left him, and ordered him to be tied down in bed.

August 7th, 11 o'Clock.

He fell fast asleep at twelve, and slept (for the first time) six hours ; but when he awoke, he still retained the worst symptoms of his disease ; the character of his delirium was changed, he was quite sullen ; he was leaning over the side of the bed with his eyes fixed on the floor, and constantly spitting out the viscid saliva with great violence. Still I retained more influence with him than any one, he even expressed a regard for me ; and at one time, as he was struggling to get his hands out of the jacket, he suddenly recollected that I had ordered it on, and became quiet, observing, that I should not have ordered it had it not been for his good. He had a little time before that taken several draughts of tea, and swallowed some bread rather greedily, immediately after a severe expression of the hydrophobia. About half past ten he became very sick, and after retching a ropy saliva, his attendants described him as becoming quite livid, the affected arm quite stiff, and the rest of his body gently agitated for about ten minutes, since which time he has been quiet and insensible. He is now lying in the arms of a friend, who is now wiping away the glary poison which he is salivating; his eye is suffused; his breathing is quick and short; he is still sick at times : he has lost the *hydrophobia* since he became *insensible*, and has swallowed some fluids without any struggle.

2 o'Clock.

He died at one o'clock, in the way of those whose nervous system has been in a state of violent excitement; his struggle was not unlike what we see at the last in nervous fevers. The face sunk, the eye glazed, the breath short and laborious, slight *sub sultus.* A little before death he became quite calm.

I had neglected to place a mirror before him, but I understood that he had several times during yesterday surveyed himself in one which hung in the room. He had nothing of the hydrophobia when passing his urine : and I have reason to think, that the fluids in producing the convulsion had always a reference to the act of swallowing : at one time, as I sat beside him, I saw the spasms, or rather a trembling about the lips, and was apprehensive of a convulsion ; he saw me eyeing him with earnestness, and told me, that his uneasiness arose from his apprehension that he should not be able to swallow the medicine which I was recommending.

N. B. The man was bitten on the 9th of December, and the disorder first shewed itself the 2d of August, an interval of nearly *eight months.*

What follows is a minute description of the symptoms that appeared upon dissecting the body of Mason ; and which investigation unquestionably proves, that much inflammation in various parts accompanies the progress and is discovered at the fatal issue of *canine madness.*

BRAIN.—The blood escaping from the longitudinal sinus, black as ink. The *surface of the brain,* a great effusion under the membrane *anachnoides.* The veins on the surface of the brain as if injected with blood, and minutely so to their utmost extremities. When a section is made, a great quantity of *black* blood escapes from the points in the medullary matter, and the cineritious matter is in a strong contrast with the medullary, being darker than usual. No intermediate lines to be observed. Substance not particularly firm, rather soft; about an *ounce* of *fluid* in the *ventricles*. *Choroid plexus* of a purple colour. The striated parts of the brain particularly distinct. Observe the general state of congestion of the *cerebellum*. *Dura mater* particularly dark.

INTESTINES.—*Intestines* distended with flatulence: the convolutions near the *pubis*, natural; towards the upper part, considerable inflammation. The small intestines all forced towards the *left side*. Omentum rather vascular. The colon much distended on the *right* hypochondrium.

STOMACH.—Little points of extravasation in the inner surface of the stomach. The *cardiac* orifice somewhat inflamed.

NECK.—*Lymphatic* glands, under the base of the jaw, particularly *large* and *livid*. *Salivary* glands, nothing particular. *Membrane* of *larynx* very much *inflamed*, and perfectly *black*. *Membrane* of *pharynx* also perfectly *inflamed*, and quite *black*.

The above account was furnished by Mr. Charles Bell, of Edinburgh.

TRAINING DOGS

FOR

The Gun.

———

Under this head I shall first observe, that, by proper attention to breeding, the sportsman will have very little trouble in training.   A well-bred dog, either setter or pointer, will generally require very little instruction, as he will, particularly if taken out young, set and back of his own accord.   For an illustration of this remark I refer the reader to what has been said under the heads of *Setter*, page 14 ; and *Pointer*, page 18.

I know it is a received opinion that those dogs which are very difficult to reduce to the required subordination, prove, when thoroughly subdued, superior to all others.—From experience, I will venture to pronounce this a hasty opinion :—These hardy, untractable animals are chiefly the offspring of the pointer and setter; and are, after all the painful flagellation, and endless trouble in training, no better than a good dog of a milder and more pliable disposition—indeed, after repeated trials of dogs of this description, I have become so disgusted with them, that I would not on any account take the trouble of another experiment.

However, in order that this chapter may be complete, it will be necessary to detail the regular progressive mode of training a dog under the supposition that many will be found amongst the very best bred animals, which require every instruction from the sportsman.

In the first place, then, it is indispensably necessary that the sportsman should procure dogs whose breed is unexceptionably good; as well-bred dogs are more than half broke the moment you take them into the field. The dog is an animal possessed of an uncommon degree of sagacity;—in short, he has *reasoning powers* to a very great extent, which may be converted to the pleasure or the service of his master; yet, in this respect, dogs will be found to vary very much; and while some will appear to exhibit *instinct* merely, others will be found to evince a degree of acuteness very similar to reason. There is a countless variety of the dog tribe, many of the non-descript ramifications of which, with an ugly and diminutive form, seem to sink much below the general level of the canine tribe in sagacity, while the nobler kind appear to rise in the scale of importance in proportion as they are judiciously bred, and afterwards cherished by the fostering care of their human protector.

The most sagacious of all the varieties of this highly interesting animal is, without dispute, the *Newfoundland dog.* His olfactory organs are of the first order; yet, as from his heavy, long, and loose form he is unable to support the fatigue of a day's range, he, on this account *alone*, is ill-calculated for the shooting sportsman. Similarly important disqualifying observations would apply to most of the other varieties of the dog, till we come to the *pointer* and *setter*, which appear altogether most admirably adapted to the purpose for which they are so generally used. We may, however, remark that the mere pointing or setting is by no means confined to these two particular kinds; on the contrary, terriers, hounds, and all dogs inclined to hunt, may be easily taught to *point* or *set*, or, in other words, to pause or stop, on their approaching game. Indeed, there are few dogs given to hunting but will point *naturally*, in the course of a little time, which arises no doubt from the following reason : as a young dog ascertains his proximity to game by his sense of smell, so, on his near approach, he is eager to seize it ; but finding, after repeated trials, that he is unable to accomplish his purpose, he becomes more circumspect or wary, and will be observed to *pause* for a short space, and then make a sudden rush to secure his object. This pause is, no doubt, for the purpose of ascertaining, by his olfactory organs, the exact spot where the game is seated ; and the observation of this very circumstance, there is not a doubt, originated the idea of the setting dog ; the sportsman carefully improving, by education, a quality which he easily discovered would so essentially conduce to the pleasures of the field.

Taking it for granted, therefore, that all dogs which will range for game will naturally pause or set, yet none of the various kinds seem so quickly to adopt this sagacious manœuvre as the pointer or setter ; nor is any one of them every way so admirably adapted as an auxiliary to the fowling piece. Next to the Newfoundland dog, on the score of powerful instinct, or animal reasoning, may be ranked the *pointer ;* his countenance is open, intelligent, and expressive ; while his speed, strength, and persevering spirit enable him to continue the chase for a length of time almost incredible.

The *pointer* and *setter*, though used for the same purpose, offer, individually, a very different object for contemplation, either as regards their external appearance, or their mode of questing for game. The setter is fleeter than the pointer ; and, as his feet are small and much protected by hair, he has a decided advantage on hard ground, or in frosty weather ; but, at the commencement of the shooting season, when the weather is oppressively hot, he suffers more from thirst than the pointer, arising, no doubt, from his long, thick, and warm coat of hair, which, though extremely convenient in cold weather, nevertheless, exposes this generous animal to great inconvenience during the intense heat of the month of August, particularly on mountains where water is seldom to be met with.   On the whole, the setter is a hardy, high-spirited animal; but he is often found troublesome to break, and can only be kept steady by incessant labour, backed, but too frequently, by *severe correction*.   For those who follow the diversion very ardently, and are out almost every day, the setter will generally be found a valuable acquisition ; but those who enjoy the fascinating amusement of shooting only *occasionally*, will find greater satisfaction in the more steady and better regulated exertions of the pointer.

The *pointer* is of foreign origin, and is known, with but slight difference of form, not only in Spain, but in Portugal, and also in France.   The pointers that have been brought immediately from Spain are heavy and clumsily formed ; those from Portugal are somewhat lighter ; while the French breed is remarkable for a wide furrow which runs between the nostrils, and which gives to the animal's countenance a very grotesque appearance.   All the pointers, however, exhibit a very different form and character from the setter : they are thick and heavy creatures, with large chubby heads, long pendant ears, and are covered with short smooth hair ; nor do they always possess that generosity of disposition which is so distinguishing a trait in the character of the setter ; in fact, they are of little value till crossed with the generous blood of these islands.   Yet the conjunction of the setter and pointer is by no means adviseable, since the production generally unites the worst qualities of the two, without any of those requisites, perhaps, for which the two breeds are most highly prized.   Sometimes, indeed, a first rate dog is produced between a setter and a pointer ; but it rarely happens ; the cross, at best, is never to be depended on ; and for one good dog thus obtained, there will be found, on an average, twenty very indifferent or bad dogs ; while not the least dependance can be placed on the offspring of the very best animals thus obtained. The most valuable dogs are, unquestionably, those produced between the Spanish pointer and the deep-flewed fox-hound or deep-flewed harrier, particularly if the progeny incline much to the pointer ; unless, indeed, speed be more the object than acute olfactory nerves, when the lighter kind of hounds will be found to answer best. The *Spanish pointer* has been already so judiciously crossed, and is arrived at such a degree of perfection, as to leave little to be desired in the way of experiment ; good pointers are now to be met with in all parts of the kingdom. Pointers are very susceptible of education, are easily broke or trained, and not so apt to forget their lessons as the setter.

Having offered these preliminary remarks on the varieties of the dog, I will now proceed to a consideration of the subject more immediately under discussion. A very mistaken notion (as before observed) has obtained currency, namely, that those dogs which it is difficult to reduce to the required subordination, ultimately prove, when thoroughly subdued, superior to all others. How such an idea could have become prevalent I am at a loss to conjecture ; but I have not the least hesitation in pronouncing it erroneous. That there have been good dogs of this description I am willing to admit,—one, perhaps, out of a hundred ; but it must be acknowledged, after all, that the *steadiness* of the very best of these hardy, headstrong dogs is seldom to be depended on ; they are always apt to spring the game, particularly when hunted in company ; and it is only by hard labour, or excessive correction, or both, that their mischievous impetuosity can be restrained.

The *first* object to be considered in training a dog is the *animal's temper* : some dogs require frequent and severe correction, while, with others, mild treatment, and even encouragement, are indispensable. The most *philosophic patience* is an admirable quality in a dog-breaker; as many otherwise excellent dogs have been ruined by ignorance and brutal passion.

Well-bred dogs generally begin to hunt at an early period, though it will sometimes happen (but not often) that a dog will continue so long before he manifests a disposition for hunting, as to induce a suspicion that he is good for nothing. Let no sportsman be too hasty in forming this conclusion. At the age of five or six months, or even earlier, you should allow your dog to accompany you when you walk out, supposing it to be in the lanes or elsewhere; and, occasionally, lead him in a cord, or couple him with another dog. He may be allowed to ramble to a certain distance, so as not to be out of call; occasionally, making him come behind you at the word *back*. The fewer words that are used in each lesson the better, which should be always the same, of the plainest sound, as well as the most distinct from each other, as the dog is guided by the sound alone; any meaning beyond what the sound and tone convey is, of course, above the capacity of a quadruped. At this period, it will not be amiss to teach him to crouch at a piece of bread, or any thing else you may think proper, and not to stir till he is ordered: this may easily be done by *gentle correction* when he does wrong, and by rewarding him when he has done right. A good time for this introductory lesson is before you feed him, and he should never be allowed to eat till he has performed his task in a satisfactory manner. The word *down* is short, and sounds well from the mouth, and is all that is necessary to make the dog crouch, except when he shows any unwillingness to execute what you desire, when *sirrah!* spoken in an angry tone, may perhaps produce obedience; if not, the whip should be administered with moderation. Further, it may be as well to teach him, at the same time, words of caution, such, for instance, as *take heed;* as well as of encouragement, as *good boy;* the latter should not be *used profusely,* but applied in the most judicious manner, as encouragement is very apt to induce a dog to commit errors. A plurality of teachers should, if possible, be avoided; one instructor being amply sufficient:

Whenever a dog is corrected, either at this period or afterwards in the field, he should not be suffered to leave you till he is satisfied that you intend him no further chastisement: for example, if a dog be guilty of so great a fault, when hunting, as to render a severe flogging indispensable, you should not allow him to run away immediately after the flagellation, but compel him to remain at your feet for some seconds or a minute, otherwise, you will not be able to catch him, perhaps, should he require a second chastisement. When a severe flogging is necessary, it is adviseable to put a cord round the neck of the dog, by which means the punishment may be administered more effectually.

After the dog has been thus brought under subjection, or reduced to the requisite obedience, at any period, from the age of eight to eighteen months, according as he is strong and healthy, he may be taken into the field, either with or without another dog, and suffered to hunt whatever he pleases, (except sheep or domestic animals,) and, in fact, to run riot. *Larks*, as they so frequently present themselves, will, most likely, be the first object of his attention; these he will spring and chase very eagerly; if *partridges* come in his way, he will do the same, with this difference only, that his eagerness will much increase; it will be still greater should he come in contact with a *pheasant*; and if a hare happen to rise before him, he will not fail to chase, with all imaginable ardour, and will, most likely, *open* in the pursuit. In this way he may be indulged till such time as he has become so attached to the sports that he may be checked without the least danger of his being *overfaced*, and thus induced to *blink* his game, or be otherwise rendered shy.

In a short period you will perceive him draw more cautiously upon the scent; on approaching his object, he will pause even at a lark; but when a partridge happens to be before him, his pause or stop will be more steady, and his manner altogether much more earnest; and the difference of the object will be very clearly manifested in his countenance.* He should now be taken out with an old steady dog, and whenever he comes to a point, the word *toho!* should be used, and afterwards the whip, should the word prove unavailing. Whenever he sets, approach him at your regular pace, but seem not in a hurry, (as, if you run, he will be very apt to do the same) and stand by him for a few seconds; if the birds do not rise he should be allowed to advance, by saying *hold up!* be mindful, however, that he does not advance too rapidly, and in order to effect this, make use of words expressive of caution, as *take heed!* When the old dog points, the young one should be taught to *back*, which may be accomplished in the following manner:—As soon as the old dog settles to a point, supposing the young one happens to be at a distance, he must be stopped, as the moment he perceives the point, he would, if left to himself, rush eagerly up: however, he must be prevented from so doing, by calling out *toho!* at the same time, holding up your hand.—If he obey not by gentle means, recourse must be had to the whip. By these means he will, most likely, soon become very steady; for dog-breaking, if attended to at a proper period, and in a proper manner, does not give half the trouble that is generally supposed. Holding up the hand is the signal for the dog to *back;* and, in a little time, whenever he sees it, he will immediately stop, though he may be at the other end of the field, or at a considerable distance.

* If, contrary to expectation, he should manifest no disposition to pause or stop, after having been taken into the field half a dozen times, every time he springs the game, he must be brought back to the spot whence it rose, and compelled to crouch; the word *toho!* must be angrily spoken, and the whip used, if, after repeated cautions, he should pay no attention.

At the same time, he should be taught to quarter his ground in a proper manner, as well as not to break fence. In beating a field, care should be taken to give him the wind; or, at least, he should never be suffered to run directly with the wind: if it blow in his face, so much the better, but a dog will hunt very well with a side wind. The dog should cross about twenty yards before the shooter, and if, after running down the field, he should not cross up again at about the distance just mentioned, he should be called to or whistled, and a wave of the hand should direct him across the field; unless indeed he catch scent, when he should be suffered, of course, to follow it. In case of attempting to *break fence*, he should be instantly whistled to or called by name, in an angry tone, using at the same time the words *'ware fence!* This will, in all probability, soon produce the requisite obedience; but should he refuse to obey the whistle or call, the *whip* must produce what more gentle means are unable to effect. If he refuses to pay attention to the whistle, he should receive a few stripes, (more or less, according to the disposition of the animal) the whistle occasionally used during the operation; and continued to be so corrected, should he not return implicit obedience when called to. Thus, he will soon become pleasingly tractable.

However, as some young dogs, are alarmed at the report of the fowling piece, it will not be amiss, on the game rising after having been properly set, to fire a pistol, which will render him familiar to the sound. If his terror should increase on the firing of the pistol, so as to frighten him from the field, the experiment should be entirely abandoned till the shooting season, when he should be coupled to another dog, or otherwise prevented from running away till a few birds are killed and shown to him.—If a bird be winged, he should be induced to foot it, and even suffered to mouth it, which is by far the best method of reconciling him to the discharge of the fowling piece.

We will suppose that the dog is already steady at partridge;

L

yet if he happens to approach a hare, he will scarcely fail to rush at her—at all events he will chase when she rises. In this case, he must be brought back to the place from whence he run, and made to crouch as before described, using the words, *'ware hare !* or *'ware chase !*

Hitherto, I have supposed that the dog breaker has been engaged with a mild, good tempered animal, which will be easily rendered tractable by the means just described ; there are, however, dogs of a very different description, which require an excess of flogging, aided by other coercive measures, in order to enforce that indispensable degree of subordination, without which, shooting, so delightful with well trained pointers, is rendered irksome and vexatious.

If repeated severe flogging fail to accomplish the object of the sportsman, recourse must be had to the *trash cord*, or rather *drag-cord*. This is a cord something like a clock line, about twelve or fourteen yards in length, to be fastened round the dog's neck, if in the fields ; on the moors the dog will run with twenty yards, while twelve or fourteen will soon tire him in enclosed grounds :* the greater the length of the cord, however, that can be used with propriety, the better : the cord may be shortened as the dog becomes fatigued. By the help of this cord, you will be able to stop him whenever you please. We will suppose that he makes a point : should he attempt to run in, you must check him as smartly as possible, making use of the word *toho !* and the whip also if you think proper. This cord will be very useful should the dog not come in when called, &c. If, after some little practice with the drag cord, the dog perseveres in springing his game, or continues otherwise refractory, the *spiked collar* must be used. The *spi-*

* On moors, the cord is drawn over the top of the heath in a great measure, and therefore runs light ; in stubble fields and rough grounds many obstacles render the dragging of the cord very hard labour.

ked collar is merely a leathern strap, through which are inserted
a dozen or more small nails, the points of which should extend
half an inch beyond the surface of the inside.   On the outside
a piece of leather must be sewed over the heads of the nails, to
prevent their starting back when the dog presses upon their points.
This is to be buckled round the dog's neck, the points of the
nails inward, and the drag cord attached to it.   Thus, when it
becomes necessary to check him on his attempting to run in, or
behaving otherwise unruly, the admonition, or rather correction,
will be much more impressive ; in a little time, his neck will be
very sore ; and he must be contumacious beyond measure if this
mode of punishment does not produce the desired effect.

The most difficult part of dog-breaking is, perhaps, the reducing of the animal to perfect obedience in respect to hares.
In the first instance, a young dog will eagerly pursue larks or
thrushes, or in fact any of the feathered tribe which he happens
to meet with ; the partridge being a larger object, and making
considerable noise when taking wing, will be pursued by him with
much more ardour ; a similar remark will equally apply to the
pheasant, which he will still more eagerly pursue : but very soon
discovering the attempt to be hopeless, he will shorten the distance of his pursuit, and ultimately abandon the chase altogether.
Not so, however, with the hare ; for perceiving that it does not
leave the ground, but runs like himself, he will not very easily
relinquish the hope of overtaking her, but will rush forward with
ungovernable ardour, and, even when lost sight of, will continue
to follow the chase by the nose.   But there are few dogs which
may not be rendered steady in respect to hares by the means
which we have pointed out ; and that where hares are numerous
much sooner, of course, than where they are seldom met with.
There is one effectual mode of reducing a dog to obedience in
this respect, should the whip, the drag-cord, and the spiked collar
fail of the desired effect.   For this purpose a living hare should

be procured, to the neck of which a cord should be fastened: to the other end of the cord (which may be six or seven yards in length) should be attached a wire, which wire should be thrust through the snout or cartilaginous part of the dog's nose. The hare will, of course, spring forward at the sight of the dog, which will not fail to cause the most acute pain to the latter; the whip should be applied at the same time, accompanied with the words, 'ware hare!* This may be regarded, perhaps, as the excess of severity, and should never be resorted to but when all milder means have been repeatedly tried in vain. To prevent an obstinate dog chasing hares, I have sometimes seen the fowling-piece used as a remedy. It may be regarded as a desperate one, which, though it will generally have the desired effect, should be used with the utmost circumspection. If a dog is to be shot at, care should be taken that he is at a sufficient distance, as well as to hit him about the rump, otherwise you run great risk of *killing* him.

In the earlier part of these remarks, I have mentioned mild-tempered dogs. It will be requisite here to observe, that well-bred dogs are occasionally met with so very shy as to require encouragement rather than correction: dogs of this description may sometimes prove excellent; but I must confess I do not like to see a *shy dog.* Animals of this sort should never be taken out with dogs that need much checking or flogging, as the very sight of the whip alarms them to such a degree that they will not stir from behind you. Nothing is more difficult than to manage very shy dogs: they must be encouraged to hunt; and if they commit an error, the means of correction are difficult, and sometimes impossible: the least severity will most likely make them *blink* †

* On all occasions of correction, the requisite word should uniformly accompany the punishment.

† *Blinking* is when a dog finds game, and, on being spoken to, draws off, and runs behind you, and frequently without being spoken to.

their game ; and when once this habit is contracted, it will require more than ordinary pains to eradicate it. Many young
dogs will be much alarmed at the report of a gun ; and yet,
when reconciled to it, prove excellent. Few shy dogs are very
prizeable ; I never saw a good one.

As I have spoken of the various methods to be employed to
render a dog steady at the point, to range, and also to *back*, I
must observe, in this place, that a dog should never be suffered
to *break fence;* or, in other words, to leave the field till you are
ready to accompany him, as much mischief may ensue from his
being suffered to ramble out of sight, or to a great distance. On
his attempting to break fence, the whistle should be used, the
dog should be called by his name, (in an angry tone,) followed
by the words, *'ware fence !*—the whip, &c. to be resorted to,
as in other cases, if necessary, to procure obedience.

Generally speaking, as little noise as possible should be made.
The voice or the whistle should never be used, but when absolutely demanded : the dog will thus hunt steadier ; and if you
accustom him to the motion of your hand, he will regularly look
for the signal whenever he is at a loss.

It is thought by some, that dogs *broke on the grouse mountains* are superior as to *ranging :* this is doubtful, if not a mistaken notion altogether. In this respect, much will depend upon
the animal himself.

Young dogs in general hunt with their noses closer to the
ground than old ones, and are apt to puzzle on the scent a considerable time after the game has left the spot. A little practice
will, however, most likely remedy these defects : if not, recourse
must be had to the *muzzle-peg,* an instrument very well known
amongst sportsmen, but which I will, nevertheless, describe.
The *muzzle-peg* is merely a piece of wood hollowed out and
formed at one end so as to fit or receive the under jaw of the
dog. From the dog's nose to the other end, projecting about

nine inches, it is merely a round stick rather thicker than a man's thumb; though some persons, instead of one of these round projecting sticks, prefer two, forming an angle with the dog's nose. At the upper end of that part which is placed under the dog's nether jaw, two longitudinal holes or slits are made, through which a strap is inserted, which is buckled behind the animal's ears; while the other end of the thick part of the muzzle-peg, or that which comes under the canine teeth, or fangs, is perforated with two holes, through which a leather thong is drawn, and tied immediately behind the fangs just mentioned. With this instrument, so fastened, the dog may be hunted without the smallest injury. At the first putting on, however, he will use every effort to rid himself of so disagreeable a companion, nor will he hunt till he has satisfied himself of the inefficacy of his utmost exertions to get free from this unpleasant restraint. At length, he will become familiar with the instrument, and run with it as unconcernedly as possible; and it will make him carry his head well up, as well as prevent him chopping young hares, or mouthing in any way. A dog that *rakes* (that is, runs with his nose close to the ground), and follows his game by the track, will generally spring it. Whenever, therefore, a young dog is seen to follow the track of a partridge (down wind in particular) he should be called to in an angry tone, *hold up!* he will then become uneasy, going first to one side and then to the other till the wind brings him the scent. If, after a short period, he should persevere in keeping his nose to the ground, and in following the track, recourse must be had to the instrument which I have just described.

Grouse, partridges, or any kind of game, lie much better to a dog that winds them, than to one which approaches by the track. The dog that winds the scent approaches the game by degrees, and that more or less as he finds it wild or otherwise, which he is enabled to discover by the scent which is emitted;

and though grouse or partridge see him hunt round them, they will be much less alarmed than when they observe him following their track, and suffer his near approach ; or, in other words, *lie well*. The reason seems evident :—the dog, I apprehend, is seen by the birds (generally speaking) as soon as he enters the field ; or, at all events, at a very considerable distance ; and the moment they perceive him approach by the track, they take the alarm, supposing themselves discovered, or, at least, very likely to be discovered ; but watching, as they assuredly do, the motions of the dog, and observing that he does not follow the track along which they have run, they conceive themselves undiscovered, and thus allow the dog to come to a steady point. It may, moreover, be further remarked, that a dog which carries his head high will always find the most game, to say nothing of finding it in a handsome style.

A YOUNG dog should be kept regularly to his work, if possible, until he become quite staunch.   Great care should be taken with him the first season he is shot over, as it seldom fails to determine his worth : at this period, numbers of otherwise valuable dogs are ruined by improper treatment, particularly by ignorant, passionate game-keepers and dog breakers : no fault, however, should be allowed to escape correction or *reproof*.   I do not mean that the dog should be flogged for every trivial mistake, but that the most trifling error should be noticed by sounds or symptoms of displeasure ; and, proceeding in this way, you should administer correction according to the degree of crime.

We will suppose the young dog broke, and taken out to be put into effectual practice all his previous instruction.   On the first shot, particularly if the dog see the bird fall, he will be very apt to break away, in which case he should be brought back to the spot whence he had run, and there making him lie down, call out, *down charge !*   He should be compelled to remain in that position till the gun is re-loaded ; and the disposition and temper of the animal should be the rule and guide of correction. A well-bred dog will generally become perfect in this lesson in a very short period.

It sometimes happens, however, that a young dog will testify every symptom of alarm on the firing of the fowling piece :— will, perhaps, run home, and be with difficulty brought again to the field. When this occurs, I consider it a very unfortunate circumstance, as it will frequently require no ordinary pains to free the dog from this unnecessary fear. There is no better' mode of effectually remedying the evil, than by convincing the animal that the discharge of the fowling piece is intended for a very different purpose than to create alarm. He must therefore, be brought back, and compelled to remain in company with the sportsman : he must, in fact, be led in a cord, to prevent his running away again ; and if an attendant be not in the field, the sportsman may tie the cord round his own body. A few birds should be killed over him as quickly as possible, which should be shown to him, and he should be allowed to mouth them, if he appears inclined to do so : if a bird happen to be winged, he should be enticed to foot it ;—thus he will very soon comprehend the true intention of the fowling piece ; his fears will subside ; and he will shortly manifest as much anxious joyful expectation at the sight and sound of a gun, as he previously testified alarm and terror.

Some persons accustom their young dogs to the report of fire-arms at a much earlier period than when taken into the field ; in fact, when they are very young. Certainly, if they endure the report of a gun or pistol at this early period, there can be little dread of their taking alarm when brought into the field ; but if a very young dog or whelp takes fright on the report of a pistol or gun, his fears will become so rooted that much greater difficulty will arise in completing his education than in the case

I have before stated. In fact, all firing of guns or pistols near him should be cautiously avoided, as a practice of this sort will but increase his alarm, unless, indeed, it were daily, and almost incessantly, resorted to. The dog must be regularly broke, and, when taken into the field with the fowling piece, treated in the manner I have described above. It is highly important to convince the dog that the fowling-piece is for the purpose of killing the game, which he is to find; and this cannot be done when shooting merely to accustom him to the sound, as no object is thus placed before him. For the same reason, I do not strongly recommend the practice of teaching dogs, when very young, to crouch in the lanes, &c. when you happen to be walking out, as the animal cannot be thus aware of the ultimate intention of his master, or conscious of the object for which he is compelled to become prostrate: this method, in fact, teaches the dog to crouch too much, and, on that account, I never practise it, or, in other words, force my pointers to endure such abject and unmeaning servitude.

Having thus gone, as plainly as possible, through what, for the sake of distinction, I will call the *regular rules* of dog-breaking, I will finish this long essay by a few desultory or general remarks, which will, I trust, be equally useful, and, at the same time, serve the purpose of collateral illustration.

In the first place, then, I would advise gentlemen *to break their own dogs,* wherever such a plan is easily practicable, and agreeable to the taste of the sportsman. Dogs thus broke, and never suffered to go out but in company with the person who trained them, will infallibly be superior to all others. They are thus accustomed to obey one person only; they become perfectly familiar with his mode and manner, and, after being shot over one season, never afterwards give the least trouble. If dogs are lent from one to another, or become subject to many masters, they cannot be expected to be perfect. For instance, I will suppose I have trained a dog, have shot over him several seasons, and he has, at length, become perfectly master of his business ; I lend him to a friend for one day, as good a sportsman, too, as myself; the dog, on being taken into the field, and perceiving a stranger, is unwilling to acknowledge his authority ; the mode and manner of my friend, too, are different from mine, and, consequently, unlike that which the dog has been accustomed to ; in fact, the sportsman and the dog do not perfectly understand each other, and a quarrel ensues : the sportsman succeeds, perhaps, in reducing the dog to obedience ; but the latter returns home, in some measure, a different animal ; he has committed various mistakes in the course of the day, most likely, and, on next going into the field, his own master will not fail to perceive that his dog is not the same, but requires, in some degree, training anew.

The less a dog is spoken or whistled to, the better. Whenever a wave of the hand or a motion will answer the purpose, the silent signal is to be preferred to noise ; and those who are well acquainted with grouse shooting will feel the force and propriety of this remark. I have often been surprised at the distance at which the human voice, in common conversation, may be heard on the moors, down the wind :—grouse will bear noise less than any other game.

A well-bred pointer seldom requires excessive correction. Setters, on the contrary, are more unruly ; and, generally speaking, render severe and frequent flogging indispensable ; they are, however, valuable where plenty of employment can be given ; but where incessant labour is not called for, the pointer is far preferable. However, no dog should be corrected in a passion ; nor, after being flogged, should he ever be suffered to run away or leave the sportsman, till he and the dog become reconciled to each other. I have seen foolish, passionate men let their dogs run away immediately the flogging is over, and aim another blow at them as they are going away; nothing can be more censurable; for, when the dog next commits a fault, and you wish to chastise him, he will not suffer you to approach sufficiently near to lay hold of him. Therefore, after correction, he should not be suffered to move, till by a word or two of caution, spoken in a mild tone, his alarm is dissipated. If a dog, either from strength or disposition, becomes difficult to chastise, by first tying his legs together, the sportsman will have a perfect command over him.

The best dogs may sometimes make mistakes—on bad scenting days, for instance; or if they happen to run down wind, particularly when it is blowing strong. On such occasions, it would be cruel to flog them, though the words expressive of caution may be used, spoken in an angry tone.

Well-bred pointers, as I have before observed, if taken into the field at a proper period, will, in general, require little breaking; they will often point and back of themselves, and, in fact, give the sportsman much satisfaction with little trouble.

The dog that first finds the game should always go up to it; and on no account should another be suffered to pass or run before him. It is like snatching his well earned reward, to say nothing of the confusion which must ensue from such a culpable practice.

I have seen dogs shot at for the purpose of rendering them steady, and particularly to prevent them from chasing hares; I cannot say I admire this method, though I have seen it used with effect: it can only be had recourse to with hardy, headstrong animals; as to shoot at a young timid dog is to ruin him at once. It is a dangerous method at best, nor should it ever be resorted to but when the dog is at a considerable distance.

A pointer or setter should never be named *Carlo, Sancho,* or, indeed, any name ending in *o,* as the word TOHO is so frequently indispensable, and, ending in the same sound, is apt to cause misunderstanding and confusion.   A dog's name should consist of one expressive syllable, which comes forcibly from the mouth, such as *Nell*, for instance, and, where more than one dog is used, their names should sound as differently as possible.

- It but too frequently happens that young dogs manifest an inclination to *hunt and worry sheep*, which must be instantly corrected. If a severe flogging have not the desired effect, the dog should either be tied to a strong ram, leaving a sufficient length of cord to allow the ram to make a run ; or they should be confined together in a barn or some building. Flog the dog till he cries out, making use of the words *'ware sheep!* The ram will not fail to commence a furious attack upon him, and will butt him most violently.   They should be kept together for twenty minutes ; the ram will not fail to continue his butting, and it may not be amiss to flog the dog several times during this period, making use of the words just mentioned at the same time.   This will, most likely, prevent the dog ever looking at sheep afterwards, unless, perhaps, where he has absolutely bitten them before this system of correction was put in practice, in which case, I am not aware of any mode of punishment or correction that can be depended on ; for, although the dog may not even notice sheep in your presence, yet he will, nevertheless, be very apt to steal away, as opportunity may offer, for the purpose of depredation :—when once dogs have *tasted mutton*, they are never to be trusted.   Indeed, I have seen an instance or two, where the dog, after being a little butted, has fiercely turned upon the ram,*

---

* On this subject, Beckford relates the following anecdote :—
A late lord of my acquaintance, who had heard of this method, and whose whole pack had been often guilty of killing sheep, determined to punish them, and to that intent put the largest ram he could find into his kennel. The men with their whips and voices, and the ram with his horns, soon put the whole kennel into confusion and dismay, and the hounds and ram were then left together. Meeting a friend soon

which he would have torn to pieces had he not been prevented; but a circumstance of this sort rarely occurs, and, in the instances to which I allude, the dogs were grown rather too old to be cured by this or any other mode short of confinement or death. If a young, dog look earnestly at, or set, a sheep, he should be corrected; and, if you find him repeat it, have recourse to the ram, as by far the most effectual mode that can be adopted. A dog should be corrected, in fact, the moment he is observed to manifest the slightest inclination even to notice sheep; as he will, if not checked, first look and set, then chase, and, ultimately, worry them.

As to poultry, the evil is not of so much magnitude, nor the disposition to worry it so difficult to subdue, as when sheep are the object; besides, poultry, by being generally about the house or premises, afford better, as well as more frequent, opportunities of observation. Young pointers are very apt to make their first essay, as it were, by worrying chickens, or pigeons, where they happen to be very tame. Early and severe flogging will, however, generally remedy the evil: if not, tie a fowl (a living one is the best, on account of its fluttering,) to the dog's tail, and tie it in such a manner, either by a cleft stick or otherwise, that it may give the dog considerable pain. Take him to a place some distance from his kennel, and, after giving him a few smart strokes with the whip, let him loose, and he will seldom fail to run home,

after, "come," says he, "come with me to the kennel, and see what rare sport the ram makes among the hounds; the old fellow lays about him stoutly, I assure you—egad he trims them—there is not a dog dares look him in the face."—His friend, who is a compassionate man, pitied the hounds exceedingly, and asked if he was not afraid that some of them might be spoiled?—"No, d—n them," said he, "they deserve it, and let them suffer." On they went—all was quiet—they opened the kennel door, but saw neither ram nor hound. The ram by this time was entirely eaten up, and the hounds having filled their bellies, were retired to rest.

howling all the way, (just as if a tin kettle were tied to him,) and terrified, beyond measure. He should, however, be followed, dragged from the farther end of his kennel, in which he will, no doubt, endeavour to hide himself, and be again well flogged; and the fowl, being taken from his tail, should be buffetted about his head.

I have met with sportsmen who teach their pointers to fetch the dead bird: I must confess I am not fond of this method; as the dog, thus accustomed to fetch the bird, is very apt to break away, on the shot, whether a bird be killed or not.

The Russian Pointer.—In concluding these observations on dog breaking, I must once more revert to the animal distinguished by the name of the *Russian Pointer*, though it has already been slightly noticed under a distinct head:—The Russian Pointer, which has of late years attracted the attention of the shooting sportsman, is one of those animals which, from external appearance, is by no means calculated to excite a prepossession in its favour. The dog in question may or may not have come originally from Russia; his thick covering of hair would seem to indicate, however, that he is well calculated to endure the rigours of a northern climate; therefore, as far as relates to the word *Russian*, the idea and the appearance seem perfectly in unison. But while I admit the word *Russian* to be appropriate to the nature of the dog, I feel much inclined to dispute the specific and particular application of *pointer.* That this rough thickly clad dog may be taught to point, there is little doubt, and the same remark may, with propriety, be extended to almost every ramification of the dog: any dog that will run and hunt may be taught to stop or point. Take a young terrier, for instance, into the field, and hunt him several days; he will be found, at first, to chase every bird that he meets with; but, after having been on the scent of partridges repeatedly, he will be seen to pause, and, after a few seconds, rush to the spot where he supposes, from the scent, the birds are situated. The fact is, that almost all dogs hunt the tenants of the air from inclination or instinct, but particularly partridges, pheasants, &c. which are much given to running, and thus afford their four-footed enemy a far better opportunity of following them than such as take to immediate flight, at once convincing the dog of the hopelessness of the pursuit.

In following birds, all dogs are actuated by a strong desire to seize them; and, after repeated ineffectual attempts, at length cunningly adopt the mode of stopping for a few seconds, in order to ensure the object by a sudden rush to the identical spot, which the information of their exquisite olfactory organs enables them to do with tolerable precision. It has been stated, that an earl of Surrey was the first who taught a dog to set; this certainly may have been the case, and I have no doubt that the observation of the *pauses* which the animal instinctively makes, first gave rise to the caution in *pointing*, which the dog now receives from the sportsman.

As I have just stated that all dogs that will hunt will set also, I shall, for the sake of elucidation, exhibit a comparative view of the subject; or in other words, attempt to show that some dogs testify greater inclination for those instinctive pauses than others. The greyhound we omit altogether, as he manifests no disposition to hunt by the nose. The *lurcher*, which will hunt by the nose, and possesses the quality above described, is not a good example, as his olfactory nerves are of a very inferior description, and he is more apt to depend upon the eye than the nose. The *terrier* has already been mentioned as pausing to prepare for a rush; the same inclination will be found to prevail in most of the mongrels, which it is impossible to classify, but which will be generally found to evince a similar disposition; while all dogs of the spaniel kind, as they have better noses, and are more inclined to range, exhibit the quality of pointing in a

still greater degree ; at the same time it must be admitted, that
the pointer, by possessing still superior olfactory organs, being
uch inclined to range, and of a docile and tractable temper, is
better subject than any of those just enumerated for improv-
ng the instinctive pause into the regular, steady, statue-like *set*,
o essential to the pleasures derived from the fowling piece.

The *Russian pointer* is merely the ugliest specimen of the
ater spaniel, with a trifling cross perhaps of the setter ; and
rom what has been stated, it will be easily perceived that he
might be taught to set.   Chance, in all probability, first intro-
uced the Russian pointer to the notice of some fanciful sports-
an : to see a dog of this description set steadily would appear
trange ; and from this very circumstance the animal might ob-
ain credit for other qualities which he did not possess.   However, though the Russian pointer was much spoken of a few
ears ago, its introduction was very limited, and attended, for
the most part, with unqualified dissatisfaction.

The writer once accompanied a gentleman on a shooting ex-
ursion, who had procured three of these Russian pointers ; and
rom seven o'clock in the morning till eleven, the dogs ranged
he fields in an unruly manner, without even making a handsome
teady *point*, though it was in the early part of September, the
cent good, and plenty of birds : the impression left on the
writer's mind was, that the dogs possessed a headstrong disposi-
ion, and a bad nose.   It is clear that the Russian pointer
ould require incessant correction, and, after all, be good for
othing.   They are low rangers, and on this account would
lways be apt to get too near their game.   Under all these
ircumstances, therefore, of uncouth appearance, bad nose, and
efractory disposition, these dogs may be safely pronounced
utterly unworthy of the notice of the sportsman.

Of Scent;

AND THE REASON WHY ONE DOG'S SENSE OF SMELLING IS SUPERIOR TO ANOTHER'S.

Scent is an effluvium which, in a greater or a less degree, is continually issuing from the bodies of animals, and other substances; but, as these remarks are intended more for the sportsman than the philosopher, I shall confine myself merely to the nature of that animal exudation by which a dog is enabled to inform his master of his approach to game. The effluvium constantly issuing from the pores of all animal substances, consists of minute particles, or corpuscles, which, driven by the wind or otherwise, and coming in contact with the olfactory nerves of the dog, enable him to discover the proximity of the object of pursuit, and, after having ascertained the direction of the vapour, he cautiously ascends, as it were, the stream, and, by practice, becomes a proficient in pointing out the identical situation of the source whence the effluvium or scent issues, and thus prepares his master for the springing of the game.

Thus sings Somerville:

> " The panting Chase grows warmer as he flies,
> And through the net-work of the skin perspires;
> Leaves a long steaming trail behind, which by
> The cooler Air condensed, remains, unless
> By some rude storm dispers'd, or rarefied
> By the Meridian Sun's intenser heat.
> To ev'ry Shrub the warm Effluvia cling,
> Hang on the grass, impregnate Earth and Skies.

M 3

With nostrils op'ning wide, o'er hill, o'er dale,
The vig'rous Hounds pursue, with every breath
Inhale the grateful steam, quick pleasures sting
Their tingling Nerves, while they their thanks repay,
And in triumphant Melody confess
The titillating Joy.   Thus on the Air
Depend the Hunter's hopes."

But to the *air* only, Somerville ought not to have attributed the origin or difference of *scent*, it depends also on the soil, and doubtless is most favourable to the hound, when the effluvium constantly perspiring from the game as it runs, is kept by the gravity of the air to the height of his *breast*, for then it neither is above his reach, nor need he stoop for it; this is what is meant when scent is said to lie *breast high*.   Experience tells us that difference of soil alters the scent: When the leaves begin to fall, and before they are rotted, scent lies ill in cover, a sufficient proof that it does not depend on the air only.   Scent also varies by difference of motion, the faster the animal goes, the less scent it leaves; when game has been ridden after, and hurried on by imprudent sportsmen, hounds will with difficulty pick out the scent, and one reason may be, that the particles of scent are then more dissipated; but if the game should have been run by a *dog, not belonging* to the pack, very seldom will any scent remain.

Scent frequently alters in the same day; it may be said to depend chiefly on two things, the condition of the ground, and the temperature of the air, which should be moist without being wet; when both are in this state, the scent is then perfect, and *vice versâ*, when the ground is hard and the air dry, there seldom will be any scent.   It scarce ever lies with a north, or an *east* wind; a *southerly* wind without rain, and a *westerly* one that is not rough, are the best.   Storms in the air seldom fail to destroy scent.   A fine sunshiny day, is not often good for hunting;

but a day warm without sun, is generally a perfect one ; there
' are not *many* such in a whole season. In some *fogs,* scent lies
high, in others not at all, depending probably on the quarter the
wind is then in. It sometimes lies very high in a *mist,* when
not too wet ; but if the wet continues to hang upon the boughs
and bushes, it will fall upon the scent and deaden it. When
the dogs roll, and also when cobwebs hang on the bushes, there
is seldom much scent. During a *white* frost, the scent lies
high, as it also does when the frost is quite gone ; at the time
of its *going off,* scent never lies. In heathy countries, where the
game *brushes* as it goes along, scent seldom fails ; yet from the
inclosures of poor land surrounding them, the scent is at times
very difficult for hounds ; the sudden change from a good to a
bad scent confuses their noses; a scent, therefore, which is less
good but less unequal, is to hounds more favourable. When
the ground *carries,* the scent is bad, for an obvious reason,
which hare-hunters, who pursue their game over greasy fallows
and dirty roads, have great cause to complain of. A remark
has been generally made, that scent lies best in the richest soils,
and those countries which are favourable to horses, are not so
to hounds ; and it has likewise been observed in some particular
spots, in almost every country, let the temperature of the air be
what it may, that hounds can never carry a scent across them.

The ingenious author of Observations on Hare-hunting, in
speaking of *scent,* says, the qualities of those portions of matter
that discharge themselves from the bodies of beasts of game,
would much better suit the experiments of a philosopher, than
a huntsman. Whether considered as an extraneous stock of odo-
riferous particles given them by Divine Wisdom for the very
purpose of being hunted ? Whether they are proper identical
parts of the animal's body, that continually ferment and perspire
from it ? Whether these exhalations are from the breath of
the lungs, or through the skin of the whole body ? are queries

that deserve the subtilty of the virtuoso. His opinion is next given upon it, and possibly the recital may tend to reconcile the various and jarring sentiments that prevail amongst sportsmen, respecting this *first* article in all their pursuits of the field, where the dog is called in as an auxiliary.

The author contends that the particles of scent evaporated must be inconceivably *small*, as he has taken many hares after a chase of two, three, four, or five hours, without being able to perceive the least difference in *weight* from those that have been killed on their forms; nor from gentlemen who have hunted box hares, could he learn, that they discovered any visible waste in their bodies, further than might be supposed to arise from the effect of discharging their grosser excrements. But admitting a loss of two or three *drachms* after so long a fatigue, yet how minute must be the division of so small a quantity of matter, when, (deducting the *number* of those particles that are lost upon the ground, dissipated in the air, and extinguished or obscured by the fœtid perspirations of the dogs and other animals,) it affords a share to so many couple of hounds, for eight or ten miles successively. To a sportsman it is needless to observe, that scent depends on the state of the weather, and is affected by its vicissitudes; a storm will in an instant destroy it, nor is this to be wondered at, if we consider these particles of scent are of an exactly equal specific gravity with those of the *air*, and which always fall and rise in just proportion to it. Huntsmen who are hasty, rate and curse those hounds, (which yesterday were the best in England,) for galloping with their noses in the air, as if their game was flown, when in fact it is in vain for them to seek the scent in any other place, the increasing weight of that fluid element having wafted it over their heads. The most terrible day for the hare is, when the air is in its mean gravity, tolerably moist, but inclining to grow drier, with a mild breeze; the moderate gravity buoys up the scent as high as the dog's breast, the vesicles of moisture serve as canals to carry the effluvium into their noses, and the gentle wind so much helps to spread it, that every hound, even at eight or ten paces distance, especially with the wind, may have a due portion.

That the same hare will, at divers times, emit finer or grosser particles, is equally manifest to every one observant of the frequent changes in a single chase. The coursing of a cur dog, is ever the occasion of a fault, and after such an accident, the hounds must be again and again put upon the scent, before they will acknowledge it for their game; the reason is, the change in the *motion* causes one in the perspiring particles. The alterations of scent in a yielding hare are less frequently productive of faults, because they are more gradual and insensibly grow smaller; but that alterations there are, every dog-boy knows, by the *old* hounds pressing forward with greater earnestness as the hare is near her end.

Motion, continues this author, is the chief cause of discharging these particles of scent, because a hare is very seldom winded whilst quiet in her form, although the hounds are so near as even to run over her; sometimes indeed she is *chopped* upon her seat, but this probably is the consequence of her own curiosity, in moving and rising up in it, to watch the proceedings of her enemies. It is very plain, the slower the hare moves, the stronger and grosser are the particles of scent she leaves, which is one reason that the morning walk will yield scent so much longer than in flight when hunted.

It is diverting to hear country fellows, on sight of a hare, cry out, she is all over in a *sweat;* the most indifferent sportsmen know to the contrary, and that on the nicest examination, no proof has ever been found, any more than of the sweating of a dog or cat. Another prevailing notion is, that the longer a hare has been hunted, the weaker the scent grows. But, continues this author, I never found such an alteration, and if any judgment is allowed to be formed from the action of the hounds, the old staunch dogs will be found to rate on, towards the conclusion of the chase, with additional vigour, surely not from decay of scent, but the contrary, and from whence they become every yard they go, more sensible of their near approach to the hare, than all the hunters in the field. Yet, should it be still maintained that the scent does really decrease the more a hare is pressed, what can it be owing to? To lay it down as fact, without offering some reason, is certainly a very arbitrary determination. Is it because she is run out of wind? If that is allowed, those who insist that the hounds hunt the *foot*, must give up the argument; for what reason can be assigned why a hare's feet, immediately preceding her death, do not leave as strong and equal a scent as at first starting from her seat?

Hares or other creatures, hard run, perform their inspiration and expiration very quick, at least in the proportion of six times to one, supposing them not urged beyond their natural pace, or to remain perfectly cool and quiet. If therefore *six* expirations under severe pursuit, are equal to *one* when a hare is just started, what difference can there be in the scent?

It may be alleged, the scent lies stronger at first, because it makes its return from a full stomach, or that at starting, the lungs having not suffered much distention, she breathes freer, which by running low to the earth intermixes better with the herbage. On the other hand, that a hare long hunted runs high, and of course emits her breath further off from the surface, therefore more liable to be sooner separated, and overpowered by the wind.

To the first part it is answered, the faster a hare runs, the longer she stretches, therefore the lower she lies to the ground; but the further the hounds are behind, and her breath (although expired ever so free,) remains a long time, in proportion to the distance, before the dogs come up to enjoy it.

In the second place, the hard pressed hare makes her stretches shorter, which brings her body naturally more upright and high from the surface, and the scent is hereby more likely to suffer from wind and weather ; but then as she breathes quick in proportion, and shortens her pace in a sensible degree, the hounds so much as she shortens, so much do they hasten, being urged on by an increasing scent. The only natural reason why a hare towards the end of the chase is often difficult to be killed, is, that she confines her works in a much shorter compass, doubles here and there, over and over, shifts, redoubles, and tries all places for rest and security, making very much *foiling* in a little space, which variety of *equal scent* puzzles the hounds exceedingly ; and if the dogs are not thorough masters of their business, or if the air be not in due balance, the difficulty will be the greater.

It is also to be remembered, that there is no small accidental difference in the very particles of scent, which are more distinguishable at one time than at another : that there is a different scent in other animals of the same species is evident, from the hounds formerly used for tracing and pursuing thieves and deer-stealers, and likewise from any common cur or spaniel, who will hunt out his master, or his master's horse, distinctly from all others ; and that it is the same with the hare, is no less visible from the *old* beagles, which will not readily change for a fresh one, unless she start in view, or unless a long fault happen, which puts them in confusion, and inclines them in despair to take up with the next scent that presents itself.

Of the influence which *frost* has upon scent, this author observes, that he has been often disappointed in the hounds hunting the trail of a hare up to her seat, and frequently been able to hunt her walk in one part of a field, and not in another; that at ten or eleven o'clock, the same walk which gave the least scent at seven in the morning, has afforded the best; but what

has been more perplexing, the hounds have only been able to
hunt it at the wrong end, or backwards, and after many hours
expectation; the fact is, that the hounds are never so far from
their game, as when they hunt it the warmest.   All these accidents are only the effect of the *hoar frost*, or very *gross dew*
(for they never happen otherwise), and from thence must the
miracle be accounted for.   At the going off of a frost, the mercury is commonly falling, and by consequence the scent sinking
into the ground.   The earth is naturally on such occasions,
fermenting, stinking, and very porous, so that it is impossible,
but that most of the particles of scent must then be corrupted,
buried, or destroyed by stronger vapours : it is common to hear
it said, the hare carries ; but that is not all, for by what has been
alleged, it is plain she is not so eagely pursued by the scent of
her feet only.   Thus having ascertained that a *thaw* tends to
corrupt the particles of scent, it leaves a fair reason to maintain,
that the *frost* fixes, covers, and preserves them.   Whether this
is done by intercepting their ascent, and precipitating them to
the ground by the gross particles of frozen dew, or whether by
protecting them from the penetrating air, is not professed to be
decided ; but the facts are certain, confirmed by experience.

It is a very well known fact, that the sense of smell varies
very much in dogs; or, to speak as a sportsman, some of them
possess better noses than others./ In dogs with broad heads, the
os æthmoides, or *sive bone*, is much larger than in narrow headed
dogs ; the *laminæ cribrose*, or the *sive* itself, is therefore more
capacious, and contains more openings; so that the olfactory
nerves, which pass through it, are divided more minutely, and
thus that exquisite acuteness of smell is produced, which is found
to obtain in the old English blood hound, and all dogs with
broad heads : this excellence or superiority of the olfactory
organs is further assisted by the largeness and flexibility of the
lips and skin about the nose, which thus admit of a much greater

extension of the olfactory nerves, and render them more susceptible of external impressions. The olfactory nerves resemble a bunch of small white cords, one end of which is connected with the brain, while the other, descending the head, spreads into numerous ramifications, reaching to the edges of the lips as well as to the extremity of the nose.

Hence the inferiority of the greyhound's sense of smell will be easily perceived : his head is narrow, while his lips are thin and compressed ; and in consequence of this inflexibility, and the contracted structure of the head, that breadth and extension of nerve are inadmissible, and to make up, as it might seem, for this defect, nature has endowed him with a celerity which is not to be met with in any other species of the dog.

All dogs, therefore, with broad heads must possess superior organs of smell ; but it does not appear that a narrow or sharp nose presents any obstacle, as the main bulk of the olfactory nerves are situated in the head ; but I think it is abundantly evident, that a very long nose (like the greyhound) must always be detrimental, since the impression of scent, externally caught, must have farther to travel to the brain, The wolf and the fox have both sharp noses; but their heads are remarkably broad and capacious :—their olfactory organs are unquestionably exquisite. Experience, in fact, fully verifies these conjectures : the dogs most remarkable for exquisite sense of smell, are equally distinguished for brood heads ; and the gradations are easily to be traced : the talbot,* the original of all our mod-

---

* To try whether a young *blood hound* was well instructed, a nobleman (says Mr. Boyle) caused one of his servants to walk to a town four miles off, and then to a market town three miles from thence. The dog, without seeing the man he was to pursue, followed him by the scent to the above-mentioned places, notwithstanding the multitude of people going the same road, and of travellers that had occasion to cross it. When the hound came to the chief market town, he passed

ern hounds, exhibits the outward characteristics of superior olfactory nerves in a very obvious and striking manner:—by crossing the talbot with something of the greyhound breed, the stag hound was produced:—the speed of the talbot was thus increased; but as the head became more compressed, the sense of smell suffered accordingly. The fox-hound is a still farther remove, and his olfactory organs are inferior to the stag-hound; and the reason, in fact, why well-bred stag-hounds distinguish the blown or hunted deer from the herd, is intirely owing to their proximity to the talbot; while the fox-hound, by being

through the streets, without noticing any people there, till he got to the house where the man he sought was, and there found him in an upper room.

Blood hounds were formerly used in certain districts lying between England and Scotland, which were infested by robbers and murderers; a tax was laid on the inhabitants for maintaining them, and there was a law in Scotland, that whoever denied entrance to one of these dogs in pursuit of stolen goods, should be deemed an *accessary*. This peculiar property of discovering the nightly spoiler by the unerring accuracy of the dog's smell, Somerville thus beautifully notices:

―――――――――Soon as the morn
Reveals his wrongs, with ghastly visage wan
The plundered owner stands, and from his lips
A thousand thronging curses burst their way:
He calls his stout allies, and in a line
His faithful hounds he leads, then with a voice
That utters loud his rage, attentive cheers;
Soon the sagacious brute, his curling tail
Flourished in air, low bending plies around
His busy nose, the steaming vapour snuffs
Inquisitive, nor leaves one turf untried,
Till, conscious of the recent stains, his heart
Beats quick; his snuffling nose, his active tail,
Attest his joy; then with deep op'ning mouth
That makes the welkin tremble, he proclaims

farther removed, is unable to distinguish the hunted or blown fox, when another fox happens to come in the way during the chase.

I have frequently thought, that the size of the ears is a criterion, in some degree, of the sense of smell. The talbot has amazing large ears; the stag-hound's are smaller; the fox-hound's, the smallest of the three.

The pointer is remarkable for a broad, capacious head, as well as for large pendant ears; and those setters distinguished for the goodness of their olfactory powers, will be found to possess a

> Th' audacious felon; foot by foot he marks
> His winding way, while all the list'ning crowd
> Applaud his reas'nings.   O'er the watry ford,
> Dry sandy heaths, and stony barren hills,
> O'er beaten paths, with men and beasts distain'd,
> Unerring he pursues; till at the cot
> Arrived, and seizing by his guilty throat
> The caitiff vile, redeems the captive prey :
> So exquisitely delicate his sense !

The above description is faithful and highly picturesque, presenting a curious picture of the blood-hound's use in ancient times, when the word *police* was almost unknown.

In speaking of the pursuit of Robert Bruce by Edward I. an old manuscript says :

> " The king Edward, with horn and *hounds* him sought,
> With men on foot, thro' marshes, moss, and mire,
> Thro' woods also, and mountains where they fought."

In 1803, the Thrapston Association for the prosecution of felons in Northamptonshire, procured and trained a blood-hound, for the detection of sheep stealers. To prove the utility of the dog, a man was dispatched from a spot where a great concourse of people were assembled, at *ten* o'clock in the forenoon, and at *eleven* the hound was laid on the scent; after a chase of an hour and a half, the hound found him secreted in a tree, many miles distant from the place of starting.

very considerable expansion of the head, though their noses may taper more than the pointer. Thus, at first glance, a bull-dog will be supposed to excel in this respect; but, on examination, it will be found that his head is rather chubby than broad, while the skin about the mouth is comparatively inflexible and compressed, his under jaw projected, and his nostrils thrown so far back as to prevent that immediate contact with external objects, which is seen to obtain in the dogs before mentioned; yet, notwithstanding all these objections, the bull-dog's sense of smell is of the superior order, which arises, no doubt from the capaciousness of his head.

The sense of smell, like most other faculties, is improved by practise. Dogs which are kept in towns, and but little exercised, will always be found inferior to such as are quartered in the country.

The Fowling Piece.

Of all the engines that were ever produced by human genius, not one has experienced a greater variety, or more improvements that the gun. It is asserted that Edward, the Black Prince, was the first who introduced great guns or cannon, at least into England; but this is doubtful.

There perhaps is nothing, says a brother sportsman, in which persons have more faith, than in the excellence of their own gun. The distance it kills, and the closeness of its throwing the shot, are inconceivable; striking a *card* with *ten* or *twenty* pellets of shot at *sixty* yards is nothing uncommon, and the merits of the shooter and his gun bid defiance to rivalship. It is no easy matter to change the opinion of such persons respecting their guns; but when a gun is said to be sure at *three* or *fourscore* yards, the measure may be safely asserted to be of the proprietor's own making. The circumstance of knocking down a partridge at *eighty* yards may happen, but very few barrels, of those that are generally used for the shooting of birds on wing, will throw shot compact enough to be certain of killing at *sixty* yards: one or two grains of shot are not sufficient so to strike a bird as to bring it to the ground; for when stript of its feathers a partridge is a much smaller object than it appears to be, and possesses many parts not vital. It is the weight of iron properly disposed in a barrel that can alone produce such an effect,* and

* So well apprised are the best gun makers of this, that they *now* recommend a weight of metal in the barrel, which a very few years since they used to denounce as a needless incumbrance.

in double guns the stoutness of the barrels is indispensable if the shooter has any regard to his own safety ; for, in light double barrel pieces, the firing of the one will frequently loosen the charge in the other barrel, and should the shot be shaken, so as to leave the powder a few inches, and the second barrel be fired with the muzzle pointing downwards, most likely it bursts.

Some time after the introduction of the fowling-piece, the Spaniárds became celebrated for the manufacture of the barrels, and Spanish barrels were eagerly sought for many years. It is possible, certainly, that Spain, at the period alluded to, might excel her neighbours in making gun barrels ; but at present she is by no means equal, in this respect, to either England or France. Spanish barrels are fallen into disrepute ; nor is it a matter of surprise, as cunning fellows, in various parts of Europe, taking advantage of the rage for these articles, poured abroad what they denominated *Spanish barrels* in profusion ; and some considerable time elapsed before the cheat was discovered.

The French make beautiful fowling-pieces ; but the English are the neatest in the world. At Birmingham, all descriptions of guns are manufactured in the greatest perfection ; what are called the best military muskets are made complete, with bayonets included, for fifteen shillings each : and there are very few gun-makers in any part of the kingdom, (London included) who do not receive every part of the fowling-piece from this place, in a rough state, which they polish and put together.

OF GUN BARRELS.

Barrels, it has been asserted, forged from steel, are lighter, safer, and shoot stronger than all others ; but a barrel maker, whose superior excellence renders him a very competent judge, and whose practice is—not to dupe his customers, has declared that he has wrought a great deal of Spanish iron, has forged barrels from *old scythes*, from *wire, needles,* and many other articles suggested by the whim of his employers ; has made barrels with a lining of steel, and formed others with a double spiral of iron and steel alternately : yet, so far as he can determine from these numerous trials, the *stub iron* wrought into a twisted barrel is superior to every other. Wherever steel was used, he found that the barrel neither welded nor bored so perfectly as when composed of iron alone.

The first object in a fowling piece is *safety*. Gunsmiths *prove* their barrels whilst in their *rough* state, and this is done with the idea that if they burst, the expence of further workmanship is saved ; the consequence is, that a single barrel, weighing nearly *five pounds*, is reduced to *three pounds* nine or ten ounces : this reduction is confided to the workman, who, if careless or in haste, may take it from the *breech*, or that part of the barrel where the greatest strength is requisite ; and when the barrels are laid together, and the rib soldered on, it is impossible to discover whether the filing has been too deep. The barrels undergo no *second proof*, and thus the gun too often becomes a *masked battery* to him who shoots with it.

So many barrels have burst, and occasioned permanent misfortunes, after having sustained the ordeal of the company's or Tower proving-house, and received their *marks* as a pledge of their safety, as evidently to shew that a barrel may bear that *one shock*, and still be very unworthy to be put into the hands of any one. The only mode of ascertaining whether a barrel is perfectly secure is, by *water-proving*, after it returns from the *proof-house*, and has apparently withstood that of fire.

There are various kinds, or rather qualities, of barrels, which pass under various denominations, such as *twisted-stub* barrels, *wire-twisted* barrels, *Damascus* barrels, and *common* barrels. *Twisted-stubs* are old horse-shoe nails twisted together; there are also *iron-twisted*, inferior to the former. *Wire-twisted* are stubs drawn into wire, and then twisted and formed into the barrel. *Damascus* barrels are iron and steel *curled* together, which give the barrel a beautiful appearance. Wire-twisted barrels are the best. Damascus barrels are inferior even to common twisted stubs; though, as they bear a foreign name, and as the peculiar curling of the iron and steel give them a pleasing appearance, they have of late been in request; and as the English gun-makers found it inconvenient to import a sufficient number, they did not hesitate to manufacture Damascus barrels, and not more than one real Damascus barrel out of a hundred is to be met with. Whether they are originally from Damascus, I am not certain, but I am willing to believe so; at all events, several of what were called real Damascus barrels, which reached this country through Russia, are much superior to the *English Damascus* barrels.

BORING of BARRELS.

I shall not attempt to describe the process of boring gun-barrels, as this work is intended not for the mechanic, but the sportsman ; besides, in every thing of this and a similar descrip-tion, five minutes' inspection would do more than a volume of words ; yet, as the *well-shooting* of the fowling-piece materially depends upon the boring of the barrel, I shall not hesitate to state what kind of bore or cylinder I have found to throw the shot with the greatest force, as well as with the greatest regu-larity. Many gun-makers, when speaking on this subject, as-sume an air of importance, and by mysterious nods and broken sentences, give you to understand, that the true and correct method of boring gun-barrels is a secret, which remains with them alone; but the fact is, that the art and mystery of boring barrels is imperfectly understood, and it not unfrequently happens, that a gun upon which every possible care has been bestowed in the boring, will not shoot so well as an ordinary or common barrel :—even the African guns, which at the time of the slave trade were furnished to the merchant, complete, for six shillings and sixpence, have been known to throw the charge remarkably well.

Some time ago, a fowling-piece came into my hands, the cylinder of which, for several inches from the breech, was a trifle wider than the remainder of the barrel. This gun shot remark-ably well, better, in fact, than any I had ever before met with ; and, conceiving this superiority must arise from the peculiarity of the bore, and having another very indifferent fowling-piece, I had the latter re-bored in the manner just described, and was

pleased to find it answer the desired purpose in a manner that
far surpassed my most sanguine expectations.   Under these circumstances, I have no hesitation in recommending the above
plan of boring barrels : the increase of width at the lower end
should be but a trifle, just sufficient to be perceived when putting in the wadding, which will, of course, slide rather easier in
that part.

THE LENGTH of the BARREL

Is another matter, which is still involved in doubt, though
abundant evidence has been obtained to prove that the antiquated
notion of long barrels carrying the farthest, is completely erroneous.   After a great number of experiments, I have found that
a barrel twenty-two inches long, of the common fowling-piece
caliber (five eighths of an inch diameter) shoots fully as strong,
if not stronger, than any other greater length, though the difference between twenty-two and twenty-eight, or even thirty inches,
is not very great ; but for any increase of length beyond thirty
inches, the difference, or the decrease of force, would very much
surprise any person who had never witnessed the experiment. I
have shortened five different barrels, gradually, inch by inch for
instance, and the result has invariably been the same ; and in
these experiments, great pains were taken in regulating the
charge, so that in this respect, no perceptible variation could take
place. Nevertheless, though a barrel twenty-two inches long
(I have never tried one shorter) may impel the charge with more

force than a greater length, yet I prefer a barrel somewhat longer, as it is pleasanter to load, and the aim may be much better taken with it : yet, for my own choice, I never would exceed thirty inches. I would not recommend a *very light* barrel, not from any fear of its bursting, since, if a gun is kept clean, there is not the *least danger*, supposing it to be properly loaded ; but on account of the recoil, which will always be much greater than in a stout barrel.

At first sight, it may be asked how it happens that a long eighteen-pounder carries farther than a shorter cannon ? To which, it may be answered, that it is possible, an increase of length might be added with advantage to the longest eighteen-pounder in the service ; since, on comparison, taking into consideration the difference of the caliber, a fowling piece barrel twenty-two inches in length is proportionably longer than any cannon whatever.

If the bore or caliber of the fowling piece be made extremely wide, it will require a greater charge, and will of course admit of a greater length of barrel.

THE ELEVATED BREECH

Is a modern invention; and consists of a sort of broad rib which runs along the top of the barrel, thicker at the breech end and tapering to the muzzle: by this contrivance, the muzzle acquires an elevation, and the shot is consequently thrown higher; for those, therefore, who are apt to shoot under or below the object, the elevated breech is to be recommended.

THE PATENT BREECH AND THE TOUCH HOLE.

On the patent breech, a great number of trifling *variations* have been made; which, however, are called *improvements* by the inventors. The difference between the patent and the common breech is, that in the former, the powder in the breech lies much looser, and is brought more nearly in contact with the priming, and the discharge is of course more instantaneous. Also, the patent breech does not require so much powder as the common breech; for, as from the reason just stated, the ignition of the powder in the barrel is quicker, so also it kindles better, as it were; and the whole charge, or very nearly so, becomes ignited; whereas, in the common breech, a much greater quantity falls from the muzzle of the fowling-piece unexploded.

FOR THE TOUCH HOLE

Platina is superior to any thing ever made use of for that purpose—it resists the action of the fire better than gold.

THE LOCK.

Gun locks appear to have arrived at that degree of perfection
as to bid defiance to improvement.—A good lock can always
be obtained for a good price.

THE STOCK.

As to the stocking of a gun, much will depend upon habit;
but, generally speaking, a person with a long neck will require
a stock much bent, a short-necked person the contrary. But, I
must confess, I am by no means partial to much bend in a stock,
as it appears to give the muzzle too great a declination, and on
this account will be apt to throw the shot below the object.

o

THE RECOIL

Arises principally from improper management. Very few guns indeed will recoil much if they are kept clean, and properly loaded. See *Proportions of Powder and Shot*—A light gun is more inclined to recoil than a heavy one.

The Percussion Gun.

———

Some years ago, Forsyth procured a patent for the application of what is called *percussion powder* to fire arms. Sportsmen regarded with astonishment the pompous advertisements,
which announced the discharge of the fowling-piece, " *without
flint, flash, or smoke.*"—The percussion powder was used merely
as the priming. The invention, however, did not at first meet
with great encouragement, for two reasons, namely, the price
appeared exorbitant; and an idea of danger naturally enough
attached itself to the use of the percussion powder, which, at
first sight, appears so calculated to produce accidental mischief.

Forsyth's invention for containing the priming, consists of
what he calls a magazine, which is attached to the outside of the
lock, and contains a chamber large enough to hold powder for
a number of primings. By a slight movement of the magazine,
a sufficient quantity for one priming is thrown into a cavity,
where it receives the stroke of the hammer, becomes ignited,
and thus discharges the gun. Forsyth has the merit of being
the first to apply percussion priming to fire arms; but, it was
evident, that his magazine was susceptible of great improvement.
The priming powder, too, concerning which he assumed an air
of mysterious secresy, deposited so great a quantity of feculent
matter, and was so excessively corrosive, that much more frequent cleaning than usual became indispensable: under these
circumstances, therefore, I was content to pursue the old method
of priming with gunpowder.

Sometime ago, a percussion gun was put into my hands by Mr. R. Gill, of Richmond, in Yorkshire, of which I made a trial, and found that it shot remarkably well—I found it, in fact, much superior to the ordinary fowling piece, and this superiority arose not intirely perhaps from the use of percussion priming, but from the excellence of the bore and firmness of the workmanship; yet, the indescribable rapidity of the discharge, the increase of force, with little more than half the common charge of gunpowder, were advantages too tempting to be abandoned; and I, therefore, resolved to adopt the percussion gun.

Manton contrived a method of firing with percussion priming very different from Forsyth's, and perhaps on the whole inferior, as the primings were made into small cakes, one of which being fixed in an iron plug, the latter was placed in the mouth of the cock, as it were, and by striking on the touch-hole (made in the end of the breech, which is in the form of an inclined plane), discharged the gun. Manton accommodated his customers with fifty of these iron plugs, which were understood to be sufficient for the day's amusement; and being primed before setting out, were carried in the pocket, and used as occasion required. Carrying these plugs was obviously an inconvenience; in fact, the contrivance altogether bore no marks of extraordinary genius. Forsyth brought an action against Mr. Manton in consequence, for an infringement of his patent, and succeeded in putting a stop to Mr. Manton's sale of these guns.

As the application of percussion powder to the fowling-piece excited so much surprise, and appeared so advantageous, it was not long before a number of inventions made their appearance, each professing to be the best mode of adopting it. To say nothing of Forsyth's magazine, Manton's pegs, or Webster's wire, twenty other plans at least might be enumerated—many of which had a very neat and even a beautiful appearance; but which were generally found defective in the field either from a hazy atmosphere or other incidents to which the shooting sportsman is peculiarly liable. At length what is called the *Copper cap plan* made its appearance, which I have used throughout three seasons, under the disadvantages of wet weather and every other untoward circumstance attending this fascinating recreation :—I have made a great variety of experiments upon the subject, and have, in fact, tried it in all possible forms; and feel not the least hesitation in asserting, that the copper cap plan is superior in every point of view to any other which has made its appearance.

Copper cap guns will unquestionably become general ; and will no doubt be manufactured by all the pretenders in the trade : I would, therefore, advise those who may feel an inclination to procure fowling-pieces on the above plan, to be careful whom they apply to, as the very best system may be brought into disrepute by ignorance and incapacity ; and, perhaps, of all other businesses, none is more replete with those baneful qualities than that of gun making.

The *copper cap plan* is very simple; is less liable to be out of repair than any other ; and is, at the same time, much more easily rectified, should any casual accident occur. Indeed, its superiority is obvious at first sight, in every point of view.

I had nearly forgot to mention, that, independent of the copper caps used for priming, my gun has also *double headed priming pins*, as well as *patch pins*, which may be substituted for them, at the will or the whim of the sportsmen.

The advantages of percussion priming are, the instantaneous discharge, which is indescribably more rapid than with the common-priming, and, of course, reduces the science of shooting (particularly at flying or moveable objects) to a degree of precision unattainable by any other mode hitherto adopted. Very little more than half the common charge of gunpowder is sufficient to load the percussion gun ; for the strong flame from the priming is driven with uncommon force through the touch-hole, and not only ignites the gunpowder much more completely, but appears to assist its force, as the percussion gun drives the shot with a degree of strength scarcely to be believed by those who have not witnessed it. In fact, the strength of the percussion priming is driven into the barrel of the fowling-piece, as there is no other way for much of the expansive fluid to escape ; whereas, in the common lock, the hammer, being driven up by the stroke of the cock, suffers the elastic force, or strength of the priming, to escape ; nor is this all—no doubt can exist, that part of the force of the charge is expelled through the touch-hole, and this rule will, in all probability, be found to obtain in a greater degree when the wind blows strong. It follows, therefore, that the percussion, compared with the common method, will produce a more instantaneous discharge, superior force, and greater precision, with a much less charge of gunpowder.

Waterproof.—Percussion guns are much more susceptible of being rendered waterproof than guns upon the old method. Nevertheless, waterproof, as far as relates to the fowling piece is not of that importance as a superficial observer might imagine. Shooting is always unpleasant in rainy weather—in heavy and incessant rain it is out of the question. In a slight drizzling rain, or for a shower, the sportsman may keep the field with a percussion gun, and will experience no *hanging fire ;* but the scent will be indifferent, nor will game lie well unless in hedges and strong covers

OF PERCUSSION POWDER,
AND THE BEST METHOD OF MAKING IT.

Percussion powder differs from common gunpowder inasmuch as it ignites with a blow, or, in other words, with excessive friction ; and contains so great a proportion of elastic fluid, that, on explosion, its expansive force, compared with gunpowder, is at least in the proportion of twenty to one, perhaps much greater.

How long the composition of percussion powder has been known amongst able and experimental chemists, I will not pretend to decide ; but its discovery is not of a very recent date ; and some years past an attempt, which was made in France to introduce oxvmuriate of potash into the manufacture of gunpowder, was attended with fatal effects.

Percussion powder may be made of oxymuriate of potash, sulphur, and charcoal ; and these are probably the component parts used both by Forsyth and Manton. I tried a number of experiments on the above ingredients, and after varying the proportion of each in every possible way, it appeared that the following were the best calculated for the purpose :—

Oxymuriate of potash, nine parts
sulphur, one part and a half
charcoal, one part

But I was surprised at the variations which might be made in the proportions or parts, without any perceptible difference in the result. One effect, however, I uniformly found, namely, excessive corrosion ; and those who have been in the habit of using Forsyth's method are very well aware of the urgent necessity of cleaning the lock immediately after using, in order to prevent the destruction of the percussion apparatus, as one night only would produce a degree of rust scarcely credible by those unacquainted with the nature of oxymuriate of potash. Whatever advantages were to be derived from the use of percussion priming they were certainly much lessened by the trouble of cleaning, as the feculent matter deposited was much greater in quantity, and adhered with more obstinate tenacity, than that which is produced by the discharge of gunpowder; I was, therefore, pleased to find that the following remedied the evil:—

> Oxymuriate of potash, one ounce
> antimony, one ounce

well pulverized, and made into a paste with spirit of wine in which a little rosin or gum mastic has been dissolved: it may be granulated by forcing it through a hair sieve when it is nearly dry, and will be fit for use without further trouble. If spirit of wine be not at hand, I believe vinegar, without either rosin or gum mastic, will answer the purpose.

In making percussion powder, I would wish to impress upon the mind of the sportsman the strong necessity of caution in the preparation. The oxymuriate of potash should be pulverized separately upon a smooth stone (or a smooth hard board will answer the purpose) but with a wooden mullar, as it would be apt to explode if rubbed with a heavy stone mullar, particularly if great velocity were used. It is of no consequence how the antimony is reduced to powder; it may indeed be purchased at the druggists in powder, but seldom sufficiently fine for the purpose. However, when the oxymuriate of potash and the antimony are ground so as to be impalpable, they may be mixed with a pallet-knife (adding the spirit of wine or vinegar) and forced through the sieve as before mentioned. I have generally used spirit of wine in which a little rosin has been dissolved in preference to vinegar, because I am of opinion, that powder thus made up is not so apt to imbibe moisture. Eau de Cologne is sup-posed to be preferable to spirit of wine; but the difference when using the powder is imperceptible. Excessive friction from iron or steel, or other very hard substances, would, no doubt, ignite this powder; but it would be a difficult matter, however hard it might be rubbed between two pieces of wood, to produce com-bustion.

It has been before observed, that if sulphur and charcoal are used with the oxymuriate of potash, a great excess of corrosion will result from the explosion: but antimony corrects or neutralizes the acidity or corrosive quality of the oxymuriate of potash, and renders the powder less injurious, in regaid to rust, than even common gunpowder; while it is, at the same time, in every other respect superior.—An ounce of oxymuriate of potash, and an ounce of antimony, will make, I should suppose, about 10,000 primings. It may be mixed up in the manner before described in a few minutes, without the least danger. The oxymuriate of potash, when bought at the chemist's, by single ounces, costs two shillings and nine-pence an ounce, and, I have no doubt, could be sold, with a reasonable profit, for much less; an ounce of antimony will cost a penny: so that, including the spirit of wine, the expense of two ounces of priming powder will scarcely amount to three shillings. For an ounce of priming-powder, Mr. For-syth charges ten shillings and sixpence (or, at least, used so to charge.) When the superior strength of percussion powder is taken into consideration, it is much cheaper than gunpowder. Two ounces of the best gunpowder will cost more than sixpence; two ounces of percussion powder will searcely amount to three shillings, while one-twentieth part will answer the purpose: but, how far it is susceptible of application to fire-arms beyond the priming has not been determined; yet the present forms of the breeches of guns are not calculated to admit of its use for the charge, on account of the very small quantity which would be admissible for that purpose. Nor, for the purposes of safety, would it be adviseable to carry percussion powder in a spring-top flask, unless the springs were altogether made of something much softer than steel. If the sportsman thinks proper to carry percussion powder into the field, independently of what he has already prepared for priming, I know of nothing more safe or more convenient, than a small wooden box.

From the following paragraph, it would appear that gunpowder may be ignited by percussion:—" From experiments made in the Laboratory of the Royal Institution it has been found, that if gunpowder be mixed with pulverized glass, felspar, and particularly with harder substances, it may be inflamed by being struck violently on an anvil, though faced with copper, and struck with a copper hammer."

For military purposes, I should think percussion powder, for priming at least, an object of the first importance. The method invented by Gill would be an incalculable advantage to the musket, as missing fire could never happen, rain would have little or no effect, while the ball would be impelled with much greater force. To great guns Gill's invention is equally applicable, at a very trifling expence.

CLEANING THE FOWLING PIECE.

This operation is so obvious and so well known, that it would appear time worse than idly spent to describe it. Nevertheless, I will take the liberty to say a few words on the subject. Those who wish to shoot with pleasure and precision must keep the fowling-piece always very clean. After returning from an excursion, though I may not have had a shot, and have only flashed the powder off prior to going into the house (a rule which I invariably observe) the first object, to which I dedicate my attention, after having taken a little refreshment, is the fowling-piece, which I clean thoroughly, not omitting the inside of the locks if rain should have overtaken me ; an operation that takes up but a few minutes, and to which nothing more is requisite in addition to the screw driver, than a spring cramp. There is no difficulty in the matter, and the only introductory lesson at all necessary is merely to look on while a gunsmith performs the operation, twice or three times at most.

OF OIL,

AND THE BEST MODE OF CLARIFYING IT.

All vegetable oils possess a harder quality, and are more apt to become cloggy, than animal oils ; and are, consequently, not so well calculated for the fowling-piece, the locks in particular. Neat's foot oil, and the oil from sheep's feet, generally contain

a considerable quantity of feculent matter ; which may be separated by the following simple process :—drop a few small pieces
of lead into the bottle, and hang it in the sun for a week or ten
days, when the residuum will sink to the bottom, leaving the oil
remarkably pure, and admirably adapted for the purpose just
mentioned. If it happens in the winter, when the sun is not
sufficiently powerful, hang the bottle near the fire, to keep the
oil perfectly fluid, otherwise, the residuum cannot sink.—Goose
grease, or the fat of fowls in general, will answer the purpose
fully as well, if clarified in the manner above described.—A
profusion of oil is not to be recommended—if the locks are
rubbed with oily flannel or tow, it will be sufficient; the inside
of the barrel should be wiped with oily flannel or tow, immediately after washing, while it is warm.—I rub the outside also,
as well as the stock, and indeed every part of the fowling-piece.

BURSTING OF BARRELS

Arises, in nineteen instances out of twenty, from the gun having
been kept in a filthy state, or at least not sufficiently clean. If
the inner surface of the barrel is suffered to rust, so as to form
specks, in washing the barrel, wet will always remain in these
specks, and thus facilitate the corrosion : the barrel, of course,
becomes weaker in these particular parts, and must ultimately
burst. Nothing is more common among farmers and country
people, than keeping guns loaded for months—if for the purpose
of protection from thieves, loaded guns are necessary, they should

be fired and cleaned every week, for two reasons, to prevent missing fire, as well as to prevent the corrosion of the inner surface of the barrel, which will take place from the action of the gunpowder alone. No gun will burst, if properly loaded and kept clean ; not even those African guns, which used to be sent out of the country without proving. All fowling pieces, even the most inferior, are now *well proved ;* indeed, a severe penalty attaches to any person who sells a barrel which has not undergone the operation of proving. I am told, but I never tried the experiment, that if clay be forced into a gun barrel, in any way so as to leave a space between it and the charge, the barrel will inevitably burst on firing : the same remark has been by some, extended to snow—thus, if the muzzle of the fowling piece happens to fill with snow, in getting over a hedge, or by any other accident to which sportsmen are liable, they say, that on firing, the barrel would burst just under the snow : which will certainly happen supposing the snow is air tight. However, there will be no harm in the sportsman examining the muzzle of his fowling piece, after leaping a ditch, or under any other circumstance, where it might be possible for snow, dirt, or any other matter, to get into it.

Shot getting loose may cause the barrel to bulge or burst.

GENERAL OBSERVATIONS

THE FOWLING PIECE.

In the choice of a Gun I would recommend every sportsman first to consider the weight he can conveniently carry, strength being a most essential point as well to the safety as the shooting of the barrels. After the weight of the barrels is fixed upon, I turn my attention to the bore and length, and recommend the former not to be too wide, as it has two or three bad tendencies : in the first place, if the bore be wide, and the weight limited, it must weaken the barrel. Seventeen gage (i. e. seventeen balls to a pound) is a good size, and I think best calculated for general use ; but, suppose the weight of your barrels is confined to 4lb or 4½lb. which is a good and proper weight for 17 gage, if barrels of the same weight are made three-fourths of an inch in bore, they are then not only much reduced in strength and rendered unsafe, but do not shoot so well for want of a proper proportion of metal according to the bore, (I allude to double barrels only;) besides, a wide-bored double gun, unless made excessively heavy, such as no gentleman would wish to carry, is very unpleasant to use, as it must be loaded according to its bore, and, for want of sufficient metal, it recoils violently ; when, on the contrary, barrels of a less bore, suppose 17 or 18 gage, the same weight as the wide-bored ones will shoot well, and be perfectly safe : strength is essential in barrels, but I do not recommend any sportsman to have too heavy a gun, that is, heavier than he can conveniently manage, for if he becomes overpowered with weight or fatigue, I think he will shoot well no more that day. If the weight is limited, the shorter your gun is, the stronger it must be; and there is no weight that a gentleman will carry, that will, in the least be any improvement to the shooting of barrels above 2 feet 5 inches, or 2 feet 6 inches long; and although many sportsmen will scarcely admit that a barrel 2 feet 2 inches, or 2 feet 4 inches, will kill equal to one of 2 feet 6, or 2 feet 7 inches, yet a short gun (well manufactured) will certainly shoot equally well, or perhaps better: I agree that all short guns do not shoot as well as long ones: because there is more judgment required in making a gun under 2 feet 5 inches, to shoot properly, and few gunmakers understand the method. For my own part, I shoot with one made by Gill, of Richmond, only 2 feet 2 inches in barrel, the shooting of which has surprised some of my sporting friends: it fires by percussion, and according to my own judgment on the most simple and best principle* of any I have yet seen: it may be properly cleaned by almost any person in three or four minutes. Of the Locks, I think nothing more need be said than to have them as well made as possible, as much depends on the good workmanship of a gun lock, let the principle of it be what it may; and, a real good lock will be as perfect with proper care, after twenty years' wear as it was the first hour; while a bad one will wear out the first season, and probably cost the owner the price of a good lock in repairs.— The next essential points about a gun, are the bend, length, and mounting of the Stock: if the gun is in every respect a piece of superior workmanship, and shoots in a superior manner, it is of little service if it be not stocked exactly to suit the person who uses it; it is therefore not only a most material thing to have the gun stocked the exact bend and length to suit the owner, but to

* It is the copper cap plan, with the locks of a peculiar construction.

have it properly *laid off*, a circumstance which gunmakers in general seem not to understand, or at least to disregard, and to which the slightest attention is never paid by the Birmingham makers. Every other particular depends chiefly on the fancy of the sportsman. In conclusion, therefore, I caution the purchaser to employ such gun-makers as are in the habit of executing good work and most particularly guns that shoot well, as there are many eminent gun-makers, who either do not understand the particular art of making guns shoot in a superior manner, or will not give themselves the trouble, the latter is equally objectionable, in my opinion, and too often applies to some of the London makers.

Gunpowder.

The first *fire* that was used in war occasioned as great, if not a more considerable, alarm, than that caused by the explosion of gunpowder. It was called the *Greek fire*, and is said to have been discovered in very ancient times. It was the invention of *Callinicus*, an architect of *Heliopolis* or *Balbeck*, who left the service of a *Caliph*, and brought the important arcanum to Constantinople in the reign of *Constantine Pagonatus*. That emperor forbade the art of making it to be communicated to any except his own subjects, and the secret was long preserved : it was, however, at length known among the nations confederated with the *Byzantines*. It is supposed to have been compounded of the gum of the pine and other resinous trees, reduced to powder with brimstone, to which were added *naptha* and other bitumens, and, according to some, the water of a fountain in the east, which had the property to amalgamate with these combustibles, and to render them more inflammable ; but this last article seems hardly possible to have been included, as in that case it could have been only made where *that water* was to be had, whereas it was in use both all over *Asia* and in *Europe*. *Anna Comena* says it was composed of *bitumen, sulphur*, and *naptha*.

The *Greek fire* was employed A. D. 883, by *Nicetas*, the high-admiral of the eastern empire, who was sent by the *Saracens* of *Crete* with a navy to assault *Constantinople :* he attacked and utterly defeated them, burning twenty of their ships by " the *Greek fire*."

Procopius, in his History of the *Goths*, calls it " Medea's oil," considering it as an infernal composition prepared by that sorceress. It is said to have been known in China, A. D. 917, three hundred years after *Constantine Pagonatus*, under the name of the " oil of the cruel fire;" and was carried thither by the Kitan Tartars, who had it from the king of *Ou*. This wonderful and destructive mixture twice preserved the metropolis of the *Eastern Romans* from the infidel armaments. The *Greek fire* is much spoken of in all the histories of the holy wars, as being frequently employed with success by the *Saracens* against the *Christians*. During the Crusades, and in the reign of Richard *Cœur de Lion*, we shall find, that it struck with dismay the most intrepid Christian knights, until a method of extinguishing it was discovered by the French. By the following description of it, given by *Joinville*, who was an eye-witness, it has somewhat the appearance of the *iron rockets*, still used in India: he says it was thrown from the bottom of a machine called a *petrary*, and that it came forward as large as a barrel of verjuice, with a tail of fire issuing from it as big as a great sword, making a noise in its passage like thunder, and seeming like a dragon flying through the air ; and, from the great quantity of fire it threw out, giving such a light, that one might see in the camp as if it had been day. Such was the terror it occasioned among the commanders of *St. Louis's* army, that *Gautier de Cariel*, an experienced and valiant knight, gave it as his advice, that so often as it was thrown they should all prostrate themselves on their elbows and knees, and beseech the *Lord* to deliver them from that danger, against which he alone could protect them : this counsel was adopted and practised; besides which, the *King* being in bed in his tent, as often as he was informed that the *Greek fire* was thrown, raised himself in his bed, and with uplifted hands thus besought the Lord, " good Lord God, preserve my people!" But the great terrors it occasioned, the effects of this fire do not seem to justify, as a mode had been found of quenching it. We are told, some of their *castellated cats*, (a covered shed, occasionally fixed on wheels, and which had crenelles and chinks, from whence the archers could discharge their arrows; it was used for covering soldiers employed in filling up the ditch, preparing the way for the moveable tower, or mining the wall; sometimes under the cover of this machine the besiegers worked a small kind of *ram*,) were set on fire, but the flames were extinguished. The *Greek fire* was thrown thrice in the night from the *petrary*, and four times from a large *cross-bow:* the blaze lighted by this composition was inextinguishable by water. *Geoffry de Vinesauf*, who accompanied Richard I. to the crusade, says of it, " with a pernicious stench, and livid flame, it consumes even flint and iron, nor could it be extinguished by water; but by sprinkling *sand* upon it the violence may be abated, and *vinegar* poured upon it will put it out." To these, some add *urine*, and even *oil*.

The following is a translation of some ancient lines, descriptive of the general opinion of its properties :

" May the fiend fly away with this odious *Greek fire !*
" Not *water* to quench it, but *sand* we require ;
" Then *vinegar's* acid its influence must lend us,
" And *lye* in its turn too must help to defend us.

" The *Pagans* alone by this pest are protected,
" 'Gainst the Christians alone are its perils directed :
" By the *Pagans* 'tis armed by most foul incantation.
" Oh ! save us, kind Saviour, from such conflagration !"

From other descriptions it appears, this composition was of an unctuous and viscid nature, sticking to the objects against which it was directed. In land engagements and sieges, it was projected by the machines of the times, and at sea by hand, enclosed in vessels or phials, in which it was also kept and transported; it was likewise sometimes fastened to the heads of arrows: sea water, instead of quenching, seemed to give it new violence and activity.

Both parties used the Greek fire at the siege of *Acre*, A. D. 1190, and Father Daniel says, " this wild fire was not only used in *sieges*, but even in *battles*, and that *Philip Augustus*, king of France, having found a quantity of it prepared in *Acre*, brought it with him to France, and employed it at the siege of *Dieppe*, for burning the English vessels in that harbour. At several other sieges in France, it was also used; and an engineer, named *Gaubert*, a native of Manté, acquired the art of making it, which luckily for mankind, has been since lost." A composition something of the same nature was some years since invented by a chymist in this country, and who has an annual allowance so long as it shall remain a secret; our government being unwilling to increase the destruction and cruelty of war: a like discovery was made formerly in France or Holland, and for the like reason suppressed. It was supposed that this was what Earl Stanhope referred to, when he said in the House of Lords, "that the French were not only in possession of a secret respecting this unquenchable fire, but meant to practise it against our navy to its certain destruction." Notwithstanding they do not appear to be fond of coming close enough to our fire of common gunpowder, to enable them to apply any of this supposed more destructive material.

Greek fire was used long after the introduction of fire arms, particularly in sieges. When the Bishop of *Norwich*, besieged *Ypres*, A. D. 1383, the garrison is said, by *Walsingham*, to have defended themselves so well with stones, arrows, lances, *Greek fire*, and certain engines called *guns*, that they obliged the English to raise the siege with such precipitation, that they left behind them their *great guns*, which were of inestimable value. A great part of that army was soon after besieged in the town of *Burburgh* by the French, who threw such quantities of

Greek fire into it, that they burned a third part of the town, and obliged the English to capitulate.

Although the invention of gunpowder with its application to fire-arms may be ranked among the most important discoveries, yet the date of that invention, with the name of the person to whom mankind are indebted for it, are both equally unknown. From the number slain in engagements previous to its introduction, what, at first view of its fatal effects, might be deemed an additional and severe scourge, has rather proved beneficial to the human race, by reducing the destruction of the species in battle within narrower limits. Formerly, when men engaged *hand to hand,* they were so intermingled, that the only criterion of victory was, the having no more of the enemy to kill : the duration of sieges* has also been considerably shortened since the use of gunpowder and artillery, by which the lives of many millions has been saved, who would otherwise have perished by hardships or disease, commonly in sieges more fatal than the sword, and in providing man with increased power over the animal world, and thus multiplying the catalogue of his food, the advantages derived from gunpowder are eminent.

* A numerous train of artillery, with a few barrels of this wonderful powder deposited in a *mine*, soon batter and throw down the strongest walls ; and indeed the greatest effects towards a victory and capitulation are brought about as much by the terror occasioned by the noise of the cannon, as the real mischief or slaughter, few men having sufficient firmness to stand their dreadful thunder ; and it is undoubtedly a fact that many a battle or town is won, more by the flight of those who are terrified at the sound of the artillery, than from the actual loss of those killed or wounded by it.—At Gibraltar, on the memorable 13th of September, 1782, the casualties amounted only to sixteen officers and men killed, and sixty-eight wounded ; a loss so trifling, as to be scarcely credible, that such a quantity of fire, in almost all its destructive modes of action, should not have produced greater effect with respect to the loss of men.

The common story respecting the invention of gunpowder and artillery is thus related : about the year 1320, one *Bartholdus Schwartz*, a German Monk, and student in *alchymy* (a pursuit then much in fashion), having in the course of his experiments mixed *saltpetre, sulphur*, and *charcoal* in a mortar, and partly covered it with a stone, it somehow took fire, and blew the stone to a considerable distance : thus, by one accident, furnishing the hints for making gunpowder, its force, and a piece of ordnance for using it ; and it is worthy of observation, that *stones* are said to have been thrown from mortars long before *point blank* shooting was attempted : possibly this story may be true ; but it does not at all follow from thence, that gunpowder was not *before known*, the same discovery having been frequently made by different persons engaged in the same study.

Many modern writers carry the *invention* of gunpowder, and even its application to *artillery*, back to very remote antiquity: The ingenious translator of the *Gentoo Laws*, finds *fire arms, gunpowder*, and *cannon*, mentioned in that code, supposed at least coeval with *Moses*. " It will no doubt (says he) strike the reader with wonder, to be informed of a prohibition of fire-arms, discovered in records of such unfathomable antiquity ; and he will probably from hence renew the suspicion which has long been deemed absurd, that Alexander the Great did absolutely meet with some weapons of that kind in *India*, as a passage in *Quintus Curtius* seems to ascertain : gunpowder has been known in *China* as well as *Hindostan* far beyond all periods of investigation." There is also, says *Mr. Grose*, the following ancient testimony to this point in *Grey's Gunnery*, printed, A. D. 1731. In the life of *Appolonius Tyanæus*, written by *Philostratus*, fifteen hundred years ago, there is the following passage concerning a people of India, called *Oxydracæ* :—" These truly wise men dwelt between the rivers *Hyphasis* and *Ganges ;* their country Alexander the Great never entered, deterred not by fear of the inhabitants, but, as I suppose, by religious considerations, for had he passed the *Hyphasis* he might doubtless have made himself master of the country all round them; but their cities he could never have taken though he had led a thousand as brave as *Achilles,* or three thousand such as *Ajax,* to the assault, for they come not out into the field to fight those who attack them, but these holy men, beloved by the gods, overthrew their enemies with tempests, and thunderbolts shot from their walls. It is said, that the Egyptian *Hercules* and *Bacchus,* when they over-ran *India,* invaded this people also: and having prepared warlike engines, attempted to conquer them; they made no shew of resistance, but upon the enemies near approach to their cities, they were repulsed with storms of lightning and thunderbolts, hurled upon them from above."

Our countryman, *Friar Bacon,* whose works were written at Oxford about the year 1270, fifty years before the supposed invention by *Schwartz,* has expressly named the *ingredients of gunpowder* as a well-known composition used for recreation, and describes it as producing a noise like thunder, and flashes like lightning, but more terrible than those produced by nature, and adds, this might be applied to the destruction of an enemy by sea and land: *Bacon* acquired this composition from a treatise on artificial fire works, written by one *Marcus Græcus;* the manuscript is still extant, and is quoted by the *Reverend Mr. Dutens,* in order to prove that gunpowder was known to the ancients; the composition therein prescribed is, two pounds of charcoal, one pound of sulphur, and six pounds of saltpetre, well pounded and mixed together in a stone mortar; this is a better mixture for powder than many late in use.

Bishop Watson, in his Chemical Essays, remarks, that the history of the discovery of gunpowder is involved in much obscurity; the most ancient authors differing from each other in their accounts of this matter; and many of them confounding two distinct enquiries :—viz. the discovery of the composition of gunpowder ; and the discovery of finding out the means of applying it to the purposes of war.

Polydore Vergil, who died in 1555, attributes the discovery of gunpowder to some very ignoble German, whose name he wishes might never be handed down to posterity. He further informs us that this German invented also an *iron tube*, and taught the Venetians the use of *guns* A. D. 1380. This, continues *Dr. Watson*, is the common account of the discovery of gunpowder : its truth, however, is rendered doubtful by what follows:

The battle of *Cressy* was fought 1346, and an historian who lived at that time is quoted by *Spondanus* as affirming, that the *English* greatly increased the confusion the French had been thrown into, by discharging upon them from their *cannon, hot iron bullets.* Three years before the battle of *Cressy*, the *Moors* were besieged by the *Spaniards* in the city of *Algeziras ;* and we learn from *Mariana* the Spanish historian, "that the besieged did great harm among the Christians with *iron bullets* they shot." The same author adds, " This is the *first time* we find any mention of *gunpowder* and *ball* in our histories." The Earls of *Derby* and *Salisbury* are mentioned by *Mariana* as having assisted at the siege of *Algeziras*, and as they returned to England in the latter end of the year 1343, it is not an improbable conjecture, that, having been witnesses of the havoc occasioned by the *Moorish* fire-arms, they brought the secret from Spain into England, and introduced the use of artillery into the English army at the battle of *Cressy*.

It was to cover the disgrace of the French arms that *Edward* was alleged to have used gunpowder, *and* to which was owing his success. This advantage the French might have resorted to, and fought the English by the same means; for father *Daniel* cites a record preserved in the Chamber of Accounts at *Paris*, to prove that the *French had*, and *used*, cannon in the year 1338. The charge in the Treasurer of War's Account in the above year was as follows: "*To Henry de Faumachon* for *powder* and other things necessary for the *cannons* which were before *Puy Guillaume*." N. B. Puy Guillaume was a castle in *Auvergne*. It is to be remarked that neither *Froissart* nor any one of the many historians who have described the battle of *Cressy* has noticed the employment of the artillery there, except *Vilani*, an Italian author.

The use of guns in Spain, Anno 1343, is proof sufficient either that *Schwartz* was not the inventor of gunpowder, or that *Kircher* and others are mistaken in fixing his discovery so late as the year 1354. There is reason, notwithstanding, to believe that both gunpowder and guns were known in *Germany*, at least forty years before the period assigned by the *Spanish* historian for their first introduction into Spain. In the Armory at Amberg in Bavaria, there is a piece of ordnance, on which is inscribed the year 1303. This is the earliest account I have yet met with of the certain use of gunpowder in war; and it seems probable enough, as the *Pope* and the Duke of Bavaria are thought to have been the first Princes who made saltpetre in Europe. It ought not, however, says *Dr. Watson*, to be concealed from the reader, that *Camerarius* quotes a Danish historian as relating, that *Christopher*, King of the Danes, was killed in battle by the stroke of a gun, A. D. 1280. Upon examining the passage quoted, it is only said that *Christopher*, the son of *King Waldemar*, was killed in the beginning of an engagement by a *gun*, a warlike instrument then lately discovered. Now it appears, that *Waldemar*, Christopher's father, did not succeed to the crown of Denmark until 1332, and that his son was killed in a naval engagement several years afterwards, probably about the time stated by *Munster* for the earliest use of gunpowder in Denmark.

There are passages in the history of the English wars, which assert the employment of artillery antecedent to the above periods. For instance, if we are to credit John Barbour, arch-deacon of Aberdeen, *Edward* III. had artillery in his campaign against the Scots, A. D. 1327, and which were described as

———" Craky's of war,

That they before heard never."

In 1339, at the siege of Stirling, the Scots used battering cannon, which certainly had been sent by their French allies. At the siege of Calais, in 1347, "gunners and artillers" appear in a MS list of the English troops in the Harleian collection. The Earl of Pembroke, who commanded a British fleet, A. D. 1372, was taken prisoner by a *Spanish* squadron superior in numbers, and which were (perhaps for the first time) provided with cannon. Indeed we are shewn that more than half a century afterwards the English ships of war had very few guns, seldom more than *two*, and those not mounted so as to be altered occasionally in their direction, a circumstance, the motion of the sea considered, which must have rendered them of little service.

In 1378 is the first authentic mention of the lately invented instruments of death to be found; for then Richard II. sent to Brest great quantities of saltpetre, sulphur, and charcoal, together with two greater and two lesser engines called cannons, and 6,000 stone bullets. *John* of *Gaunt*, who had the command of the army, attempted to take St. Maloes, but was baffled by the conduct of the Great *Du Guesclin*, although, it is said, he had a train of 400 battering cannon playing upon the town.

The Flemings in 1382, had a most dreadful piece of ordnance:—" it was (says *Froissart*) fify feet long, and threw wonderfully large stones. Its report was heard *five leagues* by day and *ten* by night; and its noise was so immense, that one would have thought that all the devils in hell had a share in it."

In 1418 *iron balls* were not used for cannon in England, since in Rymer there is an order from King Henry V. to the clerk of the ordnance, and John Bonet, a mason of Maidstone, in Kent, to cut 7,000 stone shot in the stone quarries there; but there is reason to believe that the French had at that time *iron balls* in common use, since at the attack of Cherbourg, towards the close of the year 1418, the Duke of Gloucester, who commanded the beseigers, was much annoyed by *red hot balls* fired from the town : a very singular occurrence, the state of artillery at that period being considered.

In 1428 the valiant and dreaded Earl of Salisbury fell by a cannon shot at the siege of Orleans, and was, according to *Camden,* the first English gentleman " ever slain therebye." Salisbury was reconnoitring the town from a high tower on the bridge, when the son of the master gunner of Orleans, pointed a cannon at the window and slew him ; the ball carried away one of his eyes and his cheek, and mortally wounded one Sir Thomas Gargrave.

At the siege of *Belgrade* by the Turks A. D. 1437, they were repulsed by the help of gunpowder, then used for the first time in that part of Europe. But the extreme awkwardness in the early construction of cannon, and the great cost of gunpowder, may fairly account for the preference still given to the old engines for discharging stones. Two pieces of artillery used at *Dieppe* in 1442, as represented by *Pere Montfaucon,* seem ill calculated for service ; nor does there appear throughout the century any contrivance to elevate or depress the pieces ; a deficiency which must have rendered them comparatively useless.*

---

* *Edward* IV. had field pieces when he defeated *Sir Robert Wells* at Stamford 1469, and which was the first time they were employed by an English army. " The King, (says Leland) sparkeled the enemie with his ordnance, slew many of the commons, and thereby gained the victory."—At the battle of *Flodden,* 1513, the Scots were much superior

It certainly was not for want of *bulk* that the artillery of the age failed in becoming respectable. We are told by *Monstrelet* of a piece of ordnance which sent a ball weighing 500*lbs* from the Bastille at Paris, to Charenton in 1478. The cannon too used by Mahomet II. at the siege of Constantinople were im. mense both in bulk and power. On the other hand, there was the *culverin* (a kind of light artillery, sometimes carried by *one* and sometimes by *two* men), and which was used by the Switzers at the battle of Morat, where 10,000 of them were so armed.

This weapon (an entirely different instrument from the long cannons formerly named coulouverines or *culverines*) seems to have been the parent of the musquet, and was placed on a *rest* to be discharged. But to return to the more immediate history of Gunpowder, we find from *Camden*, in his life of Queen Elizabeth, that she was the *first* that procured gunpowder to be made in England, that she might not *pray* and *pay* for it also to her neighbours. At first, gunpowder was not granulated, but remained in its *mealed* state; it was then called *serpentine* powder. In several accounts of military stores during the reign of Edward VI. and Elizabeth, there are large quantities of serpentine powder.

The making of gunpowder after the most ancient manner:—

Anno 1380, saltpetre, brimstone, charcoal, equal parts.

in ordnance: *Borthwic*, an engineer of eminence, had the direction of it. *Lewis* of France had sent him to *James* with a large present of brass cannon, on each side of which was inscribed "Machina sum Scoto Borthwic fabricato Roberto." This valuable train of artillery fell into the hands of the Earl of Surrey after the battle of Flodden, together with seven "faire culverines," called the *seven sisters*. To his successful general, *Henry* restored his father's patrimony, the dukedom of *Norfolk*; and this honourable addition to his arms, that he was permitted to bear on the bend of his arms, the upper half of a red lion, painted as in the arms of Scotland, with the mouth pierced through with an arrow.

Anno 1410, saltpetre three parts, brimstone two parts, charcoal two parts.

Anno 1480, saltpetre eight parts, brimstone three parts, charcoal three parts.

Anno 1520. The making best powder, saltpetre four parts, charcoal one part, brimstone one part.

Anno 1647. The best sort now made, saltpetre six parts, brimstone one part, charcoal one part.

The musket powder is now commonly made of saltpetre five parts, brimstone one part, charcoal one part.

The cannon powder, saltpetre four parts, one part charcoal, one part brimstone.

The *Bishop of Llandaff*, in his essay on the Composition and Analysis of Gunpowder, states, " that in the proportion in which they are combined, the manner of mixing, the goodness of the ingredients, and the drying of the powder after being made, its strength and excellency consists. Saltpetre, in its crude state, whether it be brought from the East Indies or made in Europe, is generally, if not universally, mixed with a greater or less portion of common salt: now a small portion of common salt injures the goodness of a large quantity of gunpowder; hence the very finest saltpetre becomes necessary to be used in its formation. The purest sulphur is that sold in the shops under the name of flowers of sulphur; but the roll sulphur being much cheaper than the former, and being also of a great degree of purity, it is the only sort which is used in the manufacturing of gunpowder. With relation to the charcoal, it has been for the most part believed that the coal from soft and light woods was better adapted than the hard and heavy ones to the making of gunpowder : thus *Evelyn* says of the hazel, that ' it made one of the best coals used for gunpowder, being very fine and light, till they found alder to be more fit.' An eminent French chemist (*M. Baume*) has shewn from actual experiment, that this opinion in favour of coal from *light* wood is ill founded : he affirms, that powder made from lime tree coal, or even from the coal of the pith of the alder tree, is in no respect preferable to that made from coal of the hardest woods, such as guiacum and oak. This remark, if confirmed by future experience, may be of service; as it is not always in the power of gunpowder makers to procure a sufficient quantity of the coal of soft wood.

" The mixture of the materials of which gunpowder is made should be as intimate and uniform as possible ; for in whatever manner the explosion may be accounted for, it is certain that the three ingredients are necessary to produce it. In order to procure this accurate mixture, the ingredients are previously reduced into coarse powders, and afterwards ground and pounded together, till the powder becomes exceedingly fine ; and when that is done the gunpowder is made. But as gunpowder, in the state of an impalpable dust, would be inconvenient in its use, it has been customary to reduce it into grains, by forcing it, when moistened with water, through sieves of various sizes.

" The necessity of a complete mixture of the materials, in order to have good gunpowder, is sensibly felt, when such as has been dried, after being accidentally wetted, is used. There may be the same weight of the powder after drying that there was before it was wetted ; but its strength is greatly diminished, on account of the mixture of the ingredients being less perfect. This diminution of strength proceeds from the water having dissolved a portion of the saltpetre (the other two ingredients not being soluble in water) ; for upon drying the powder, the dissolved saltpetre will be crystallized in particles much larger than those were which entered into the composition of the gunpowder, and thus the mixture will be less intimate and uniform than it was before the wetting. This wetting of gunpowder is often occasioned by the mere moisture of the atmosphere. Great complaints were made concerning the badness of the gunpowder

used by the English, in their engagement with the French fleet
off Grenada, in July 1779 ; the French having done much
damage to the masts and rigging of the English, when the
English shot would not reach them. When this matter was
inquired into by the House of Commons, it appeared that the
powder had been injured by the dampness of the atmosphere;
it had concreted into large lumps, in the middle of which the
saltpetre was visible to the naked eye. If the wetting of gunpowder has been considerable, it is rendered wholly unfit for
use ; but if no other foreign substance has been mixed with it,
except fresh water, it may be made into good gunpowder again,
by being properly pounded and granulated. If the wetting has
been occasioned by salt-water, and that to any great degree, the
sea salt, upon drying the powder, will remain mixed with it, and
may so far vitiate its quality that it can never be used again in
the form of gunpowder. However, as by solution in water, and
subsequent crystallization, the most valuable part of the gunpowder, namely, the saltpetre, may be extracted, and in its
original purity, even from powder that has been wetted by sea-
water, or otherwise spoiled, the saving damaged powder is a
matter of national economy, and deservedly attended to in the
Elaboratory at Woolwich.

" The proportions," continues *Dr. Watson,* " in which the
ingredients of gunpowder are combined together are not the same
in different nations, nor in different works of the same nation,
even for powder destined to the same use. It is difficult to obtain
from the makers of gunpowder any information upon this subject: their backwardness arises not so much from any of them
fancying themselves possessed of the best possible proportion, as
from an affectation of mystery, common to most manufacturers,
and an apprehension of discovering to the world that they *do
not use so much saltpetre as they ought to do,* or as their com-
petitors in trade *really do use.* Saltpetre is not only a much

dearer commodity than either sulphur or charcoal, but it enters also in a much greater proportion into the composition of gunpowder than both those materials taken together; hence there is a great *temptation* to *lessen* the quantity of the *saltpetre*, and to *augment* that of the other ingredients; and the fraud is not easily detected, since gunpowder, which will explode readily and loudly, may be made with very different quantities of saltpetre.

" *Baptista Porta* died in the year 1515 : he gives three different proportions for the making of gunpowder, according as it was required to be of different strength, the quantities of the several ingredients contained in one hundred pounds weight of each sort of powder.

	WEAK.		STRONG.		STRONGEST.
Saltpetre	$66\frac{2}{3}$*lb.*	.	75*lb.*	.	80*lb.*
Sulphur	$16\frac{2}{3}$		$12\frac{1}{2}$		10
Charcoal	$16\frac{2}{3}$	.	$12\frac{1}{2}$	.	10
	100		100		100

" It is somewhat remarkable that in these three powders the sulphur and charcoal are used in equal quantities. *Cardan* died about sixty years after *Baptista Porta,* and during that interval the proportions of ingredients of gunpowder seem to have undergone a great change. Cardan's proportions are expressed as follows :

	GREAT GUNS.		MIDDLE SIZED.		SMALL.
Saltpetre	50*lb.*	.	$66\frac{2}{3}$*lb.*	.	$83\frac{1}{3}$*lb.*
Sulphur	$16\frac{2}{7}$		$13\frac{1}{2}$		$8\frac{1}{3}$
Charcoal	$33\frac{1}{3}$		20		$8\frac{1}{2}$
	100		100		100

" For great and middle sized guns, we see a much greater proportion of charcoal than of sulphur was here used : at present it is in most places the reverse ; or at least the charcoal no where exceeds the sulphur. The proportions were as under, for the best kind of gunpowder in England, France, Sweden, Poland, and Italy.

ENGLAND.	FRANCE.	SWEDEN.	POLAND.	ITALY.
Saltpetre 75*lb.* .	75*lb.* .	75*lb.* .	80*lb.* .	76½*lb.*
Sulphur 15 .	9½	16 .	12 .	12½
Charcoal 10 .	15½ ,	9 .	8 .	12½
* 100	100	100	100	101½

" Several experiments have been made in France to ascertain the exact proportions of the several ingredients which would produce the strongest possible powder, and the result has been in favour of

Saltpetre	80*lb.*
Charcoal	15
Sulphur	5

And from hence it appears that in a certain weight of saltpetre the powder would produce the greatest effect when the weight of the charcoal was to that of the sulphur as three to one. On the other hand, experiments are produced from which it is to be concluded that in a certain weight of saltpetre the best powder is made when the sulphur is to the charcoal as two to one. From these different accounts it seems as if the problem of determining the very best possible proportion was not yet solved.

" In drying gunpowder, after it is reduced into grains, there are two things to be avoided, too much and too little heat. If the heat is too great, a part of the sulphur will be driven off, and thus the proportions of the ingredients being changed, the goodness of the powder, so far as it depends upon that proportion, will be injured. In order to see what quantity of sulphur might be separated by a degree of heat not sufficient to explode it, I took," says *Dr. Watson*, " twenty-four grains of the pow-

* These were said to be the proportions of government powder.

der marked FF in the shops, and placing it on a piece of polished copper, I heated the copper over the flame of a candle; the gunpowder soon sent forth a strong sulphureous vapour, and when it had been dried so long that no more fume or smell could be distinguished, the residue weighed nineteen grains, the loss amounted to five grains. The remainder did not explode by a spark like gunpowder, but like a mixture of saltpetre and charcoal, and it really was nothing else, all the sulphur having been dissipated. Gunpowder was formerly dried by being exposed to the heat of the sun; and this method still obtains in France, and in some other countries: afterwards a way was invented of exposing it to a heat equal to that of boiling water; at present it is most generally in England dried in stoves heated by great iron pots; with any tolerable degree of caution, no danger of explosion need be apprehended from this method. All the watery part of the gunpowder may be evaporated by a degree of heat greatly less than that in which gunpowder explodes, that degree of heat having been ascertained by some late experiments to be about the six hundredth degree on *Fahrenheit's* scale, in which the heat of boiling water is fixed at two hundred and twelve. There is more danger of evaporating a part of the sulphur in this mode of drying gunpowder than when it is dried by exposure to the sun.

" The necessity of freeing gunpowder from all its moisture is obvious from the following experiment, which was made some years ago before the Royal Society. A quantity of gunpowder was taken out of a barrel and dried with a heat equal to that in which water boils, a piece of ordnance was charged with a certain weight of this dried powder, and the distance to which it threw a ball was marked. The same piece was charged with an equal weight of the same kind of powder, taken out of the same barrel, but not dried, and it threw an equal ball only to one half the distance. This effect of moisture is so sensible, that some officers have affirmed that they have seen barrels of gunpowder which was good in the morning, but which became (by attracting, probably, the humidity of the air) entirely spoiled in the evening. To keep the powder dry, by preventing the access of the air, it has been proposed to line the barrels with *tin foil*, or with thin sheets of *lead*, as tea boxes are lined. Would it not be possible," asks *Dr. Watson*, " to preserve powder free from moisture, and from the loss of a part of its sulphur in hot climates, by keeping it in glazed earthen bottles, or in bottles made of copper or tin, well corked? The disposition to attract the humidity of the air varies in different sorts of powder; it is the least in that which is made from the purest saltpetre. Pure saltpetre, which has been dried as gunpowder is dried, does not become heavier by exposure to the atmosphere; at least, so far as my experiments have informed me, not amounting to above one seventy-second part of its weight. I rather think," continues Dr. Watson, " that it does not acquire any increase of weight; however, in order to judge with more certainty concerning the effect of sea salt when mixed with saltpetre, in attracting the humidity of the air, I made the following experiment: five parts of pure saltpetre, in powder, were exposed for a month to a moist atmosphere, but I did not observe that the saltpetre had gained the least increase of weight; for the same length of time, and in the same place, I exposed four parts of saltpetre mixed with one of common salt, and this mixture had attracted so much moisture, that it was in a state of fluidity "

Of all the powders which have fallen under my observation, Messrs. Lawrence & Son's, of Battle, is the best. Some time ago, a powder was pompously advertised, with "*Sir Humphrey Davy*" attached to it, which did not answer the expectation intended to be excited by the name of so great a chemist; and still farther to continue this feeling, the price was doubled. It is probable, that Sir Humphrey Davy had nothing to do with the manufacture of this article ; nor is it likely, that either he or any other chemist should be so well acquainted with the process of making this combustible, as those who are in the constant habit of attending to it in all its different stages. Good powder is distinguished by the instantaneity of its ignition, by the clearness of its burning, as well as by its tinging the pan with a gold colour, and depositing little or no residuum or feculent matter; and these qualities Lawrence's powder possesses in an eminent degree.* In damp weather, however, powder will not

* "The late very fine breeding season had, with me, raised expectation to the tip-toe; and, amongst other preparatory matters, I determined to try the strength of different gunpowders, some of which are offered to the notice of the sportsman under high-sounding denominations. I, in the first place, made use of an instrument, called a *powder-tryer*, specially made for the purpose; and, after a number of experiments, not quite so satisfactory as I could wish, I had recourse to the fowling-piece; and, by weighing the charge, both powder and shot, with all possible accuracy, and firing at sheets of smooth close paper, I at length arrived at a result more satisfactory than that which I had derived from the tryer. The powder manufactured by Pigou and Co. and that made by Curtis and Harvey, as well as that made by Lawrence of Battle, are excellent, though, from repeated trial, the last was evidently the strongest, while the combustion seemed to deposit less feculent matter or residuum. Of six different samples of gunpowder which I tried, the three which I have mentioned were so far superior to the rest, that the latter are not worthy of enumeration ; and in order that they all might be fairly tried, I had kept the samples in the same dry cupboard for several weeks prior to the experiments. Powder kept in a damp place, or even exposed to the action of the atmosphere, will lose much of its force, burn comparatively dull, and the explosion is followed by a greater deposition of extraneous matter or filth.

From these experiments, I was led to make a trial of *percussion powder*, in order to ascertain how far it might be applicable for the charge as well as the priming ; and for this purpose I had again recourse to the powder-tryer, fearful lest unpleasant consequences might ensue from prematurely firing it in the barrel of the fowling piece. However, I burn so well, nor so clear; while the pan, instead of receiving the gold-coloured tinge from the explosion, will become foul, and exhibit strong marks of imperfect combustion. In hot or

derived nothing very satisfactory from my attempts with percussion powder, which not only deposited a very great quantity of residuum, but appeared to operate in a way altogether different from gunpowder. The ignition of the quantity of percussion powder, with which I filled the tryer, produced a kind of liquid fire, which issuing backwards through the touch-hole, in considerable quantities, and emitting sparks, as it were, of the same fluid, repeatedly burnt my hand. I could not ascertain the strength of the percussion powder, so much more, comparatively, of the fire uniformly re-issuing from the touch-hole, than what is found to be the case with gunpowder. It is true, it generally moved the wheel of the tryer (though not always), but never drove it nearly so far as the explosion of gunpowder uniformly effected. Nor does the detonation appear either so loud, or so instantaneous. I fired two ounces of percussion powder in the open air, by kindling it with a red hot poker, and the result followed which I have just mentioned, viz. the explosion was neither so loud nor so quick as gunpowder; while the board upon which it was laid, was much burnt, and a great quantity of feculent matter deposited. If a thimble full of percussion powder be ignited upon a plate, the combustion will break the plate; the same quantity of gunpowder kindled upon a plate, will explode more rapidly, and without breaking the plate.

Finally, from the result of my experiments, I felt a perfect conviction, that percussion powder (at least in its present state), however admirably it may act as a priming, is by no means calculated for the charge; unless, indeed, the explosion can be rendered much quicker, as well as the combustion much cleaner. Should any of your readers be disposed to try experiments upon this subtle composition, I would strongly advise them to be very cautious in their proceedings.

N.B. Percussion powder will ignite when brought in contact with highly-concentrated sulphuric acid: I have tried the experiment many times. If the head of a pin be dipped in highly-concentrated sulphuric acid, and applied to the priming in a copper cap, it will ignite immediately, but not so instantaneously as when struck with a hammer, nor will the combustion be so complete."—*Annals of Sporting, vol.* II.

dry weather, powder will burn remarkably well; I make a point, particularly when the atmosphere is hazy or heavy, to air my powder, as well as my gun before going out; and, for this purpose, I never suffer the flask to be out of my own hand—by holding the flask (a copper one) a short distance from the fire, the powder will be well aired in one or two minutes.

For ascertaining the strength of powder, gunsmiths generally make use of an instrument, which, I believe, is called a *trier*, and from which may be obtained tolerably accurate results: I prefer the fowling piece for this purpose: by adjusting the charge very exactly, and firing at paper many sheets in thickness, and at given distances, much satisfaction may be obtained, not only as to the quality of the powder, but of the manner in which the gun throws the shot.

THE POWDER FLASK.

A copper flask is preferable to any other.

SHOT.

For general use, I prefer No. 5, as it will answer every purpose, snipe shooting excepted, for which I should use much smaller. No. 6 or 7 will be found large enough for the early part of the partridge season; but I cannot agree with General Hanger, that No. 2 is decidedly preferable for all occasions, and from one end of the season to the other.—Upon trial, I found that I could scarcely average three shots in a card (four inches by three) at the distance of thirty-two yards, with No. 2. With No. 5, I averaged 8; and the latter, too, were driven with a force more than sufficient for the purpose. Upon increasing the distance to forty-one yards, I could seldom put in more than one pellet of No. 2; No. 5, at the same distance, averaged four; No. 6 averaged five.

FORCE OF PERCUSSION PRIMING

COMPARED WITH GUNPOWDER.

At the distance of thirty yards, the percussion gun threw the shot round and well, and perforated, completely, twenty nine sheets of strong writing paper, with shot, No. 5:—with common priming and patent breech, nineteen sheets were perforated. When shot, No. 2 was used, it perforated two or three sheets more than No. 5, and tore the paper in a slug-like manner.— *See note, page* 192, &c.

PROPORTIONS of POWDER and SHOT.

If you overload a gun with 'powder, the shot will scatter amazingly, and but few pellets will strike the object. If an insufficient quantity of powder is used, the shot will not be driven with the requisite force. But it is more than probable, that a trifling variation will be found in all guns; or, in other words, it will be a difficult matter to find two guns (though of the same length and caliber) which require precisely the same charge. The best method of ascertaining the proper load for the fowling-piece is, by firing at sheets of paper at given distances, and the progressive result will instruct the sportsman whether to increase or diminish the powder or shot, or both.—The general error in loading guns, I am inclined to think, is using too much powder, which not only scatters the shot prodigiously, but renders the recoil extremely unpleasant—it is quite a mistaken notion to suppose, that a distant object is better reached by a large load of powder, or that the force of the shot is thus increased; for, however paradoxical it may appear, it will be found, on experiment, that (to say nothing of the scattering of the shot, by which a small object will generally be missed) those pellets which strike the mark are not so strongly driven as when a reduced, but a correct, portion of powder is used. There is a certain proportion both of powder and shot with which a gun will shoot better than any other; these proportions are easily ascertainable in the manner just described; and, when ascertained, can be adopted.

If percussion priming is made use of, very little more than half the common load of powder will answer the purpose, see page 163.

WADDING.

Wadding punched from hat or common card will answer the purpose, but these articles are inferior to soft millboard, about the thickness of three cards. If cork were so cut as to fit the caliber of the fowling-piece, there is little question but it would be superior to any other kind of wadding; but, in this case the assistance of a regular cork cutter will be required, as I think, from some trials which I made, that cork cannot be punched. The thick soft millboard is preferable to any which I have ever used; though an old hat will make excellent wadding.

Shooting.

There is perhaps no amusement whatever, where success is so anxiously desired or so confidently anticipated, as by a young shooter on the approach of the 12th of August or the 1st of September. It is a most fascinating recreation; though the disappointments which almost uniformly attend the noviciate are extremely mortifying; yet hope sustains the spirit; every subterfuge is resorted to, on which to fix the blame of miscarriage, while the true reason is studiously kept out of sight:—the powder is bad, or the shot, or perhaps the fowling piece is crooked; the game rises too near or two far off—every thing, in fact, will in turn be wrong, or at least be made to serve as a salvo, rather than the real cause candidly acknowledged, namely, lack of skill, or rather, want of steadiness, in the sportsman.

To acquire the art of shooting flying, poor inoffensive swallows are often put in jeopardy: how far this practice is calculated to promote the intended object, I will not pretend to determine exactly; but very little practice will enable any person, I should suppose, to become a very expert swallow shooter. The flight of these birds is regulated by the winged insects upon which they feed, and the elevation of the latter is determined by the state of the atmosphere. When swallows fly about ten or fifteen yards from the ground, they are easily shot; the distance being completely within reach, and as every now and then they turn or become stationary for a moment, a slender share of skill is sufficient to bring them down.—Every thing that accustoms the tyro to the use of the fowling-piece will more or less pro-

Eng.d by T. Landseer from a Sketch

Edwin

DOWN CHARGE.

Nov.1.1823. Published by Sherwood. Jones & C.°

mote the object, and swallow shooting will no doubt assist; but in preference to destroying these very useful birds, whose appearance associates the beauties of spring and summer to the mind, I would certainly recommend shooting at sparrows and starlings, as they are very mischievous, and their flight, particularly the latter, resembles in some degree that of a partridge. But, allowing that practice of, this sort will assist, it will not attain, the ultimate object; nor does, in fact, the secret or skill consist merely in the dexterity of shooting flying—the alarm which is caused by the sudden spring of game, and the noise which ensues, throw the young sportsman so completely off his guard, and create such a trepidation, that some practice is at least indispensable, before these difficulties can be overcome; nor, until the game is approached with the utmost coolness, the sudden spring, &c. regarded with indifference, and the object selected with deliberation, will the sportsman be able to bring down the object with almost unerring certainty. I will suppose a man to be an expert swallow-shooter—let him approach a covey of partridges, prepared to fire—the birds rise suddenly, with great noise and confusion, and the swallow-shooter will be so completely bewildered, that they are sure to escape; or if he hit one, it will be merely an accident.

A young shooter, on the first of September, is prepared for the field almost before the gray of morn will enable him to distinguish any distant object :—he directs his hasty steps to the place where he expects to find a covey.—The dog *sets*, and, aware that the birds are under his nose, the tyro approaches the important spot with irregular step and a palpitating heart—the dog is motionless as a statue; his master has advanced one step before him, with such an increase of trepidation, as to be scarcely able to breathe—the awful stillness of a few seconds is interrupted by the sudden spring and screaming of the covey, and the shooter becomes so confused as to be incapable of levelling at any individual bird, and the whole fly away, leaving the sportsman much chagrined at the disappointment. On the re-currence of several of these disappointments, the dog will become uneasy, and will not hunt with his wonted cheerfulness: the fall of the bird gives as much pleasure to'the dog as to the shooter; and a capital dog, if no game be killed to him, will become careless, and eventually good for nothing. Practice, however, will soon overcome the obstacles just mentioned; and with an ordinary share of self-command, no person need despair of be-coming a tolerable shot. By way of illustration, I will, once more, suppose the young shooter in the field, with two dogs: he perceives one drawing on the scent, and settling to a point—let him call out *toho!* holding up his hand at the same time: the word will induce greater care in the first dog, and if the other should not be aware of the game, he will immediately look about him, and seeing his master's hand, will keep his position (no matter what his situation may be, either before or behind the shooter) or, to speak as a sportsman, will *back.* I will sup-pose both the dogs perfectly steady—let the sportsman advance, deliberately, up to the setting dog; and, if the game should not spring, let him go before the dog—if the birds should run, in-stead of taking wing, he will be aware of the circumstance, by the dog following; but if the dog follows or *foots* too eagerly, he should be checked by the words *take heed!* These are anx-ious moments, but the sportsman must, nevertheless, summon all his fortitude, and continue as calm as possible, with his thumb on the cock: when the game springs, pull up the cock, select an individual object—if the bird flies straight forward, it is a very easy shot; let the sportsman direct his eye down the barrel, and the instant he perceives the bird on a line with the muzzle, let him pull the trigger; in levelling, however, the aim should be directed rather above, than below, the object; for the shot, if correctly thrown, will form its centre from the centre of the muzzle of the fowling piece : nevertheless, in this respect, allow-ance must be made for the trim of the gun, or for the manner in which it throws the shot, with which I am supposing the sports-man perfectly acquainted : the *elevated breech* too will have con-siderable influence—*see page* 156. If the bird should fly directly across, or only partially so, and thus describe the segment of a circle, the aim must be directed before the object ; if with a com-mon gun, four inches ; with a percussion gun, two inches, sup-posing the distance to be about thirty yards. The average of shots is perhaps from twenty to thirty yards, though forty is quite within reach, and even fifty, particularly with a percussion gun—*see this Article, page* 159. When the bird flies in the shooter's face, as it were, or towards him, he should let it pass before he attempts to fire, or he will be almost certain to miss.

In what manner soever the object might present itself, I will suppose it comes down ; and though it should fall directly in view of your dogs, they must not stir. The sportsman will direct his attention to the covey, and, after *marking down*, will proceed to re-load. At the commencement of the season, part of the covey will frequently remain ; if, therefore, the dogs are not steady on the shot, mischief must ensue. I would not suffer my dogs to follow a winged bird till I had re-loaded ; I would much sooner lose the bird than injure my dogs ; though very few winged birds will be lost with good dogs.

Let me caution the sportsman, in loading, to keep the fowling-piece at arm's length, and not hang his face over the muzzle. Also, if he uses a double gun, let him examine, whether by any means the other barrel has become cocked—indeed, whether he has fired or not, he ought to see that the cock or cocks are se-cure, before he places the fowling-piece on his left arm for the purpose of advancing, which should be carried with the trigger forward, and as nearly perpendicular as possible. A gun is a dangerous instrument, and therefore care is indispensable.

It is not an easy matter to prevent a dog chasing a hare, unless he is in the constant habit of seeing them. I do not hesitate to shoot a hare on her seat, if I happen to observe her, and am in want of a hare, in order to prevent the dogs chasing, which will not fail to make them unsteady for an hour or two afterwards, particularly if she happens to be lamed. In shooting at a running hare, the fowling-piece should be levelled forward, as a hare will carry away a great quantity of shot, if struck about the buttocks:—a trifle kills them if hit in the head, or just behind the fore-leg.

The great secret of shooting feathered game is the attainment of philosophical calmness: a hare even, whose progressive motion is attended with little or no noise, yet starts so suddenly as to disconcert the inexperienced; but the rising of a pheasant, particularly out of a bush, will not fail to startle any stranger to the diversion: Fabricius of old, who testified no symptom of astonishment at the sudden appearance of an elephant, would not have been proof against surprise had a pheasant risen before him.

In aiming, I have met with one or two gentlemen who do not shut one eye, and have, nevertheless, been very fair shots. Savages, in some parts of the world, are very expert with the bow and arrow at moving objects—the emperor Commodus excelled in this respect, and with arrows headed with broad sharp barbs, was able to cut off the head of an ostrich at full speed; yet, neither the native savages, nor the more savage Roman, shut one eye, or even looked down the arrow, but directed their attention to the object. There is a strong sympathy between the action of the hand and the organs of vision, and I have no doubt, that by practice the union just mentioned will become so perfect, as to produce the effect of almost unerring certainty. In this way I account for good shots, who regard the object with both eyes, without looking down the fowling piece. Nevertheless, I always shut one eye in aiming, and have not the least hesitation in recommending the practice. But I have met with others, who shut *both* eyes when they pull the trigger; and others again, who jerk back their heads at this moment—such are not likely to become dead shots !

It may not be amiss to observe, that a sort of unconscious or involuntary motion or movement of the arms and body accompanies the level, which should not be checked till after the piece' is discharged—if stopped at the moment of pulling the trigger, the bird, most likely, will fly away. Also, for a very long shot, the level should be higher than usual, as the shot will not fly' any very great distance before it begins to curve downwards. In levelling, the fowling piece should be held firmly to the shoulder, the left hand placed either close to the trigger guard, or a few inches in advance : the former is perhaps safer, in case the barrel burst; but I, nevertheless, prefer the latter, in order to prevent the gun becoming point heavy. I always ram *well home*—the powder, in a patent breech, if not more than a proper quantity is used, will always lie loose (and thus ignites much better) as the wadding cannot be forced farther than the top of the breech (and the closer the wadding fits the better) ; the shot should certainly be well rammed. The fowling piece, too, will require wiping out once or twice in a hard day's shooting ; also on going out in the morning, it should be aired by firing a little powder : if percussion priming is used, it will be necessary to place wadding over the powder in the barrel, or it will be apt to be driven out unexploded, such is the force of percussion priming, that it drives the atmospheric air with such violence before it, as to expel the powder before the fire reaches it.

Flints should be changed frequently, to prevent missing fire —this is avoided with the percussion priming.

It sometimes happens, that a sportsman may cock the gun, and, not firing, have occasion to let down the cock—in doing which, he should let the cock pass, and, bringing it back to the half-cock, make it *tell* well into the tumbler. A gun (particularly a double) is a dangerous instrument, and should be used with the utmost caution.

For partridges, a brace of good dogs is quite sufficient at once; but they should be used to hunt together, and perfectly acquainted with each other; otherwise they will be jealous and commit many mistakes. To beat a country in a sportsman-like manner, a person should not go straight through it: but form circles, as it were, traversing well the ground, and taking care to give the dog the wind as much as possible; at the same time the sportsman should not be afraid of beating the ground over twice, where there is any reason to believe there is game. He who patiently beats and ranges his ground over and over again, will generally kill the largest quantity of game; and will be sure to find it where it has been left by others. A hare will frequently suffer a person to pass within a few yards of her, without stirring; and birds will often lie so close, as to suffer themselves almost to be trod upon before they will attempt to rise.

It will be proper to observe in this place, that the shooter should never strike either bush or hedge, or indeed any thing, with his fowling-piece. Should he use the butt-end for this purpose, it is possible the cock may be caught by some branch, and thus cause the piece to be fatally discharged; on the contrary, should a bush, &c. be struck with the muzzle-end, the sportsman will be very liable to lose his shot. It is a good method to examine occasionally, in shooting in general, whether by any means the shot has moved.

If the sportsman use a double gun, and has discharged one of the barrels, he should, after ramming the wadding on the powder in re-loading, put the ram-rod down the barrel that has not been discharged, which will be less trouble than placing it under his arm, or otherwise; he can then put in the shot; and on taking the ram-rod out of the other barrel, he can instantly ascertain whether the shot has moved. In discharging one barrel of a double gun, the shot in the other will frequently be loosened, if paper or any such pliable wadding be used; but with card I never knew this to happen, though I invariably examine with the ram-rod, in the method above described, in order to avoid every possible danger.

Horses, where they can be used in shooting, no doubt diminish the fatigue; and if birds fly straight forward, it is very easy to shoot while on the saddle; the same remark will apply if the birds rise or fly to the left: but the case is very different if they rise and make off on the right—the horse's head must then be instantly turned to that direction, or the game escapes. For this purpose, ponies are used, which have been so accustomed to the sport, as to be perfectly reconciled to the firing of a gun: However, on many of the grouse mountains, riding is altogether impracticable.

On an excursion to the Highlands, the sportsman should provide himself with a case, containing every thing necessary, not only to clean his fowling piece, but also to repair those parts which are liable to become broken or out of order, such as breaking of the cock, main-spring, &c. as gunsmiths, or indeed any person capable of doing these jobs, are seldom to be met with in the Highlands of Scotland. On grouse shooting excursions in general, similar preparations should be made.

As to the colour of the shooter's dress, green is supposed to be the best in the early part of the season, and when winter approaches, a kind of light brown, resembling stubble: this last colour will be found to answer throughout the season.

Grouse shooting is very laborious, and requires both judgment and experience, particularly in mountains the sportsman is a stranger to. As the season is frequently very hot, it becomes highly necessary to be clothed accordingly. The lighter the dress the better, taking care at the same time to let the garments next your skin chiefly consist of flannel. A flannel shirt and drawers are the best that can be used for this purpose, and ought, in fact, to be considered as indispensably necessary. Flannel, though so capable of administering warmth, is, notwithstanding, a bad conductor of heat; and, therefore, if the sportsman habituates himself to wear it, he will experience but little increase of heat in the summer on that account; at the same time it must be allowed, that nothing will so effectually absorb the moisture which arises from excesssive perspiration, and consequently there can be no better preventive against taking cold. Some persons have an aversion to wearing flannel next the skin, and to such I would recommend calico, on account of its possessing a quality of absorption superior to linen. In hot weather, to walk among the heath till violent perspiration ensues, and then to become stationary for a little time (which will undoubtedly sometimes be the case in grouse shooting) is almost a sure method of taking a violent cold, if a linen shirt is worn next the skin; to say nothing of the disagreeable sensation it excites, by sticking to one's back.—Short boots, that lace close, but which are easy to the legs and feet, are to be recommended: for shoes, when you walk on the mountains, gather the tops of the heath, which will be very apt to rub the skin off your feet. It will be adviseable also to rub some tallow on your heels, the bottoms of your feet, and the joints of your toes, before you go out in the morning, which will not only cause you to walk easy, but prevent that soreness otherwise consequent to a hard day's grouse shooting.—It need scarcely be mentioned that the liquor flask is a very necessary appendage; to the bottom of which should be attached a tin cup, which will enable the sportsman to allay his thirst by mixing water with his brandy or rum: rinsing the mouth will perhaps be found occasionally to answer the desired purpose. But on no account drink cold water alone; the fatal consequences of which, when a person is in a violent per-spiration, are well known.

In bad weather, the birds will generally be found about midway on the hills; and in case of very bad weather, the butts of the mountains are the places they resort to : but in fine weather they will be found near the tops.

Grouse go to water immediately after their morning flight, which is the proper time to begin the day's diversion : from that time till the extreme heat of the day comes on, good sport may be obtained; as also from half past three till sun-set. Should the sportsman, however, be inclined to continue in the dead time of the day (which is from about eleven till three) let him be careful to hunt all the deep cracks he meets with, as grouse frequently creep in these to shelter themselves from the excessive heat of the sun; at this time also, they may frequently be found in mossy places.

In this diversion, be careful to give your dogs the wind, and also to try the sides of the mountains which are most sheltered: if it blows hard you will be certain to find the birds where the heath is longest; and when this unfortunately happens to be the case, they generally take long flights, and these too, are for the most part *down* the wind, which is the very reverse of what most other fowls are known to do.

On finding a pack of grouse, the old cock is generally the first that makes his appearance, and the first to take wing : if he has not been much disturbed, he will run out before the dogs, making a *chucking* noise, and will frequently get up and *challenge*, without seeming to testify any symptoms of fear for himself; but by this he warns the hen and the poults, which immediately begin to run and separate. The hen generally runs as far as she can from you, in order to draw your attention off the poults; and if the poults are strong enough to shift for themselves, she will some-times make off altogether, in which case good diversion will gene-

rally follow. The main object, however, should be to kill the old
cock, which will most likely enable you to pick up the young
ones, one after another, as in the beginning of the season they
lie very close, particularly after hearing the report of a gun, which
terrifies them to such a degree, that you may sometimes take
them up with your hand from under the dog's nose. When this
happens, the ground cannot be beaten too carefully. If the
night should have been wet previous to the day of shooting,
grouse will not *lie*.

Of all shooting, none is so laborious, either for man or dog*
as that of *grouse ;* the sportsman ought, therefore, to be provided with plenty of dogs, in order to rest them alternately ; and
one brace, or a brace and a half, of good ones at a time will be
sufficient.

* " The most essential point about the dog is a good foot; for, without
a good, firm foot, he can never hunt long. I never look at a dog which
has a thin, flat, wide, and spread foot ; they are not worth two-pence.

" It has been a constant custom with me to wash my pointers' feet
with strong salt and water after the day's sport. I have found my error,
and am convinced that it is a wrong practice. I never altered my method
until three years ago. A gamekeeper in Suffolk, seeing that a boy was
washing my dogs' feet with strong salt and water, (his name was Cooper)
said to me : ' Sir, I think you do wrong to wash your dogs' feet in salt
and water at this early part of the shooting season, (it was the first week
in September) at this time, Sir, when the ground is uncommonly dry,
and as hard as a rock. If you will feel their feet, you will find there is
a considerable degree of feverish heat in the dogs' feet, from having
hunted all the day on hard and dry ground. A dog, Sir, in such weather,
should have his feet suppled and comforted. As long as the ground is
dry and hard, I always wash my dog's feet with warm soap and water,
and clean them well, particularly between the toes, and balls of the feet ;
this comforts his feet, allays the heat, and promotes the circulation in
the feet. In the more advanced period of the season, when the ground
is very wet, then salt and water may be proper.' I approved much of
the reasons he gave ; it shewed the sense of his practice, and the folly of
mine : since that period I have taken his advice."—*General Hanger.*

To insure an abundance of grouse, care should be taken, prior to the pairing season, to destroy a number of the male birds, as, at the close of the shooting season, a preponderance of cocks will be uniformly found. It is well known to sportsmen that the cock bird is always the first to take wing; he cautiously avoids the approach of the shooter, and hence the reason why so many male birds are always left. If, therefore, at the commencement of the breeding season, more cocks are left than can find mates, furious battles ensue, much confusion is produced, and the nestling and incubation suffer in consequence. To this cause may perhaps be attributed the scarcity of grouse last year in particular spots; for as to the epidemic, so much spoken of, it amounted to very little indeed, as I met with neither shepherd, watcher, nor keeper, who had met with half a dozen diseased birds. Nothing of the kind had at all been seen on those mountains, which formed the scene of my diversion; on the contrary, birds were abundant, very finely grown, as well as very strong on the wing. On the moors in Durham, however, as well as on some in Yorkshire and Westmoreland, I last year noticed a greater number of hawks than were consistent with the well-being of the game.

It is a prevalent opinion that a very dry breeding season is detrimental to grouse; this I conceive to be a notion hastily adopted, and which will not bear the scrutiny of investigation. And, whilst this opinion is so inconsiderately taken up, it is as strenuously maintained that the season cannot be too dry for partridges. Now I should be glad to know the reason, why a wet season should be conducive to the health of young grouse, and yet detrimental to young partridges? They are not exactly the same birds, it is true; but they are, in some measure, allied to each other, while there is a striking similitude in their habits. In a dry breeding season, partridges are sure to be abundant; for a very good reason, their eggs are not chilled by the wet, nor

s 3

do the young birds suffer, for the same reason; and it will take
something more, in the shape of argument, than an inconsiderate
assertion, or the dictum of ignorance, to convince reasonableness
that the case is not precisely the same with grouse. The mountains distinguished bv the name of Westhope-fells, Westmorland, are remarkably wet, and for this reason, (according to the
prevalent notion,) as the season (1820) had been uncommonly dry,
they should have produced an abundance of game, or, at least,
much more than other mountains, which were equally remarkable
for being dry. This was not the case; for, on the 13th of August,
when we ranged Bollyhope-fells, which are very dry, I found the
grouse much more abundant, in the proportion of four to one.

As grouse, however, are found only in particular parts of the
country, the pursuit of these fine birds is by no means so general
as partridge shooting. Grouse are out of the reach of Cockney
sportsmen : though many tradesmen resident in large towns, con-
trive to enjoy, now and then, the pursuit of the partridge, they
seldom venture upon a grouse shooting excursion, on account
of the distance, perhaps, as well as the expense necessarily attendant upon it. The highlands of Scotland abound in grouse;
they are also found on the Welsh mountains, and in Ireland;
in the north of England, in Lancashire, Derbyshire, Staffordshire, and other contiguous places, especially among the moors
and mountains of Yorkshire, where these birds are found in sufficient numbers to afford excellent diversion. For several weeks
prior to the 12th of August, dog-carts may he frequently seen
on the road to the north, laden with that sagacious animal which
so essentially contributes to the success of the chase; and, as the
time approaches, equipages on a smaller scale may be observed
in great numbers, all directing their course to the scene of action.
About the 10th or 11th, the roads become crowded with sportsmen and their attendants, who travel principally in gigs, in the
bottom of which is generally seen a convenient receptacle for

several pointers. The more humble pursuers of the chase seize the opportunity offered to them by numerous extra stage coaches of reaching their destination in time ; and thus by the eve of the 12th, every one is at his post, palpitating with the eager expectation of to-morrow's sport, and uttering the most fervent ejaculations for fine weather.

Grouse when sent to a distance should be packed air tight, and not drawn.

I am not aware that I can give those who have never visited the moors a better idea of a grouse shooting excursion, than by sketching one of my own visits to the moors :—Myself and my companion reached Bowes, a small town in Yorkshire, on the confines of Durham, about three o'clock in the afternoon of the 12th (this day falling on a Sunday, in 1821, and the shooting not commencing till Monday) and having mounted ponies, provided for the purpose, we left the high road, and, with but a slight knowledge of the country, set out in search of a small village, called *Chapel in Weardale,* in Westmorland. In order to reach the *point d'appui* as soon as possible, by the advice of a rustic, whom we met, we attempted to cross a considerable extent of moorland : for this purpose, we followed a path pointed out to us, and traced it for a considerable distance, till at length, it dwindled into a sort of sheep-walk, and shortly afterwards vanished altogether. Still we kept onward in the direction that had been pointed out, till, the lowering appearance of the horizon threatening unfavourable weather, scarcely sufficient light remaining to enable us to avoid the bogs which frequently obstructed our progress. It was but an indifferent bridle road at best ; and as we became enveloped in the dusk of the evening, we found ourselves in the midst of boundless moorlands, dotted here and there with lead mines, which we could but just discover by the aid of the murky twilight ; not a human being was to be seen on this dreary waste. After wandering about for some time in a state of uncertainty, we discerned through the gloom, at a short distance, two uncouth figures, which appeared to be stalking towards us. They approached, and, like guardian genii, accompanied us to a road (a rough one certainly) by which we ultimately reached our place of destination, at a quarter past eleven o'clock, after a most uncertain and irksome journey. Having made arrangements for the following day, we retired to rest at twelve, and had not been in bed more than an hour before the trampling of horses and the whistling of dogs, &c. sufficiently indicated the anxiety of brother sportsmen to be on the mountains at the peep of morn, to see the first rising and flight of a grouse. The mountains in this neighbourhood, which principally belong to the Bishop of Durham, rise, for the most part, very abruptly, and to great heights ; they are, nevertheless, much inclined to bog; and walking over them is attended with no ordinary fatigue. We rose a little before two o'clock, and after making a hasty, but not a very hearty, breakfast, we mounted our ponies, and, accompanied by our guides, directed our steps up a long, winding, steep ascent, which led to the wished-for spot. The weather was hazy, and the gray of the morn enabled us to see the dense fog, which hung, like rolling smoke, in volumes, round the tops of the mountains. No one but a true sportsman can picture to the mind that eager, that impatient anxiety which is felt at a moment like this ; particularly, as from report, we had reason to believe that abundance of game lay before us. But this anxious feeling is not confined to the sportsman :—his dog partakes it in a greater degree, if possible, than himself. The motion of his tail, his crouching curves, his impatient whine, the blandishment of his expressive eye, all confess the delightful anticipations which animate his eager hopes.

Grouse shooting may be placed at the head of the list of what the French would significantly enough call *la chasse au fusil*. In fine weather nothing can equal grouse-shooting : in wet weather

it is attended with much vexation, as the game will not suffer
the approach of either dog or sportsman ; the reason of which
is, that the heath being laden with wet the birds will not run,
but remain stationary, and take wing on the most distant alarm :*
when birds will run they may be approached, otherwise they are
extremely shy.

Our diversion in the early part of the morning did not equal
our expectations, for numerous parties were scattered over the
mountains, and the ground on which we commenced operations
had been already ranged. Several ardent sportsmen had ascended the hills at midnight, ranging the summits of the mountains in order to drive the birds into the valleys, and thus be enabled, the moment the dawn of day admitted sufficient gray light,
to commence their amusement at a distance from the fog, which
almost uniformly caps the summits of lofty hills at this time.
However, it was not broad day-light by any means, when a
solitary fine old cock cheered our spirits by his chattering, and
fell to rise no more. In every direction the heath was enlivened
by the ranging of dogs, an occasional whistle, and the almost
continual firing of guns.

We had been led to believe that the breeding season having
been tolerably fine, grouse would be found in abundance ; and
this was strictly true ; but we felt the full effect of coming late
upon the ground, and for several hours met with nothing but
odd birds. I never recollect traversing grouse mountains where
the walking was more unpleasant, more irksome, or more fatiguing. The birds were strong on the wing and wild, which
consequently rendered the pursuit much more laborious ; in
fact, the fatigue was excessive, and at eleven o'clock, we sat down
to dine beneath enormous masses of awfully projecting rock ;

---

* Contrary, however, to general rule, grouse will sometimes lie well
when the heath is wet.

and with our heads reclined against one of these *solid*, not *downy*, pillows, we enjoyed a véry comfortable nap.   And here young sportsmen should be cautioned against lying at full length, or sleeping on the ground, unless it be uncommonly dry, as well as against drinking cold water when heated to excess; it being better to alleviate thirst with a little diluted spirit, or if the flask should be prematurely exhausted, by washing or rinsing the mouth at the first spring or rivulet.   The most fatal consequences have often resulted from a disregard of these precautions. Like giants refreshed, we sprung from our slumbers, and pursued our sport till we could no longer distinguish the flight of a bird; better success than we expected to meet stimulated exertion and left us no time to think of fatigue.   As the evening closed in, however, we sought our ponies in the valley below, and'although they were not more than several hundred yards off, we could scarcely reach the spot from excessive fatigue.   Arrived at our homely inn, we made a hearty supper, took a cheerful glass, talked over the day's sport, and threw ourselves into the arms of Mr. Morpheus, who strewed his poppies over us without much solicitation.   On demanding our account in the morning from " mine host," we found that his name should have been " *Woodcock, by the length of his bill*," his charges very much resembling those of *Peacock*, at the London Tavern, although the accommodations were of a very different description.

The Bishop of Durham has a great extent of moor-land in this part of the country, and is very liberal in giving permission to sportsmen to range his mountains; but, at the same time, his hilly domain is overrun by the most audacious and determined set of poachers to be found in any part of the kingdom; who, when pursued, seek protection in the bowels of the very mountains on which they have committed their depredations.   The miners are, almost to a man, poachers; and so desperate are they, that the bishop's gamekeeper confessed to me that he was compelled to wink at much of their depredation. The mode adopted by the lead-miners of procuring grouse is with the dog and fowling-piece ; the *net*, so effective in the destruction of the partridge, being, with respect to these birds, quite out of the question. The poachers frequently sally forth in such bodies as to bid defiance to the united strength of the *watchers* in any particular district ; and appear to pursue the diversion, not for the sake of profit alone, but with all the eagerness and zest of true sportsmen. Moreover, they generally commence *their* season a week prior to the 12th of August, and send horse loads of grouse to different large towns, to watering places, and particularly to Harrowgate ; at which last place, the grouse are frequently sold for as much as ten shillings a brace. On the 12th of August, and for several days following, the miners abandon poaching and act as guides to the sportsmen ; one of them served me in this capacity, and from him I learned the particulars just mentioned ; he was recommended for the purpose by the bishop's gamekeeper, and proved himself an excellent attendant.

The Earl of Darlington's moors are contiguous to the Bishop of Durham's. The earl is much more strict than the bishop in preserving game ; but in spite of all his exertions, the miners frequently sally forth and commit extensive depredations with impunity. I am of opinion, that men of great landed property adopt in general very erroneous modes for the purpose of preserving their game ; nor have I the least doubt that I could point out and carry into practice a much more *effective* as well as a much more *pleasant* method, of rendering nugatory the efforts of poachers, and at a much less expense than is generally incurred ; though I am free at the same time to confess, that my plan would apply to enclosures, rather than grouse mountains ; and that I should certainly feel no great inclination to be brought in contact with the miners in the neighbourhood of Chapel-in-Weardale.

Spittle, near Bowes, in Yorkshire, may be regarded as a sort of general rendezvous for those sportsmen who either do not choose to ask, or are unable to obtain, permission to range more particular domains. At this place, there is a great extent of moor, which is claimed by a number of proprietors, who possess no paramount right, and therefore are unable to prevent a general unsolicited range, which uniformly takes place. At the same time the mountains are much better travelling than they will be found in many other places, and being surrounded by excellent preserves scarcely ever fail to abound in game. Spittle is also a general resort for dog dealers and *dog stealers ;* and the sportsman who visits this neighbourhood unprovided with this very essential assistant in the chase, may be accommodated exactly according to his means, or the price he is willing to give. But, though this may be a general practice, it is one " more honoured in the breach than the observance ';" and that sportsman who depends upon such suspicious means, will hardly fail to experience disappointment.

Ten brace of grouse may be bagged on the 12th of August, on the Bowes moors, on which, at this period, a general flashing is kept up from one extremity to the other. At some distance further Lord Stanley occupies some excellent moors, at a place called Mucar (I am not certain as to the spelling of the name) and in the early part of the season generally averages twenty brace per day. His Lordship, however is much annoyed by poachers ; and, as a curious instance of this sort occured three years ago, I will take the liberty of relating it :—his Lordship's watchers had frequently observed a stranger, accompanied by one dog only, who, in defiance of all authority, took the diversion of grouse shooting on his Lordship's preserve. The watchers had repeatedly approached this unasked and unwelcome visitor ; but when they came within a hundred yards of him, he uniformly altered his position, or moved on, and moved so quickly too, that he appeared with ease to distance his pursuers; he would also frequently stop, and have the audacity to kill game in their sight; and then darted forward again with the swiftness of the roe. After many attempts had proved ineffectual, the matter was reported to his Lordship, who desired that he might be informed of the next time the trespasser made his appearance. A very short period elapsed before it was reported to his Lordship that the *man in the dark-green jacket* (the colour he always wore) had again offered himself to observation. Lord Stanley was soon brought in sight of the depredator, and at the moment when he had approached within about two hundred yards of the poacher (whose dog at the moment was pointing), he saw him deliberately bring down a bird. This was too much to be borne; his Lordship darted towards the spot: the man in the dark green jacket, however, *pocketted his bird,* and, in a few seconds, fairly distanced his pursuer, and had no sooner gained a sufficient distance, than he again commenced ranging for game. His Lordship being a good foot-man, determined to make up in a persevering chase what he had lost at starting, and therefore continued the pursuit. Again he approached the poacher, but only to witness the *fall of another bird;* and in this manner the contest lasted for more than an hour and a half, when Lord Stanley acknowledged the superior dexterity of the *man in the, dark-green jacket,* by abandoning all further efforts to come to close quarters with him.

During the whole of the season grouse are regularly conveyed by the stage coaches to all the large towns, and particularly to Manchester and Liverpool. For this purpose there are certain days appointed, when quantities of these birds are brought to particular houses by the road side, at which the coachmen and guards call; and this unlawful traffic is continued with as much regularity, if not with as much publicity, as the authorized dealings in any other species of marketable commodity. Abundance

T

of game is thus conveyed from Yorkshire and the northern parts
of England to places situated at a distance, or more to the
southward; and when the weather becomes cold, and the game
will keep, immense quantities are brought from Scotland. The
quantity of grouse killed in England will not bear a comparison
with the numbers annually destroyed in Scotland, where this
game *literally abounds*. Last year (1820) Sir Thomas Graham
(now Lord Lynedoch) bagged seventy brace per day, for the
four first days of the season.

I shall conclude this sketch with some observations as to the
dog best calculated for the pursuit of grouse. Various opinions
exist on this subject; some preferring the setter, and others the
pointer. Although excellent dogs of both kinds are to be met
with, there are some leading characteristics which eminently
distinguish the long and the short haired dog. The setter is a
hardy, impetuous, unruly animal; which, if taken into the field
while very young, will frequently set intuitively; but no sooner
does he acquire strength, than he shows a turbulent spirit, and
can only be kept sufficiently obedient by constant exercise. On
account of their long coat, setters are more affected by heat,
and consequently sooner become thirsty than their sleek thin-
coated rival; and, in very dry weather, suffer very much from
want of water on the grouse mountains. The well bred pointer,
on the contrary, is a docile creature, very easily reduced to obedience, and, when once well trained, requires neither very hard
work, nor severe correction, to keep him submissive and tractable. The pointer, however, is more liable to become foot-sore,
either from the wiry lacerations of the heath, or from running
upon hard or stony ground; consequently, in a sharp frost, he
is unable to hunt: the olfactory organs of the pointer are unquestionably superior to, and more acute than, those of the setter; which will generally be found pre-eminently conspicuous
in a harsh dry wind, blowing from north or easterly directions,

at which time the scent will be found very difficult of recognition.*

* *The following appeared in the Annals of Sporting, vol.* II. *page* 298, *addressed to the Editor* :—

SIR,—" You must know I am but a young sportsman at present; a mere novice in the science of shooting ; till the present season I never saw a grouse on the wing : but, being ardently attached to the sport, I determined on visiting the moors of Yorkshire, though my residence was at the distance of almost two hundred miles. For a month before the 12th of August I could scarcely think of any thing but the moors, of which, however, I had formed a very erroneous idea. I thought they must bear some resemblance to Charnwood Forest, in Leicestershire, and was never more surprised than when, on reaching Yorkshire, I beheld the very different aspect presented by the abrupt and mountainous moorlands to the plains and gentle ascents of the forest just mentioned. If I saw no "cloud-capt towers," I beheld very plainly cloud-capt hills : for the first time in my life I saw the summits of the mountains enveloped by the clouds, beneath which the dark and sombre hue of the lower parts of these heathy hills conveyed, at the distance of a mile, a very fallacious idea of their real form and appearance.

" Your correspondent T. in a late number, speaks much of the anxiety felt by sportsmen on the approach of the 12th of August, which, I assure you, was experienced by me in its fullest force. Like him, I rose at midnight, between the 11th and 12th, and ascended the mountains before I could discern the flight of a bird : up to this moment I had never seen a grouse on the wing, (as I have above observed,) and I now heard them chatter for the first time in my life. It was the grey of the morn : and I could hear these birds in various directions, and observed several variations in their cry or call, one of which was an excellent imitation of the words "*come back ! come back ! come back !*" These matters may appear trifling to an old grouse-shooter, but they were quite new to me, and forced themselves on my attention ; my situation was altogether novel, nor do I think any thing can be more interesting to a young sportsman who visits the moors for the first time, than to listen to the calling of the grouse a little before day-light.

" Almost up to the knees in ling or heath, I commenced my operations. My dogs, though excellent, were strangers to grouse-shooting as

The best time for partridge shooting is from two hours after sun-rise until eleven o'clock ; and from half-past three o'clock

well as myself, nor did they at first seem to relish the diversion ; they run in to the first pack or brood, and raised it out of distance ; six dark-coloured birds rose, and, skimming over the top of the heath, were quickly out of my sight ; indeed, in colour they appeared so nearly to approximate the ling over which they flew that they proved a puzzling mark for me when they were completely within gun-shot. More birds were raised in a similar manner ; and I soon discovered that grouse must be approached with much more caution than partridges ; I also found that they rose in a different manner, and that the sport was not at all similar to that of the midland counties.

" I was extremely anxious (as you may suppose, Mr. Editor) to kill a bird : I fired six shots, and had the mortification to see the birds uniformly fly away ; indeed, when I pulled the trigger I was always in doubt, for I could not discern the object half so clearly as if a partridge had been before me. I met, at length, with several grouse not half grown, and was fortunate enough to break the wing of one of these *squeakers !* I seized the prize with eagerness, but it was very young, very small, unsatisfactory in every point of view, and only served to increase my vexation. I began to lament that I had visited the moors ; that I had made so long a journey to seek a diversion which now appeared to me so inferior to what might be obtained at home ; and, to add to my chagrin, while making these irksome reflections, I happened to get *ingulphed in a bog* nearly up to my middle ! I could not help venting my grief aloud : I cursed my own folly for having taken a journey of *two hundred miles,* which I now conceived could not fail to end in the bitterest disappointment. With the assistance of my attendant and guide, I got tolerably well cleared from the wet and filth which adhered to my clothes when I emerged from the bog, and I hesitated for some minutes whether or not to quit the mountains, and immediately return home : the idea that my friends would have the *laugh against me* alone determined me to continue for some time longer upon these dreary and uncultivated wilds.

" An hour or two elapsed, during which I fired repeatedly, but was not fortunate enough to bring down a bird. Arrived at a spring of fine clear water. I sat down in despair, determined, after taking a little refreshment, to leave the moors and return home. I had been walking until it is dark. When the weather is very dry, especially at the beginning of the season, as soon as the sun becomes very powerful, the scent is dissipated, and the dog's abilities are put to the test to no purpose. In the middle of the day, partridges cease to feed or run, and place themselves by the side of some sunny bank in order to bask.

In general they have their separate feeding and sleeping places; but it frequently happens, that they remain all day or

over broken and boggy ground for some hours, sometimes nearly up to my knees in ling, sometimes up to the ancles in dirt and water, bad crossed a number of deep and yawning ravines, been once nearly smothered in a bog, had ascended a number of steep hills, and was, in fact, become completely fatigued, as well as severely mortified by a succession of unlooked-for disappointments. However, I had scarcely seated myself, when the *chattering of a grouse* attracted my attention; I observed the bird approach; I rose—it was crossing me at the distance of thirty or forty yards—I fired—it fell! I ran to the spot with all the eagerness of ardent expectation. I seized the prize with rapture—viewed it with delight. I instantly felt a full flow of spirits—my fatigue had vanished, and I determined on continuing my range, regardless of the fine clear spring, and my late intended refreshment.

" The bird I killed was a fine old cock; and, in the coure of something less than an hour, I succeeded in killing three other young, but fine birds. My spirits were now raised to the highest pitch of exultation, and I felt confident that before night I should bag at least *ten brace.* I did not, however, realize these sanguine expectations; but, with more than half the number, I quitted the mountains, at seven o'clock, delighted, after all, with my day's diversion.

" On the *second day* I commenced my operations with renewed vigour, and was more fortunate than on the first. I had become, in some degree, accustomed to the rising and flight of the game—I could distinguish it better; I became, also, in some measure, familiar with the mode of traversing the mountains; and, after spending a few more days in this way, I returned home with this conviction, that *grouse-shooting* is very laborious, but that it affords, at the same time, *the finest diversion in the world !* "

all night where they fed the preceding evening or morning ; yet it much oftener happens that they change their ground. At day-break, they *call*, and, when collected, generally take their flight to the stubbles, which, if high and thick enough to afford them shelter, will most likely induce them to remain there till disturbed: however, in dry weather in particular, they are frequently to be found at this time among potatoes. After feeding in the evening they again *call*, and fly to the place where they intend to remain for the night. When they are *calling*, they seldom *lie* well, or, in other words, will not permit the sportsman to approach within gun-shot.

My pointers *stand*,
How beautiful they look! with outstretched tails,
With heads immoveable, and eyes fast fixed,
On fore leg raised and bent—the other firm,
Advancing forward presses on the ground.

FOWLING, *a Poem*.

Although I have been a sportsman for more than twenty years, I still retain much of that anxious feeling of anticipation in which young shooters indulge themselves on the eve of the first of September, and which arrives at its greatest height when the gray dawn of the next day appears, but which is seldom completely realized by the events which succeed. Young and indifferent shooters, on this occasion, calculate on performing wonders; and in order to qualify themselves for the sport, they generally, for several preceding weeks, practise at swallows,— " a custom more honoured in the breach than the observance ;" for a person may become a most expert swallow shooter, (as I have before observed, and here repeat, as it is a circumstance, which cannot be too deeply impressed on the mind of the tyro) and yet not bring down a partridge once in a dozen shots : and nothing can be more ill advised, or even cruel, than the worse than useless slaughter of these birds, which daily destroy millions of noxious insects. The flight of swallows is quick and capricious, and yet their destruction is easily attainable by the fowling piece. The sportsman takes his station with calmness and even *non-chalance;* and selecting his object from the number that are fluttering about him, deliberately waits for the precise moment, when his victim may be destroyed with almost unerring certainty. With *game* the affair is quite different; the object is larger, much larger, but the exact spot whence it will spring is not ascertainable, while the sudden rush and noisy confusion accompanying the rise, so astonish the tyro, or the bungler, that the fowling piece is discharged not only too soon, but generally at random. Hence it will easily be perceived that little or no analogy can exist between swallow shooting and partridge shooting. The secret of shooting may be easily explained, as it is comprised merely in *coolness* and *deliberation;* these, however, are not so easily attained as the superficial observer might be led to suppose. A friend of mine, who has followed this diversion for forty years, still continues a very indifferent shot: the rise of a covey never fails to dissipate his previous mental resolves, and he has, nineteen times out of twenty, the mortification of seeing the game go away untouched; but it must be observed, that, to say nothing of his firing too soon, he has contracted a habit, which must for ever preclude any thing like certainty in shooting :—no sooner does his finger touch the trigger, than he shuts *both* his eyes! And yet, though conscious of this preposterous defect, and aware that if a bird fall from his gun, it is merely the effect of accident, should he be shooting in company, and happen to fire at the same time as his companion, he will not fail to claim the merit of having *killed the bird:* indeed, to judge from his conversation over the bottle, a stranger would suppose, that, as a shot, he was equal to Sir John Shelley. I have seldom met with a bad shot who was not extremely anxious to be thought otherwise; and who would not, in his cups, relate, with much self-satisfaction and infinite glee, a hundred shooting exploits, which never had existence but in his own prolific brain.

The moment the light of the morning will enable the young shooter to discern the flight of a partridge, he is impatient to rush to the scene of action, and is all uneasy eagerness, while his more experienced companion *finishes his breakfast.* The resort of a covey or two is previously known ; the sportsmen, therefore, direct their steps to an appointed spot, where the dogs come quickly to a point. The shooters advance—the tyro with trepid eagerness and a palpitating heart ;—his veteran companion with philosophic coolness. They arrive at the desired spot, abreast of the foremost dog ; and, for a few seconds, in almost breathless anxiety, nearly choked with expectation, the tyro expects the game to spring :—the covey rises, with screams and confusion, and, at the same instant, the tyro's gun is ineffectually discharged—while his companion, deliberately selecting his object, with one eye shut, and the other steadily directed down the barrel, the bird no sooner appears at the end, than the trigger is drawn, and the partridge falls. This scene is well described by the author of " FOWLING" :—

> Full of th' expected sport my heart beats high,
> And with impatient step I haste to reach
> The stubbles, where the scattered ears afford
> A sweet repast to the yet heedless game.
> How my brave dogs o'er the broad furrows bound,
> Quart'ring their ground exactly. Ah ! that point
> Answers my eager hopes, and fills my breast
> With joy unspeakable. How close they lie !
> Whilst to the spot with steady pace I tend,
> Now from the ground with noisy wing they burst,
> And dart away. My victim singled out,
> In his aerial course falls short, nor skims
> Th' adjoining hedge o'er which the rest unhurt
> Have passed.

PHEASANT SHOOTING WITH SPRINGERS.

I have occasionally met with tolerable shots who have asserted that they do not shut one eye when drawing the trigger, but uniformly direct both eyes to the object; others, again, will be found who declare that they look directly at the bird, regardless of running their eye down the gun-barrel. With a sportsman of this latter description, I happened to be shooting for several days in the month of August : he shot well, and asserted that he merely kept his eye on the bird, without directing a Cyclop-peep down the barrel of the fowling-piece. Of the correctness of this assertion I could not avoid expressing my doubts, as he shot much better than I conceived it possible for any one to do who followed the random mode just mentioned. I, therefore, determined to ascertain the point from personal observation ; and with this view watched his motions for several successive shots : he was a cool deliberate shooter ; but I had the satisfaction of observing that he had no sooner selected his object, than he bent his cheek to the stock, and maintained that usual position till he had pulled the trigger. This I remarked to him ; and he ultimately confessed that such was the real state of the case, though he was unconscious of the circumstance till it was so clearly pointed out to him. I am of opinion that it is scarcely possible to become an expert or dead shot, without closing one eye, and taking a deliberate aim with the gun-barrel down the other.

Pheasant shooting is ver laborious, and requires the sportsman to be properly equipped for a cover ; and, in my opinion, strong woollen cloth gaiters are preferable to leather, as, in wet weather, the latter are very uncomfortable, and the former are a sufficient guard against the briars, &c.

If the night before you shoot be wet, the droppings of the trees will compel the pheasants to quit the woods ; and in this case the hedge-rows and furze covers should be tried very carefully, and good sport will most likely be obtained. This bird is much attached to almost all sorts of covers, especially to the sides of pits where alder trees are growing.

Of all dogs, none are so good for this sport as the setter. Pointers are frequently too tender to follow this bird through the brambles, which is not the case with a good setter; but care should be taken never to let them range out of gun-shot. The small springing spaniel is frequently used in pheasant shooting, and may answer tolerably well in the beginning of the season, or where the birds have not been much disturbed; but are by no no means equal to the setter. The springer is too noisy for this diversion.

In hedge-rows, pheasants lie remarkably well; and in this case a pointer or a setter will of course make a very steady point, and you must perhaps shake the bush before the bird will rise; but it is different in covers, where these birds frequently run a considerable distance, and it becomes necessary to encourage your dog; though one a little used to this sport will need no encouragement.

Naturalists observe, "Of all game birds, pheasants are shot most easily, as they always make a whirring noise when they rise, by which they alarm the gunner, and, being a large mark, and flying very slow, there is scarcely any missing them." The sportsman cannot but smile at this last sentence. A pheasant is shot easily enough by an old and an experienced sportsman; but I much doubt whether the tyro stands not a better chance of success when a *twiddling* snipe rises before him. That the pheasant is a "*large mark*" every one will readily allow; that its flight is by no means rapid is equally incontestible; but the tremendous bustle and whirring noise, which they make in rising, so agitates the inexperienced sportsman, that he not only fires too soon, but, generally without taking aim, and has to endure the mortification of seeing the bird fly away unhurt. A cock pheasant, when *pushed* from a bush or thicket, generally rises perpendicularly, till he has cleared every obstacle, before he goes off horizontally. The moment for shooting is when he assumes the horizontal direction. If a novice in the art fire at the bird while he is rising, he will, nineteen times out of twenty, throw the shot below the bird. With an experienced shot, the mode of rising is of little consequence.

> " Ah ! what avail his glossy, varying dies,
>   His purpled crest, and scarlet-circled eyes,
>   The vivid green his shining plumes infold,
>   His painted wings, and breast that flames with gold ?"

The hen pheasant, when pushed, seldom rises so high as the cock, or yet takes so long a flight. A cock pheasant will sometimes fly to a considerable distance ; and whenever this happens, as the act of flying is very laborious to this heavy bird, he is not able to rise again for some time. If the sportsman can mark down a pheasant, after one of these long flights, and hasten to the spot, he will find the bird to rise with great difficulty, and fly to a very short distance, or, perhaps, he will be unable to rise at all. Indeed, pheasants seem conscious of their incapacity to maintain a long flight, and, therefore, prefer running, wherever practicable, in preference to taking wing ; however, after a long flight they are difficult to find, as, on these occasions, they generally drop into a bush or thicket, and remain for a considerable time (if undisturbed) without moving.

Woodcocks arrive in Great Britain in flocks ; some of them in October, but not in great numbers till November and December, though they are sometimes seen as early as September. They generally take advantage of the night, being seldom seen to come before sun-set. The time of their arrival depends much upon the prevailing winds ; they are unable to struggle with the boisterous gales of the northern ocean, and therefore wait for the advantage of a favourable wind.

They feed on worms and insects, which they search for, with their long bills, in soft grounds, and moist woods, feeding and flying principally in the night. They go out in the evening, and generally return in the same direction, or through the same glades, to their day retreat.

An erroneous notion generally prevails that the woodcock lives by *suction;* which has probably arisen from the bird's being occasionally observed to thrust his long bill into the earth. As I am not aware that any naturalist has truly described the mode of feeding of the woodcock, I shall relate a few particulars from actual observation. Most writers observe, that, to obtain food, the woodcock thrusts his long bill into the ground, and thus coming in contact with small worms and insects, he is enabled, by means of his semi-serrated beak, to squeeze the dirt out of his mouth, and then swallow the food. It is possible, certainly, that the woodcock may, by *boring,* obtain small worms and insects, and, after cleansing them from the dirt, swallow them; but his general and regular mode of feeding is as follows :—having pierced the ground with his long bill, and shaken the surrounding earth, all the worms in the immediate vicinity make their way to the surface and are greedily swallowed. If a person force a stick or spade into the ground, and move it about, he will quickly perceive the worms within reach of the motion appear at the surface, manifesting great alarm and eagerness to escape from danger : instinct, therefore, no doubt, impels the woodcock thus to procure his food. In a severe frost, this bird is driven to shades and protected places, where the ground still remains sufficiently soft to admit of the operation of *boring.* The woodcock appears to crush the worm to a jelly as it passes up his bill; and, either from this circumstance, or from extraordinary powers of digestion, whatever the bird swallows seems to become almost instantaneously that exquisite table delicacy known by the name of *trail.* If a woodcock be *flushed* while feeding, in the very act of swallowing a worm, and be shot, at the distance of thirty yards from the spot whence he rose, the worm will be found changed into a jelly-like substance, the *trail* I have just mentioned. The woodcock is seen to feed early in the morning, and at dusk in the evening; but this must not be understood in a literal sense. This bird is on the wing at the very dawn of the morning, and feeds as soon afterwards as he can discover food; he will then generally continue in the place where he has fed, if sheltered, or seek the protection of some cover or hedge; and, if undisturbed, will remain in the same situation till late in the afternoon, when he feeds again, and afterwards takes a short flight or two to his resting place for the night.

The greater part of them leave this country about the latter end of February or the beginning of March.—They retire to the coast, and if the wind be favourable, set out immediately; but, if contrary, they are often detained for some time, and thus afford good diversion to those sportsmen who reside near the sea.

Woodcocks generally weigh from twelve to fourteen ounces, and are chiefly found in thick covers, particularly those with wet bottoms, and underneath holly bushes; they are not, however, fond of covers where there is long grass growing in the bottom, and at the roots of the trees.

The sight of the woodcock is very indifferent in the day time, but he sees better in the dusk of the evening and by moonlight; and it may also be remarked, that woodcocks will lie much better the day following a moonlight night, than when it has been preceded by a very dark one: the reason is obvious —the bird has been enabled by the light of the moon to make a plentiful repast, and the next day is lazy and unwilling to fly; whereas, when the darkness of the night has rendered it impossible for him to satisfy the calls of hunger, he is constantly uneasy, and on the alert in search of food, which he never attempts

U

to seek in the day time, but when necessity compels him.—— Shooting woodcocks is a very pleasant amusement in woods which are not too thick ; and, if they are cut through in several places, it renders it more easy to shoot this bird in his passage when he rises, and also to mark him with greater certainty ; and and woodcocks will generally be found near the openings or roads through the woods, if there are any. In this diversion a good marker is of essential service ; for with his assistance it will be difficult for a woodcock to escape ; as he will generally suffer himself to be shot at three or four times before he takes a long flight.

Springers are frequently used for this diversion—see the head *Springer* ; and give notice when the cock rises by barking : these animals, when well trained, may answer very well : and, in fact, they are better adapted for this than pheasant shooting.

The woodcock is a clumsy walker, and rises heavily from the ground, which I believe is the case with most birds that have long wings and short legs. This bird, as well as the snipe, it is said, rises from its bill.* When a woodcock is found in an

* It frequently happens that an opinion once generally received, however ridiculous its origin or absurd in itself, if it be not of a nature to excite inquiry, becomes a sort of *common law*, from the circumstance of its being handed from one generation to another with implicit credit, untainted by the most remote suspicion. Thus, in those parts of the country where I have resided, the idea that the snipe rose from its bill, or that in rising from the ground to fly, this bird pushed itself up by its long bill, so as to be able to use its wings, was the uniform and mistaken belief. Indeed, I should never have suspected this opinion but for an accidental circumstance, which occurred last winter, when in shooting at a snipe, I wounded it very slightly, merely fracturing the extreme end of one of its wings : the bird came to the ground, but made many efforts to rise again, and absolutely contrived to raise itself a yard or more repeatedly. By the time I had re-loaded my gun, the snipe had got to a considerable distance, principally, however, by

open field, in a hedge row, in the pass of a wood, or an unfrequented lane, he generally skims the ground slowly, and is
very easily shot; in fact, thus circumstanced, he is the easiest
of all shots; but it is occasionally otherwise, particularly when
he is flushed in a tall wood, where he is obliged to clear the
tops of trees before he can take a horizontal direction.

There are three different sizes of snipes, the largest of which,

running. As I approached, for the purpose of taking it up, its efforts
were again repeated, during which I distinctly observed that it did not
rise from its bill, but threw itself into the air in the same manner as a
crow or any other bird, by springing from its feet: but, in justice I
ought to remark, that the circumstance was first noticed by a much
younger sportsman than myself, with whom I happened to be in company, and but for him, in all probability, the bird would have been
pocketed, *sans ceremonie*, and the matter (trifling enough certainly)
still have remained enveloped in an ignorance equal to the mistaken
fancy which originally invented it. However, while I stood watching
the bird's attempts to escape, I noticed another peculiarity in it:—exhausted, as it soon became by its impotent efforts to fly, it then tried to
get away by running; and, when we approached very near, it repeatedly spread out its little tail like a fan, and erected it after the manner
of a turkey cock; at the same time, I was fully convinced, from the
length of its legs when it stood erect, that it was not at all necessary for
the snipe to put its bill to the ground in order to rise, had I not witnessed its repeated attempts to fly.

When seen on the ground, the snipe is a very pretty bird; and
though its bill, compared with its size, seems out of all proportion, yet,
from the manner in which it carries its head, it presents nothing of that
grotesque appearance which the enormous length of its bill would induce one to expect.

In the course of all my shooting excursions, I never recollect observing a snipe on the ground prior to its rising, though I have shot some
hundreds. I am inclined to think they are scarcely ever seen till on
the wing, and this circumstance, aided by the coincidence of an enormous length of bill, has, in all probability, given rise to the supposition
before mentioned.

however, is much smaller than the woodcock.—The common snipe weighs about four ounces, the jack snipe is not much larger than a lark, the great snipe weighs about nine ounces, but is seldom met with.

Snipes are to be found all the winter in wet and marshy grounds, particularly where there are rushes; they are frequently met with on mountains and moors among the heath; but a severe frost forces them to the springs and running streams. · Numbers of these birds remain with us all the year, and breed in our marshes, laying generally six eggs the latter end of May.

The snipe is generally regarded as a difficult shot; and it must be allowed that it requires practice to surmount this difficulty, which arises from the zig-zag manner in which the bird flies immediately after rising. The best method to pursue in this diversion is to walk down the wind, as snipes generally fly against it; and if a snipe rises before the sportsman, it will not fly far before it turns, and describes a sort of semi-circle, which will afford more time to take aim, by thus remaining longer within gun-shot. If, however, the bird should fly straight forward, it will be highly proper to let it get some little distance, as its flight will become much steadier. The slightest wound is sufficient to bring these birds to the ground.

An old pointer is the best in snipe shooting. To accustom a young dog to snipes, slacks his mettle, and renders him of little use for partridge or grouse, owing to getting a number of points with little exertion. However, when these birds are plentiful, a dog is unnecessary, as walking them up will answer equally well.

In closing this chapter on shooting, I will introduce some judicious remarks upon the subject generally, from Daniel's Rural Sports:—

"In the reign of Charles the First no person shot flying: what is now termed poaching was the gentleman's recreation;

and so late as within eighty years an individual who exercised the art of shooting birds on the wing was considered as performing something extraordinary, and many persons requested to attend his excursions, that they might be eye-witnesses of it. Since that period the practice has been more common, and is at present almost universal; so that lads of sixteen bring down their birds with all due accuracy. To prescribe any extensive rules for the attainment of this art may now be deemed superfluous, and therefore they will be reduced into a very narrow compass.

" In shooting, it is to be ever remembered, that the hand is to obey the eye, and not the eye be subservient to the hand. Both eyes should be open,* and the object fired at, the instant the muzzle of the gun is brought up, and fairly bears upon it; the sight becomes weakened by a protracted look along the barrel at a bird, and it is for this reason that birds which spring at the marksman's feet, and fly off horizontally, are frequently missed; his keeping the aim upon them so long fatigues the eye, and the finger does not obey the eye so readily as when employed at a first glance. It is not here meant that a bird is to be blown to atoms as soon as it tops the stubble, but that a marksman is first to make himself a thorough judge of distance: with that knowledge in open shooting, he will never put the gun to his shoulder until the bird has flown a proper length, and then fire the instant the sight of it is caught.

* This I regard as a mistaken notion.—I have already noticed the subject. However, let any person point a gun to a fixed object; by shutting one eye, and directing the other down the barrel, he will easily perceive that the level is true: by directing both eyes down the barrel, he will not only perceive a degree of confusion, as it were, but the aim will be with more difficulty, as well as more uncertainty, directed to the object. Nevertheless, I am willing to admit that there are those who shoot remarkably well, who keep both eyes open. Yet, a rifle man or sharp shooter always closes one eye; if therefore the latter mode is preferable with a ball, why not in shooting at game with shot?

". To kill birds flying cross either to the right or left, allowance must be made by the shooter both for the distance he is from them, the strength of the bird, and also the velocity of the object itself. The motion of a partridge, for instance, in November, will be greatly accelerated to what it was two months before. Practice alone can teach these minutiæ, which if fixed at any given space, or attempted to be uniformly regulated upon paper, might lead the marksman erroneously in the field.

" It may however be mentioned that in a cross shot to the right, the difficulty is very much increased if the right leg is first when the bird rises; the gun cannot then be brought but a very trifle beyond a straight line to the right, and frequently gentlemen stand with their feet thirty inches apart when in the act of firing, a position that effectually prevents their bringing their gun to bear upon a crossing object. When dogs point, or when game has been marked and expected to spring, the walk should be with short and easy steps ; the body can then be easily turned upon the legs, as if on a pivot, and the bird commanded even if it should fly quite round the sportsman.

" The science of aiming accurately will be of little service, except the gun is held steady from all starting or flinching in the action of firing ; it is to small purpose to traverse the gun with the celerity of a bird flying rapidly in a transverse direction, if the person suspends that motion when he touches the trigger to pull it. In this interlapse, between the beginning of the pull and the appulse of the shot to five and thirty or forty yards distance, (be the pull and stroke of the cock as short, and the fire as quick, as possible) any bird of game will, in a serene day, gain progressively in its flight above two yards, and with a rough wind considerably more. Quickness of sight and steady aiming will never constitute a marksman, unless the motion of the gun corresponds with them, and receives no check whilst in the act of drawing the trigger.

" Should different guns be employed, the shooter should have all the locks made, if possible, to require exactly the same pull to bring them to action ; there is nothing deceives or disconcerts him more than shooting one day with a stiff, and the next with an easy going lock : the transition from that which goes off with a slight to that where a hard touch is necessary will often cause the most expert to miss his bird.

" Always hold the gun with the left hand close to the guard (and not forward upon the barrel to strongly grasp it near the entrance of the ramrod, notwithstanding it has been so strenuously recommended) : all the requisite steadiness in taking aim, and even of motion, in traversing the flight of a bird, can be obtained by thus holding the heaviest pieces ; and, in case of a barrel bursting, the certainty of having a hand or arm shattered by grasping the barrel is reduced to a chance of escaping the effects of such an accident, by placing the hand close to the guard beneath it.*

" With double guns a danger arises from the shooter who fires but one barrel, and kills his bird, forgetting to uncock the other previous to his reloading that which has been discharged : to obviate this, let him invariably uncock† the second barrel be-

---

* In September 1806, Mr. Banister lost the top of three fingers, and the thumb and other parts of the hand were much torn by the bursting of his gun. He had unfortunately placed his hand forward upon the barrel : it is hoped the misfortune to this gentleman may operate forcibly against so dangerous a practice ; for with the hand in that position, should any barrel burst, it is next to a miracle but the party is dreadfully wounded, whereas, by the hand being kept close to the guard, there have been numberless cases where barrels have flown to pieces, without injury to the persons who held them.

† One barrel only should be cocked at a time ; after the first barrel has been fired, the gun should be taken from the shoulder and the other cocked, should a second shot present itself; which would obviate the danger above mentioned.

fore he sets the butt of the gun upon the ground; a sense of self-preservation will soon render this habitual; and a man who is so absent or so eager as to disregard this practice, had better confine himself to carrying a cane instead of a gun.

" After discharging one barrel, be careful to secure with the ramrod the wadding of the other, which from the recoil usually becomes loose: this is not only needful to prevent the shot from falling out, but is an act of safety, lest there should be a space between the shot and the wadding, that will endanger the barrel: it likewise prevents mistakes in loading; and no objection can be made to it, but the accidental fall of a shot into the loaded, whilst pouring them into the fired, barrel, and which may occasion some trouble in withdrawing the ramrod: in such a a case, turn the muzzle into the hand, and keep the ramrod home upon the charge, and the stray shot will easily be extricated.

" When uncocking a gun, never remove the thumb from the cock until after having let it pass down beyond the half bent, and gently raising it again, the sound of the sear is heard catching the tumbler.

" Carrying the gun in a safe position, and well securing the lock, are the first articles a young sportsman should learn, and never cease to regard: the result of neglecting other observances is, generally, no more than missing the object; but carelessness in the handling, or position of the gun, are too frequently attended with the most melancholy catastrophes: however probabilities may be calculated from, a proper attention to the muzzle prevents the possibility of mischief from one source. When a keeper of the Earl of Chesterfield's was preparing for the field in January 1789, and stooping to buckle on his spur, as he sat with his gun resting on his knee, and the muzzle close to his cheek, it seemed improbable that a part of the lock should break at that particular point of time; but his instantaneous death was the terrible effect of his not having guarded against what was possible. The muzzle of the gun pointing obliquely upwards between the left elbow and left cheek, if the piece fires ever so often by accident, can never do harm ; and from this position it may be presented with more ease, expedition, and correctness, than from any other.

"Beware of the muzzle of the gun being kept hanging downwards ; when so carried, the shot is apt to force its way from the powder, especially in clean barrels ; if it happen that a space of sixteen or eighteen inches is thus obtained, and the gun fired with its point below the horizon, it is ten to one but the barrel bursts. There are other perilous consequences besides those that generally accompany the diruption of a barrel, for the men, horses, and dogs, are in perpetual danger of being shot, when a gun is carried in the beforementioned pendent manner.

"In shooting with a stranger, who keeps his gun cocked, and the muzzle usually pointed to the left, plead for the right hand station, and that you cannot hit a bird flying to the left; with a gamekeeper, take the right hand without ceremony. In getting over a fence, constantly endeavour to go last, notwithstanding the usual assurance of ' My dear Sir, I am always remarkably careful :" and if a person beats bushes with a cocked gun, get out of his company as a shooter, with all possible expedition.

"Recollect, both in the house* and in the field, always to con-

* At Dr. Bennet's, vicar of Chapel-en-le-Frith, a person in 1803 left his gun loaded. A servant girl, unconscious of its being charged, presented it in a sportive manner at another girl, and instantly shot her dead. The unintentional author of this accident was so affected that she has remained in a melancholy state ever since. This is one selected out of the too numerous and fatal effects from wantonly handling fire-arms : and it ought to be recollected, that should any previous quarrel between the parties be brought forward, the laws of the country may bring the unhappy survivor to an ignominious end.

Two recent instances, (which are mentioned with the wish of increasing the caution necessary to be observed in all cases where fire-arms

sider a gun as loaded, and never suffer it to be pointed for a moment towards any human being.

" Never display skill by firing close to the head of either man or beast, whether a companion's or a favourite pointer's. A story is told of two persons shooting together, when one of them, an exhibiter in this way, put several shots into his friend's arm, who made suitable outcries. In the course of the day the compliment was returned, with interest, by the wounded man :—' You're a pretty fellow (exclaimed the man last hit) to be so vociferous about my shooting you this morning; why, d—n me, I have half your charge now in my leg.'—' Very likely, (replied the other, coolly,) but I killed my hare, and your bird was missed.'

" In shooting alone with a double gun, it frequently occurs, that the attention is taken up by a wounded bird, and the opportunity of a second shot is neglected; or, upon a second bird being shot at, the first is lost, although, if observed, it might have been easily retrieved. In company, the *marker* to a double

are handled,) occurred in August and September, 1806 ; the first where the son of Mr. Turkin, at Taunton, a young gentleman about seventeen years old, had fired one of the barrels of his double-barrelled gun, and returned to the house, thoughtless of the other being loaded.—It accidentally went off, and the contents were lodged in the arm and side of his sister, a most amiable girl, two years older than himself; and although every assistance was immediately procured, a few hours terminated her existence.—The latter was in the county of Bucks, when Mr. Pincott, a hop-factor at Clapton, was shot in the following manner :—he went out shooting with a gentleman at whose house he was visiting; having occasion to get over a hedge during their diversion, the deceased, who was a man of agility, first passed over, and in order to assist his friend, gave him the butt end of the piece to help him up the bank: the gun discharged, and lodged its contents in the body of Mr. P. who immediately expired. This is a practice very frequently adopted; but it is to be hoped this accident will operate so as to show the danger, and to prevent its being ever again resorted to, gun should keep his eye upon the first bird, if wounded, and leave the second to the shooter himself.

The marker should however recollect that the harder a bird is hit, especially at long distances, when only one or two grains have taken place, the less visible signs of it are observed, unless the bird drops the legs, or instantly *towers;* for which reason the marker's eye should be kept on the bird so far as it can be seen: it frequently happens, that a bird falls dead, four or five hundred yards from the place where first struck, and is as frequently lost for want of proper attention to its flight. When a bird is seen to drop its legs at the instant of firing, and fly off with an undulating motion, or tower to a great height, both these are certain signs of death, and are generally occasioned by a contusion on the *vertebræ;* for if the spine is injured, *paralysis* ensues. If the brain is contused, the bird towers, but the legs are not pendent."

Of the Forest Laws.

As we find a passion for the chase was coeval with human existence, so at the earliest periods of civilization, a jealous distinction marked the privilege of hunting; and, at length, positive laws were enacted, by which the chase became a sort of monopoly, appropriated to the use or the pleasure of those, who, either from birth or fortune, had attained a pre·eminence among their fellow beings.

The Romans appear to have delighted in a miserable apology for field sports, viz. they procured great numbers of wild beasts and birds from the East, which were driven promiscuously into the circus, and exhibited to the view of the people, tearing each other to pieces; while the Emperor Commodus, and several of his imperial brethren, condescended, on these occasions to astonish the spectators by a display of their skill in archery. These masters of the world, however, were specially provided with such situations, that, while they attempted to transfix a panther, the oppressed and infuriate animal could use neither his teeth nor claws in his defence. But Forest or Game Laws were unknown at this period; and though partridges and hares were most probably in existence, no special statutes were enacted for their protection.

After a lapse of some centuries, the Roman empire was annihilated by the barbarians of the north; who, emerging through the dark forests of Germany, at length established themselves in the more cultivated parts of Europe, and introduced the feudal system, to which the petty states of Germany bear a faint resemblance. These barbarians were governed by a number of warlike princes, but were, nevertheless, extremely jealous of their rights, and possessed a generous liberty unknown to their civilized neighbours, and perhaps incompatible with the extreme refinements of the most polished state of society. Hunters from necessity as well as choice, with their conquests they introduced a passion for the chase; and when their subsistence no longer depended upon the pursuit of wild animals, they followed the chase as an amusement, and hence originated laws for the preservation of what has since been known under the denomination of *game*.

It would appear, that laws were known on the subject of field sports, as early as the times of the Saxon dominion in this country, which were, however, extremely mild compared with those enacted in after times by Canute, and more particularly by William the Conqueror.

Canute, the Dane, instituted what are called the Forest Laws, or, at least, I am not aware of any written evidence on the subject farther back than the time of this monarch; but whatever censure may be due to regulations, which at the present time would be insupportable, must not be laid solely to the account of the Dane, as the nobility were despotic on their own estates, and ruled, not only more absolutely, but more tyrannically, than the king himself. Thus, while various forests were appropriated to the use of royalty, the nobility, in imitation of the monarch, had each either his forest, chase, park, or purlieu, over which he exercised unbounded authority; in fact, these forest laws appear to have been instituted in compliance rather with the wish of his nobility, than from the spontaneous inclination of Canute. The first charter of the forest, it seems, was granted by this monarch at Winchester, in the year 1062; and, as a few extracts from Manwood's Forest Laws will be both amusing and

instructive, I trust there needs no' farther apology for their introduction :—

I, Canutus, king, with the advice of my nobility, do make and
establish, that both peace and justice be done to all the
churches of England, and that every offender suffer according
to his quality and the manner of his offence.

'1. There shall be, from henceforth, four, out of the best of
the freemen, who have their accustomed rights secure, (whom the
English call pœgened) constituted in every province in my
kingdom, to distribute justice, together with due punishment, as
to the matters of the forest, to all my people, as well English as
Danish, throughout my whole kingdom of England, which four
we think fit to call the chief men of the forest ; (now called verderors.)

2. There shall be under every one of these, four out of the
middle sort of men (whom the English call lespegend, and the
Danes, young men) placed, who shall take upon them the care
and charge as well of the vert as the venison, (now called regarders.)

3. Again, under every one of these, shall be two of the
meaner sort of men, whom the English call tine men; these shall
take care of the vension and vert by night, and undergo other
servile offices, (now called foresters, or keepers.)

4. Also, every one of the chief men, or verderors, shall have
every year out of our ward (which the English call michni) two
horses, the one with a saddle, the other without ; one sword, five
lances, one head-piece, one shield; and two hundred shillings of
silver.

5. Every one of the middle sort of men, or regarders, one
horse, one lance, one shield, and sixty shillings of silver.

6. Every one of the meaner sort of men, or foresters, one
lance, one cross-bow, and fifteen shillings of silver.

7. That all of them, as well chief men or verderors, middle

sort of men or regarders, and meaner sort of men or foresters, shall be free and quit from all provincial summons and popular pleas (which the English call hundred laghe), and from all taxes concerning the wars or weapons (which the English call warscot) and from all foreign plaints.

8. That the causes of the middle sort of men or regarders, and the meaner sort of men or foresters, and their corrections, as well criminal as civil, shall be adjudged and decided by the provident wisdom and discretion of the chief men or verderors. But the enormities of the chief men or verderors, if any such shall be, we ourselves will cause to be punished according to our royal displeasure.

9. These four (chief men or verderors) shall have a royal power (saving in our presence), and four times in the year the general demonstrations of the forest, and the forfeitures of vert and venison (which the English call mechehunt) where they shall all of them hold claim, or challenge of any thing touching the forest, and shall go to a threefold judgment (which the English call gang fordel) and thus the threefold judgment shall be obtained : the party shall take with him five others, and he himself shall make the sixth, and so by swearing, he shall obtain a threefold judgment or triple oath. But the purgation of fire, or fiery ordale, shall be by no means admitted, unless in such cases where the naked truth cannot otherwise be found out.

10. Whosoever shall offer any violence to the chief men or verderors of my forest, if he be free, he shall lose his liberty, and all that he hath ; and if he be a villain, his right hand shall be cut off.

11. If either of them shall offend again, in the like case, he shall be guilty of death.

12. In the like manner, if any person shall contend in suit with one of the chief men or verderors, he shall forfeit to the king as much as he is worth.

13. If any person shall break the peace before the middle sort of men, or regarders of the forest, he shall pay to the king ten shillings.

14. If any person shall be taken offending in the forest, he shall suffer punishment according to the manner and quality of his offence.

15. The punishment and forfeiture shall not be one and the same of a freeman and one that is not free, of a master and of a servant, of one that is known and of one that is not known; nor shall the management of causes, either civil or criminal, of the beasts of the forests, and of the royal beasts of the vert and of the vension, be one and the same: for the crime of hunting has been of old reputed (and not undeservedly) amongst the greatest offences that could be committed in the forest; but that of vert is esteemed so little and trivial, (except as it is a breach of our royal chase) that our constitution of forest laws doth scarcely take notice of it; nevertheless, he, that offends therein, is guilty of one of the trespasses of the forest.

16. If any freeman shall course or hunt a beast of the forest, either casually or wilfully, so that by the swiftness of the course, the beast doth pant, and is put out of breath; such freeman shall forfeit ten shillings; and if he be not a freeman, he shall forfeit double; but if he be a bondman, he shall lose his skin.

17. But if a royal beast be killed by any of them, the freeman shall lose his freedom, the other his liberty, and the bondman his life.

18. My bishops, abbots, and barons, shall not be challenged for hunting in my forest, except they kill royal beasts; and, if they do, they shall make satisfaction according to my pleasure, without knowing the certainty of the forfeiture.

19. I will that every freeman may, as he pleaseth, have and take venison or vert, upon his own grounds, or in his own field, being out of my chase; and let all men avoid and forbear taking my venison or vert, in every place where it is mine.

A forest is a franchise royal, created by the king, and by him set apart, and appointed for the generation, feeding, and nourishment of wild beasts of venery and chase, and also for beasts and fowls of warren ; (no subject can have, or enjoy a forest, without special grant from the king, under the great seal of England) having particular laws, privileges, and officers belonging thereunto, for the preservation and continuance thereof, and of the vert and venison therein.

2. It is a circuit of ground, stored with great woods, and thickets for the shelter, residence, and safety of wild beasts, and fowls of the forest, chase, and warren ; and is also replenished with fruitful pastures, and lands for their continual feeding and subsistence ; being privileged to rest, and abide therein under the king's protection, for his royal pastime, diversion, and pleasure.

3. A forest is circumscribed, or bounded with irremovable and indelible marks, meers, and bounds, known and preserved either by matter of record or by prescription.

4. It consists of eight things, viz. 1. of soil, 2. of covert, 3. of laws, 4. courts, 5. judges, 6. officers, 7. game, 8. bounds.

Note, a forest is not a place privileged generally for all manner of wild beasts or fowls, but only of those that are of forest, chase, and warren ; the wild beasts of the forest, or beasts of venery, being these five and no other, viz. the hart, the hind, the hare, the boar, and the wolf. And although the hart and the hind are beasts of the same kind, or species, yet, nevertheless, they are accounted two several beasts, because they are of two several seasons for hunting : the season for hunting the hart being in the summer, and the time for hunting the hind beginning when the season of the hart is over.

*Of a frank chase, a park, and a free-warren, what they are,
and how they differ from each other.*

1. A frank, or free chase, is a franchise next in degree unto
a forest, being an open place for the keeping of game, and in
that respect something resembling it, yet with this difference,
that a chase hath neither the same kinds of game in it, nor any
particular laws belonging to the same, proper to a chase only;
for, whereas the beasts of forest are the hart, hind, hare, boar,
and wolf; the beasts of chase are none of them, but other five,
viz. the buck, the doe, the fox, the martern, and the roe; in like
manner, all offenders in a chase are punishable by the common
law of this realm, and not by the forest laws. Besides, a chase
hath no such officers as a forest, viz. verderors, regarders, (or
rangers) foresters, or agistors; nor hath it any courts of attachments, swainmote, or justice-seat appertaining thereunto, all the
officers belonging to a chase being only keepers, as they are
called in a park, but such are termed foresters in a forest.

2. As a chase is next in degree unto a forest, and in some
sort resembling it, so is a park to a chase, being in many respects the same; for there is no diversity between them, save
only that a park is inclosed, and a chase lies always open without inclosure.

3. Lastly, the next franchise, in degree unto a park, is the
liberty of a free warren; the beasts and fowls whereof are four,
viz. the hare, the cony, the pheasant, and the partridge, and no
other (being such as may be taken by the long-winged hawks,
according to Budœus), for as a forest is the highest and greatest
in dignity of all franchises, so it doth surpass them all for extent
and comprehensiveness, including in it a frank chase, a park,
and a warren; for which reason, the beasts of chase, and
the beasts and fowls of warren, are as much privileged within
the forest, as the beasts of forest are; every forest being in
itself a chase, though a chase be not a forest, but a part of it;

and so the like may be said of a park and a warren : and there-fore the hunting, hurting, or killing any of the beasts or fowls of chase, park, or warren, within the limits of the forest, is a trespass of the forest, only punishable by the laws of the forest, and not otherwise.

And because the laws made for the preservation and continu-ance of forests, and purlieus thereof, and the vert, venison, and fowls therein, are particularly applicable unto, and only proper for forests, and no other places ; therefore we shall begin with a brief account of the laws that relate to the king's forest only, and afterwards proceed to discourse of such other laws, as have been since made for preservation of the game of hunting, hawk-ing, fishing and fowling, in the chases, parks, warrens, woods, or other grounds, fisheries, or vivaries, within England and Wales, belonging to the subject.

Of the FOREST LAWS in GENERAL.

It is reported by ancient historians, that forests have been always in this kingdom from the first time that the same was in-habited ; and the author of Concordantia Historiarum tells us, that Gurguntius, the son of Belyn, a king of this island, did make certain forests, for his pleasure, in Wiltshire ; and that divers other kings have done the like, since his time. Which forests, the kings of this realm have always maintained and pre-served (with divers privileges and laws appropriated thereunto) as places of pleasure and delight for their royal pastime and diver-sion.

And when it happened that any offenders entered into those privileged places, and committed any trespass thereon, they had very severe punishments inflicted upon them, according to the laws then in force, which were very grievous and altogether uncertain, according to the arbitrary and unlimited will of the king : and thus those laws were executed, and their punishments continued, until about the year 1016, when Canutus, the Dane, became king of this realm ; who, delighting much in forests, did establish certain laws, or constitutions, peculiar only to forests. By which it appears, that before his time, all wild beasts and birds were only the kings, and that no other person might kill or hurt them: the kings of England having, by their prerogative royal, a right and privilege in such things as none of their subjects could challenge any property in ; and such were then said to be the king's, as wild beasts, birds, &c. in whose lands or woods soever they were found. Whereupon the said Canutus made a law, that every freeman might, at his pleasure, have and take his own vert and vension, or hunt upon his own ground, or in his own fields, being out of the king's chase ; but that all men should forbear to have or take the king's vert or game in every place where his highness should have the same.

Also, it appears, by the laws of St. Edward, the Confessor, that he did confirm the said laws of Canutus, by a sanction made in his time, to this effect :—That it should be lawful for every one of his subjects to enjoy the benefit of his own hunting, that he could any way have or make in his own lands, woods, or fields ; so that he did forbéar to hunt the king's game in his highness's forests, or other privileged places, on pain of losing his life for such offence.

Which laws were afterwards confirmed by William the Conqueror, as appears in the 27th chapter of the book, wherein his laws were collected and digested ; and so were continued by him all his time.

After whose death, William Rufus, his son, in like manner continued the same laws during his life.

And after his death, king Henry the first, his brother, succeeding him to the crown, by his charter, confirmed all the laws of the forest made by St. Edward the Confessor, as appears by the book kept in the Exchequer, called Liber Rubrus, cap. 1. Legum Suarum: which laws of the forest so continued during all the life time of the said Henry the first.

After whose decease, king Stephen, by his charter confirmed all the said laws, privileges, and customs granted by St. Edward the Confessor, and Henry the first, and continued the same during his life.

After whose death, king Henry the second succeeding him, did, by his general charter, confirm the aforesaid laws of the forest in many particulars, but not without great alterations and additions. For he doth, in and by his said charter, recite and declare the nature of the laws of the forest, and in what sense they were taken and used, or how interpreted or construed in times past, and wherein they do differ from the common law of the kingdom ; and that the kings of England, before that time, and he himself, even then, might make a forest in any place of the realm, where they or he pleased, as well in the lands and inheritances of any of their or his subjects, as in their or his own demeasn lands. Which unlimited and unaccountable power, claimed by the kings of England in those times, by colour of the forest laws, over the birth-rights and inheritances of their subjects, was a mighty and insupportable grievance to those whose lands were so afforested ; their pastures and the profits of the lands being then devoured by the king's wild beasts of his forests, without any recompense for the same.

The punishments for offences against the forest laws were often exceeding great for a small offence, and the forfeiture according to the king's pleasure, not regarding the quantity of the trespass, nor according to the course of the common law.

Which rigorous execution of the forest laws continued during the life of Henry the second, and both the reigns of Richard the first and king John ; every one of which kings did daily increase those oppressions, by making more new forests in the lands of their subjects, to their great impoverishment.

And this mischief was not at all remedied until the making of Charta de Foresta by Henry the third, published in the ninth year of his reign, which was afterwards confirmed and enlarged by Edward the first, his son; whereby it is provided, that all forests that Henry the third, Richard the first, and king John had forested and made of the land, meadows, pastures, or woods of any of their subjects (being not the demeasn lands of the crown) should be disafforested again. For those three kings last mentioned, had (in their times) afforested so much of their subjects' lands, that the greatest part of the kingdom was then converted into forests.

FOREST COURTS, &c.

There be three principal courts usually kept for matters of the forest, viz. the court of attachments, the court of swainmote, and the high court of the lord justice in eyre of the forest, called the justice-seat ; being each of them of a several and different nature.

The court of attachments is the most inferior of them all, for therein the officers do nothing but receive the attachments of the foresters, and enrol them in the verderors' rolls, that they may be in readiness against the time that the court of swainmote is kept; and for that this court cannot determine any offence or trespass, if the value thereof be above 4d.

Next in degree above the court of attachments, is the court of swainmote, though much inferior to the justice seat of the forest: for when the presentments of the court of attachments and the court of swainmote have had their proceedings, according to the assizes and laws of the forest, yet cannot the court of swainmote determine the same, or assess fines for any offences contained in such presentments, or give judgment thereupon (other than to pronounce them convicted.) But such presentments and convictions must be delivered in to the lord justice in eyre of the forest, the court of justice seat, on the first day of sitting of the said court, when the same are called for, according to the laws and ordinances of the forest: the swainmote is a court unto which all the freeholders within the forest do owe suit and service.

The next is the most supreme court of the forest, called the justice-seat, or general sessions, wherein the lord chief justice, or lord justice, doth sit; for unto him it only belongs to give judgment in this court of all offences, and to assess fines, and punish offenders, this court being as the fountain head, unto which the other court of attachments and swainmote are but (as it were) two conduit pipes to convey the matter and causes of the forest, that from thence judgment may be had, and given thereupon.

The office of lord chief justice of the forest, is a place of great honour and authority, executed always by some of the chiefest of the nobility, who is of the king's privy council. When he is made lord chief justice in eyre of the forest by the king's special commission, he hath, by that means, as great authority as any justice of oyer and terminer hath to hear and determine matters of common law, if not greater: for then he may punish all trespasses and offences of the forest according to the laws of the same, and may hear and determine all claims touching the liberties and franchises within the forest, as to such as have parks, warrens, &c. therein; also of them that claim to be quit of asserts and purprestures, or of such as do claim leets, hundreds, goods of felons, fugitives and outlaws, felo's de se, waifs, estrays, deo-dands, and such like immunities, and other liberties within the forest, as likewise of such persons that claim to kill hares, and other beasts of chase and warren within the forest.

He hath also an absolute authority to determine all offences within the forest, either of vert or venison; for such offences shall not be determined before any other justices, except such as are appointed by commission under the great seal, to aid and assist him in the execution and performance of his office.

When the justices of the forest have obtained their commis-sion for holding the court of justice seat of the forest, they make out their precept to the sheriff of the county wherein the forest lies, and the justice seat is kept, commanding him to summon all the prelates, nobility, knights, gentlemen, and freeholders that have lands within the bounds of the forest, and out of every town and village four men and a reve, and out of every borough twelve lawful men; and all persons that claim to hold pleas of the forest before the justices; to appear (such a day and place) before the justice in eyre of the forest or his deputy, to hear and do such things as appertain to the pleas of the forest. And likewise that the said sheriff do make proclamation in all boroughs, and other towns, fairs, markets, and other public places throughout his bailiwick, that all persons who claim to have any liberties, franchises, or free customs of the forest, may be there, at the same time and place, to make good their claims; and that all persons attached, since the last court, touching vert or venison, and their pledges and mainpernors, who had a day given them until this court for their appearance, be there also to stand to, and abide the judgment of the court; and that the sheriff be there with his bailiffs, to execute such matters as ap-pertain to his office, and certify the justice of the forest concern-ing the premises.

OF HUNTING, &c. WITHIN THE FOREST.

The king, and such persons only as have any sufficient warrant or authority by charter or grant from his majesty, or his ancestors, may hunt and hawk within the forest, and no other: also, all such persons as have any lawful claim allowed in eyre, in respect to any grant to hunt or hawk within the forest, may use the same accordingly.

But if any knight, esquire, or gentleman doth dwell within the regard of the forest, and be lord of the manor there, yet he may not hunt or hawk therein, except he hath a lawful claim for so doing allowed him in eyre, as aforesaid; because, by the laws of the forest, no person may hunt or hawk within any part of the forest that is within the regard of the forest, though it be within his own fee, except he hath a sufficient warrant so to do: and, therefore, they must forbear to hunt or hawk in their own grounds, if they be within the regard of the forest; because it is a trespass of the forest so to do, unless they have good warrant for the same.

But by the charter of the forest, anno. 9 H. 2, cap. 11, every arch-bishop, bishop, earl, or baron, coming to the king by his commandment, and passing through any of his majesty's forests, it shall be lawful for any such prelate, or peer, to kill one or two of the king's deer therein, by the view of the forester, if he be present, or otherwise cause a horn to be blown for him, that he may seem not to steal the king's deer. And the same they may do in their return home from the king. By which it appears, that those prelates and peers have, by the said charter, a lawful license to hunt in the king's forests, but yet with this restriction,

Y

that such prelate, or nobleman, must be sent for by the king.
2. He must be an arch-bishop, or bishop, earl, or baron. 3.
Such hunting must be made by the view of the forester. 4. If
the forester be absent, a horn must be blown.

Then, as to the licenses to hunt or hawk in the king's forests,
chases, parks, or warrens, these things ought to be considered.
1. How such licenses ought to be used. 2. The difference
between a license of profit, and a license of pleasure, and a
license in law, and a license in fair.

As to the first, the king being the chief monarch of this realm
(unto whom the government and regulation of forests, and such
like places of royal pastime and recreation do principally appertain) may himself grant licenses to hunt and hawk in any of his
majesty's forests, chases, parks, or warrens, unto any of his subjects, according to his royal will and pleasure.

Secondly, whosoever hath any special authority derived from
his majesty in that behalf, under the great seal of England, may
in like manner grant licenses, in some respect, and in some places,
to hunt and hawk in his majesty's forests, chases, parks, or warrens ; as the lord chief justice in eyre of the king's forest,
may grant a license, or give a warrant, to any nobleman, or gentleman, that hath a manor or freehold therein ; for the first to
hunt and hawk in his manor, or lordship, and the other in his
freehold, according to the purport or intent of such grant or
warrant.

In like manner, a subject that is lord of a forest, may grant
a license to whom he pleaseth to hunt and hawk in his forest.
But no person can grant any license, or give warrant to any man
to hunt and hawk in the king's forests, other than the king
himself, or his chief justice in eyre of the forest ; or such
other persons as have the like authority from the king, by some
special grant to do the same. For if any of the king's foresters
(or other officers) should attempt or presume to do the same (ex

officio;) not only such forester (or other officer) but all those who shall hunt or hawk with him there, by colour of such license, or warrant, would be all trespassers, and liable to the punishments of the forest laws.

Neither can any forester (or other such officer) hawk or take any fowls of warren, as pheasants and partridges, within his walk, in the forest, because his office is to preserve and not destroy them; and therefore he cannot give or grant any warrant, or license, to another to hawk, or take any fowls of warren within his walk or liberty; for if he do, although he hold his office by patent from the king, or some other person as hath power to grant the same, yet is such act such a disuse or abuse of his authority, that it is a cause of forfeiture of his office.

In licenses to hunt or hawk within a forest, chase, park, or warren, there is this difference to be considered, whether such license be of profit or for pleasure only. For a license of profit is, where a man hath a lawful warrant to kill and carry away with him the game that is taken by him, either by hunting or hawking in any of those places above mentioned; but a license of pleasure is only where a man hath a warrant to hunt or hawk in a forest, chase, &c. but doth not thereby acquire any property in the game he takes, and so hath not any authority to carry away the same with him; neither can he that hath only a license of pleasure, hunt or hawk with any more persons in his company than himself: but he that hath a license of profit may hunt or hawk with his friends and servants in his company, and carry away with him the game he hath taken to his own use.

OF THE PURLIEU, OR POURALLEE, OF THE FOREST.

A purlieu, or pourallee, is a circuit of ground adjoining unto the forest, circumscribed with immoveable boundaries, known only by matter of record; this compass of ground was once forest, and afterwards disafforested by the perambulations made for the severing the new forests from the old. This pourallee began at the first after this manner, viz. when king Henry II. came first to be king of England, he took such great delight in the forests of this kingdom, that (being not contented with those he found here, though many and large) he began, within a few years after his coming to the crown, to enlarge divers great forests, and to afforest the lands of his subjects, that any way were near adjoining unto those forests, and so they continued during his reign.

After whose death, king Richard I. succeeding him to the throne, within some short time after his coming to the crown, began to follow the example of Henry II. his father, not only in the delight and pleasure he took in forests, but also in daily afforesting the lands of his subjects that any way lay near to his forests; by means whereof, the enlarging of forests did daily increase during his reign.

After whose decease, king John, his brother, coming to the crown, did, in like manner, soon afterwards begin, by little and little, to follow the examples of his father and brother, in afforesting the lands of his subjects, that lay any way near unto his forests, so that the greatest part of the lands of the kingdom was become forest. And thus they continued until the seventeenth year of his reign, at which time, in regard this grievance was not particularly injurious unto a small number, or the meanest persons, but generally to all degrees of people, divers noblemen and gentlemen finding a convenient opportunity, repaired to the king, and besought him to grant unto them, that they might have all those new afforestations that were made by Henry II. Richard I. and himself, disafforested again : all which king John seemed not willing to do, but promised to grant accordingly, and at last consented to subscribe and seal to such articles concerning the liberties of the forest, which they then demanded, being for the most part, in such sort, as are now contained in the charter of the forest of the said king John, dated at Runingse-mede, or Ryme-mead (Runnymede, between Staines and Windsor, the 15th of June, in the eighteenth year of his reign.) —But before any disafforestation was made upon this grant, king John died at Newark Castle, in Nottinghamshire.

After whose death, Henry III. his eldest son, at the age or nine years, succeeded to the throne, so that by reason of his minority, nothing was done until the ninth year of his reign, at which time the two charters were made, and confirmed by the said Henry III. called Magna Charta and Charta de Foresta, and caused to be sent into every county throughout the kingdom, to be published and proclaimed.

And for the better accomplishing and performing of those articles of Charta de Foresta, as concerned the disafforestation of such woods and lands as were afforested by Henry II. Richard I. and king John, the said Henry III. ordered inquisitions to be taken by substantial juries for severing the new forests from the old ; and thereupon two commissioners were sent to take those inquisitions, by virtue whereof many great woods and lands were not only disafforested, but improved to arable land by the owners thereof. So that now, after this charter thus made and confirmed, some of these new afforestations were perambulated, and after such inquisitions taken, the certainty was made known by matter of record, which were the old and which were the new forests. Nevertheless, the greater part of the new afforestations were still remaining to be disafforested during the life of king Henry III.

After whose decease, Edward I. his eldest son, succeeded him unto the crown, who, being often besought, and petitioned as well by the nobility as commonalty of this kingdom, to confirm the aforesaid liberties, which his father had granted, was graciously pleased to confirm the same according to his request. And now all things having been granted, performed, and confirmed concerning the said two charters, viz. Magna Charta, and Charter de Foresta, the same were delivered, signed, sealed, and confirmed, to the sheriff of London, to be proclaimed, which was accordingly done in St. Paul's church yard, in the presence of a numerous concourse of people there met together. Whereupon the lords and commons soon after began to put the king in mind of granting commissions to persons fitly qualified for the same, that perambulations might forthwith be made for all new afforestations, that they might be disafforested, according to the first and third articles of Charta de Foresta.

Whereupon three bishops, three earls, and three barons, were appointed by the king to take care of and see those perambulations performed, who caused them to be made accordingly, and inquisitions to be taken thereupon, and returned into the court of chancery; whereby the king was ascertained, what woods and lands were ancient forests, and what were newly afforested; and caused all those that were ancient forests, to be meered and bounded with irremovable boundaries, to be known by matter of record for ever. And likewise those woods and lands that had been newly afforested, the king caused to be separated from the old, and to be returned into chancery by marks, meers, and bounds to be known, in like manner, by matter of record, for ever.

By which it appears, how the purlieus, or pourallees, had their first beginning; for, all such woods and lands as were afforested by Henry II. Richard I. or king John, and by perambulations severed from the ancient forests, were, and yet are, called pourallees, viz. woods and lands severed from the old forests, and disafforested by perambulation; pourallee, in French, being the same as perambulation in Latin.

But, notwithstanding, such new afforestations were disafforested by perambulation, whereby the same became pourallee, or purlieu; yet they were not thereby so disafforested as to every man, but that they do, in some sense, continue forest still, as to some persons, though disafforested, in some sort, as to others. For by the words, Charta de Foresta, if the king had afforested any woods or lands of his subjects, to the damage of them whose they were, they should be forthwith disafforested again; that is, only as to those persons whose woods and lands they were, who, as the proper owners thereof, might fell and cut down the woods at their own pleasure, without any license from the king, as also convert their meadows and pastures into tillage, or otherwise improve their grounds to the best advantage. In like manner, they might hunt and chase the wild beasts of the forest towards the same, so that they do not forestal the same in their return thither; but yet no other person could claim such benefit in the pourallee, but only the proper owner of the soil thereof; so that the same remains forest still, as to those who have no property in the lands therein: for the owners of the woods and lands therein may suffer the pourallee to remain forest still, if they be so minded, notwithstanding such disafforestation) as appears by the statute of 33 Edward I. cap. 5.) as some have thought it most expedient for them, because thereby they had the benefit of common within the forest, which otherwise, by having their lands severed from the forest, by way of pourallee, they were excluded from: which doth prove, that the woods and lands in the pourallee are disafforested only for the owners thereof, and not for every one to hunt and spoil the wild beasts there at his pleasure; for if they chance to wander out of the forest into the pourallee, yet the king hath a property in them still against every man, except the proper owner of the ground wherein they are; for such person has a special property in them, ratione soli, but yet so that he may only take them by hunting, or chasing with his greyhounds or dogs, without any forestalling, or foresetting them in their course back again towards the forest; for the king hath always rangers in the pourallee to attend such wild beasts of the forest, as come there, and re-chase them back into the forest; which proves, that though the wild beasts of the forest do by chance stray into the pourallee, yet the king hath a property still in them, or otherwise the ranger could have no lawful authority to re-chase them into the forest.

The Forest Laws may now be regarded as obsolete; they may be said to have naturally become defunct, since the forests have ceased to exist. However, we may hence very easily trace the origin of the Game Laws. Whatever forest regulations might have been adopted by the Saxons, the English appear to have been comparatively content under their dominion; and though Canute may be accused of having instituted laws in respect to the forests and wild beasts, which reflect no credit on his memory, it does not appear that they were rigorously enforced in his time. The Normans not only rendered these unjust enactments much more oppressive, but appear to have exercised the greatest cruelties, and, with savage delight, to have rioted amidst the misery and desolation of the unfortunate English.

On this subject, Blackstone observes, "Another violent alteration of the English constitution consisted in the depopulation of whole counties, for the purpose of the king's royal diversion; and subjecting both them, and all the ancient forests of the kingdom, to the unreasonable severities of forest laws imported from the continent, whereby the slaughter of a beast was made almost as penal as the death of a man. In the Saxon times, though no man was allowed to kill or chase the king's deer, yet he might start any game, pursue, and kill it, upon his own estate. But the rigour of these new constitutions vested the sole property of all the game in England in the king alone; and no man was entitled to disturb any fowl of the air, or any beast of the field, of such kinds as were specially reserved for the royal amusement of the sovereign, without express license from the king, by a grant of a chase or free-warren: and those franchises were granted as much with a view to preserve the breed of animals, as to indulge the subject. From a similar principle to which, though the forest laws are now mitigated, and by degrees grown entirely obsolete, yet from this root has sprung a bastard slip, known by the name of the Game Law, now arrived to and wantoning in its highest vigour: both founded upon the same unreasonable notions of permanent property in wild creatures; both productive of the same tyranny to the commons: but with this difference, that the forest laws established only one mighty hunter throughout the land, the game laws have raised a little Nimrod in every manor. And in one respect the ancient law was much less unreasonable than the modern: for the king's grantee of a chase or free warren might kill game in every part of his franchise; but now, though a freeholder of less than £100 a year, is forbidden to kill a partridge upon his own estate, yet nobody else (not even the lord of a manor, unless he hath a grant of free-warren) can do it without committing a trespass, and subjecting himself to an action."

Notwithstanding the excessive rigour of the forest laws, the lower orders of the English could never be prevented from committing depredations ; and though time has so much altered the face of the country, as well as its political institutions, as to render the forest laws a dead letter, yet the passion for the chase appears unabated, and the most severe exercise of the complex enactments of the game laws, has been found inadequate to the intention, as poaching, so far from being prevented, is extensively and audaciously practised, and appears even to increase in proportion as the laws for its suppression are multiplied and rendered more severe.

The Game Laws.

The statutes which are denominated the " Game Laws," far from harmonizing with the general spirit of British legislation, are as remarkable for the petty tyrannical spirit which pervades them, as for the injustice in which they are founded; and yet, paradoxical as it may appear, whenever in the senate attempts have been made to soften their severity, many of the opposition have distinguished themselves by their decided hostility to such laudable intentions; nor have they been content to stop here, but have, on the contrary, eagerly embraced every opportunity of rendering an odious system still more disgusting—so much for patriotism!

Geese, ducks, the common barn-door fowl, and indeed, all domestic poultry, have been reclaimed from a state of nature; nor can the least doubt be entertained that partridges and pheasants might be rendered equally submissive; yet, no sooner is a motion for this purpose brought before the notice of parliament, than the *patriots* take the alarm; and though they will talk much about the rights of the subject, they seem, at all events, determined that the working part of the community shall not taste of a dainty which they choose to keep for themselves. I do not mean to assert, that when Mr. Brandt brought this subject before the House of Commons, that the opposition to his enlightened proposal arose from the *patriots* alone; many of the ministerialists no doubt, were unwilling to sanction the motion; in these it might be said to be consistent; but what must be thought of men, who, at elections and public meetings, load ministers with the most rancorous abuse, declaim in bitter terms on the invaded rights of the people, the galling oppression under which they are sinking, and rave about reform almost as madly as Platoff did for Buonaparte's head; yet, only let the *reform of the game laws* be distantly hinted, and they immediately strain every nerve to continue a system at variance with reason and justice, but which enables them, as land-holders or lords of manors, to play the petty tyrant on a scale contemptible enough, but well suited to the narrowness of their contracted ideas!

While poaching has most alarmingly increased, the means resorted to for the preservation of game are not only disgusting, but extremely dangerous; and though accidents are of frequent occurrence, and valuable lives occasionally lost, by steel traps and spring guns, yet the system is obstinately pursued in this enlightened age, and in a country too which boasts so much of the freedom of its institutions, and the inherent rights of the human race!

If a partridge could, like a sheep, be kept in a paddock, then indeed the right of private property would be claimed with justice; but as no limits can be put to its motions, as it is seen on the ground of one man this hour, and on that of another the next—may feed on the corn of the peer in the morning, and ravage the poor man's crop in the evening—what can be more ridiculous or unjust than to claim as a right that which, in the very nature of things, can belong to no particular person whatever.

Colonel Wood, a few years back, brought this subject before the House of Commons with a view to remedy the evil here complained of, but he did not succeed; and the more recent attempt of Mr. Brandt (fresh in the recollection of the reader, no doubt) though entertained for some time, and triumphantly debated, as far as reason and justice were concerned, was, nevertheless, ultimately rejected. This enlightened statesman had no intention to abridge the privileges of the rich, but merely wished to extend the liberty of the poor, and thus put a stop to the present frightful system of poaching. According to his plan, the farmer would be at liberty to breed game for the market in the same manner as domestic poultry or rabbits, without, however, restricting the land owners from making any agreement they thought proper with their tenantry : hence the great would be still enabled to preserve what quantity of game they thought proper; yet, as the proposition would evidently annihilate that odious distinction of qualification, and in all probability render partridges as plentiful as common poultry, it was not to be endured : and though neither the hostility of ministers, nor any thing like sound argument, was urged against the measure, it was lost, notwithstanding ; and an attempt made to raise on its ruins the following—" to authorise the sale of game under certain restrictions :—Lords of manors and gamekeepers authorized by deputation to kill game, may sell game to licensed persons. Justices may grant licences to certain persons, upon entering into a recognizance. Justices empowered to revoke licences, upon proof of the conditions of the recognizance being broken. Licensed persons selling game to affix a ticket to the same, signed with his name. Persons obtaining certificates under false pretences liable to penalties. Not to affect former acts for the preservation of game."

This, which went merely to enable great land owners to derive a pecuniary profit from the sale of game, and increase perhaps the grievance complained of, did not pass into a law, owing, however, more to the late period of the session at which it was introduced, than to any intention of the proposers ; and even when, for this reason, it was reluctantly abandoned, notice was given that it would again be brought before the House at the first convenient opportunity.

There are many causes to which the great extent of poaching is to be attributed, and it will be necessary to glance at these

z

before I describe my plan for preventing this infraction of the law so uniformly deplored, although from very different motives.

In the first place, it will be readily admitted that there is an inherent attachment to field sports in human nature, but particularly in this country; so much so, indeed, that even the *well-fed citizen* is observed, occasionally, to quit the solacing and balmy comforts of a snug fire side and domestic ease, and exert himself beyond his usual custom, merely to enjoy the diversion of *shooting a few sparrows!* The *rustic* seems to imbibe a relish for the chase from the earliest period of life; but his desire, in the first instance, arises much less from a wish to be possessed of the game than from a thirst to enjoy the pleasure of pursuing it; nor is it till after an enticing lure has been repeatedly exhibited to his view, that he even contemplates the union of *profit* with pleasure; and no one follows a profession with more delight than the poacher.

Persons in the middle classes of life, as tradesmen in large towns, who are attached to field sports, as well as those who are fond of the pleasures of the table, but chiefly the former, look with an envious eye upon those privileges and distinctions, which the rich, as it respects game, have appropriated to themselves: not one amongst the numerous enactments on this head, however, excites such unmingled disgust as that which relates to *qualification*. On this account, therefore, since these persons are thus unjustly excluded, as they conceive, from a little rational enjoyment, *they encourage poaching*, not only without the least hesitation, but as a kind of duty; and instances are not wanting where they have accompanied the poachers to the borders of the identical domain, and have even shared, occasionally, in the forbidden pleasure of nocturnal havock.

Hence it will be readily seen that they who follow the business of poaching have always the advantage of a willing market, good prices, and ready money for their illicit commodities; and, while the traffic is thus encouraged, and the security from detection increased to a very great degree, owing to the jealous feeling of those who foster it, as well as the light in which it is unfortunately viewed by the community in general, it will be no easy matter to frame any legal restraints which shall operate as an effectual check to poaching. Indeed, since the penalties have been increased to a very great degree of severity, poaching, instead of being checked in its baneful operation, appears to have increased—proceeding exactly in an inverse ratio.

From experience, then, we may safely conclude that an excess of severity, in legal enactments, tends rather to encourage than to depress poaching: prudence, therefore, should induce us to look for a remedy of a conciliatory nature rather than those irritable caustics which, though, for a time, they may cicatrize the wound, it still remains unsound at the bottom, and ultimately bursts out with increased virulence. Now, if as I have already observed, the farmer were allowed to breed game and bring it regularly to market in the same manner as domestic poultry, the poacher would not only be under-sold, but more strictly watched by the occupier of the land. And, however wild partridges and pheasants may appear, there is no doubt, that by persevering for a few generations they would be brought to propagate in the farm yard as familiarly as domestic poultry. All our present domestic fowls were unquestionably reclaimed from a state of nature. Nothing could be more easy than to breed hares in abundance, though in a state of half confinement. Such a system, in my opinion, would operate most essentially in checking a vice which every reflecting mind must seriously lament, and which very often leads to the most mischievous, as well as the most deplorable, consequences; it would, also, have the good effect of putting an end to those jealousies and heart-burnings so frequently manifested by the middling classes of tradesmen, already alluded to. If to this were added something more equitable or more satisfactory, in regard to *qualification*, I have no hesitation in declaring my firm conviction, that poaching would nearly, if not altogether, cease. At the same time, far from reducing the price of the certificate, I would have it increased. It is a good and legitimate source of revenue : it is, in fact, a oluntary tax, and therefore in the eye of reason and justice, appears unexceptionable.

Admitting, then, for the sake of argument, that the measures just proposed would answer the end in view, it is but fair that we should examine the other side of the question, in order to see how far such regulations would affect what have been hitherto considered as the peculiar privileges of the great and wealthy classes of society. In the first place, I conceive, it will be readily admitted, that game, under such circumstances, would abundantly increase ; and while the regular market might be thus well supplied, the noble and wealthy sportsman would experience an increase rather than a diminution ; and, if economy were an object, a considerable expense might be saved in keepers. The law of trespass should remain precisely as it is at present—it is an excellent law ; and would operate, in the case I propose, as it does at this moment, as a protection to the land-holder, and, consequently, as a sufficient guard against the illegal destruction of game. Landholders would still possess the right of granting leases upon such specific conditions as might give satisfaction to both parties ; as, at present, a clause is generally inserted respecting the game. Therefore, upon every view of the case, while the proposed system would render game abundant, it would not abridge, in the most remote degree, the amusements of the higher orders : it would infringe no privilege ; and would, I have no doubt, in a little time, effectually destroy the now-growing evil of poaching. Moreover, most of those who give encouragement to poaching, and which they now regard as no crime, could then view it in no other light than absolute robbery, and though they might purchase game from a poacher with indifference, or perhaps with delight, they would shudder at the idea of being connected with professed thieves!

At present, poaching is by no means confined to the lower orders; for it is a certain fact, however difficult the proof might be, that there are to be found in higher life, those who do not hesitate to supply the market clandestinely with game.

I am no enemy to the rich, nor would I encroach on the rights of any class of men; but I cannot help regarding the distinction in the qualification for killing game as most unjust—why, in the name of all that is reasonable, should the merchant be debarred from the pleasures of the chase?—It is very well known that the revenue arising from merchandize or moveable property is far greater than that derived from land; and therefore, since it pays more towards the support of government and the protection of the country, why should it not entitle its possessor to the same privileges as the land-holder?—I do not mean to say, that a merchant ought to have the privilege of entering upon the grounds of any person without the consent of the owner—quite the contrary: property should and must be held sacred, or anarchy will ensue. But as the matter stands at present, an unqualified person is liable to be prosecuted, even should he be sporting with the consent of the owner of the ground, and in possession of a game certificate!

Many of these strict game preservers, though they may have an immense extent of land, yet, if they find any of the neighbouring land-holders indifferent as to the game, they volunteer their services for what is called its preservation; or, in other words, they manifest the utmost anxiety to prevent a partridge from falling into plebeian hands; and while they rigorously enforce the most odious part of the law against any of the inferior order who happens to do any thing more than look at the game,

z 3

they are not scrupulously exact in every legal point themselves, but strain every nerve to render oppression still more oppressive!

In general, these tyrannical Nimrods will be found *Whigs*. I have experienced liberality from the *Tories* in respect to game; but never from the *Whigs:* and when I hear the latter, with inflated pride, boast so much of patriotism, the game laws flash across my mind; nor can I help suspecting the intentions of men, whose private practice is so much at variance with their public profession.

That some alteration must, at no distant period, take place in respect to game is abundantly evident; much good may result from a judicious and liberal revision of the statutes, without the least injury to the just right of any class or order of men.

Lord Cranbourne having brought the subject of the Game Laws before the House of Commons in the spring of 1823, during the printing of the present edition, for an account of the proceedings thereon, we refer the reader to the end of the volume.

TRESPASS,

Which is the entry by one person upon the ground of another, without the owner's consent; and even though no real injury may be sustained by the owner of the land, it is a trespass, nevertheless. It is a *wilful* trespass where the person has been warned not to come upon the ground; and *malicious*, where the intention to distress or injure the owner is evident.

In the sense we are here to consider it, trespass applies to *qualified*, as well as *unqualified*, persons, though not in an equal degree. The existing statutes relative to this subject, are fundamentally just and laudable; though it cannot be denied, that they have been frequently resorted to (on account of game) merely as a colour to the basest intention, and have thus become the instruments of legal oppression.

An action of trespass may be supported for any unlawful entry on land, although no notice has been given; but in that case, if the damages recovered be under forty shillings, and only the general issue has been pleaded, the plaintiff will in general recover no more costs than damages; whereas, when a trespass has been committed after notice, it is usual for the judge on the trial to certify that it was wilful; in which case the plaintiff will be entitled to full costs, however small the damages.

It is enacted, by 43 Eliz. and 22 and 23 Car. 2. c. 9. that where the jury, who try an action for trespass, give less damages than 40s. the plaintiff shall be allowed 40s. damages only, unless (8 and 9 Will. and Mary, c. 11.) it shall appear that the trespass was wilful and malicious, and is so certified to be by the judge; in which case the plaintiff shall recover full costs.

However, 4 and 5 Will. and Mary, c. 23. s. 10, enacts, that every inferior tradesman, apprentice, or other dissolute person, may be sued for going upon another man's ground to hunt, &c. though he do no injury; and if found guilty, shall pay full costs of suit. The reason for which, is to discourage the temptation which might otherwise be afforded them of neglecting their proper business in pursuit of sport, to the injury of themselves and families.

Who are " *Inferior Tradesmen*," has not been legally defined. Upon the prosecution of a huntsman for being out with his master's hounds, it was decided that the huntsman did not come within the meaning of the statute as an " inferior tradesman" or " dissolute person." In the case *Buxton* v. *Mingay*, the question was, whether the defendant, a surgeon and apothecary, not qualified to kill game, came within the description of an inferior tradesman. For the plaintiff it was said, that amongst tradesmen no line can be drawn with respect to who are superior and who are inferior; but that the distinction which the legislature intended, was between those who were qualified and those that were not; so that in this respect every tradesman is inferior who is not qualified. For the defendant, it was urged, that every case of this kind ought to be determined on its particular circumstances and left to the jury, whether the defendant is an inferior tradesman or dissolute person within the statute. The court being equally divided, no rule was made.

A lord of a manor, unless he have a right of free-warren, (which is very seldom the case) is as liable as any other man to the penalties just enumerated; or, in other words, he cannot sport upon the lands of another, even in his own manor, without permission from the owner or occupier of the land: a tenant can notice his landlord off the estate which he occupies, unless a a clause in the lease (which is generally the case) gives the landlord the privilege to sport. If a manor is to be strictly preserved, every occupier of land throughout such manor should sign a paper drawn up in the following manner:

SIR,

I do hereby give you notice, and require you not to enter, or cause or procure to be entered, any of my closes, lands, or premises, situate and being in the parish of ——, or elsewhere, in the county of ——, with horses, dogs, or otherwise, in order to beat for, follow, or pursue, any game, or for any other purpose whatsoever; and in case you do not as yet know the local situation of such, my said closes, lands, and premises, I hereby give you notice, that the same will be pointed out and shewn to you, upon reasonable application at my dwelling-house, situate at ——. And I do hereby further give you notice, that in case, after you being served with this notice, you shall commit any trespass upon any part of my said closes, lands, or premises, you will not only be proceeded against as a wilful and malicious trespasser, pursuant to the statutes in that case made and provided, but will also be otherwise prosecuted for such offence according to law.* Dated this —— day of ——, in the year of our Lord ——.

SYLVESTER SOREHEAD.

To Mr. Peter Popemoff.

The oral notice of either gamekeeper or lord of a manor is insufficient; but is deemed legal from the occupier of the land where the sportsman happens to be found. In all other cases, a written notice, similar to the above sketch, and signed by all the occupiers of the land in the manor, must be given to the trespasser.—A gamekeeper cannot demand the name of a sportsman, or a sight of his certificate, without first producing his own deputation and certificate; a gentleman must first produce his own certificate, before he is authorised to see the certificate of another person. In default of certificate, the name and address must be given; and any fictitious name adopted, or evasion resorted to, subjects the party to a penalty of 20l.

* The notice may in general be in the above form, but where there will be no difficulty in so doing, it may be advisable either to point out the names or abuttals of the closes in the notice, or to annex a sketch of them. It was held, in the case of Sellon v. the huntsman of the Berkeley hunt, sittings at Westminster, K. B. after Trinity term, 1816, that a general printed notice stuck up, purporting to be a notice that "the Stanmore Association" would prosecute all persons trespassing, but not signed by the plaintiff, nor addressed to the defendant, is not a legal notice not to trespass. In order to establish the notice in evidence, it is not necessary to give notice to produce the original notice, but it suffices to produce a duplicate made at the time; by Chambre, Justice, in the year 1802. 2 Bla. Comm. Christian's edition, 147, with notes, 3 Bla. Comm. 215, note b, 2 Campb. Rep. 110.

It is supposed by some, that a person may continue to sport on the same manor all day, though he has been warned off in the morning. This cannot be the case—he may go through the manor to some road, but should he persevere in continuing his diversion for any unnecessary length of time, he becomes a *wilful* trespasser.

At the summer Hertford assizes, 1809, the Earl of Essex, *v.* the Hon. and Rev. Wm. Capel. The plaintiff declared in trespass, for breaking and entering certain closes of the plaintiff, and that with hounds, dogs, and horses, he hunted, sported, and went in, along, and over, the said closes, and trod down and destroyed, the grass and herbage of the plaintiff. The defendant pleaded several pleas. 1st. the general issue, which he afterwards withdrew. 2d. that as to breaking and entering the close, called Cashiobury Park, the defendant, with divers other persons, who, as well as the defendant, were qualified to keep hounds, had found a fox in a certain place, called Bricket Wood, not being the close of the plaintiff, and that a fox being a noxious animal, he hunted it with his dogs, hounds, and horses, and that the hunting the fox with dogs, hounds, and horses, was the only way of killing the fox. In the 3d plea, it was stated, that such pursuit of the fox, with dogs, hounds, and horses, was the most effectual and proper way of killing the fox. To these pleas the plaintiff replied, that hunting the fox, was not the only, or the most effectual way of killing and destroying it; and further stated, that the trespasses were committed, for the sport and diversion of the chase, and for the purpose of amusement and pleasure only. To these replications, the defendant rejoined, that the trespasses were not committed for diversion and amusement, but as the only and most effectual and proper way of killing and destroying the fox.—Shepherd, Serjeant, for the plaintiff, contended, that the only question was, whether it was the defendant's object, to rid the country of noxious vermin, or whether he hunted for the sake of amusement? If it was merely for amusement, the law does not sanction it. Even in the enjoyment of a man's own property, the maxim of law is, that every man must so use his own, as not to injure his neighbours; if that is the law, with respect to the enjoyment of property, then, unquestionably, as to the enjoyment of an amusement, the principle is doubly applicable, and no one can say, that under the pretence of destroying a noxious animal, it is lawful to trespass over every species of property a fox may go through. I should extremely doubt, whether, after starting a fox on one piece of land, persons have a right to follow it on the lands of another, even if they do it, for the destruction of the animal. In Fentham r. Gundry, the judgment of the court proceeded upon the plaintiff's admitting, that the way taken by the defendant was the only one to destroy the vermin, and therefore the action could not be supported.

Lord Ellenborough said, " the defendant states in his plea, that the trespass was not committed, for the purpose of the diversion and amusement of the chase merely, but as the only way and means of killing and destroying the fox. Now, if you was to put it upon this question, which was the principal motive? Can any man of common sense, hesitate in saying, that the principal motive and inducement, was not the killing of vermin, but the enjoyment of the sport and diversion of the chase? and we cannot make a new law, to suit the pleasures and amusements of those gentlemen, who choose to hunt for their diversion. These pleasures are to be taken only, when there is the consent of those who are likely to be injured by them; but they must be necessarily subservient to the consent of others. There may be such a public nuisance by a noxious animal, as may justify the running him to his earth, but then you cannot justify the digging for him afterwards, that has been ascertained and settled to be law; but even if an animal may be pursued with dogs, it does

not follow, that fifty or sixty people have, therefore, a right to
follow the dogs, and trespass on other people's lands. I cannot
see what it is, that is contended for by the defendant. The
only case which will at all bear him out, is that of Fentham *v.*
Gundry; if it be necessary, I should be glad that that case should
be fully considered. I have looked into the case in the year
book. 12 Hen. 8. pl. 9. That seems to be nothing more than
the case of a person, who had chased a stag from the forest into
his own land, where he killed it, and on an action of trespass
being brought against the forester, who came and took the stag,
he justified, that he had made fresh suit after the stag, and it
was held, that he might state that he was justified, and the plaintiff took nothing by his writ. This is the case upon which that
of Fentham *v.* Gundry is built, but it is founded only on an *obiter
dictum* of Justice Brooke, and it does not appear to me to be
much relied on; but even in that case, it is emphatically said by
the judge, that a man may not hunt for his pleasure or his profit,
but only for the good of the common weal, and to destroy such
noxious animals as are injurious to the common weal. Therefore, according to this case, the good of the public must be the
governing motive." The Jury, under his Lordship's direction,
found a verdict for the plaintiff.

A word or two on the *legal property* which qualified persons
have in the game of which they are in pursuit may not be altogether uninteresting; indeed, they are indispensably necessary.
In general, it continues so long *only* as the game remains *within*
the limits of the manor or liberty of the owner; yet it is held, that
if after having been started upon a person's own grounds, it be
pursued and killed on those of another, it will nevertheless be the
property of him who started it, because the possession which he
gained by finding it within his *own liberty* is *continued* by the
immediate pursuit. 11 *Mod. Rep.* 75. But if it is started on
another man's ground, and killed there, it will belong to him on

whose ground it was killed, this property arising *ratione soli*. *Lord Raym*. 251.

Moreover, if, having been started on another person's ground, it be killed on that of a *third person*, it will belong neither to him on whose ground it was started, nor to him on whose ground it was killed, but to the person who killed it, though he be guilty of a trespass on the grounds of both the other persons.

But if a stranger starts game in the *chase or free warren* of another man, and hunts it into the liberty of another, the property will continue in the owner of the chase or warren, and the keeper may pursue and retake it; for whilst the keeper pursues it, it does not in law pass into a new liberty.

On the 12th of May, 1782, the following question of law was determined in the Court of Common Pleas, viz. one gentleman brought an action against another, for trespassing upon the waste of his manor, by remaining there after notice to quit. Upon the trial it was insisted that the waste was not that kind of property, as to be so strictly sacred from a trespass as a manor; but it was over-ruled by the court.

At the summer assizes held at Bury, 1804, two causes were decided before Mr. Justice Heath and Special Juries, in which Lord Rous was plaintiff, and Sir Henry Smyth, Bart. and William Gill, Esq. two gentlemen of considerable property in Essex, were defendants, for a trespass upon the land of his lordship, after the parties had received from him a written refusal to a note requesting permission to shoot, and after a verbal notice had been given them by his lordship's gamekeeper to leave the premises. The Judge, after animadverting upon the improper conduct of these gentlemen, informed the Jury that he should certify upon the record that the trespasses were wilful and malicious, which would entitle the plaintiff to his costs, in consequence of which the Juries gave nominal damages only. This decision will correct a very mistaken notion, that no trespass can be deemed wilful or malicious, unless a formal written notice be previously delivered; and proves, that the mere entering another person's land, without consent, constitutes a trespass, and will entitle the plaintiff to a verdict, although no damage be actually sustained.

A qualified person cannot justify committing trespasses in the lands of any other person without his consent, whether such person be or be not lord of a manor. If he commit a trespass upon land in possession of any other person, he is liable to an action of trespass, let the damage be ever so small, which I suppose is the reason of giving notice, in order to entitle the plaintiff to full costs; but this notice will not entitle any person thereto, but he who gives the notice, though plaintiff be tenant to the person who gives it, and no person but the occupier of the lands can maintain action of trespass; and he may maintain trespass against any person entering thereon, and if notice hath been given to keep off, the person coming on afterwards will be a wilful trespasser *; and his looking for game will be no defence, though I should think that pursuing it (as hares by hounds after starting) would be defence, but even this is much doubted.

CASE.—The plaintiff in an action of trespass was lord of the manor, defendant had freehold property in the same manor, and was entitled to common of pasture and turbary; he had received notice not to treepass on the moors belonging to the manor, for the purpose of hunting, shooting, &c.; the question was, whether, after the above notice, defendant could lawfully enter and kill game upon the commons and waste lands within the manor?

* If it appears on the trial that the trespass, however small, was committed after notice, and the Jury gives less than forty shillings damages, the judge is bound under the stat. 8 and 9 Will, 3. c. 11. s. 14. to certify, that the trespass was wilful and malicious, in order to entitle the plaintiff to his full costs. 6 *Term Rep.* 11.

OPINION.—The circumstances of the defendant having a right of pasture and turbary, and a right of getting stones and slates on the moors, commons, and wastes within Caton, in respect of his estates, these will not justify his entrance upon those moors to kill game. If he has a right to enter to kill game there, it will be by virtue of a prescription for that purpose, or of a grant from the owner of the manor, or reputed manor, so to do ; and such a prescription may be established by strong evidence of an uninterrupted course of usage, or of a usage in despite of prohibitions to the contrary, or exercised, under circumstances shewing it to have been used as a claim of right, and not allowed or connived at as a courtesy or indulgence. The fact of the other freeholders of Caton (the manor) having been in the same habit of sporting within the manor, and of doing so not only on the commons, but on the enclosed lands also, is unfavourable I think to the defendant's establishing what he has done as a right in himself to sport upon the manor; and I think in all probability the result of what has been done by the freeholders of Caton, and by the defendant amongst the rest, will, on investigation, be deemed to have been founded on courtesy, and indulgence, and connivance, and not on right. If, however, the defendant can shew such a strong uninterrupted or adverse course of sporting on the waste lands of the manor, as will induce a Jury to believe it founded on a privilege annexed to his estate in Caton, he cannot give that enjoyment in evidence in support of such a right under the general issue, but must plead it specially, as a prescriptive right appurtenant to his estate, which is the only mode by which he can have an opportunity of trying that question.—G. S. H. Gray's Inn, 11th February, 1800.

QUALIFICATION.

The first time we meet with any defined qualification, is in the time of Richard II. when 40s. per annum was deemed sufficient. Prior to the time of Richard II. it would seem, that every man was entitled to kill game upon his own land; and those who possessed the right of freewarren could legally kill game upon any land within their franchise, though it might belong to another person. But by the 13th of Richard II. c. 13, no *layman* who hath not lands or tenements of 40s. per annum, or *clergyman* not being advanced to £10 a year, shall keep any greyhound or hunting dog, nor use any instruments whatever for taking or destroying *gentlemen's* game, on pain of one year's imprisonment.

The 1st of James I. c. 27, rendered it indispensable for a person to possess an estate of £10 per annum, or goods to the value of £200, in order to acquire a qualification; unless he were the son of a lord or a knight, or the heir apparent of an esquire. In a few years afterwards, the qualification sum was raised to £40 a year, by the 7th of James I. c. 11.

The most important, however, of the statutes on this head, and which alone, in fact, deserves the attention of the sportsman; is the 22nd and 23rd Charles II. c. 25. This is the most modern, is uniformly acted upon at the present day, and has consequently rendered the preceding enactments a dead letter. By this, every person not having lands or tenements, or some other estate of inheritance in his own or his wife's right, (a) of the clear (b)

(a) This is not to be understood of a tenant by curtesy, but of one whose wife is living.—Vide Co. Lit. 351.

(b) On this word it has been held, that the estate must be clear of yearly value of £100; or for a term of life, or having lease or leases of 99 years, or for any longer term, of the yearly value of £150, other than the son and heir apparent of an esquire, or other persons of higher degree (c) and the owners and keepers of forests, parks, chases, or warrens, being stocked with deer or conies for their necessary use in respect to the said forests, parks, chases, or warrens, are declared to be persons, by the law of this realm, not allowed to have or keep for themselves, or any other person, (d) guns, bows, greyhounds, setting dogs, ferrets, coney dogs, lurchers, hays, nets, low bells, hare pipes, gins, snares, or other engines for the taking and killing of conies, hares, pheasants, partridges, or other game, but shall be prohibited to have, keep, or use the same

The 5 Anne, c. 14. s. 4. may be regarded as a prop or strengthener to the preceding; by this statute it is enacted, if any person not qualified as before stated, shall keep or use (e)

all mortages or incumbrances created by the owner, or by those under whom he claims.—Caldecot's Cases, 230.   But an equitable estate of that value is sufficient.—Ibid.

(c) Esquires are—1. The younger sons of noblemen and their heirs male for ever. 2. The four esquires of the king's body. 3. The eldest sons of baronets, or knights of the Bath, and knights bachelors, and their heirs male in the right line.   A justice of the peace is also an esquire for the time he holds his commission, but no longer.—Blount.   Persons of higher degree than esquires are colonels, serjeants at law, and doctors in the three learned professions; but neither esquires, nor any of these, are qualified, unless they have the requisite estate mentioned in the preceding part of the act; though their sons are qualified without any estate whatever.—1 Term Reports, 44.

(d) An unqualified person, therefore, cannot keep the dogs of a qualified person.

(e) These words being in the disjunctive, the bare keeping of one of these dogs is an offence, 1 Stra. 496; as to the using, it has been determined, that walking about with an intent to kill game, is a using, within this statute.

any greyhounds, setting-dogs, hays, lurchers, tunnels, or any other engines, (f) to kill and destroy the game, and shall be thereof convicted upon the oath of one witness, by the justice of peace where such offence is committed, he shall forfeit the sum of £5, one half to go to the informer, and the other half to the poor of the parish, to be levied by distress, (g) under the warrant of a justice, and for want of (h) distress, the offender shall be sent to the house of correction for three months, for the first offence; and for every after offence, four months; and any justice of the peace, or lord or lady of manors, are allowed to take away hare or other game, and likewise any dogs, nets, or any other engines which shall be in the custody of any persons not qualified to keep the same, to their own use.

And by 22 and 23 Car. 2. cap. 25. section 2, it is provided, that gamekeepers, or any other persons, by warrant of a justice of the peace, may, in the day time, search the houses, or other places of any such persons prohibited by this act to keep or use any dogs, nets, or other engines aforesaid, and the same seize and keep for the use of the lord of the manor; or otherwise to cut in pieces or destroy the things so prohibited.

By 4 and 5 W. and M. c. 23. it is enacted, that if any inferior tradesman, (i) apprentice, or other dissolute person, shall

---

(f) It has been held, that a gun is not such an engine, the bare keeping of which is penal; it must moreover be shewn to be used for the destruction of game. 2 Stra. 1098. It is also observable, that though using a gun and a dog are both separately penal, yet, per Lord Kenyon, Ch. Justice, if a person go out with a gun and a dog the same day, he is subject to but one penalty. 7 Term Rep. 152.

(g) Goods destrained for penalties under the game laws are not repleviable.

(h) The justice cannot commit, if the offender have effects sufficient to answer the penalty.

(i) It hath been adjudged, that if any person be an inferior tradesman, within the meaning of this act, it makes no difference as to his qualification by estate. 1 Lord Raym. 142.

hunt, hawk, fish, or fowl, (unless in company with the master of such apprentice duly qualified) such persons may be sued for wilful trespass, on coming on any person's ground, and if found guilty shall pay full costs.

At Winchester assizes, three years ago, a cause was tried under the game laws, in which Mr. Ward, a gentleman of considerable property in the Isle of Wight, and lord of the manor of Northwood, was plaintiff, and Mr. Hart, a gentleman residing at Cowes, defendant. The question was, whether the defendant, who was possessed of landed property above 100*l.* per annum, but not assessed under the property tax acts to that amount, was qualified to kill game. The judge, Mr. Baron Graham, summed up the evidence in the most impartial manner, and the jury found their verdict for the defendant.

Hooker *v.* Wilks. This was an action of debt, on 8 Geo. I. c. 19. for the penalty of £30, for using a hound to destroy the game; and, after a verdict for the plaintiff, the judgment was arrested; for 5 Ann. c. 14. has not the word hound, and the words other engines, come after nets, &c. and are applicable only to inanimate things. And this being a penal law, cannot be extended. The statute 22 and 23 Car. II. c. 25. has indeed the general words, or any other dogs to destroy game; but this is not a conviction on that statute*. 2 Stra. 1126.

King *v.* Filer. Conviction on 5 Ann. for keeping a lurcher

---

* But, although this statute has those general words, it is impossible to convict any offender under it in any penalty, because none is thereby given. The act does not declare that no person shall keep or use any greyhound, &c. or any other dogs to destroy game; but the general words are found in the enacting clause, which gives authority to lords of manors to appoint gamekeepers to search the house of any person suspected to have any greyhounds, setting-dogs, ferrets, coney-dogs, or other dogs to destroy hares or conies. No penalty can therefore be recovered under 5 Ann. against those who keep any dog not mentioned in that statute.

to destroy game, not being qualified. Mr. Eyre excepted, that it was not shewn he made use of the dog to destroy game; and it may be only kept for a gentleman who was qualified, it being common to put dogs out in that manner.—By the court, the statute is in the disjunctive, keep or use; so that the bare keeping a lurcher is an offence; and so it was determined in the case of King *v.* King, which was a conviction for keeping a gun; and it was not doubted by the court, whether the keeping was not enough to be shown; but the only question they made was, whether a gun was such an engine as is within the statute; and in that case a difference was taken as to keeping a dog, which could only be to destroy game, and the keeping a gun, which a man might do for the defence of his house.—The conviction was confirmed.

This decision was further confimed by the case of the King *v.* Hartley, E. 22 Geo. III. in which Lord Mansfield said— In this act there are two offences described, a keeping and a using; and the legislature means that there may be a keeping to destroy, which is not of necessity to be proved by a using for that purpose. If it were so, it would be tautologous; for such evidence would be a proving of the offence. The keeping therefore of a thing prohibited being an offence under the act, it is necessarily *prima facie* evidence of a keeping for the purpose prohibited; and it is incumbent on the defendant to shew that it was kept for another purpose; as, in the present case, that it is a house-dog, a favourite dog, or a particular species of greyhound.—Caldecott's cases, 175.

Respecting the form of the conviction, it has been holden, that if it be only alleged that the defendant had not, at the time of the commission of the offence, any lands or tenements, or any other estate of inheritance of the clear yearly value of 100*l.* or for term of life, &c. nor was in any other manner qualified, empowered, licensed, or authorised by the laws of this realm, either to take, kill, or destroy any sort of game whatsoever, without expressly negativing that the defendant had an estate of inheritance of the clear yearly value of 100*l. in right of his wife*, the proceedings will be defective. All the qualifications mentioned in 22 and 23 Car. 2. c. 25. s. 3. must receive an express and specific negative.

It has been shewn, that a diploma to give a right to sport in England must be conferred either by the university of Oxford or Cambridge. With respect to the evidence which must be given to prove this qualification, we find Lord Kenyon stating an instance within his own recollection where it was relied on, which seems of considerable importance. In that case, the books from the university which contained the act of the corporation conferring the degree were produced in evidence, and holden to be sufficient for the purpose, as being the best kind of proof which the nature of the case afforded. On the other hand it has been holden, that the mere production of a diploma, sealed with a seal purporting to be the seal of a university, and proved only by a witness to the acknowledgments of the parties, where names were affixed to it, of its authenticity, is not sufficient evidence to authenticate the instrument, so as to shew that a degree has been actually conferred. At least, an examined copy from the university books should be given in evidence. And though it is not necessary to prove the seal of a corporation in the same manner as that of an individual, by producing the witness who saw it affixed, it must be shewn to be the instrument used by the corporate body whose authority it professes to bear, because otherwise any instrument with a seal to it might be produced as the seal of a corporation.

Notwithstanding the 44 Geo. 3. c. 54. s. 26. enacts, that all officers in corps of volunteers, having commissions from lieutenants of counties, shall rank with the officers of his majesty's regular forces, it has been holden, that the statute merely intends

military rank ; and, therefore, a commission of captain of volunteers, signed by the lord lieutenant of a county, does not confer
the degree of esquire, so as to give to the son of the party, thus
commissioned, a qualification to pursue game.

Kent Assizes. Maidstone, Wednesday, March 16, 1814.—
Kingsnorth v. *Breton and another.*

The Common Serjeant stated, that this was an action against
the Rev. Dr. Breton, a magistrate, and Mr. Jemmett, a solicitor
of great practice in the county, for causing the plaintiff's dog to
be killed. The facts of the case were, that the plaintiff was
summoned by Mr. Toke, a magistrate, to attend to answer a
charge for keeping a lurcher. He attended accordingly, when
the defendant, Dr. Breton, Mr. Toke, Mr. Brett, and two other
magistrates were present, Mr. Jemmett acting as their clerk.
Some investigation took place, at the end of which Dr. Breton
told the plaintiff that he was convicted in the sum of 5*l.* and that
the dog was forfeited, and should be destroyed. A constable
of the name of Norley was then called, and desired to destroy
the dog ; but he hesitating, Mr. Jemmett repeated the order,
and said he would pay him for so doing. Norley then took the
dog out into the town of Ashford, where the magistrates were
sitting at the Saracen's Head Inn, and he was shot in the market
place. The plaintiff borrowed of a friend on the spot the sum
of 5*l.* to pay the fine.

Mr. Serjeant Best contended, that all this proceeding was
warranted under the statute of Queen Anne, in which the Lord
Chief Baron concurring, the plaintiff was nonsuited.

ADJUDGED CASES.

It has been determined that the clause in the stat. 22 and 23 Car. 2. c. 25. relative to qualification by freehold estate, terminates with the words per annum; and that a life estate, being of an inferior quality, ought to be coupled with leasehold, whereof one hundred and fifty pounds a year is necessary to constitute a qualification. A clergyman's benefice is a life estate. Lowndes *v.* Lewis. Caldecott's Cases, 188.

A person having an estate of one hundred and three pounds a year, mortgaged a part of it to the value of fourteen pounds a year, which being copyhold, was surrendered to the mortgagee, who was thereupon admitted tenant, but never entered on the premises, the mortgager continuing in possession and paying interest. It was held that the mortgager, under these circumstances, was not a qualified person. Wetherall *v.* Hall. Caldecott's Cases, 230.

In the case of Jones *v.* Smart, after much argument it was decided, that a diploma conferring the degree of doctor of physic, granted by either of the universities in Scotland, does not give a qualification to kill game under stat. 22 and 23 Car. 2. c. 25. and that an esquire, or other person of higher degree as such, is not qualified under that act, though the son of an esquire, or the son of other person of higher degree, is qualified. 1 Term Rep. 44.

It is remarkable, that on this construction a son who holds a qualification in the right of his father, may be deprived of it by succeeding to his father in the estate, if under the required value; and the son, during his father's life, may for the same reason be qualified in right of an unqualified father. Lofft's Gild. Evid. 1125.

A doctor of physic of the English universities is not qualified as such. 1 Term Rep. 44.

The King *v.* Utley. This was an information before a justice of the peace, and a conviction of the defendant thereon, because he was neither qualified by property, under 22 and 23 Car. 2. nor the eldest son of an esquire, or of other person of higher degree, nor within the exemptions of the act. Counsel moved to quash the information for the insertion of the word *of*. He said, the precedent in Burn, from which this conviction was copied, was faulty and not warranted by law, for the construction put on the words of the statute by inserting the word *of*, would prevent an esquire, or a knight, or the person superior to an esquire, from being qualified by degree. Buller, J. said, it appeared to him, that the legislature had taken it for granted, that an esquire, or other person of higher degree, would of course have sufficient estate to qualify him. Conviction confirmed. 1 T. R. 45.

The lord of a manor, who is worth one hundred and twenty pounds a year, the demesnes of which are granted to another for life, is not thereby qualified to kill game, within the 22 and 23 Car. 2. c. 25.; for the words having an estate, &c. signify an estate in possession. Mallock *v.* Eastley. 7. Mod. 482. per Abney, justice. This very point was expressly determined in the king's bench upon a very great debate some years ago, where a young gentleman in Essex, who had ninety pounds a year in possession, and one hundred and fifty pounds in reversion, expectant on the death of his mother, was yet held not to be qualified. Ib.

An estate of the value of one hundred and fifty pounds per annum, holden by the defendant in his own right, under a lease for ninety-nine years, to trustees, if the defendant and others should so long live, is a sufficient qualification to kill game under the stat. 22 and 23 Car. 2. c. 25. s. 3. Earl Ferrers *v.* Henton. 8 Term Rep. 506.

Booth *v.* Pinnock, Esquire. This was an action on the game laws, brought against Mr. Pinnock, under the direction of the Right Hon. Lord Berkeley. The defendant had shot a hare on his lordship's grounds, which was proved. But inasmuch as the defendant was a gentleman of fortune, Lord Kenyon thought they ought to go further, and shew he was not qualified.

Mr. Erskine, for the defendant, said, he was instructed to state, that the defendant was summoned to appear before a magistrate; that the noble lord was personally present; that upon that occasion, Mr. Pinnock produced a settlement that was made on his wife, who was within six weeks of being of age, by which it appeared that she was tenant for life, without impeachment of waste, of an estate of upwards of one thousand pounds a year. When that marriage settlement was produced, the magistrate asked Lord Berkeley if he would wait. "No," said his lordship, "go on, and convict." And after the defendant was convicted of the penalty, the plaintiff brought this action.

Lord Kenyon, after being made acquainted with the contents of the marriage settlement, was clearly of opinion that the defendant was qualified.

With respect to a received notion among many of the citizens of London, that they have a right to hunt, hawk, and shoot in Middlesex, &c.* arising from their charter, it must be observed,

---

* Fitzstephen says, they have liberty of hunting in Middlesex, Hertfordshire, all Chilton, and in Kent, to the Waters of Grey.—Stephanides Disc. London. This account differs from the clause in the royal charter granted to them by Henry I. which runs thus:—"The citizens of London may have chases and hunt as well and as fully as their ancestors have had; that is to say, in the Chiltre, in Middlesex, and Surry." These Exercises were not much followed by the citizens of London at the close of the sixteenth century, not for want of taste for the amusement, says Stowe, but for leisure to pursue it. Strype, however, so late

that in about seven years after King Charles the II. had confirmed to the citizens all their liberties and privileges, the qualification act was made, enacting " that all and every person not having, &c. are declared to be unqualified persons." And that in the said act there is no reservation or exception in favour of the citizens of London. But, there was a statute made, 2 W. and M. c. 8. to reverse a judgment given in the court of king's bench against the mayor, aldermen, &c. of London ; and by that statute all the privileges which had been forfeited were re-granted and confirmed.

Dog Cause.—In the court of king's bench, at Westminster, Jan. 10, 1822, an appeal against the decision of an Essex jury (under direction from the judge to that effect) was heard, and the verdict obtained at the assizes against defendant, for keeping a setter dog, was now set aside. At the trial the presumption was that the mere possession of a dog used in destroying game was proof enough of its being so used ; but Mr. Justice Best suggested that a man might be a breeder of such dogs without using them as game-dogs. And Mr. Justice Bailey thought, if a pointer were kept in a yard chained up by day, and let loose at night, being so trained as to guard the premises, he was to be considered as a yard-dog and not a game dog. The name of the cause is " Haywood v. Horner."

as the reign of George I. reckons among the modern diversions of the Londoners, "Riding on horseback and hunting with my Lord Mayor's hounds, when the common-hunt goes out."

CERTIFICATE.

The first act relative to game certificates was passed in 25th of Geo. III. This statute (c. 50. s. 8.) levies a penalty of twenty pounds upon persons pursuing or taking game without a certificate; and states further, that the certificate hereby directed to be taken out shall not authorize any person to pursue or take game, unless duly qualified by estate or otherwise. Also, the party thus offending to be liable to the same penalties as are inflicted by former acts now in force.

The list of game includes the following: *heron, pheasant, partridge, heath-cock, moor-game, mallard, duck, wigeon, teal, woodcock, snipe, quail, and landrail; as also hares and rabbits.* This act was passed in the 48th of Geo. III. and inflicts the before-mentioned penalties for the pursuit or destruction of any of the animals just mentioned, by persons not duly authorised.

There is an exception, however, in respect to woodcocks and snipes taken in nets or springes; as also in regard to conies taken in warrens or inclosed grounds, by the proprietors of such places; or by any persons in lands in his or her occupation, either by himself or herself, or by his or her direction or command.

By this act also, a different method of issuing certificates was ordered to be adopted. Instead of applying to the clerk of the county, the sportsman must pay three pounds fourteen shillings and sixpence into the hands of the collector of the duties for the parish, ward, or place where he resides; the collector gives a receipt for the money, and on carrying this receipt to the clerk of commissioners, acting for the district, a certificate will be given in exchange for the collector's receipt, without any further fee.

This act likewise (s. 7.) provides that, should a gamekeeper quit his master or mistress before the expiration of the season for which his certificate has been obtained, the same certificate will be sufficient for the successor of such gamekeeper, provided the name of such newly appointed person is indorsed upon it, which the clerk to the commissioners is to do, upon application for that purpose, free of expense. Also, land-holders, legally authorised to appoint gamekeepers, may grant deputations to the servants of other persons for that purpose, whose certificates may be renewed in the same way.

Further, by this act, s. 10. the sportsman, when using dog, gun, &c. must produce his certificate, if demanded, to the assessor, collector, commissioner, or gamekeeper, inspector, or surveyor, or other person assessed as aforesaid ; or the owner, landlord, lessee, or occupier of the land upon which he may be found sporting ; and must allow the persons so demanding the same, not only to read, but to take a copy of, his certificate, if they think proper. But in case the sportsman has not his certificate about him, he must declare to the person demanding, his christian and surname, and place of abode ; as also the parish or place where the certificate has been issued. A refusal or evasion, by fictitious name or otherwise, subjects the offending party to the penalty of twenty pounds.

By this act too (s. 12.) a person sporting without a certificate, is liable to pay the duty for the year, and forfeit the sum of twenty pounds over and above, which is to be assessed by way of surcharge, in the district where the offence shall be committed. And finally, (s. 11) the commissioners are to cause the names and residences of the persons taking out certificates to be published annually in the newspapers circulated in each county.

N. B. The royal family are exempt from the provisions of this act.

Laws

TO PREVENT THE DESTRUCTION OF WINGED GAME, &C.
AT IMPROPER SEASONS OF THE YEAR, CHRISTMAS
DAY, SUNDAY, &C.

It is provided by 9 Anne, c. 25, s. 4. that if any person shall, with hays, tunnels, or other nets, destroy, in the *moulting season* (that is, between the 1st of June and the 1st of October) any wild duck, teal, wigeon, or other water fowl; such persons shall forfeit five shillings, and the nets, &c. used in taking such fowl to be destroyed.

The proper season for shooting grouse (called *red game*) is from the 12th of August to the 10th of December; that for heath fowls (commonly called *black game*) begins on the 20th of August, and ends on the 10th of December; for bustards the season commences on the 1st of September, and ends on the 1st of March. The penalty for destroying any of these birds (by the 13th of Geo. III. c. 55. s. 2.) buying, or selling, or carrying, or even having in possession, at any other season of the year, is any sum not exceeding twenty, nor less than ten pounds, for the first offence; for every subsequent offence, a sum not exceeding thirty pounds, nor less than twenty. One half the penalty to be paid to the informer, and the other to the poor of the parish; to be levied by distress, if not immediately paid: and in case no distress is to be had, the offender to be committed to the house of correction, and kept to hard labour for any period nor exceeding six months, nor less than three. However, by the 43d of Geo. III. c. 112. the season for *black game* in the

New Forest, Hampshire, does not begin till the 1st of September.

Also (by 4 and 5 Will. and Mary, c. 22. s. 11.) no person is allowed, between the 2nd of February and the 24th of June, to burn any gaig, ling, heath, furze, goss, or fern, on any mountains, heaths, or other places where moor game and heath fowls breed, upon pain of being committed to the house of correction for any time not exceeding one month, nor less than ten days.

The season for shooting *partridges* begins on the 1st of September, and ends on the 1st of February ; that for *pheasants* commences on the 1st of October, and ends at the same time as partridge shooting : the penalty attached to the taking, destroying, carrying, or having in possession, at any other period of the year, any of these birds, is five pounds for every pheasant or partridge ; unless, however, such pheasant or partridge was taken at the proper season of the year, and kept in a mew or breeding place. The whole of this penalty to be paid to the informer with full costs of suit.

As to woodcocks, snipes, quails, landrails, and rabbits, there is no specified time for their destruction, though snipes as well as quails breed in this country. In fact, it does not appear, that either woodcocks, snipes, or rabbits, are that species of game, the bare possession of which, in an unqualified person, is penal, unless it can be proved that the two first were *shot,* and the last caught in a place other than a warren, &c.

By the 35th, therefore of Geo. III. c. 80. s. 1. it is provided, that if any person shall take or destroy any hare, pheasant, partridge, moor-game, or heath-game, between seven o'clock at night and six in the morning, from the 12th of October till the 12th of February ; and between nine o'clock at night and four in the morning, from the 12th of February to the 12th of October ; such person, upon conviction before a justice of the peace, upon the oath of one witness, shall forfeit a sum not exceeding twenty pounds, nor less than ten ; for every subsequent offence, a sum not exceeding thirty pounds, nor less than twenty —half to the informer, the other half to the poor. Also, should a person be found *using* a dog, net, &c. with an *intent* to destroy the game above-mentioned, at the specified prohibited times, he will be liable to the same penalties.

By s. 6. also of the same act, a person who shall take or destroy any of the last-mentioned animals on a Sunday, or on a Christmas day (in the day time) or *use* dog, &c. for that purpose, will be liable to the same penalties as are inflicted for destroying game in the night, and to be convicted in the same manner.

Thirty-nine and 40 of Geo. III. c. 56. enacts, that if two or more persons be found in a forest, park, wood, plantation, field, meadow, or other open or enclosed ground, between the hours of eight o'clock at night and six in the morning, from the 1st day of October to the 1st of February ; or between the hours of ten at night and four in the morning, from the 1st day of February to the 1st of October, having any gun, &c. for the purpose and intent to take or destroy, any hare, pheasant, partridge, moor or heath game ; or if any person shall be found with fire-arms, or other weapons aiding or assisting any such person as aforesaid ; it shall be lawful for the owner of the place where any such persons are found, or his servants, or in fact any person, to apprehend such offenders, and deliver them into the custody of a peace officer, by whom they are to be conveyed before a justice of the peace ; who is authorized to commit such offenders to the house of correction, there to suffer such punishments as are directed to be inflicted on rogues and vagabonds. Or in case such offenders make their escape, any justice, on the oath of one credible witness, may issue his warrant for their apprehension ; and such persons, upon being apprehended, may be committed, upon the oath of one credible witness, the same as though he had been taken on the spot.

Free warren is a franchise, erected for the preservation or custody (which the word signifies) of beasts and fowls of warren ;
which, being *feræ naturæ*, every one had a natural right to kill
as he could : but upon the introduction of the forest laws, at the
period of the Norman conquest, these animals being looked upon
as royal game and the sole property of our savage monarchs, this
franchise of free-warren was invented to protect them ; by giving
the grantee a sole and exclusive power of killing such game so
far as his warren extended, on condition of his preventing other
persons.   A man therefore that has the franchise of a warren, is
in reality no more than a royal gamekeeper ; but no man, not
even a lord of a manor, could by common law justify sporting on
another's soil, unless he had the liberty of free-warren.   This
franchise is almost fallen into disregard, since the new statutes
for preserving the game ; the name being now chiefly preserved
in grounds that are set apart for breeding hares and rabbits.
There are many instances of keen sportsmen in ancient times,
who have sold their estates, and reserved the free-warren, or right
of killing game, to themselves ; by which means it comes to pass
that a man and his heirs have sometimes free-warren over another's
ground.

A person having a grant of free warren possesses a sole and
exclusive right of taking and destroying game within its limits.
If a person have a free warren in another's lands, the owner of
such land cannot permit a qualified person to kill game thereon ;
the consent of the owner of such free warren must be obtained, or
the person taking or killing game will be a trespasser, and will
be punishable as such.

Lord Dacre *v.* Tebb.   Black. Rep. 1151.   Trespass for
hunting in a free warren.   On not guilty pleaded and tried by
a special jury, the defendant was found guilty of breaking and
entering plaintiff's free warren, and chasing and hunting one
hare ; damages six-pence ; not guilty as to the residue.   It was

moved for the plaintiff that he should have full costs, on the ground, that the stats. 22 and 33 Car. 2. (which restrict costs in trespass, where the damages are under forty shillings, unless the freehold or title to the land came in question,) did not extend to this action; in which there could be no question relating to the land, but merely to the free warren. For the defendant it was alleged that title to the land might be so involved with the title to the free warren, that both might come in question. —By the court In an action merely for breaking free warren, it is impossible that the title of the soil can ever come in question; for though both may concur in one person, yet the title to the free warren is always collateral to that of the land; for a man may have a free warren in another man's land. Besides, the hare so hunted was the personal property of the owner of the free warren; and if any injury be done to personal property, that will take it out of the statute, and intitle the plaintiff to full costs. And the rule was made absolute for taxing full costs.

At the summer assizes at Abingdon, 1802, a cause was tried, Westbrook, gent. of the parish of Bray, (situate in Windsor-forest,) was plaintiff, and a gamekeeper of his majesty's the defendant. The action was brought to try the right of the defendant, as one of the king's keepers, to kill game within the enclosed grounds of the plaintiff, situate in, and surrounded by, the wastes, commons, and within the boundaries of the said forest. When, without adverting to the laws relative to forests only, (with which the question was totally unconnected,) the court held it good, that the king, possessing a free warren over the whole, possessed likewise the privilege of appointing a keeper to kill game upon any and within every part of the said free warren, without the least exception as to enclosed lands the property of others. The jury instantly found for the defendant, by which the right is fully confirmed.

He who hath a free warren may bring trespass against any

but the owner of the soil for hunting there.   2 Ro. 111. 550. 2 Salk. 637.

A person may have a warren in another's land, for one may alien the land and reserve the franchise; but none can make a warren, and appropriate those creatures that are *feræ naturæ*, without license from the king, or where a warren is claimed by prescription.   8 Rep. 108. 11 Rep. 87.

No one can make a warren in his own land without the king's license, because he cannot appropriate to himself *feræ naturæ*, which are *nullius in bonis*.   11 Co. c. 87. 2 Inst. 199.

A warren may lie open, and there is no necessity of enclosing it, as there is of a park.   4 inst. 318.

But a man cannot prescribe for a warren in the lands of a stranger, which are not within his seignory.   2 Rol. 265. c. 52.

And if the king grants B. a warren within his manor, he shall have it only in the demesnes, not in the land of the freeholders.

————

BUYING AND SELLING GAME.

It is enacted by the 5th of Anne, c. 14. s. 2. that if any higler, chapman, carrier, innkeeper, victualler, or alehouse-keeper, shall have in his possession any hare, pheasant, partridge, moor or heath game (unless where such carrier is transporting such game for a qualified person) or shall buy, sell, or expose for sale, any such hare, &c. such offending person shall forfeit the sum of five pounds : and the oath of one witness shall be a sufficient conviction—half the penalty to the informer, and the other half to the poor of the parish : to be distressed for, if necessary ;

and in default thereof, the offender to be committed to the house of correction for three months; and for the second and every subsequent offence four months.

Also, s. 3. of the same act allows any person buying and selling game, to inform against any other peron so offending, and to be allowed the same benefit as any other informer; and himself discharged from the above-mentioned penalties.

By s. 4. the lord of the manor, or justice of the peace, may take to his own use any game which shall be found in the custody or possession of any unqualified person; unless protected by some qualified person.

If any person, whether qualified or unqualified, shall sell or expose for sale any hare, pheasant, partridge, moor or heath game; every such person shall be liable to the penalty of five pounds for every hare, &c. on the oath of one witness—half to the informer, and half to the poor of the parish where the offence was committed: to be levied by distress, if necessary; and for want thereof, the offender to be committed to the house of correction for three months for the first, and four months for every subsequent offence. Or, if any of the above-mentioned game be found in the house, shop, or possession of any poulterer, salesman, fishmonger, cook, or pastry-cook, the same shall be deemed an exposing thereof to sale.

The last statute upon this subject cuts both ways with a vengeance :—By 58 Geo. III. c. 75, the *buyer* (whether qualified or not) of any partridge or any other description of game, is liable to a penalty of five pounds for every head of game he may purchase; and may be convicted on the oath of the very person who sold him the game; who, for his information, will not only be borne harmless, but entitled, without further trouble, to half the penalty; and is at liberty, if he thinks proper, to sue for and recover the whole.—A greater temptation to roguery could not have been devised !

TRACING HARES IN THE SNOW, &c.

An old statute (14 and 15 Henry VIII. c. 10) inflicts a penalty of six shillings and eight-pence for tracing and killing a hare in the snow. The 1st of James 1. c. 27. inflicts three months' imprisonment on the offender for tracing or *coursing* a hare in the snow; unless the offending party pay to the church-wardens, for the use of the poor, twenty shillings for every hare; or within one month after commitment, become bound with two sureties, in twenty pounds each, not to offend again in like manner. Two witnesses are necessary in this case, as also two justices of the peace.

The same penalty, by the same act, is also inflicted for taking hares with hare-pipes, snares, or any other engines; two witnesses are necessary to convict the offender, before two justices.

Also, by the 22nd and 23d of Charles II. c. 25. if any person be found using or setting any snare or other engine for the purpose of taking hares, he shall make the injured party such recompence as the justice shall appoint, and pay down immediately, for the use of the poor, a sum not exceeding ten shillings; otherwise to be committed to the house of correction for a time not exceeding one month. In this case, the oath of one witness, before one justice, is sufficient; but it must be done within one month after the offence is committed.

APPOINTMENT OF A GAMEKEEPER, AND HIS AUTHORITY.

By the 22nd and 23rd of Charles II. c. 25. s. 2. lords of manors and other royalties, *not under the degree of an esquire,** may, by writing under their hands and seals, appoint gamekeepers within their manors and royalties, who then become authorized to seize all guns, greyhounds, setting dogs, or any other dogs for killing hares or rabbits; as well as snares, nets, &c. for the purpose of taking hares, partridges, or other game, which may be found within their respective manors, used by unqualified persons.—This act, however, does not authorize gamekeepers to kill game, but merely to preserve it.

The 5th of Anne, c. 14. s. 4. however, enables lords of manors to appoint a person to kill game. But, if he sell game, he is liable, on the oath of one witness, to be sent to the house of correction for three months, and kept to hard labour.

Twenty-five Geo. III. c. 5. s. 2. enacts that every deputation of a gamekeeper granted to any person in England or Wales, shall be registered with the clerk of the peace in the county where the manor lies, for which such person is appointed. A neglect of this, as also of taking out a certificate of such registry, incurs the penalty of twenty pounds. But gamekeepers to the royal family are exempt from the operations of this act.

The following is the form of a gamekeeper's deputation or appointment :—

" Know all men by these presents, that I, SIMON SULKY, of

---

* Willes, J. in the case of Jones, *v.* Smart, said, that a lord of a manor is not an esquire by virtue of his manor or royalty, though in common acceptation he may be considered as such.

————, in the county of Lancaster, esquire, lord of the manor of————, in the same county, have nominated, deputed, authorized, and appointed, and by these presents, do nominate, depute, authorize, and appoint, GEORGE GRABEM, of————, to be gamekeeper of and within my said manor of————, with full power, licence, and authority to pursue, take, and kill any hare, pheasant, partridge, or other game whatsoever, in and upon my said manor of————, for my sole and immediate use and benefit; and also to take and seize all such guns, bows, greyhounds, setting-dogs, lurchers, or other dogs, ferrets, trammels, low-bells, hays, or other nets, harepipes, snares, or other engines, for the pursuing, taking, or killing of hares, rabbits, pheasants, partridges, or other game, as shall be used within the precincts of my said manor, by any person or persons, who by law are prohibited to keep or use the same. In witness whereof, I have hereunto set my hand and seal this 24th day of July, 1819.

" SIMON SULKY."   (Seal)

" Sealed and delivered in the presence of
TIMOTHY TWIST, of———— aforesaid."

If a gamekeeper be qualified in his own right, he has no occasion to enter his deputation. But a gamekeeper is not authorized, by any statute, to seize game which he may find in the possession of poachers, even on his manor, though it is lawful for him to take their dogs, nets, or other implements. Also, gamekeepers, if found killing game off the manors for which they were appointed, are liable to the same penalties as unqualified persons. The only difference, in this case, between them is, that a gamekeeper's gun and dogs are not seizable; while those of an unqualified person may be taken.

Vere *v.* Lord Cawdor and King. M. 50. G. 3. In this, which was an action of trespass for shooting and killing a dog

of the plaintiff, there was a plea of not guilty, and special plea
that Cawdor was lord of the manor, and the defendant gamekeeper; that the dog was running after, chasing, and hunting
divers hares, for the preservation of which the gamekeeper shot
and killed the said dog.

To this plea there was a demurrer : and after argument, Lord
Ellenborough, J. C. said, the question is, whether the plaintiff's
dog incurred the penalty of death for running after a hare in
another's ground ? And if there be any precedent of that sort,
which outrages all reason and sense, it is of no authority to
govern other cases. There is no question here as to the right
of the game. The gamekeeper had no right to kill the plaintiff's dog for following it. The plea does not even state that
the hare was put in peril, so as to induce any necessity for killing
the dog in order to preserve the hare.—Judgment for the plaintiff. 11. E. R. 568.

By 48 Geo. III. c. 93. s. 2. lords of manors are enabled to
appoint and depute any person as gamekeeper whatever, whether acting in that capacity to any other person or not, or the
servant of any other person, qualified or unqualified, to kill game
within a specified manor for his own use, or for the use of any
other person or persons to be specified in such appointment or
deputation, whether qualified or not; nor need such person to
be entered or paid for as the male servant of the lord or lady
who gives the deputation.

Sect. 3. of this act gives the same authority as a regular
gamekeeper.

Thompson v. Christall.—The defendant, one of the Earl of
Sefton's gamekeeper's, who resides at Kirkby, near Liverpool,
having admitted to have had in his possession two game dogs
belonging to the plaintiff, which he, the defendant, afterwards
destroyed, or otherwise disposed of, the plaintiff brought this
action in the Court of King's Bench, and the defendant having

suffered judgment to go against him by default, the case came
before the Sheriff at Preston, upon a writ of inquiry, when the
jury, after a full investigation of the circumstances, gave the
plaintiff £20 damages, besides the costs.

If a gamekeeper shoot an unqualified person's dog, who thereupon shoots the gamekeeper's, and behaves insolently, the judge
will direct very considerable damage.   2 Atkyn's Rep. 190.

Although by stat. 22 and 23 Car. II. c. 25. s. 2. a gamekeeper (so authorised) may search for dogs and engines, and
seize the same for the use of the lord, or destroy them; yet it
hath been adjudged, that an authority from the lord of the manor
is not of itself sufficient for this purpose, but that he ought to
have a warrant from a justice of peace.   Comberbach 183.   Car-
penter v. Adams.   At least it may be safe to have such a warrant, especially if any houses are to be entered and searched;
for it would be to allow too great a stretch of power to gamekeepers, to permit them, in their vigilant discretion, to search
whatever houses or places they should think proper; as also to
constitute them judges, whether the person falling under their
suspicion is or is not qualified to kill game.

Rogers v. Carter.   The plaintiff being gamekeeper within
the manor of Ringwood, in beating for game within the said
manor sprung a covey of partridges, which he shot at within the
said manor.   They took a second flight, and he pursued them
out of the manor, but could not find them.   As he was returning to the manor of Ringwood, he was met by the defendant,
who asked if he had a qualification?   The plaintiff answered, I
have a deputation from the lord of the manor of Ringwood.
The defendant replied, you are now out of the manor; and demanded his gun, and took it from him.   The plaintiff did not
shoot out of the manor, but was three quarters of a mile out of
the manor with his gun and dog, with an intention to shoot at
game.   By the court.—The question is, whether the defendant

had a right to take the plaintiff's gun from him, while he was sporting for the purpose of killing game out of the manor of Ringwood? And we are all of opinion he had no such right. If he had killed game where he was not a gamekeeper, he might have been convicted in the penalty of 5*l*. but he was entitled to keep and have dogs, gun, and nets, any where; and a gamekeeper's gun cannot be seized, either in going to or returning from the manor, or in any other place. 2 Wils. 387.

The lord of a hundred or wapentake cannot grant a deputation to a gamekeeper. The Earl of Ailesbury *v.* Pattison. 1 Dougl. 28.*

It seems, gentlemen receiving deputations to be gamekeepers are not chargeable with the duty on servants, under 25 Geo. III. c. 43. Several lords of manors granted deputations to divers gentlemen to be gamekeepers within their respective manors; and being surcharged for the said gentlemen gamekeepers, they appealed against the surcharge. The surveyor urged, that in the terms of the act, all gamekeepers are rateable without distinction or exception; and that they, therefore, in their present capacity as gamekeepers, could have no pretence to any exemption: but the commissioners were of opinion, that the said gentlemen, considered as gamekeepers, did not come within the meaning of the act as servants, and therefore not rateable; and with that opinion the judges concurred.

* Sir Thomas Gage claims and exercises a paramount free warren over all the extensive manors in Suffolk, from Ipswich nearly to Newmarket. His keepers invariably go upon each at the beginning of the season, and kill a single bird, merely to maintain this singular supremacy.

STATUTES RELATING to RABBITS.

By 3 Jac. 1. c. 13. s. 2. If any person shall, by night or by day, unlawfully enter into any park or grounds, enclosed with a wall, pale, or hedge, and used for the keeping of conies, and unlawfully hunt, take, chase, or slay, any conies within such park or ground, against the will of the owner, and shall be thereof convicted, at the suit of the king or the party, at the assizes or sessions, he shall suffer three months imprisonment, pay treble damages and costs to the party, to be assessed by the justices before whom he shall be convicted, and shall find sureties for his good behaviour for seven years, or remain in prison till he does.

And by 22 and 23 Car. 2. c. 25. s. 4. If any person shall at any time wrongfully enter into any warren or ground lawfully used for keeping or breeding of conies, though the same may be not enclosed, and shall take, chase, or kill any conies against the will of the owner or occupier, not having lawful title so to do, and shall be thereof convicted within one month after such offence, by confession, or oath of one witness, before one justice, he shall yield to the party grieved treble damages and costs, and suffer three months imprisonment, and so long after till he find sureties for his good behaviour.

And by 5 Geo. 3. c. 14. it is enacted, That if any person shall enter into such warren or grounds in the night time, and take or kill any coney, against the will of the owner or occupier of the said ground, or shall be aiding or assisting therein, and be thereof convicted at the assizes, he shall be transported for seven years, or suffer such other punishment, by whipping, fine, or imprisonment, as the court shall award.

And by 9 Geo. 1. c. 22. If any person, being armed and disguised, shall appear in any warren or place where hares or conies are usually kept, or unlawfully rob any such warren, or shall, though not armed and disguised, rescue any person in custody for such offence, or procure any person to join him therein, he shall be guilty of felony without benefit of clergy.

By the stat. 22 and 23 Car. 2. it is provided, That no person shall kill or take, in the night, any conies upon the borders of a warren, or other grounds lawfully used for the breeding and keeping of conies, except such person be the owner of the soil, or lawful possessor of the ground, whereupon such conies shall be killed, or be by him employed, upon pain of such satisfaction as the justices aforesaid shall award, and also pay to the overseers for the poor a sum not exceeding ten shillings, or, in default thereof, to be committed to the house of correction for a term not exceeding one month.

And by the same act, any person convicted of setting or using any snares, or other like engines for the taking of conies, shall be liable to the same penalties as in the last-mentioned section.

A man cannot have an action of trespass on the case for another man's conies breaking into his grounds, because they are in their natural liberty when they are out of the warren, but the owner of the soil may lawfully kill them while they are on his ground. Cro. Eliz. 547. 5 Co. 104.

The lord of the soil may make burrows in a common, and stock them with rabbits; and therefore a commoner cannot justify chasing them thence, *damage fesant*, for he ought to come there but to use his common : but if the lord surcharge the common, he is liable to an action for so doing. Cro. Jac. 195. 208. 229.

Rex *v.* Yaites.—Yaites was convicted of killing rabbits in a private warren by inquisition taken before a justice of the peace, and was fined twenty shillings a rabbit. And it was moved to quash the inquisition, because the justices of the peace have no authority to set a fine upon a man for such offence. For the statutes 22 and 23 Car. 2. c. 25. s. 4. give treble costs and damages, but no fine. And the statute 4 and 5 Will. and Mary, c. 23. extends only to game, which cannot be extended to rabbits kept in a private warren. And of this opinion was the whole court, and therefore the inquisition was quashed. 1 Ld. Raymond, 151.

If the lord hath a right to put conies upon the common, and by an excess in number surcharges the common, and by the number of burrows made by the conies, prevents the commoner's cattle from depasturing the common ; an action in such case is the proper remedy, and the tenant may not of his own accord fill up the burrows and remove the nuisance. Cooper v. Marshall, 1 Burr. 259:

Conies in a warren shall go to the heir, and not to the executor. Co. Litt. 8.

Pigeons.

Any person who shall shoot, or destroy in any manner, any pigeon, shall on conviction before two justices, on the oath of two witnesses, be committed to gaol for three months; or pay for the use of the poor twenty shillings for every pigeon; or, within one month after commitment, find sureties not to offend again.

However, by 2 Geo. II. c. 29. one witness and one justice are sufficient: to forfeit twenty shillings to the person who prosecutes, or be committed to the house of correction and kept to hard labour for any term not exceeding three calendar months or less than one. Notwithstanding, a man has a right to shoot any pigeons he may find destroying his corn.

A very severe statute was passed in 1816. It runs thus:—Whereas, the laws now in force having been found insufficient to prevent idle and disorderly persons from going out armed in the night-time, for the destruction of game: And whereas such practices are found, by experience, to lead to the commission of felonies and murders: For the more effectual suppression thereof, it is enacted, that if any person or persons shall unlawfully enter into, or be unlawfully found in, any forest, chase, park, wood, plantation, close, or other open or inclosed grounds, in the night time, that is to say, between the hours of eight of the clock at night and seven in the morning, from the 1st day of October to the 1st day of March, or between the hours of ten at night and four in the morning, from the 1st day of March to the 1st day of October, in each and every year, having any gun, net, engine, or other instrument, for the purpose and with the intent to destroy, take, or kill, or shall wilfully destroy, take, or kill, any hare, rabbit, pheasant, partridge, heath fowl, commonly called black-game, or grouse, commonly called red-game, or any other game; or if any person or persons shall be found with any gun, fire-arms, bludgeon, or with any other offensive weapon, protecting, aiding, abetting, or assisting any such person or persons as aforesaid, every person so offending, being thereof lawfully convicted, shall be adjudged guilty of a misdemeanor, and shall be sentenced to transportation for any term not exceeding seven years, or shall receive such other punishment as may, by law, be inflicted on persons guilty of misdemeanors, and as the court before which such offenders may be tried and convicted, shall adjudge; and if any such offender or offenders shall return into Great Britain, before the expiration of the term for which he or they shall be so transported, contrary to the intent and meaning hereof, he or they so returning, and being thereof duly convicted, shall be adjudged guilty of felony, and shall be sentenced to transportation for the term or terms of his or their natural life or lives.

A justice, on information before him, on the oath of any credible witness or witnesses, may issue his warrant for the apprehension of such offender or offenders; and if upon the apprehension of any such offender or offenders it shall appear to such justice, on the oath of any credible witness or witnesses, that the person or persons so charged hath or have been guilty of any or either of the said offences, it shall and may be lawful for such justice to admit such person or persons so charged to bail, and in default of bail, to commit such person or persons to the county gaol, until the next general quarter sessions of the peace, or the next general commission of gaol delivery.

Mutiny Act.

———

According to this, if any officer or soldier shall kill any kind of game, poultry, or fish, and be convicted on the oath of one witness, before a justice, an officer* so offending shall forfeit five pounds to the poor of the parish; but if a soldier be thus convicted, the commander in chief of the place shall pay twenty shillings for every such offence; and if not paid within two days after demand by the constable or overseer of the poor, he shall forfeit his commission.

* This of course is supposing such officer not to be qualified.

Dog Laws.

It is a nuisance for any ferocious or mischievous dog to be at arge and unmuzzled, and the owner may be indicted.

An action may be maintained against a man for keeping a dog *accustomed* to bite sheep ;—if it can be proved that he has ever bitten one before, it is deemed a sufficient proof of his being *accustomed* so to do. Should the dog of one man fall upon that of another, he is justified in using violence, even to the death of the offending dog, if it appear probable that he could not otherwise rescue his own dog. If any person take up a lost dog, he must restore him on being demanded by the owner, or an action in trover may be maintained against him, in which he will be liable to damages and costs.

The 10th of Geo. III. c. 18. enacts, that if any person shall steal any dog, or dogs, of any kind whatsoever, from the owner, or from any person entrusted by the owner with such dog or dogs, or shall sell, buy, receive, harbour, detain, or keep any such dog or dogs, knowing the same to be stolen, every such offender, convicted on the oath of one witness, before two justices, shall for the first offence, forfeit a sum not exceeding thirty, nor less than twenty pounds, at the discretion of such two justices ; together also with the charges previous to and attending such conviction, to be ascertained by the said justices. In case such penalty be not immediately paid, such justices may commit the offender to the house of correction, for a time not exceeding twelve, nor less than six, calendar months ; or till the penalty be paid. For a second offence, the offender shall forfeit a sum not exceeding fifty, nor less than thirty, pounds; together also with the charges.

No dog to be liable to the duty until six months old.

Nov. 1780. Johnson v. Overall. The declaration stated, that the defendant discharged a certain gun loaded with gunpowder and bullets, and shot a certain dog of the plaintiff. The defence was, that only four sorts of dogs are in law of any value, and those specified. Dog in the declaration not specified, and therefore did not appear of any value.—Plaintiff nonsuited.

To an action of trespass for killing plaintiff's dog, the defendant may plead, that the dog chased the rabbits in his warren, or the deer in his park; but not that he chased a hare into defendant's land. 2 Morg. 265.

A dog is such a creature as a man may have a property in, and an action has been brought for taking a hound, and the plaintiff recovered. The like of a bloodhound, greyhound, pointer, setter, spaniel, and lurcher.

If a person hunt upon the ground of another, such other person cannot justify killing of his dogs; as appears by 2 Roll. Abr. 567. But this has been over-ruled; and in the case of Wadhurst v. Damme, Cro. Jac. 44. it was held, that a warrener may justify killing a mastiff dog in the warren pursuing the conies, to prevent his destroying them. So, if a dog run after deer in a park. 3 Lev. 28.

It is no justification in trespass for killing a mastiff, that he run violently upon the defendant's dog and bit him; but the defendant should state further, that he could not otherwise separate the mastiff from his dog. 1 Sannd. 84.

And a man may justify an assault in defence of his dog. Cro. Eliz. 125.

And delivery of a dog will be a good consideration for an *assumpsit.* Ibid. Owen. 93.

It having been once made known to the owner that his dog

bit a man, he appears to be answerable for a subsequent mischief, though the person bitten had given some accidental occasion for it, as by treading on the dog's foot; for it was owing
to his not hanging the dog on the first notice. And the safety
of the king's subjects ought not afterwards be endangered. 2.
Stra. 1263.

OF DESTROYING THE EGGS OF WILD FOWL AND WINGED GAME.

By 25 Hen. 8. c. 11. it is enacted, that no person, from the
1st day of March to the 30th day of June, shall destroy or
convey any eggs of wild fowl from any nest where they shall be
laid, upon pain of imprisonment for one year; and of forfeiting
for every egg of any crane or bustard, 20d.; for every egg of
bittern, heron, or shovelard, 8d.; for every egg of wild duck,
teal, or other wild fowl, 1d.

And by Jac. 1. c. 27. s. 2. any person who shall take the
eggs of any pheasant or partridge out of the nest, or wilfully
break or destroy the same, shall, on conviction before two justices, by confession, or oath of two witnesses, be committed to
gaol for three months, unless he pay to the churchwardens, for
the use of the poor, 20s. for every egg; or, within one month
thereafter, become bound with two sureties in 20l. each, not to
offend again.

ADJUDGED CASES.

Sussex Assizes, 1808.—Hebben *v.* Luff. This was an action to recover a penalty, for a breach of the game laws, on the statute of the 9th of Anne, Cap. 25. sect. 2, which gives a penalty against any unqualified person, having game in his possession, and makes the mere having of it, evidence of an exposure to sale. Mr. Courthorpe having stated the law, next produced evidence of the fact, which was proved by two game-keepers, who being on the watch early in the morning, heard the screams of a hare, upon which they looked about, and discovered a hare in a trap, not far from the cottage of the defendant; they lay in wait, expecting that the person who set the trap, would come to see what it produced : they saw the defendant come to the trap, and take the hare out : upon this they came out of their concealment, but the defendant seeing them, threw the hare away, and denied that he had had it; they, however, found the hare at a little distance from him.

Mr. Serjeant Best submitted to the court, that this was not such a possession, as the act meant, when it made possession, an exposure to sale.

The judge, on referring to the act, declared he did not wish to extend the game laws, but the words were so very positive, that he did not know how to get over them, it in express terms made all possession of game, by an unqualified person, an exposure to sale.—The jury found the defendant, guilty.

At Leicester assizes, an action of trespass, commenced by Earl Ferrers against Mr. Randall Lovell, for shooting in his lordship's preserves, at Thrussington, was tried at nisi prius; the plaintiff obtained a verdict; and the judge (Mr. Baron Graham) gave a certificate, under the 8 and 9 W. 3. c. 11, for costs, declaring, that the species of trespass for which the action was brought, (notwithstanding the defendant had not been previously warned to keep off the plaintiff's lands) was wilful and malicious, and the plaintiff in consequence entitled to costs, although the damages were under forty shillings.

In the case of Warneford v. Kendall, the possession of game by a servant, employed to detect poachers, who took it up after it had been killed by strangers on the manor, in order to carry it to the lord, is not a a possession within the penalty of the game laws. Lord Ellenborough, C. J. the question is, whether the possession of the defendant were such as to constitute an offence? He did not claim the hare as his property, nor acquire the possession of it for himself, but for his master, on whose manor it was taken; and if this be an offence, no case can be stated in which an unqualified person can innocently come in contact with game. It may as well be said, that if a qualified man returning home with a bag of game was to fall from his horse, another could not lawfully take up the bag in order to assist the owner. The case of Molton v. Cheeseley (the fact then proved was, that a pheasant had by accident been killed by the defendant's dog, and the defendant had carried it away, and two penalties were sought to be recovered, one for having the pheasant in his possession not being qualified, the other for keeping a dog to kill game. Mr. Justice Buller is said to have ruled, that the plaintiff could go for one penalty only, and that two penalties could not be recovered under this statute for the same act done by the defendant) must have been imperfectly stated.—Grose, Le Blanc, and Bailey, justices, assented, and the former observed, that the possession of the game by the defendant, was rather for the purpose of protecting the game than in breach of the laws for preserving it.—Rule absolute. East's Rep. p. 19.

Lord Albemarle *v.* Brooke.—This was an action tried at the Norfolk assizes, for the recovery of penalties under the game laws, to the amount of 700*l.* The defendant is a poulterer and wholesale dealer in game, at Thetford, represented to be connected with the poachers and gamekeepers in his own neighbourhood, on the one hand, and with the poulterers in Leadenhall-market, on the other. The interception of his commerce had created as much alarm in Leadenhall-market as the stagnation of the trade between this country and the north of Germany had occasioned amongst the merchants at the royal exchange. The defendant had the means, as a poulterer, of carrying on this trade 'to a great extent, and with much facility. On the 7th of December last, he brought to the waggon-office, at Thetford, three baskets, called flats, one of which weighed two cwt.; on the road this flat was removed to make room for more luggage, and on its removal, part of the game fell out of it, namely, four partridges, two pheasants, and two hares. The witness on the part of the plaintiff, to prove this fact, and the delivery of the flat into the waggon by the defendant, personally, was the waggoner. An attempt was made to discredit his testimony, but it did not succeed. Lord Ellenborough observed, that having game in one's possession, not being qualified, was sufficient evidence of an exposure to sale, to bring the party within the penalties of the act.—Verdict for plaintiff, damages 40*l.* being 5*l.* for every head of game which had fallen out of the basket.

In Scotland, the case of the Earl of Hopetoun *v.* Wright, after very serious discussion before the supreme court of session, was thus settled, that no tenant, whatever may be the endurance of his lease, is entitled to be considered as a qualified person, so as to shoot game, even on his own farm, without the permission of his landlord.

Church *v.* Sturdy.—This was an action tried at the Exeter assizes, 1811, to recover the value of a hare, wherein a verdict had been given for the plaintiff. Some hounds to which Mr. C. was a subscriber started a hare, and run her on the grounds of the defendant, where a labourer caught her alive, whereupon the defendant came up and took her from him, as being found on his land. Mr. Church demanded the hare, which Mr. Sturdy refused to deliver. Mr. Serjeant Lens moved to have a new trial. He contended, that as the hare was not killed by the plaintiff's hounds, no right of action accrued, because no right of possession was vested in the plaintiff, unless either his dogs caught or killed it in running.—That with respect to him, it was at all events *feræ naturæ*, and if an action lay *at all*, it must have been against the man who had given it to Mr. Sturdy. The court granted a rule, observing, " that the plaintiff was situated pretty much alike with his hounds and with his attorney; with his hounds he had a death in view, and lost his game; with his attorney a verdict, and lost his cause.

At the Stafford spring assizes, 1804, an action for killing game by coursing, the defendant not being qualified, Williams, serjeant, for the plaintiff, insisted, (and in this he was confirmed by Mr. Justice Lawrence) that though a qualified person may take his servant or servants to assist him to kill game, he cannot qualify them to kill it, neither will his presence protect an unqualified person, not being his servant, who goes for the purpose of taking the amusement of coursing. But if such person take an active part, by beating across the fields, or in open lands, and join in the diversion, in the same manner as a qualified person, he is as much liable to the penalties as if no such qualified person were present. The learned judge observed, that the contrary was the usual practice, but that practice would not alter the law.

In 1809 was laid before an eminent counsel this query :— " Two parties were coursing, and being threatened with an information, though in each of these parties there was one who possessed both a qualification and a certificate, and to whom the dogs that run belonged. Your opinion is requested, whether those persons who were neither qualified nor certificated are liable to any penalty, notwithstanding they were in company with a qualified man ? and if they are so liable, can there be more than two penalties recovered, or will separate penalties attach on each individual ?" Answer.—" I think that each person is not guilty of a separate offence, nor liable to a separate penalty ; but the offence committed by each party is one joint offence only, (supposing them all to be unqualified) for which they are liable to one penalty for each party ; that is, two penalties for both the parties using the dogs, not being qualified. Each person may be guilty of a separate offence, for coursing without a cer-tificate, who can be deemed to be a person, who, on that occasion, uses any of the dogs without a certificate. But the mere joining in the sport with a qualified or certificated person, who has the use and command of the dogs and of the sport, is not such a using of them, by the person so joining, as to subject him to any penalty."

And this opinion has been confirmed to be right by the fol-lowing case :—

Lewes *v.* Taylor. East's Term Reports, Trinity Term, 52d Geo. III.—This was an action of debt, for penalties upon the game laws, tried at the last Aylesbury assizes, before Heath, J. One count, charged the defendant for the penalty of 5*l.* upon the stat. 5 Anne, c. 14. for using a greyhound to kill game, not being qualified. In support of which, it was proved, that W. Goldby, a farmer, who was, by his own estate, qualified to kill game, went out with greyhounds and other dogs to course and kill hares : that the defendant, who was not qualified, was in company with Goldby when he coursed and killed a hare ; that the defendant took an active part in the sport, by beating the bushes, in order to find a hare ; and after the hare had been killed by a greyhound, he alighted from his horse, went over a gate,

and took up the hare. Upon the evidence the learned judge
was disposed to have nonsuited the plaintiff; but upon the
authority of a case, decided by Mr. Justice Lawrence, at Stafford, in 1804, in which an unqualified person partaking of the
sport in company with one who was qualified, was held not to
be protected from the penalty of the statute, he suffered the
plaintiff to take a verdict for the penalty of 5*l.* with liberty to the
defendant to move the court and set it aside, and enter a nonsuit, if the evidence did not support the charge. Storks accordingly moved the court for this purpose, and referred to the case
of King *v.* Newman*, where, upon an information being moved
for in this court against magistrates, for having unduly convicted two unqualified persons in penalties upon the game laws, for
using greyhounds to kill the game, though they offered to prove
in their defence that they were out at the time with a qualified
person, to whom the dogs belonged, Lord Mansfield expressed
a strong opinion against the conduct of the magistrates, and
only discharged the rule upon the terms of their paying the whole
costs of the application.—And in Molton *v.* Rogers† Lord Ellenborough also gave his opinion, that an unqualified person,
joining in the sport with the owner of the dogs, who was quali-
lified, was not liable to the penalty.

King now appeared to shew cause against the rule ; but the
court expressing a decided opinion in favour of the defendant,
he submitted to it, without further discussion. Lord Ellenborough, C. J. This is no evidence against this defendant,
upon the charge of using a greyhound for killing the game. The
dogs belonged to a qualified person, who was out with them at
the time. This is not a solitary amusement ; and there is
nothing to prevent a qualified person from taking others with

* Hil. 13. G. 3. Loft's Rep. 178, see Rex *v.* Taylor, 15, East, 402.

† Four Esp. A. P. Cas. 217.

him, to aid him in the pursuit of game, and he is the person using the dogs.—The others have no use of them further than his servants, and contemplating with him the pleasures of the chase. The learned judge's first thoughts were best. If, indeed, an unqualified man used his own greyhound for the purpose of coursing, though in the company with a qualified man, the case would admit of a different consideration. But there can be no ground for recovering the penalty against this defendant, who went out with the dogs of another, who was qualified, and which other was using them himself. The defendant's picking up the hare after it was killed is no using of the dogs to kill the game. We had occasion to consider this question very lately, in the case of a servant, Rex v. Taylor, 15. East, 463. The other judges agreed ; and Bailey, J. noticed, that the words of the statute of Anne, are keep or use any greyhounds, &c. but this defendant neither kept the dog, nor was it under his control at the time it killed the hare. Rule absolute for entering a nonsuit.

In 1812, at the Justices' Room, Stafford, an information was brought—Fox v. Hill, for using a greyhound to kill game, not being qualified. It appeared, that the defendant and others, were coursing with two greyhounds on Lord Ferrers' land, and that one of the party was his lordship's gamekeeper, whose qualification, it was submitted, on behalf of the defendant, extended to the others. The magistrates, however, were of opinion, that though a qualified person is authorized by law to take as many of his servants or other unqualified persons to attend him as are necessary for the purpose of assisting in raising the game, without subjecting them to any penalty ; yet a gamekeeper, who is merely qualified in right of another, has no such authority, his qualification being personal and confined to himself only. The defendant was accordingly convicted.

An action was brought against a person for entering another's free-warren : the defendant pleaded that there was a pheasant

on his land, and his hawk pursued it into the plaintiff's ground.
It was resolved, that this doth not amount to a sufficient justi-
cation; for in this case he can only follow his hawk, and not
take the game.   Poph. 162.

Though it is said to be otherwise where the soil of the plaintiff is not a warren.   2 Roll Abr. 567.

With respect to the penalty which goes to the poor of the
parish where the offence was committed: in some places a man
may stand in one parish or county, and shoot in another; and
in such a case, the place where the offence was committed is
where the party stood when he shot, and not where the object
was which he shot at.   Shaw. 339.   M. 3. W. King *v.* Alsop.

A person was indicted on 23 Eliz. c. 10. for taking partridges,
cum retiis; and it was quashed, because it should have been
cum retibus, 3 Bulst. 178.

Skill *v.* Tarr, Taunton assizes, 1801.   This was an action to
recover the penalty of £5 for killing a pheasant without being
qualified, and £20 for so doing, without having taken out a certificate.   It appeared that the defendant's dog had sprung a
pheasant, which he followed into an adjoining field, where the
dog stood, and that the defendant knocked it down with a rake
as it was rising.   The counsel for the defendant argued against
a rake being considered such an instrument for killing game as
was intended by the statute; but the learned judge found a verdict for the plaintiff to the amount of the penalties.

In an action of trespass, the plaintiff declared for taking *phasianos suos,* in such a place, on trial, upon not guilty pleaded,
a verdict was found for the plaintiff.   It was moved, in arrest
of judgment, that the declaration was naught, in using the word
suos, pheasants being *feræ naturæ,* in which the plaintiff could
have no property; but the court gave judgment for the
plaintiff, for they said that they would intend the pheasants were

dead; and in that case the plaintiff undoubtedly had a property in them, and might call them, *phasianos suos.* Anon.

Molton *v.* Cheeseley, East. Term, 28 Geo. III, 1788. This was an action of debt,* brought to recover from the defendant two penalties of £5 each, under the stat. 5 Ann. 14.—The first was, for having a pheasant in his possession, not being qualified. The second was, under another clause of the same statute, for keeping a dog for killing and destroying game.

When the case was opened, Buller, J. ruled that the plaintiff could go for one penalty only; for that both offences being by the same act, one penalty only could be recovered. The case then proved on the part of the plaintiff was, that a pheasant had been killed by accident by the defendant's dog, but that he had carried it away. Buller, J. said, that if it appeared that the bird was killed by accident, that was no offence; and in such case it should be left where it was killed: but if it was taken away, it subjects the party to the penalty for having game in his possession. The plaintiff therefore recovered one penalty of £5 for this offence.

In an action *qui tam,*† on the game laws, it is sufficient to say, that a person is not qualified generally, without shewing that he had not one hundred pounds a year, or any other estate which makes a qualification. In a conviction it is otherwise. Bluet *qui tam,* and *v.* Needs. 2 Comyn's Rep. 522.

All penalties on the game laws, sued for in Westminster hall,

---

* By stat. 8 Geo. I. c. 19. when any person shall be liable to any penalty under the game laws, by conviction before a justice of peace, it shall be lawful for any person either to proceed to recover the said penalty, by information before a justice, or to sue for the same by action of debt.

† Where qui tam is mentioned, the penalty is given half to the informer, and the other half to the poor of the parish, and when the *qui tam* is taken away, the whole penalty is given to the informer.

shall go to the informer, and no part to the poor of the parish.

In an information on the game laws, charging the defendant with keeping and using a dog, and also a gun on the same day, he can only be convicted in one penalty. Rex *v.* Lovett. 7 Term Rep. 152.

It is no objection to an information on the game laws, that it is not *qui tam.* Ibid.

If the evidence be given on the same day that the defendant appeared and pleaded, it will be intended that the evidence was given in his presence. Ibid.

The statute 4 and 5 W. and M. c. 23. makes an inferior tradesman liable to full costs in an action for hunting on another's ground, notwithstanding his being qualified by an estate. Bennett *v.* Talbois.. 1 Lord Raym. 150.

In the case Gardner *v.* Hanson, Home Circuit, July 29, 1803, it appeared that the plaintiff was a farmer, residing at Great Bromley; and the defendant was his neighbour, and lord of the manor. The action was brought to recover the value of two greyhounds, which the defendant had seized and converted to his own use. To this declaration the defendant had pleaded specially that he seized the dogs and detained them only until the plaintiff should prove himself qualified by law to use them. The proof first given by the plaintiff was of the taking of the two dogs by the defendant's gamekeeper. To justify this the warrant was produced, by virtue of which they were taken. This warrant was signed by two justices, and granted on the oath of Killibach, the defendant's gamekeeper, who swore that the plaintiff kept two greyhounds, and that he was not qualified by law to use them. The justices therefore ordered them to be seized. This warrant the justices granted without any summons to the party, or giving him any opportunity of proving his qualification. The plaintiff now proved that he was in possession of 150 acres of land, of the value of one guinea an acre, besides

cottages on it to the further value of £25 per year. This estimation was endeavoured to be reduced by the defendant, by
shewing that it had been surveyed and valued at 15s. per acre;
but the surveyor who made a survey of the parish stated, that
it was only done by way of equalising the rate, and that Mr.
Hanson's land was at the same time rated at 15s. an acre,
although he must know that it was of greater intrinsic value,
and the plaintiff's land was adjoining to the defendant's. It
was next attempted to be shewn that the land was mortgaged
for £500. The discharge of this incumbrance being also
shewn—

The learned judge said, the plaintiff was certainly entitled to
a verdict; but he added, the conduct of the two justices granting
the warrant was very extraordinary. It seemed upon the oath
of a common fellow of a gamekeeper, who took upon himself
to swear, that by law a person was not qualified to keep sporting
dogs, they, without any further inquiry, or without any summons
calling upon the party to shew his qualification, issued a warrant
to seize the dogs.—Verdict for plaintiff—damage £40.

The informer cannot be a witness. Lord Raym. 1545.
Andr. 240.

A BIRD'S-EYE VIEW OF THE GAME LAWS.

Qualification.—Either a freehold, copyhold, or an equitable estate of inheritance of the annual value of 100*l.* in the party's own right, or that of his wife; or a life estate, or leasehold property for at least 99 years, of the annual value of 150*l.* But heirs apparent of esquires; persons of higher degree than that of esquire; lords of manors, owners and keepers of forests, chases, parks, and warrens; as also gamekeepers duly authorised by lords of manors, or other royalties, not under the degree of an esquire; —may take and kill game without any qualification as to estate; (stat. 22 and 23 Cha. II. c. 25; 5 Ann, c. 14; 48 Geo. III. c. 93.) And the 54 Geo. III. c. 141, does not require any qualification from persons aiding and assisting qualified persons in taking or killing game, provided that the act of aiding and assisting be done in the company or presence, and for the use, of such qualified persons.—See 16 East's Rep. 49, and 15 Ibid, 460. Penalty for taking or killing game without qualification, 5*l.* for each offence; (5 Ann c. 14. The like penalty is imposed on unqualified persons keeping or using dogs and engines for taking game, (Ibid.)

Certificate-Duty, 3*l.* 13*s.* 6*d.* for a qualified person; 3*l.* 13*s.* 6*d.* for every gamekeeper not being a servant assessed to the duty on servants; and 1*l.* 5*s.* for every gamekeeper duly registered as gamekeeper. Penalty for taking or killing game without certificate, 20*l.* and certificate-duty, (52 Geo. III. c. 93.)

But no certificate is requisite to take snipes and woodcocks in net or springs, or rabbits, in enclosed grounds by the proprietors or occupiers thereof.

Collectors of taxes, owners and occupiers of lands, &c. gamekeepers, and persons assessed to the game duty, may demand of others using a dog, gun, &c. to produce their certificate; refusal to comply, or producing a false certificate, or giving a false name and place of residence, or place of assessment, incurs a penalty of 20*l.* (48 Geo. III. c. 55.)

SEASONS FOR THE TAKING OF GAME.

Heath Fowl, or Black Game, begins 20th August, ends 10th Dec. (13 Geo. III. c. 55.) But in the New Forest, Hants, Somerset, and Devon, begins 1st Sept. and ends 10th Dec. (43 Geo. III. c. 112 ; 50 Geo. III. c. 67.) Penaly for taking at any other time, first offence 20*l.* aad every subsequent offence 30*l.*

Grouse, or Red Game, begins August 12th, ends 10th Dec. Penalty at other seasons, first offence 20*l.* and every subsequent offence 30*l.* (13 Geo. III. c. 55.)

Partridges, begins 1st Sept. ends 1st Feb. } Penalty at other seasons 5*l.*
Pheasants, begins 1st Oct. ends 1st Feb. } (2 Geo. III. c.19 ; 39 Geo. III. c. 34.)

Wild Fowl, viz. Wild Ducks, } begins 1st October and ends 1st June.
Teal, Widgeon, and other } Penalty at other seasons 5*l.* (9 Ann, c.
Water Fowl, } 25 ; 10 Geo. II. c. 32.)

Bustards, begins 1st Sept. ends 1st March. Penalty at other seasons, first offence 20*l.* and for every subsequent offence 30*l.* (13 Geo. III. c. 55.)

Hares may be taken at any time of the year, provided in the day time.

Game must not be pursued or taken between the hours of seven at night and six in the morning from October 12th to February 12th ; or between nine at night and four in the morning from February 12th to October 12th ; or on a Sunday or Christmas-Day ; on penalty of 20*l.* for the first offence, 30*l.* for the second, and 50*l.* for every subsequent offence ; (13 Geo. III. c. 80.)

UNLAWFUL DESTRUCTION OF GAME.

Deer.—To hunt, take, or kill any deer in forests or enclosed grounds, transportation for seven years, (16 Geo. III. c. 30, 42 Ibid c. 107 ;) if in unenclosed grounds, 50*l.* (42 Geo. III. c. 107 ; 51 Geo. III. ; if disguised, capital felony, (9 Geo. I. c. 22.)

Hares.—To take or kill hares in the night, 20*l.* for first offence, and 30*l.* for second offence, (13 Geo. III. c. 80;) to trace in the snow, or take in snares, 20*l.* or three months' imprisonment, (1 Jam. I. c. 27;) if found setting snares, 10s. or one month's imprisonment, (22 Cha. II.;) and if disguised, felony, (9 Geo. I. c. 22.)

Rabbits, to take or kill in warrens in the day time, treble damages, or three months' imprisonment, (22 and 23 Cha. II. c. 25;) if in the night, transportation for seven years, or whipping, fine, or imprisonment, (5 Geo. III. c. 14;) if disguised, capital felony, (9 Geo. I. c. 22.)

Partridges and Pheasants, to shoot at or kill with gun or bow, or to take with nets, dogs, or engines, 20s. or three months' imprisonment, (1 Jam. I. c. 27; 7 Jam. I. c. 18;) if in the night 20s. for every pheasant, and 10s. for every partridge, (23 Eliz. c. 10.)

Heath Game, Grouse, or Moor Game, { to shoot at or kill with gun or bow, 20s. or three months' imprisonment, (1 Jam. I. c. 27;) if in the night, 5*l.* (9 Ann, c. 25.)

Wild Ducks, Wild Geese, and other Water Fowl, { to shoot at or kill, 20*l.* or three months' imprisonment, (1 Jam. I. c. 27;) to take with nets, &c. from 31st May to 31st August, 4d. and one year's imprisonment.

Herons, to shoot at or kill, 20s. or one month's imprisonment, (I Jam. I. c. 27;) to take the young out of nests, 10s. (19 Hen. VII. c. 11;) and to take any heron, except with hawking or long bows, 6s. 8d. (Ibid.)

Pigeons, to shoot at, kill, or destroy, with dogs, nets, &c. 20s. or three months' imprisonment, (1 Jam. c. 27; 2 Geo. III. c. 29.)

Swans, to steal, whether marked or unmarked, felony.

Hawks, to disturb or destroy in their nests, 10*l.* (11 Hen. VII. c. 17;) and to steal, felony, (37 Edw. III. c. 19.)

Wilfully to destroy the eggs of Pheasants or Partridges, 20s. for every egg, or one month's imprisonment, (1 Jam. I. c. 27;) of Cranes or Bustards, 20d.; of Bitterns, Herons, or Shovelards, 8d.; of Mallards, Teals, or other wild fowl, 1d. (25 Hen. VIII. c. 11;) of Swans, 20s. (1 Jam. I. c. 27;) or of Falcons, Goss-hawks, &c. treble damages and three months' imprisonment, (5 Eliz. c. 21; and to take the eggs of any falcon, &c. found upon the party's own lands, incurs fine and imprisonment for a year and a day, (11 Hen. VII. c. 17.)

To enter any forest, chase, park, or open or enclosed ground, between six in the evening and seven in the morning from the 1st of October to the 1st of February, between seven in the evening and five in the morning from February the 1st to April the 1st, and between nine in the evening and four in the morning for the rest of the year, armed, and having nets, &c. transportation for seven years. Offenders may be apprehended by any person. (57 Geo. III. c. 90.) Gamekeepers may seize all game unlawfully taken; and guns, nets, dogs, (except hounds, 1 Barnew. and Alders. Rep. 134,) &c. used by unqualified persons; and they, as also constables and peace-officers, may, by warrant, enter houses of suspected persons not qualified to search for game; (22 and 23 Cha. II. c. 25; 4 and 5 Will. and Mary, c. 23; 9 Geo. I. c. 22.) Officers or soldiers destroying game, without leave of the lord of the manor, forfeit 5l. (58 Geo. III. c. 75.)

BUYING AND SELLING GAME.

To sell or expose to sale Hares, Pheasants, Partridges, Moor or Heath Game, or Grouse, penalty 5l. or three months' imprisonment, (28 Geo. II. c. 12.) Unqualified persons, (9 Ann, c. 25;) poulterers, &c. (25 Geo. II. c. 12;) carriers, innkeepers, victuallers, (5 Ann, c. 14;) having game in their possession, to be deemed exposing it to sale. But carriers having in their possession game belonging to qualified persons are not subject to penalties. And by statute 58 Geo. III. c. 75, to buy game, penalty 5l. or six months' imprisonment. To buy or sell deer, penalty 40s. (5 Ann, c. 14.) Gamekeepers selling or exposing to sale game, penalty 5l. or three months' imprisonment, (9 Ann, c. 25.) Persons having destroyed game, discovering within three months any carrier, innkeeper, or victualler, having bought or sold, or offered to buy or sell, or had in his possession any game, are exempt from penalty, (5 Ann, c. 14.) And by the 58 Geo. III. c. 75, any peron having bought or sold game, discovering within six months any person guilty of a like offence, is entitled to the same exemption.

N. B. Some doubt having been entertained whether rabbits are to be considered game, it may be proper to observe that the first statute which required a certificate for killing them was the 52 Geo. III. c. 93; but it is not penal to expose them to sale, for the statutes relative to this matter do not mention them in their enumeration.

REMARKS.

I have endeavoured to give as lucid a view as possible of what are called the Game Laws; but, as they are neither founded in justice, nor supported by reason, it is impossible to exhibit them either in a very clear or a very favourable light. At first view, the qualification appears absurd; and if we proceed to examine the matter more minutely, we shall soon discover that it will not bear the scrutiny of investigation. In a free, commercial country, it must be particularly obnoxious; for what can be more unreasonable or more arbitrary, than the invidious distinction which is thus exhibited between the landed and commercial interests? A man, with a small freehold of £100 per annum, is legally qualified to keep game dogs, and pursue the diversions of the field; when a man in trade, possessed of property to the amount of many thousands, is denied the same privilege. It has been argued, that, as the game is supported by (or fed upon) the lands, so the owners, and they alone, are entitled to chase and kill it. But this doctrine will be found altogether futile and even ridiculous; since, in the first place, property in houses is a qualification equal to grass or corn fields, and consequently the argument instantly vanishes. Game, strictly speaking, can be called the property of no person: it respects neither the fields of the rich nor the gardens of the poor; its excursions are unlimited, and it feeds every where. If it can be called property at all, it is the property of the country; and, since commerce pays comparatively so much greater a proportion towards the support of the state, the rights of the tradesman ought at least to be equal with those of the landholder.

The use of spring guns and steel traps for the preservation of game appears as abominable as it is unlawful.

Aquatic & Fen Birds.

It was not originally the intention of the author to have entered into the subject of shooting farther than what related to those animals denonimated *game;* but as what are called wild fowl frequently present themselves during winter to the attention of the sportsman, and as those gentlemen who reside near the fens and marshes frequently amuse themselves in those places when superior sport is unattainable, in order to render the " Shooter's Companion" as complete as possible, I shall sketch the history of aquatic and fen birds, as well as describe the most approved mode of following the diversion of wild fowl and fen shooting. Those birds which frequent the fens but are not web footed will first come under consideration.

The progressions of nature from one class of beings to another, are always by slow and almost imperceptible degrees. She has peopled the woods and the fields with a variety of the most beautiful birds ; and, to leave no part of her extensive territories untenanted, she has stocked the waters with its feathered inhabitants also : she has taken the same care in providing for the wants of her animals in this element, as she has done with respect to those of the other ; she has used as much precaution to render water·fowl fit for swimming, as she did in forming landfowl for flight; she has defended their feathers with a natural oil, and united their toes by a webbed membrane; by which contrivances they have at once security and motion. But between the classes of land-birds that shun the water, and waterfowl that are made for swimming and living on it, she has formed a very numerous tribe of birds, that seem to partake of a middle nature ; that, with divided toes, seemingly fitted to live on land are at the same time furnished with appetites that chiefly attach them to the waters. These can properly be called neither land-birds nor water fowl, as they chiefly derive their sustenance from watery places, and yet are unqualified to seek it in those depths where it is often found in greatest plenty.

. This class of birds, of the crane kind, are to be distinguished from others rather by their appetites than their conformation. Yet even in this respect they seem to be sufficiently discriminated by nature : as they are to live among the waters, yet are inca-pahle of swimming in them, most of them have long legs, fitted for wading in shallow waters, or long bills proper for groping in them.

, Every bird of this kind, habituated to marshy places, may be known, if not by the length of its legs, at least by the scaly sur-face of them. Those who have observed the legs of a snipe or a woodcock, will easily perceive my meaning ; and how different the surface of the skin that covers them is from that of the pigeon or the partridge. Most birds of this kind also, are bare of feathers half way up their thigh ; at least, in all of them, above the knee.—Their long habits of wading in the waters, and having their legs continually in moisture, prevents the growth of feathers on those parts ; so that there is a surprising difference between the leg of a crane, naked of feathers almost up to the body, and the falcon, booted almost to the very toes.

The bill also is very distinguishable in most of this class. It is, in general, longer than that of other birds, and in some finely fluted on every side ; while at the point it is possessed of extreme sensibility, and furnished with nerves, for the better feeling their food at the bottom of marshes, where it cannot be seen. Some birds of this class are thus fitted with every convenience : they have long legs, for wading ; long necks, for stooping ; long bills, for searching ; and nervous points, for feeling. Others are not so amply provided for ; as some have long bills, but legs of no-great length; and others have long necks, but very short legs. It is a rule which universally holds, that where the bird's legs are long, the neck is also long in proportion. It would indeed be an incurable defect in the bird's conformation, to be lifted upon stilts above its food, without being furnished with an instrument to reach it.

If we consider the natural power of this class, in a comparative view, they will seem rather inferior to those of every other tribe. Their nests are more simple than those of the sparrow; and their methods of obtaining food less ingenious than those of the falcon; the pie exceeds them in cunning; and though they have all the voraciousness of the poultry tribe, they want their fecundity. None of this kind, therefore, have been taken into man's society, or under his protection; they are neither caged like the nightingale, nor kept tame like the turkey, but lead a life of precarious liberty in fens and marshes, at the edges of lakes and along the sea-shore. They all live upon fish or insects, one or two only excepted.

All this class, therefore, that are fed upon insects, their food being easily digestible, are good to be eaten; while those which live entirely upon fish, abounding in oil, acquire in their flesh the rancidity of their diet, and are, in general, unfit for our tables. To savages, indeed, and sailors on a long voyage, every thing that has life would appear good to be eaten; and we often find them recommending those animals as dainties, which they themselves would spurn at after a course of good living. Nothing is more common in their journals than such accounts as these—"this day we shot a fox—pretty good eating: and this day we shot a heron—pretty good eating: and this day we killed a turtle"— which they rank with the heron and the fox, as "pretty good eating." Their accounts, therefore, of the flesh of these birds, are not to be depended upon; and when they cry up the heron or the stork of other countries as luxurious food, we must always attend to the state of their appetites who give the character.

THE DOTTEREL.

The length of the dotterel is about ten inches. The bill is not quite an inch long, and is black. The forehead is mottled with brown and grey: the top of the head is black; and over each eye there is an arched line of white, which passes to the hind part of the neck. The cheeks and throat are white; the back and wings are of a light brown inclining to olive, each feather margined with pale rust colour. The fore part of the neck is surrounded by a broad band of a light olive colour, bordered below with white. The breast is of a pale dull orange; the middle of the belly black; and the rest of the belly and the thighs are of a reddish white. The tail is olive brown, black near the end, and tipped with white; and the outer feathers are margined with white. The legs are of a dark olive.

These birds are migratory: appearing in flocks of eight or ten, about the end of April; and staying all May and June, when they become very fat, and are much esteemed for the table. They are found in tolerable plenty in Cambridgeshire, Lincolnshire, and Derbyshire; but in other parts of the kingdom they are scarcely known. They are supposed to breed among the mountains of Westmoreland and Cumberland.

The dotterel is in its manners a very singular bird, and may be taken by the most simple artifice. The country people are sometimes said to go in quest of it, in the night, with a lighted torch or candle: and the bird on these occasions will mimic the actions of the fowler with great archness. When he stretches out an arm, it stretches out its wing; if he moves a foot, it moves one also; and every other motion it endeavours to imitate. This is the opportunity that the fowler takes of entangling

it in his net. Willoughby however cites the following case:—
six or seven persons usually went in company to catch dotterels.
When they found the bird, they set their net in an advantageous
place ; and each of them holding a stone in either hand, they
got behind it, and striking the stones one against the other, roused
it from its natural sluggishness, and by degrees drove it into the
net. The more certain method of the gun has of late superseded both these artifices.

THE WHEAT EAR.

This bird visits England annually in the middle of March,
and leaves us in September. The females come first, about a
fortnight before the males ; and they continue to come till the
Middle of May. In some parts of England they are found in
vast plenty, and are much esteemed. About Eastbourne, in
Sussex, they are taken in snares made of horse-hair, placed beneath a long turf. Being very timid birds, the motion even of
a cloud, or the appearance of a hawk, will immediately drive
them into the traps.

These traps are first set every year on St. James's day, the
twenty-fifth of July ; soon after which they are caught in astonishing numbers, considering that they are not gregarious, and
that more than two or three are scarcely ever seen flying together. The number annually ensnared in the district of Eastbourne alone, is said to amount to nearly two thousand dozen.
The birds caught are chiefly young ones, and they are invaria-

bly found in the greatest number when an easterly wind prevails: they always come against the wind. A gentleman informed Mr. Markwick, that his father's shepherd once caught eighty-four dozen of them in a day. Great quantities of them are eaten on the spot by the neighbouring inhabitants; others are sent up to the London poulterers, and many are potted, being as much esteemed in England as the ortolans are on the continent of Europe.

The vast plenty of these birds on the downs about Eastbourne, is supposed by Mr. Pennant to be occasioned by a species of fly, their favourite food, that feeds on the wild thyme, and abounds on the adjacent hills.

A few of the birds breed in the old rabbit-burrows there. The nest is large, and made of dried grass, rabbets' down, a few feathers, and horse-hair. The eggs are from six to eight, and are of a light colour.

THE RUFF and REEVE.

The ruff is about a foot in length, with a bill of about an inch. The face is covered with yellow pimples; and the back part of the head and neck are furnished with long feathers, standing out somewhat like the ruff worn bv our ancestors; a few of these feathers stand up over each eye, and appear not unlike ears. The colours of the ruffs are in no two birds alike: in general they are brownish, and barred with black; though some have been seen that were altogether white. The lower parts of the belly and the tail coverts' are white. The tail is tolerably long, having the four middle feathers barred with black; the others are pale brown. The legs are of a dull yellow, and the claws black.—The female, which is called the reeve, is smaller than the male, of a brown colour, and destitute of the ruff on the neck.

The male bird does not acquire his ruff till the second season, being till that time in this respect like the female: as he is also from the end of June till the pairing season, when nature clothes him with the ruff, and the red pimples break out on his face; but after the time of incubation the long feathers fall off, and the caruncles shrink in under the skin so as not to be discerned.

These are birds of passage; and arrive in the fens of Lincolnshire, the isle of Ely, and the East Riding of Yorkshire, in the spring, in great numbers. Mr. Pennant tells us, that in the course of a single morning there have been above six dozen caught in one net: and that a fowler has been known to catch between forty and fifty dozen in a season.

The males are much more numerous than the females, and they have many severe contentions for their mates. The male chooses a stand on some dry bank, near a plash of water, round which he runs so often as to make a bare circular path: the moment a female comes in sight, all the males within a certain distance commence a general battle; placing their bills to the ground, spreading their ruff, and using the same action as a cock: and this opportunity is seized by the fowlers, who, in the confusion, catch them, by means of nets, in great numbers.

An erroneous opinion prevails very generally, that ruffs when in confinement must be fed in the dark, lest the admission of light should set them to fighting. The fact is, that every bird, even when kept in a room, takes its stand, as it would in the open air; and if another invades its circle, a battle ensues. A whole room full of them may be set into fierce contest by compelling them to shift their stations ; but, after the disturber has quitted the place, they have been observed to resume their circles, and become again pacific. In confinement their quarrels originate in the circumstance of the pan containing their food, not being sufficiently large to admit the whole party to feed without touching each other. When the food has been divided into several pans, the birds have continued perfectly quiet.

The reeves lay four eggs, in a tuft of grass, about the beginning of May ; and the young are hatched in about a month.

It is not known with certainty in what country these birds pass the winter.

THE KNOT.

This bird, which frequents the fens, is taken in the same manner as the ruffs and reeves. The knot is said to have been a favourite dish with Canute, king of England ; and Camden observes, that its name is derived from the monarch Knute or Knout, as he was called, which, in process of time, has been changed to Knot. These birds are caught in Lincolnshire, and other fenny counties by nets, into which they are decoyed by stale birds, carved and painted so as to represent themselves, and placed within the range of the nets : their numbers are so considerable that Mr. Pennant states fourteen dozen to have been taken at once. They are fattened in the same way as the ruffs, and by some are supposed to excel that bird in flavour. The season for taking them is from August to November, after which they in general disappear with the first frosts. The weight of the knot is four ounces and a half, length from nine to ten inches, breadth from sixteen to twenty inches. Bill one inch and a quarter, black at the tip, and dusky ash fading into orange towards the base. Tongue extends to the very end of the bill, and is sharp and horny at the point. Irides hazel; from the bill to the eye a dusky line; over the eye a white one: the top of the head, neck, back, and wings, ash-colour; lower order of coverts tipped with white, and edged a little way up with the same, making a bar across the wing when extended; greater quills darker, with white shafts: lower part of the back and tail coverts dark ash-colour, mixed with white, forming spots like crescents: tail ash-coloured; the under part from the throat to the vent, white, with small dusky spots on the throat and breast; the sides under the wings, the belly, thighs, and vent, crossed with dusky lines; ridge of the wing white; the thighs feathered very nearly to the knee; the legs are short, in some are blueish ash-colour, in others reddish yellow; the toes are divided without any membrane. These birds, however, like others of the same genus, vary considerably from each other in their appearance at different seasons of the year, as well as from age and sex. Knots have been observed about lake Baikal, and Mr. Pennant mentions a specimen which came from New York.

THE GODWIT

is taken at the same time, and in the same manner, with the ruffs and knots, and when ready for market, each sells for five shillings and upwards. In the spring and summer it resides in the fens and marshes, where it rears its young and lives upon small worms and insects. During these seasons it only removes from one marsh or fen to another, but when the winter sets in with severity (for the godwit continues with us the whole year), it seeks the salt-marshes, and the sandy shores by the sea-side, which for a great space are uncovered at the ebbing of the tide, where it walks like the curlew, and feeds upon the insects which there abound.

This bird is rather bigger than the woodcock, being in length from sixteen to eighteen inches, and between the tips of the extended wings twenty-eight inches broad. The weight twelve ounces. Bill four inches long, bending a little upwards, black at the point, gradually softening into a pale purple towards the base; the under mandible the shortest; the tongue sharp; the nostrils oblong; and the ears large. A whitish streak passes from the bill to the eye; the head, neck, and upper parts of a dingy reddish brown, each feather marked down the middle with a dark spot. The fore part of the breast is streaked with black: in the female the throat and neck are grey or ash-coloured; the belly, vent, and tail, are white, the latter regularly barred with black; the six prime quill feathers are black, edged on the interior sides with reddish brown. In some birds the rump is white, and the chin nearly so; the legs are not very long, naked to the middle of the second joint, and are generally dark-coloured, inclining to a greenish blue.

The godwit is met with in various parts of the continent of Europe and Asia, as well as in America: at Hudson's Bay, the red godwit in particular is so plentiful, that Mr. Atkinson, long resident at York Fort, killed seventy-two at one shot!

PLOVERS.

There are three sorts of these birds, which are objects of the sportsman's pursuit; the golden, the grey, and the peewit or lapwing.

The golden plover is the size of the turtle; its weight nine ounces; length eleven inches, breadth twenty-four; the bill is short and black; the feathers on the head, back, and wing coverts, are dusky, beautifully spotted on each side with light yellowish green; round the eyes and the chin almost white; sides of the head, the neck, and sides of the body, the same as the upper parts, but much paler; the breast brown, marked with greenish oblong strokes; the middle feathers of the tail barred with black and yellowish green; the greater quills are dusky; the legs black; and it wants the back toe, by which it is distinguished from other birds of its kind. There is some variety seen in the colour of the belly; this is owing to the season: about the beginning of March, the appearance of black in the breast is first seen, increasing by degrees, until that part becomes a full black; but after the time of incubation, this tint again disappears, and the belly is white. The male and female differ very little, and in the young birds the spots are not of a full yellow, but incline more to grey.

M. Baillon, who has observed these birds in Picardy, asserts that their early plumage is grey; that at their first moult in August and September, they get some feathers of a yellow cast, or which are spotted with that colour; but it is not until after some years that they acquire their fine golden tint. He adds, that the females are hatched entirely grey, and only when old assume a little yellow; and that it is very rare to see their feathers

2 F 3

so uniform and beautiful as the males. No longer need the distinction of tints in this species of birds be remarked, since this gentleman has proved, that the varieties result from the difference of age and of sex.

This elegant bird inhabits England the whole year, and breeds on several of our unfrequented mountains; is very common on those of the isle of Rum, and others of the loftier Hebrides; also on the Grampian, and all the heathy hills of the islands and highlands of Scotland: millions are found in the Orknies, from which they never entirely migrate; they lay four eggs, two inches in length, more pointed in shape than those of the lapwing, and of a pale cinereous olive, blotched with blackish spots; they make a whistling noise, and fly in small flocks, and by a skilful imitation of the note, may be enticed within shot. They frequent, in November, meadows and commons; and there was once an instance of a warrener near Bristol killing eleven at one shot. Their flesh is sweet and tender; they are dressed like the woodcock, with their trail, and are excellent eating.

The golden plover is common in all the northern parts of Europe. It is numerous in America, from Hudson's Bay to Carolina; migrating from one part to another according to the seasons. Is met with to the south as far as Aleppo; and if, says Latham, the species is not mistaken, in the island of Batavia and in China. Our last voyagers found them at Owhyhee, Tongataboo, and also York islands, but of a smaller size.

THE GREY PLOVER

is about twelve inches long and twenty-five broad, and weighs
seven ounces; the hill is black, about an inch long: in the roof
of the mouth is a double row of spinous appendages pointing
inwards; the head, back, and wing coverts, are of a dusky brown,
edged with greenish ash-colour, and some with white; the cheeks
and throat white, marked with oblong dusky spots; the belly,
thighs, and rump, white; the exterior webs of the quill feathers
black; the lower part of the interior webs of the first four white:
the tail is short, does not project beyond the wing, and is marked
with transverse bars of black and white; the legs are of a dirty
green; the back toe extremely small. This bird is in no great
abundance, in England;* they generally come in small flocks
about October, and leave this country about March: in cold
and frosty weather they seek their food on such lands as lie near
the sea; in open weather they feed in ploughed fields, especially
if sowed; and, having fed, fly to some plash of water to wash
their beaks and feet; a habit which is also common to the woodcocks, the lapwings, the curlews, and many other birds which
feed on worms; they sleep chiefly in the day in calm weather,
passing most of the night in running up and down after the

---

* Mr. Gilpin speaks of them as sometimes abounding in the New
Forest. " Plovers of different kinds (says that gentleman) are common in
its heathy parts. I have sometimes seen large flocks of the grey species,
and admired them as they encircled the air; in their regular flight they
in some degree resemble water-fowls, but are not so determined in their
course, wheeling about and forming various evolutions: at times they
appear scattered and in confusion, until closing together, as if by some
word of command, they get again into form."

worms, which then creep out of the ground: at that time they make a small cry, as if to keep their flock collected till day-break, when they unite and fly to the coast; they are sometimes taken in nets at their first coming, and the fowler is cautious to set his nets to play with the wind; for instance, when the wind is easterly, that they may play westerly. The north-west is the worst wind to take them; all sea-fowl fly against the wind, whenever they design to rest on the land. The preferable places for setting the nets are in large common fields of green corn, and near to water, for there they are sure to resort to clean their beaks and feet: their flesh is very delicate. In Carolina they are seen in the valleys, near the mountains, in great numbers, but seldom alight; are also very common in Siberia, appearing there in autumn in vast flocks, coming from the extreme north, where they breed.

———

THE LAPWING or PEEWIT.

This bird is too well known to need any description here. It is found in most parts of Europe, as far northward as Iceland. In the winter it is met with in Persia and Egypt.

The chief food of the Lapwings is worms; and sometimes they may be seen in flocks nearly covering the low marshy grounds in search of these, which they draw with great dexterity from their holes. When the bird meets with one of those little clusters of pellets, or rolls of earth; that are thrown out by the worm's perforations, it first, gently removes the mould from the mouth of the hole, then strikes the ground at the side with its foot, and steadily and attentively waits the issue: the reptile, alarmed by the shock, emerges from its retreat, and is instantly seized. In the evening the lapwings pursue a different plan: they run along the grass and feel under their feet the worms, which now come forth invited by the coolness of the air. Thus they obtain a plentiful meal; and afterwards wash their bill and feet in the small pools or rivulets.

" I have seen this bird (says Dr. Latham) approach a worm-cast, turn it aside, and, after making two or three turns about, by way of giving motion to the ground, the worm came out, and the watchful bird, seizing hold of it, drew it forth."

They remain in England the whole year. The female lays four eggs on the dry ground, near some marsh, upon a little bed which she prepares of dry grass. These are olive-coloured and spotted with black. She sits about three weeks; and the young are able to run within two or three days after they are hatched. The parent exhibits the greatest attachment to them; and the arts used by this bird to allure boys and dogs from the place where they are running, are extremely amusing. She does not wait the arrival of her enemies at the nest, but boldly pushes out to meet them. When as near as she dare venture, she rises from the ground with a loud screaming voice, as if just flushed from hatching, though probably at the same time not within a hundred yards of her nest. She now flies with great clamour and apparent anxiety; whining and screaming round the invaders, striking at them with her wings, and sometimes fluttering as if she was wounded. To complete the deception, she becomes still more clamorous as she retires from the nest. If very near, she appears altogether unconcerned, and her cries cease in proportion as her fears are augmented. When approached by dogs, she flies heavily, at a little distance before them; as if maimed; still vociferous, and still bold, but never offering to move towards the quarter where her young are stationed. The dogs pursue in expectation every moment of seizing the parent; and by this means actually lose the young, for the cunning bird having thus drawn them off to a proper distance, exerts her powers, and leaves her astonished pursuers to gaze at the rapidity of her flight.

There are few readers acquainted in any degree with the country who will not recollect how justly the following lines describe the manners of this bird;

> ———Hence, around the head
> Of wand'ring swains, the white-wing'd plover wheels
> Her sounding flight; and then directly on,
> In long excursion, skims the level lawn,
> To tempt him from her nest.

The following anecdote exhibits the domestic nature of the lapwing, as well as the art with which it conciliates the regard of animals materially differing from itself, and generally considered as hostile to every species of the feathered tribe. Two lapwings were given to a clergyman, who put them into his garden; one soon died, but the other continued to pick up such food as the place afforded, till winter deprived it of its usual supply. Necessity soon compelled it to draw nearer the house, b which it gradually became familiarized to occasional interruptions from the family. At length one of the servants, when sh had occasion to go into the back-kitchen with a light, observed that the lapwing always uttered his cry of "*pee-wit*" to obtain admittance. He soon grew more familiar: as the winter advanced, he approached as far as the kitchen, but with much caution, as that part of the house was generally occupied by a do and cat, whose friendship, however, the lapwing at length con ciliated so entirely, that it was his regular custom to resort to the fireside as soon as it grew dark, and spend the evening and night with his two associates, sitting close by them and partaking of the comforts of the warmth. As soon as spring appeared he discontinued his visits to the house, and betook himself to the garden; but on the approach of winter he had recourse to his old shelter and friends, who received him very cordially. Security was productive of insolence; what was at first obtained with caution, was afterwards taken without reserve: he frequently amused himself with washing in the bowl which was set for the dog to drink out of; and while he was thus employed he shewed marks of the greatest indignation if either of his companions presumed to interrupt him. He died in the asylum he had thus chosen, being choaked with something that he had picked up from the floor.

THE BITTERN, or MIRE-DRUM.

Those who have walked in an evening by the sedgy sides of unfrequented rivers, must remember a variety of notes from different water-fowl: the loud scream of the wild-goose, the croaking of the mallard, &c. &c. But of all those sounds, there is none so dismally hollow as the booming of the bittern. It is impossible for words to give those who have not heard this evening-call an adequate idea of its solemnity. It is like the interrupted bellowing of a bull, but hollower and louder, and is heard at a mile's distance, as if issuing from some formidable being that resided at the bottom of the waters.

The bird, however, that produces this terrifying sound, is not so big as a heron, with a weaker bill, not above four inches long. It differs from the heron chiefly in its colour, which is in general of a paleish yellow, spotted and barred with black. Its windpipe is fitted to produce the sound for which it is remarkable; the lower part of it dividing into the lungs is supplied with a thin loose membrane, that can be filled with a large body of air and exploded at pleasure. These bellowing explosions are chiefly heard from the beginning of spring to the end of autumn, and, however awful they may appear to us, are the calls to courtship or expressions of connubial felicity.

. From the loudness and solemnity of the note, many have been led to suppose that the bird made use of external instruments to produce it, and that so small a body could never eject such a quantity of tone. The common people are of opinion that it thrusts its bill into a reed, that serves as a pipe for swelling the note above its natural pitch; while others, and in this number we find Thomson the poet, imagine that the bittern puts its head under water, and then violently blowing produces its boomings. The fact is, that the bird is sufficiently provided by nature for this call, and it is often heard where there are neither reeds nor waters to assist its sonorous invitations.

It hides in the sedges by day, and begins its call in the evening, booming six or eight times, and then discontinuing for ten or twenty minutes, to renew the same sound. This is a call it never gives but when undisturbed, and at liberty. When its retreats among the sedges are invaded, when it dreads or expects the approach of an enemy, it is then perfectly silent. This call it has never been heard to utter when taken or brought up in domestic captivity; it continues under the control of man a mute forlorn bird, equally incapable of attachment or instruction. But though its boomings are always performed in solitude, it has a scream which is generally heard upon the seizing its prey, and which is sometimes extorted by fear.

This bird, though of the heron kind, is yet neither so destructive nor so voracious. It is a retired timorous animal, concealing itself in the midst of reeds and marshy places, and living upon frogs, insects, and vegetables; and though so nearly resembling the heron in figure, yet differing much in manners and appetites. As the heron builds on the tops of the highest trees, the bittern lays its nest in a sedgy margin, or amidst a tuft of rushes. The heron builds with sticks and wool; the bittern composes its simpler habitation of sedges, the leaves of water-plants, and dry rushes. The heron lays four eggs; the bittern generally seven or eight, of an ash-green colour. The heron feeds its young for many days; the bittern in three days leads its little ones to their food. In short, the heron is lean and cadaverous, subsisting chiefly upon animal food; the bittern is plump and fleshy, as it feeds upon vegetables, when more nourishing food is wanting.

It cannot be, therefore, from its voracious appetites, but its hollow boom, that the bittern is held in such detestation by the vulgar. " I remember, in the place where I was a boy, with what terror this bird's note affected the whole village; they considered it as the presage of some sad event, and generally found or made one to succeed it. I do not speak ludicrously; but if any person in the neighbourhood died, they supposed it could not be otherwise, for the night-raven had foretold it; but if no body happened to die, the death of a cow or a sheep gave completion to the prophecy."

Whatever terror it may inspire among the simple, its flesh is greatly esteemed among the luxurious. For this reason it is as eagerly sought after by the fowler as it is shunned by the peasant; and as it is a heavy rising, slow winged bird, it does not often escape him. Indeed, it seldom rises but when almost trod upon, and seems to seek protection rather from concealment than flight. At the latter end of autumn, however, in the evening, its wonted indolence appears to forsake it. It is then seen rising in a spiral ascent, till it is quite lost from the view, making at the same time a singular noise very different from its former boomings. Thus the same animal is often seen to assume different desires; and while the Latins have given the bittern the name of the star-reaching bird, the Greeks, taking its character from its more constant habits, have given it the title of the lazy bird.

THE REDSHANK, or POOL SNIPE,

resides the greater part of the year in the fen and marshy countries, where it is pretty common; and there it breeds and rears its young, laying four whitish eggs, tinged with olive, and marked with irregular black spots, most numerous at the large end. When disturbed, it has nearly the actions of a lapwing, in flying round its nest, which it is said to do in such regular circles, the nest being in the centre, whether the circuits be larger or smaller, insomuch that an attentive observer will find it by this circumstance. The redshank is in length twelve inches, in breadth twenty-one, and weighs about six ounces: the bill is two inches long, slender, and like a woodcock's; of a dark red at the base, and black towards the point: the tongue is sharp and undivided; the upper mandible longer, and sometimes crooked at the very tip: irides reddish hazel; a whitish line passes over and encircles each eye, from the corner of which a dusky brown spot is extended to the beak. The head, and hind part of the neck, dusky ash-colour, spotted with brown: back and scapulars glossy olive brown: wing coverts ash-colour, mixed with dusky and brown, and marked with whitish spots: the bastard wing and primary quills are brown; the inner webs of the latter are deeply edged with white freckled with brown, and some of these quills next the secondaries are elegantly marked near their tips with narrow brown lines, pointed and shaped to the form of each feather. Some of the secondaries are similarly barred, others are white: the throat and forepart of the breast are marked with short dusky spots; the under parts from the breast, and the lower parts of the back and rump, white, marked with minute dusky spots: tail coverts and tail crossed with narrow bars of black, twelve or thirteen on each feather: legs orange red, and measure, from the end of the toes to the upper bare part of the thigh, five inches and a half: claws black. In some birds both the rump and belly are of a pure white. The red-shank is common in many parts of Europe, as high as Finland; is likewise found in Siberia, and is indigenous also to the continent of America.

THE CURLEW

is common in England, where it is to be met with at all seasons. In the winter haunting the sea coast and marshes in great numbers, where they live upon the worms, marine insects, and different fishy substances, which they find upon the beach, and

among the loose rocks and shallow pits left by the retiring tide.
Their summer residence is upon the heathy, mountainous, boggy
moors, where their food consists of worms, slugs, flies, and insects, which their long bills enable them to pick out of the soft
mossy earth, and here they breed.   The female (which is rather
bigger, but whose plumage is nearly like the male's) makes her
nest upon the ground, in a dry tuft of rushes or grass, of such
withered materials as are found near, and in April lay four eggs,
of a pale olive colour, marked with brownish spots.   These birds
vary much in size, as well as in the different shades of their
feathers, some of them weighing not more than twenty-two, and
others thirty-seven ounces.   In some, the white parts of the
plumage are clearer than in others, which are more uniformly
grey, and tinged with pale brown : they utter a very shrill cry,
that may be heard at a considerable distance.

The common length of the curlew is two feet, and from tip
to tip from three feet to forty inches; the bill is about seven
inches long, of a regular curve, and tender substance at the
point; the tongue sharp, and very short, extending not further
than the angle of the lower chap; the upper mandible is black,
gradually softening into brown towards the base, which of the
under mandible is flesh coloured ; the feathers of the head, neck,
upper part of the back and wing coverts, are of a pale brown;
the middle of each feather black, edged and deeply indented
with pale rust colour, or light grey; the breast, belly, and lower
part of the back, dull white, marked with conjunct lines of black,
the two former with oblong strokes more thickly set : quills
black, spotted on the inner webs with white; tail reddish white,
barred with black; the legs are bare a little above the knees, of
a dusky blueish colour; the toes are thick, and flat on the under-
side.   The curlew flies swiftly.   The flesh of the curlew has
been characterised as being very good, and of a fine flavour ; by
others the direct reverse' has been maintained.   The truth is,

that while they live inland, and on the moors, and are in health and season, scarcely any bird excels them in goodness ; but when curlews return to and continue some time on the sea-shores, they acquire a rank and fishy taste.

Curlews are found in most parts of Europe ; they abound in all the plains and open marshes, or heath grounds of Russia and Siberia ; also in Kamtschatka, Lapland and Iceland, in general retiring north to breed, and returning to the south as autumn approaches. In Italy and Greece, and perhaps much further south, they are met with, as flocks are seen passing over the island of Malta, spring and autumn.

THE STONE CURLEW.

Of the stone curlew (Charadrius Oedicnemus) Mr. White gives the following account :—That it lays its eggs, which are short and round, of a dirty white, spotted with dark bloody botches, usually two, never more than three, on the bare ground, so that the countryman in ploughing his fallows often destroys them. The young run as soon as they are hatched like partridges, and are withdrawn to some flinty field by the dam, where they skulk among our grey spotted flints, which are so exactly of their colour, as to be such a security, that unless he catches the eye of the young bird, the most accurate observer may be deceived. Oedicnemus is a most expressive name for them, since their legs seem swelled like those of a gouty man, yet they run with the swiftness of a greyhound, and sometimes stop suddenly, holding the head and body motionless. After harvest, Mr. W. says, he has shot them before the pointers in turnip fields. When it flies, this bird stretches out its legs straight behind like an heron. A Sussex friend, to whom Mr. W. applied for further information respecting the stone curlew, states, "that they live with us all spring and summer, and at the beginning of autumn prepare to depart by getting together in flocks. They seem to me a bird of passage, that may travel into some dry hilly country south of us, probably Spain, because of the abundance of sheep-walks in that country; for they spend their summers with us in such districts. I believe they are not fond of going near the water, but feed on earth worms, that are common on sheepwalks and downs. There is reason to think, that the old do not feed the young ones, but only lead them about at the time of feeding, which, for the most part, is in the night."

OF THE WATER-HEN AND THE COOT.

Before we enter upon water fowls, properly so called, two or three birds claim our attention, which seem to form the shade between the web-footed tribe and those of the crane kind. These partake rather of the form than the habits of the crane; and, though furnished with long legs and necks, rather swim than wade. They cannot properly be called web-footed; nor yet are they entirely destitute of membranes, which fringe their toes on each side, and adapt them for swimming. The birds in question are the water-hen and the bald-coot

These birds have too near an affinity not to be ranked in the
same description. They are shaped entirely alike, their legs are
long, and their thighs partly bare; their necks are proportion-
able, their wings short, their bills short and weak, their colour
black, their foreheads bald and without feathers, and their habits
entirely the same. These, however, naturalists have thought
proper to range in different classes, from very slight distinctions
in their figure. The water-hen weighs but fifteen ounces, the
coot twenty-four. The bald part of the forehead in the coot is
white; in the water-hen it is of a beautiful pink colour. The
toes of the water-hen are edged with a straight membrane, those
of the coot have it scolloped and broader.

The differences in the figure are but slight; and those in their
manner of living still less. The history of the one will serve for
both. As birds of the crane kind are furnished with long wings,
and easily change place, the water hen, whose wings are short,
is obliged to reside entirely near those places where her food lies:
she cannot take those long journies that most of the crane kind
are seen to perform; compelled by her natural imperfections,
as well perhaps as by inclination, she never leaves the side of the
pond or the river in which she seeks for provision. Where the
stream is selvaged with sedges, or the pond edged with shrubby
trees, the water-hen is generally a resident there: she seeks her
food along the grassy banks, and often along the surface of the
water. With Shakespeare's Edgar, she drinks the green mantle
of the standing pool; or, at least, seems to prefer those places
where it is seen. Whether she makes pond-weed her food, or
hunts among it for water-insects, which are found there in great
abundance is not certain. I have seen them when pond-weed
was taken out of their stomach. She builds her nest upon low
trees and shrubs, of sticks and fibres, by the water-side. Her
eggs are sharp at one end, white, with a tincture of green, spotted with red. She lays twice or thrice in a summer; her young

ones swim the moment they leave the egg, pursue their parent, and imitate all her manners. She rears in this manner two or three broods in a season; and when the young are grown up she drives them off to shift for themselves.

As the coot is a larger bird, it is always seen in larger streams, and more remote from mankind. The water-hen seems to prefer inhabited situations: she keeps near ponds, moats, and pools of water near gentlemen's houses; but the coot keeps in rivers and among rushy margined lakes. It there makes a nest of such weeds as the stream supplies, and lays them among the reeds, floating on the surface, and rising and falling with the water. The reeds among which it is built keep it fast, so that it is seldom washed into the middle of the stream. But if this happens, which is sometimes the case, the bird sits in her nest, like a mariner in his boat, and steers with her legs her cargo into the nearest harbour: there, having attained her port, she continues to sit in great tranquillity, regardless of the impetuosity of the current; and though the water penetrates her nest, she hatches her eggs in that wet condition.

The water-hen never wanders: but the coot sometimes swims down the current till it even reaches the sea. In this voyage these birds encounter a thousand dangers: as they cannot fly far, they are hunted by dogs and men; as they never leave the stream, they are attacked and destroyed by otters; they are preyed upon by kites and falcons; and they are taken in still greater numbers in weirs made for catching fish; for these birds are led into the nets while pursuing small fish and insects, which are their principal food. Thus animated nature affords a picture of universal invasion! Man destroys the otter, the otter destroys the coot, the coot feeds upon fish, and fish are universally the tyrants of each other!

THE WATER-RAIL,

although a shy and solitary bird, is sufficiently common in this kingdom, but it is only seen during the winter in the northern parts. It is found chiefly on the edges of ponds and rivulets, much overgrown with sedges, reeds, and other coarse herbage, among which it may find shelter on the appearance of an enemy, and also feed in secret security : it runs, occasionally flirting up its tail, through its tracks with similar swiftness to what the land rail exerts in the meadows and corn-fields; and also shews an equal aversion to take flight as that bird does ; and possesses more means of disappointing the sportsman, whose patience it generally exhausts, and distracts his dog, seldom rising until after it has crossed every pool, and skulked through every avenue, within the circle of its retreats : when once flushed, it is, however, easily shot, flying very indifferently, and with its legs hanging down : it will, at times, take to the water, swimming tolerably well, and is often seen running on the surface, where there are any weeds to bear it up.

The eggs of the water-rail, according to Latham, are more than an inch and a half long, of a pale yellowish colour, marked all over with dusky brown spots, nearly equal in size, but irregular. The flesh is of a delicious flavour.

The length of the water-rail is twelve inches, breadth fourteen, and weighs three ounces and a half; the bill is slightly curved, one inch and three quarters long, of a dusky black colour, but reddish at the base ; irides red ; the top of the head, hinder part of the neck, back, scapulars, coverts of the wings and tail, are black edged with dingy brown ; the under parts from the chin to the middle of the belly, ash-colour ; in some, supposed to be

young birds, margined with white ; the side feathers are beautifully crossed with black and white, and slightly tipped with reddish brown ; the inner side of the thighs, the belly, and the vent,
are pale brown, sometimes specked with blueish ash-colour ;
under tail coverts white ; quills dusky ; the tail consists of twelve
short black feathers, edged and tipped with dusky red ; some of
those on the under side barred with black and white. The legs,
which are placed far behind, dusky red; the toes long, and without any membrane to connect them.

The water-rail is found in Lancashire, and the northern parts
of England, and is plentiful in the marshes of Sweden, Norway,
Russia, and in the western part of Siberia, and throughout the
continent of Europe ; from whence, during the severity of
winter, it migrates southward, even into Africa.   Buffon says,
they pass Malta in the spring and autumn ; and in confirmation
adds, that "the Viscount de Querhëint saw a flight of them at
the distance of fifty leagues from the coasts of Portugal, on the
17th of April, some of which were so fatigued that they suffered
themselves to be caught by the hand."

THE GREBE.

To these birds, with long legs and finny toes, I will add one
species more, with short legs and finny toes ; I mean the grebe.
The entire resemblance of this bird's appetites and manners to
those of the web-footed class, might justly induce me to rank it

among them; but as it resembles those above described, in the peculiar form of its toes, and bears some similitude in its manners also, I will for once sacrifice method to brevity. The grebe is much larger than either of the former, and its plumage white and black; it differs also entirely in the shortness of its legs, which are made for swimming, and not walking: in fact, they are from the knee upward hid in the belly of the bird, and have consequently very little motion. By this mark, and by the scolloped fringe of the toes, may this bird be easily distinguished from all others.

As they are thus, from the shortness of their wings, ill formed for flying, and from the uncommon shortness of their legs utterly unfitted for walking, they seldom leave the water, and chiefly frequent those broad shallow pools where their faculty of swimming can be turned to the greatest advantage, in fishing and seeking their prey.

They are chiefly, in this country, seen to frequent the meres of Shropshire and Cheshire, where they breed among reeds and flags, in a floating nest, kept steady by the weeds of the margin. The female is said to be a careful nurse of her young, being observed to feed them most assiduously with small eels; and when the little brood is tired, the mother will carry them either on her back or under her wings. This bird preys upon fish, and is almost perpetually diving. It does not shew much more than the head above water, and is very difficult to be shot, as it darts down on the appearance of the least danger. It is never seen on land: and though disturbed ever so often, will not leave that lake, where alone, by diving and swimming, it can find food and security. It is chiefly sought for the skin of its breast, the plumage of which is of a most beautiful silvery white, and as glossy as satin. This part is made into tippets; but the skins are out of season about February, losing their bright colour; and in breeding-time their breasts are entirely bare.

WATER BIRDS.

The general conformation of the aquatic birds, exhibits fully the fitness of their destination to that element in or near which their lives are entirely spent. The body of the swimmers is arched beneath, and bulged like the hulk of a ship; and this figure was perhaps copied in the first construction of vessels: their neck, which rises on a projecting breast, represents the prow; their short tail, collected into a single bunch, serves as a rudder; their broad and palmated feet perform the office of oars; and their thick down glistening with oil (which entirely invests them) is impenetrable by humidity, and at the same time enables them to float more lightly on the surface of the water. The habits and economy of these birds correspond also with their organization: they never seem happy but in their appropriate element; they are averse to alight on the land; and the least roughness of the ground hurts their soles, which are softened by the perpetual bathing. The water is to them the scene of pleasure and repose, where all their motions are performed with facility, and where their various evolutions are traced with elegance and grace. View the swans moving sweetly along or sailing majestically with expanded plumage upon the wave! they gaily sport: they dive and again emerge with gentle undulations, and soft energy; expressive of those sentiments which are the foundation of love.

The life of aquatic birds is, therefore, more peaceful and less laborious than that of most other tribes. Smaller force is required in swimming than flying; and the element which they inhabit perpetually yields them subsistence: they rather meet with their prey than search for it; and often a friendly wave conveys it within their reach, and they seize it without trouble or fatigue. Their dispositions also are more harmless, and their habits more pacific. Each species congregates through mutual attachment. They never attack their companions, nor destroy other birds; and, in this great and amicable nation, the strong seldom oppresses the weak.

The bill in this tribe (which comprehends swans and geese, as well as ducks) is strong, broad, flat, and generally furnished at the end with a kind of nail: the edges of the mandibles are marked with sharp serratures. The nostrils are small and oval. The tongue is broad, having the edges fringed near the base. The toes are four in number, three before and one behind; the middle one is the longest.

As swans are occasionally met with in this country during winter, (particularly in severe weather) I will just sketch their history.

THE WHISTLING SWAN.

The whistling or wild swan is somewhat smaller than the tame species. The bill is three inches long; yellowish white to the middle, but black at the end. The whole plumage is white, and the legs are black.

This species is an inhabitant of the northern regions; never appearing in England except in hard winters, when flocks of five or six are now and then seen. · Martin says, that in the month of October, swans come in great numbers to Lingey, one of the

Western isles, and continue till March, when they return northward to breed. A few continue in Mainland, one of the Orkneys, and breed in the little islands of the fresh-water lochs; but
the principal part of them retire at the approach of spring.
They are called the countryman's almanack; for their quitting
the isle is said to presage good weather, and their arrival the reverse.

In Iceland, these birds are an object of chase. In the month
of August they lose their feathers to such a degree as not to be
able to fly. The natives, at that season, resort in great numbers to the places where they most abound; and are accompanied with dogs, and active and strong horses, trained to the
sport, and capable of passing nimbly over the boggy soil and
marshes. The swans will run as fast as a tolerably fleet horse.
The greater number are taken by the dogs; which are taught
to seize them by the neck—a mode of attack that causes them
to lose their balance, and become an easy prey.

Notwithstanding their size, these birds are so extremely swift
on the wing, when in full feather, as to make them more difficult to shoot than almost any other; it being frequently necessary to aim ten or twelve feet before their bills. This, however,
is only when they are flying before the wind in a brisk gale; at
which time they seldom proceed at the rate of less than one
hundred miles an hour: but when flying across the wind or
against it, they are not able to make any great progress.

 This species has several distinctions from that called by us the
tame swan: but the most remarkable one is, the strange form
of the windpipe; which falls into the chest, then turns back like
a trumpet, and afterwards makes a second bend to join the lungs.
By this curious construction, the bird is enabled to utter a loud
and shrill note. The other swan, on the contrary, is the most
silent of all the feathered tribes; it can do nothing more than
hiss, which it does on receiving any provocation.—The vocal

swan emits its loud notes only when flying, or calling : its sound is, *whoogh, whoogh,* very loud and shrill, but not disagreeable when heard high in the air and modulated by the winds. The Icelanders compare it to the notes of the violin : they hear it at the end of their long and gloomy winter, when the return of the swans announces also the return of summer ; every note therefore must be melodious which presages a speedy thaw, and a release from their tedious confinement.

It was from this species alone that the ancients derived their fable of the swan's being endowed with the powers of melody. Embracing the Pythagorean doctrine, they made the body of this bird the mansion of the souls of departed poets ; and then attributed to the birds the same faculty of harmony which they had thus possessed in a pre-existent state. And the vulgar, not distinguishing between sweetness of numbers and melody of voice, thought that real which was only intended figuratively.— The mute or tame swan never frequents the Padus ; " and I am almost equally certain, (says Mr. Pennant) that it never was seen on the Cayster, in Lydia ; each of which are celebrated by the poets for the great resort of swans. The Padus was styled *Oloriferus* from the numbers of these birds which frequent its waters ; and there are few of the poets, either Greek or Latin, who do not make them its inhabitants."

THE TAME or MUTE SWAN.

The mute swans are found wild in Russia and Siberia : in England they are very common in a domestic state. They are seen in great plenty on the Thames ; where they are esteemed royal property, and it is accounted felony to steal their eggs. In the reign of Edward the IV. swans were held in such estimation, that "no person who did not possess a freehold of the clear yearly value of five marks" was permitted to keep any.

ʃ Nothing can exceed the beauty and elegance with which the swan rows itself along in the water, throwing itself into the proudest attitudes imaginable before the spectators ; and there is not perhaps in all nature a more lively or striking image of dignity and grace. In the exhibition of its form, we see no broken or harsh lines, no constrained or abrupt motions, but the roundest contour and the easiest transitions imaginable : the eye wanders over every part with pleasure, and every part takes new grace with new postures.

> The swan, with arched neck
> Between her white wings mantling, proudly rows
> Her state with oary feet.

It exhibits, however, but an inelegant appearance on land.

The swan will swim faster than a man can walk. It is very strong, and at times extremely fierce : it has not unfrequently been known to throw down and trample upon youths of fifteen or sixteen years of age ; and an old swan, we are told, is able to break the leg of a man with a single stroke of its wing.—A female, while in the act of sitting, observed a fox swimming towards her from the opposite shore : she instantly darted into the water, and, having kept him at bay for a considerable time with her wings, at last succeeded in drowning him ; after which, in the sight of several persons, she returned in triumph. This circumstance took place at Pensy, in Buckinghamshire.

Swans are very long-lived, sometimes arriving at the great age of a hundred years. The flesh of the old birds is hard and ill-tasted ; but that of the young, or cygnets, was formerly much esteemed.

The swan makes its nest of grass, among reeds; and in February begins to lay, depositing an egg every other day till there are six or eight. These occupy six weeks in hatching. Dr. Latham says, he knows two females that for three or four years past have agreed to associate ; and have had each a brood yearly, bringing up together about eleven young: they sit by turns, and never quarrel.—When in danger, the old birds carry off the young ones on their backs.

———

THE WILD GOOSE.

Wild geese inhabit the fens of England ; and are supposed not to migrate, as they do in many countries on the continent. They breed in Lincolnshire and Cambridgeshire : they have seven or eight young ; which are sometimes taken, and are easily rendered tame.

They are often seen in flocks of from fifty to a hundred, flying at very great heights, and seldom resting by day. Their cry is frequently heard while they are imperceptible from their distance above. Whether this be their note of mutual encouragement, or only the necessary consequence of respiration, seems somewhat doubtful; but they seldom exert it when they alight in their journeys. On the ground they always arrange themselves in a line, and seem to descend rather for rest than refreshment; for, having continued in this manner for an hour or two, one of them with a long loud note sounds a kind of signal to which the rest always punctually attend, and rising in a group they pursue their journey with alacrity. Their flight is conducted with vast regularity: they always proceed either in a line a-breast, or in two lines joining in an angle at the middle. In this order they generally take the lead by turns; the foremost falling back in the rear when tired, and the next in station succeeding to his duty.— Their track is generally so high, that it is almost impossible to reach them with a fowling-piece; and even when this can be done, they file so equally that one discharge very seldom kills more than a single bird.

They breed in the plains and marshes about Hudson's Bay in North America: in some years the young ones are taken in considerable numbers; and at this age they are easily tamed. It is, however, extremely singular, that they will never learn to eat corn, unless some of the old ones are taken along with them; which may be done when these are in a moulting state.

Our common tame goose is nothing more than this species in a state of domestication.

THE BERNACLE GOOSE.

The bill of this bird is very short and black, crossed with a flesh-coloured mark on each side. Part of the head, the chin, throat, under-parts, and upper tail-coverts, are white; and the rest of the head and neck, and the beginning of the back, are black. The thighs are mottled. Round the knee, the feathers are black; and the lower feathers of the back are the same, edged with white.. The wing-coverts and scapulars are blue-grey;

the ends black, fringed with white at the tip. The rump, tail, and legs, are black.

, The Bernacle geese are not uncommon on many of the northern and western coasts of this kingdom, in winter ; but they are scarce in the south, and only seen in inclement seasons. They leave our island in February, and retire northward to breed.

Of all the marvellous productions which ignorance, ever credulous, has so long substituted for the simple and truly wonderful operations of nature, the most absurd, and yet not the least celebrated, is the assertion of the growth of these birds, in a kind of shell, called *lepas anatifera* (goose-bearing shell), on certain trees on the coasts of Scotland and the Orkneys, or on the rotten timbers of old ships.

Numerous writers have mentioned and credited these circumstances : one of these, Maier, who has written a treatise expressly on this bird, says, that it certainly originates from shells : and, what is still more wonderful, that he himself opened a hundred of the goose-bearing shells in the Orkneys, and found in all of them the rudiments of the bird completely formed !

OF THE GANNET, OR SOLAND GOOSE.

The Gannet is of the size of a tame goose, but its wings much longer, being six feet over. The bill is six inches long, straight almost to the point, where it inclines down, and the sides are irregularly jagged, that it may hold its prey with greater security. It differs from the cormorant in size, being larger; and its colour, which is chiefly white ; and by its having no nostrils, but in their place a long furrow that reaches almost to the end of the bill. From the corner of the mouth is a narrow slip of black bare skin, that extends to the hind part of the head ; beneath the skin is another that, like the pouch of the pelican, is dilatable, and of size sufficient to contain five or six entire herrings, which in the breeding season it carries at once to its mate or its young.

These birds, which subsist entirely upon fish, chiefly resort to those uninhabited islands where their food is found in plenty, and men seldom come to disturb them. The islands to the north of Scotland, the Skelig islands off the coasts of Kerry in Ireland, and those that lie in the north sea off Norway, abound with them. But it is on the Bass island, in the Frith of Edinburgh, where they are seen in the greatest abundance. " There is a small island," says the celebrated Hervey, " called the Bass, not more than a mile in circumference. The surface is almost wholly covered during the months of May and June with their nests, their eggs, and young. It is scarcely possible to walk without treading on them : the flocks of birds upon the wing, are so numerous, as to darken the air like a cloud ; and their noise is such that one cannot without difficulty be heard by the person next to him. When one looks down upon the sea from the precipice, its whole surface seems covered with infinite numbers of birds of different kinds, swimming and pursuing their prey. If, in sailing round the island, one surveys its hanging cliffs, in every crag, or fissure of the broken rocks, may be seen innumerable birds, of various sorts and sizes, more than the stars of heaven, when viewed in a serene night. If they are viewed at a distance, either receding, or in their approach to the island, they seem like one vast swarm of bees."

They are not less frequent upon the rocks of St. Kilda.

Martin assures us, that the inhabitants of that small island con-
sume annually near twenty-three thousand young birds of this
species, besides an amazing quantity of their eggs. On these
they principally subsist throughout the year; and from the number of these visitants, make an estimate of their plenty for the
season. They preserve both the eggs and fowls in small pyra-
midical stone buildings, covering them with turf-ashes, to prevent
the evaporation of their moisture.

The gannet is a bird of passage. In winter it seeks the more
southern coasts of Cornwall, hovering over the shoals of herrings
and pilchards that then come down from the northern seas; its
first appearance in the northern islands is in the beginning of
spring, and it continues to breed till the end of summer. But,
in general, its motions are determined by the migrations of the
immense shoals of herrings that come pouring down at that
season through the British channel, and supply all Europe, as
well as this bird, with their spoil. The gannet assiduously at-
tends the shoal in their passage, keeps with them in their whole
circuit round our island, and shares with our fisherman this ex-
haustless banquet. As it is strong of the wing, it never comes
near the land; but is constant to its prey. Wherever the gannet is seen, it is sure to announce to the fishermen the arrival of
the finny tribe: they then prepare their nets, and take the herrings by millions at a draught; while the gannet, who came to
give the first information, comes, though an unbidden guest,
and often snatches its prey from the fisherman even in his boat.
While the fishing season continues, the gannets are busily employed; but when the pilchards disappear from our coasts, the
gannet takes its leave to keep them company.

The cormorant has been remarked for the quickness of his
sight; yet in this the gannet seems to exceed him. It is possessed of a transparent membrane under the eye-lid, with which
it covers the whole eye at pleasure, without obscuring the sight

in the smallest degree. This seems a necessary provision for the security of the eyes of so weighty a creature, whose method of taking its prey, like that of the cormorant, is by darting headlong down from a height of a hundred feet and more into the water to seize it.—These birds are sometimes taken at sea, by fastening a pilchard to a board, which they leave floating. The gannet instantly pounces down from above upon the board, and is killed or maimed by the shock of a body where it expected no resistance.

These birds breed but once a year, and lay but one egg, which being taken away, they lay another if that is also taken, then a third; but never more for that season. Their egg is white, and rather less than that of the common goose, and their nest large, composed of such substances as are found floating on the surface of the sea. The young birds, during the first year, differ greatly in colour from the old ones; being of a dusky hue, speckled with numerous triangular white spots; and at that time resembling the colours of the speckled diver.

The Bass island, where they chiefly breed, belongs to one proprietor; so that care is taken never to fright away the birds when laying, or to shoot them upon the wing. By that means they are so confident as to alight and feed their young ones close beside you. They feed only upon fish, as was observed; yet the young gannet is counted a great dainty by the Scots, and is sold very dear; so that the lord of the islet makes a considerable annual profit by the sale.

WILD DUCK.

See page 58.

THE TEAL

is one of the most delicate birds that graces our tables, and has been sold for seven, and frequently sells for five, shillings a couple.

The male teal weighs about twelve ounces, the female nine; the length is fourteen inches, the breadth twenty-three; the bill is a dark lead colour, tipped with black; irides pale hazel; from the bill to the hindpart of the head is a broad bar of glossy changeable green, bounded on the under part with a cream-coloured white line, and edged on the upper side with pale brown; the rest of the head and the upper part of the neck are of a deep reddish chesnut; forepart of the neck and breast dusky white, marked with roundish black spots; belly white, middle of the vent black; the wing coverts brown, quills dusky; the exterior webs of the lesser marked with a vivid green spot; above that another of black, and edged with white; the legs dirty lead colour. The female is of a brownish ash-colour; the lower part of the neck, and sides over the wing, brown, edged with white; the wing has a green spot like the male; the belly and vent both white.

It was at no very remote period supposed not to breed in England; but Mr. White, in his history of Selborne, has established the fact by some young teals being brought to him, which were taken in a pond on the verge of Wolmer forest. It it also known to breed in the mosses about Carlisle, as well as in Lancashire, and also in several parts of Cumberland. In France, where it stays throughout the year, it makes its nest in April, among the rushes on the edges of ponds, and which is composed of the tenderest stalks of the rushes, with the addition of the pith, and a quantity of feathers. The nest is of a large size, and placed on the surface of the water, so as to rise or fall with it; the eggs, to the number of from twelve to seventeen, are as large as those of a pigeon, of a dirty white, marked with small hazel spots: it is said to feed upon the grass and weeds which grow on the edges of waters it frequents; it will also eat the seeds of the rushes, and small fish; and the insects with which all stagnant waters are so abundantly stored. The teal is found to the north as high as Iceland, and is mentioned as inhabiting the Caspian sea to the south, and is every where deemed most excellent food.

Hearne says, like the mallard, they are found in considerable numbers near the sea coast at Hudson's bay, but are more plentiful in the interior parts of the country, flying in such large flocks, that he has often killed twelve or fourteen, and has seen both English and Indians kill many more at one shot. At their first arrival they are poor, but generally esteemed good eating. He describes the teal as the most prolific of the water fowl at Hudson's bay, having often seen the old ones swimming at the head of seventeen young when not much larger than walnuts. The teal remains in these parts so long as the season will permit; for in his passage from Cumberland house to York fort 1775, he, as well as his Indian companions, killed them in the rivers they passed through so late as the twentieth of October; they were then entirely covered with fat, delicately white, and might truly be called a luxury.

THE WIGEON

is in length twenty inches, and weight twenty-four ounces; bill narrow, of a blueish lead-colour, an inch and a half long, tip black; the top of the head is cream-colour, over the bill almost white; head and neck light bay; the plumage of the back, and sides under the wings, undulated with black and white lines; wing coverts brown, more or less mixed with, and in some birds almost white; the greater quill feathers dusky; the outermost webs of the middle feathers of a fine green; the tips black, the last striped with black and white; the two middle feathers of the tail are longer than the others, black and sharp pointed, the rest ash-coloured; the belly white; vent feathers black; legs dusky lead colour.

The head of the female is of a rusty brown, spotted with black; the back is of a deep brown, edged with a paler; the tips of the lesser quill feathers white; the belly white.

This species is common on most parts of the old continent; it is caught as low as Egypt, from the middle to the end of November, by nets in the marshes before the departure of the waters; it is also found at Aleppo, during the winter, in plenty; observed likewise in the Caspian sea and its neighbourhood; and in most parts of Europe, as far as Sweden. It abounds in England during the winter months, and is caught in the decoys; it is said not to breed in France; nor is it certain they breed in this country. Both sexes are alike until the following spring after hatching, (this obtains in the pintail, the gadwall, and the shoveller, who are all grey and have no beautiful feathers when young,) when the males about March gain their full plumage, but lose it again the end of July, and with it in some measure

2 I

their voice, which they regain, and always use during their flight, in the winter season, and which is thought to be like the sound of a fife. Their flesh is much esteemed, and they are easily domesticated in places where there is much water, and are greatly admired for their beauty, sprightly look, and active frolicksome motions.

DIVERS,

as they are termed, consist of the scoter, scaup, golden eye, morillon, and others of the duck kind, and are not meant to particularly signify those birds to which naturalists have given the name of divers.

They vary much both in plumage and size, some weighing two pounds and a half, and others a pound less. In hard weather they frequent the shores and the tide rivers in great plenty, and are almost always at that season fat and in good condition; they do not fly in such large flocks as many of the duck species, and usually close to the surface of the water, and bear very hard blows from the shot without dropping, unless struck upon the head or wing.

The day seems to be spent by these birds between diving and flying to small distances over the water, which they do so low as often to dip their legs in it : they swallow their food whole, and soon digest the shells, which are found crumbled to powder among their excrements. They have been kept tame for some time, and will feed on soaked bread. The flesh tastes fishy in the extreme, and from this cause is allowed by the Roman Catholics to be eaten on fast days and in lent; and, indeed, must be a sufficient mortification.

THE PINTAIL.

This bird is less than the wild duck; its length is twenty-eight inches, breadth thirty-eight, and its weight twenty-four ounces.

The form of the pintail is slender, and the neck long: bill long and black, on the sides blueish; the head, for an inch of the neck before, rusty purplish brown; nape dusky; forepart and sides of the neck white, a little mottled with dusky, the white rising upwards on each side at the back part like ribbands; part of the neck, and back, greyish white, finely barred with black; sides of the body the same, but paler; scapulars black, long, pointed, and margined with very pale cream-colour; wings pale dusky brown; across them, first a pale rufous bar, then a broad deep copper-coloured one, edged with black, and below this is a narrow one of white; the two middle tail feathers are black, and more than three inches longer than the rest, and end in a point; the exterior feathers of the tail are ash-coloured; the under parts of the body are white; vent black, the sides of it white; legs and feet small and lead-coloured.

The female is smaller; head and neck dusky, minutely streaked with brown, spotted with black; tail as in the male, but the two middle feathers not so far elongated.

This species is pretty common during winter in England, especially in severe weather, when it is very fat; the flesh is superior in its delicate flavour to any other wild fowl. In the month of February only these birds are found in great abundance in Connaught, in Ireland. Upon the continent, in the northern parts of which it breeds, it is extremely numerous. It is abundant at the Lake Baikal, in Asia, and is often seen in large flocks on the sea-coasts of China, where it is caught in snares. In America it is not uncommon, being plentiful at New York, where it is called blue-bill; from thence found as far north as Hudson's Bay, where it is supposed to breed.

THE POCHARD.

This species, like the pintail, and some others, is common both to the old and new continent. With us it frequents the fens, as well as the coasts and tide rivers; in which last it is taken sometimes extremely fat in the severest weather. It is not ascertained whether they breed in England; but in France one has been shot in the month of July. Their food is small fish and shells: they are found south as far as Egypt, about Cairo, and in Carolina during the winter. They have a hissing voice; their flight is more rapid than that of the wild duck, and the noise made by their wings is quite different; the flocks observe no particular shape in flying, as the duck, in triangles, but form a close body.

The pochard is about the size of a wigeon, weighs one pound twelve ounces; its length is nineteen inches; breadth, two feet and a half; the bill is broader than the wigeon's, of a deep lead-colour, with a black tip; irides, orange; the head and neck deep chesnut, with a small triangular spot of white under the centre of the lower mandible; the lower part of the neck and breast, and upper part of the back, dusky black; scapulars and wing coverts nearest the body of a greyish white, elegantly marked with narrow lines of black; the exterior wing coverts and quills, dusky brown; secondary quill feathers regularly edged with a stripe of white; the belly, ash-coloured and brown; vent feathers, and coverts of tail, black; the tail consists of twelve short feathers of a deep grey; the legs lead-coloured. The female has the head of a pale reddish brown; the breast is rather of a deeper colour; wing coverts and belly, cinereous; the back marked like that of the male.

These birds are eagerly bought by the London poulterers, under the name of dun birds, as they are deemed excellent eating: the greater part of what appear in the markets are caught in decoys.

Wild Fowl Shooting.

In fen shooting, the principal object is the wild duck; it is true, wigeon and teal are frequently met with; and at certain seasons all those birds which I have described under distinct heads; and as wild ducks generally breed in and frequent marshy places, the sportsman has, of course, to pursue his game in situations where wet feet seem unavoidable, unless the marshes will admit small boats, which renders the diversion of duck shooting much more pleasant. This, however, is not always the case; and some sportsmen attempt to preserve their legs and feet from the water by enormous boots,* which are very fatiguing as well as uncomfortable. I have uniformly found that wet feet are of little consequence while the sportsman keeps moving about; but the moment he arrives at any place where he intends to stop for a time, he should always put on a pair of dry stockings, and also a pair of dry shoes, with which he should take care to provide himself, if at any distance from home.

For the diversion of duck-shooting, a water-spaniel, which has been taught to fetch and carry, will answer the purpose as well perhaps as any other kind of dog; though I use an old pointer bitch, which was never taught to fetch and carry, or to take the water, and yet a better animal for the purpose just mentioned cannot exist. The first day I took her into the field upon a shooting excursion, I happened to kill a bird as it flew across a pit. I had two other pointers with me, that had been shot over several seasons, that I could not, after every kind of entreaty,

* In order to render them impervious or water-proof, see receipts at the end of the volume.

induce to enter the water: the young bitch, however, after looking at the bird very attentively, which was not quite dead, but fluttered occasionally, to my surprise, took the water without the least solicitation, and brought me the bird as carefully as possible; and ever since then she has fetched a bird or a duck out of the water without hesitation, and will swim across water when she supposes an object is to be attained; but she invariably turns away with contempt if a stick or a stone be thrown in with a view to induce her to fetch it.

The latter end of August is, perhaps, the best time for this diversion, as the young ones are then able to fly tolerably well, without, however, being capable of sustaining those long flights which carry them away from the sportsman completely: when the young ducks become very strong on the wing they are not easy to be approached, and are ever afterwards found the most suspicious animals in nature. These birds are fond of those situations where the margin of the water is deeply fringed with sedges and aquatic plants, and where, on the least alarm, they secret themselves from human observation. In beating for the game, as little noise as possible should be made, whilst the dog should never be allowed to go out of gun shot, unless, from particular circumstances, a greater extent be rendered indispensable. A sceptic might be induced to ask why the flavour of a wild duck is superior to that of a domestic duck? this fact arises, I apprehend, from their unlimited freedom. The same remark equally applies to the partridge, compared to the domestic fowl, and indeed to every animal in a state of nature, compared to the same or a similar kind reduced to obedience by man. It was formerly customary to have, in the fenny parts of the kingdom, particularly in Lincolnshire, an annual driving of the young ducks before they were able to fly. For this purpose numbers of people assembled, who beat over a great extent of water, and forced the birds into a net placed at the spot where the sport

was to terminate. By this wholesale murderous plan, two
hundred dozen have been taken at one place in a day. This
method, which bade fair to extirpate the breed of wild ducks
altogether, has, however, I believe, been abandoned,—indeed it
has been abolished by act of parliament.

In hard winters, good sport may be had in wild fowl shooting.*

* The following Letter appeared in the Annals of Sporting, vol. 1. p.
315, addressed to the Editor ; and as it embraces my ideas on the subject,
I therefore insert it.

THE PERCUSSION GUN.—SEA FOWL SHOOTING.

SIR,—I am aware that the percussion gun has been already noticed
in your excellent miscellany, (see No. I. p. 10, No. III. pp. 147—149,)
but as there is a species of shooting to which this invention seems adapted
in a greater degree, perhaps, than any other, and which you have not
mentioned, I take the present opportunity of making it known to your
readers. As my residence is at the mouth of a large river, I frequently
take the diversion of shooting sea-fowl. The flight of the gull is slow,
its wings are very expansive, and it consequently offers a good mark for
the shooter : nevertheless its feathers are so hard, that it will carry away
a considerable quantity of shot, unless it be struck in a vital part, or
have its wings broken. It is not, however, a dainty for the table ; it may
be eaten when skinned, though, even in this case, it still retains a strong
oily flavour. If, after the skin be stripped off, the bird is parboiled, and
afterwards broiled, the unpleasant flavour will be much lessened. After
all, the sea-gull is not nearly so unpalatable as the heron, which was
formerly considered not only as a dainty, but is specially enumerated in
the list of royal game. The gull, of which several varieties visit the
shores of Great Britain, is the most common object that presents itself
to the sportsman at the mouths of great rivers; yet there is a great variety
of other aquatic game, which is frequently met with in the same situations, particularly ducks of various descriptions, which are more difficult
of approach than the gull, and on this account are generally shot at
from greater distances : here the percussion gun has a decided advantage
over the common fowling-piece. Birds of the duck kind, as well as
other sea-fowl, may be frequently seen at considerable distances, sitting
on the beach, perhaps, or on the point of some projecting rock. If fired

Lakes, with a marsh on one side, and a wood on the other, are seldom without vast quantities of wild fowl; and where a couple

at from a flint gun, the instant they observe the flash in the pan, they take wing, and are thus frequently missed. The advantage of a percussion gnn is, in this case, strikingly manifest, as there is scarcely any perceptible flash at the touch-hole, while the discharge is so much quicker, so very instantaneous, that the birds are struck before they can possibly get on the wing. At the same time, these shy birds may be reached at much greater distances than with the common flint lock, owing to the very superior force with which the shot is thrown from the percussion gun; a fact which I could not credit, till, from repeated experiment, it was no longer possible to entertain a doubt on the subject; the advantage of this mode of discharging the fowling-piece is still more evident when used for the purpose of shooting what are called divers. I was scarcely ever able to kill one of these birds with a flint lock; for though they will allow the shooter to approach within a short distance (as if conscious of their power to escape), yet the very instant they see the flash from the pan, they disappear, and are under the water in a moment: they are easily killed, however, with the percussion gun, for the reasons already stated.

In the Isle of Man, puffins are met with in great abundance; they are fat, oily, and altogether very strongly flavoured and unpleasant to the taste, in defiance of every possible care and pains in cooking them; they deposit their eggs in holes of the ground, in the interior of the island, many of which are picked up by the inhabitants, and sold principally in the Liverpool market. The Isle of Man seems, indeed, the particular resort of sea-fowl; as, independently of the large quantity of puffins, which frequent the interior, for the purpose of breeding, birds of the gull kind are in still greater abundance, if possible, and, in the breeding season, may be seen in myriads flying and screaming among the craggy rocks on the shore, on the ledges, and in the crevices of which they hatch and bring up their young. They are often very wantonly destroyed, and that too, sometimes, before the young brood are able to provide for themselves. Thoughtless sportsmen coast the island in boats for the purpose of shooting these birds; and the moment a gun is fired among the rocks, numbers of gulls immediately issue from the crevices, and hover over the shooter's head, within gun-shot, and the sportsman may continue to fire till he has either loaded the boat or tired himself.

are seen at one time, this is a sufficient inducement to bring hundreds of others. These birds, which fly in the air, are often lured down from their heights by the loud voice of one from below. To this call, all the stragglers resort: and, in a week or a fortnight's time, a lake that before was quite naked, will be black with water-fowl, that have left their Lapland retreats to keep company with our ducks, which continue with us during the whole year. Wild ducks breed in this country, in some places, to a considerable extent; but by far the greater portion of those seen during the winter season, come from the remote countries of the north.

Those birds of the duck kind which migrate to this country on the approach of winter, are seldom found so well tasted, or so fat as those that continue with us the year round: their flesh

The gull is a bold, familiar bird; and, when domesticated, is supposed to be of essential service in gardens, from the quantity of worms and grubs which it will devour. It will readily associate with the domestic duck, and soon becomes attached to the place where it is kept. A person at Douglas, in the Isle of Man, having reared a young gull, it became very familiar, and yet was placed under no restraint whatever. Its wings were suffered to grow, and it was allowed to follow its own inclination as to the extent of its flights. It became very well known in the neighbourhood, and no one molested it. At the approach of spring, however, it disappeared, and was considered to be lost; but, after the lapse of a week or two, the gull again returned; and, after being fed, flew away. Nevertheless its visits were often repeated; and it was ultimately discovered that its absence had arisen from its being engaged in the propagation of its species. On the return of winter it again took up its old abode; and again absented itself in spring. This practice the bird has continued for some years, with this difference only, that its domestic visits, during the summer, are more frequent; but it never fails to shelter itself under human protection from the hardships and perils of winter. It has been frequently seen in company with its mate and their young, which, however, keep at a distance, whenever it approaches its semi-annual habitation.

is often lean, and still oftener fishy, which flavour it has, probably, contracted in the journey, as their food in the lakes of Lapland, where they descend, is generally of the insect kind. As
they unite the power of flying with that of swimming, they have
an opportunity of resting and feeding in their long journies
across the ocean, and hence, perhaps, derive their fishy taste.
They are generally observed to arrive in England in flocks, and,
as soon as they have chosen their situation, they retire to that
part of the lake where they are inaccessible to the sportsman ;
they may be frequently seen huddled together, and are, for the
most part, very noisy. They thus continue during the day ;
but, on the approach of evening, they separate into small parties, and fly for the purpose of seeking food. This is, also, the
case at the dawn of day, as the gray of the morn no sooner
enables the ducks to distinguish objects, than they fly away to
feed. They then approach the margin of the lake, the marshy
ground, and particularly those stubbles which are situated near
the edge of the water. On these occasions, they afford much
diversion, or, at least, they are easily shot. Few sportsmen,
however, properly speaking, give themselves the trouble to attend
what is called the *flight*, that is, the flying of the ducks at
morning and evening, as this sport is very different from the pursuit of the partridge. In the latter case, all is motion and activity ; in the former, the shooter must approach the edge of
the water, and, taking his station in a convenient place, as much
concealed as possible, either by sitting down, crouching, or otherwise, and there patiently wait the approach, or passing, of the
game, sometimes, perhaps, for hours together, without having a
single shot. Duck-shooting, therefore, or what is called *flighting*,
is chiefly followed by the peasantry who reside on the borders of
the marsh, many of whom earn a subsistence by it during the
winter : these persons also catch a large quantity of snipes, &c.
by means of small snares.

Indeed, the pursuit of wild ducks appears so much disregarded by sportsmen, that gentlemen, who are the proprietors of extensive marshes, seldom think of disturbing the rustics in their occupation of duck-shooting. We do not say that the latter are allowed to approach the parks or pleasure-grounds of great men, where wild ducks are protected as ornamental to pieces of water; but, that such as are proprietors of marshes, in the general sense of the term, seldom prevent the rustics from pursuing their profitable amusement. It not unfrequently happens, however, that hares and rabbits come to feed, as well as ducks, in the dusk of the evening, particularly when the marsh happens to be situated at no great distance from strictly-preserved grounds, where game in general is found in great abundance. The best station that can be taken for shooting ducks is in a stubble, at a little distance from the water, where the ditches that surround the stubble empty themselves into the marsh, but, however, generally contain water sufficient to afford the ducks an opportunity of swimming up them. Here the ducks will resort in preference to any other situation, while the banks and the bushes afford facilities for concealment to the shooter that will be sought in vain in the open marsh. Under these circumstances, nothing is more common than for hares to visit the stubble just described, and they are then far more easily shot than ducks. On the approach of a hare, the shooter need only remain quiet; if he has any doubt of killing her as she passes, let him give a slight whistle, when she will not only pause but raise herself on her haunches, for the purpose, it would appear, of listening: nothing can be more easy than to shoot her in such a situation. This circumstance is, by no means, generally known; and many gentlemen, I have no doubt, who are extremely rigorous in the preservation of their game, allow the duck-shooter to pursue his avocation, unmolested, with the most perfect indifference.

Vast numbers of ducks are taken in Picardy, in France, particularly on the river Somme, where it is customary to wait for the flocks passing over certain places ; when the sportsman, having a wicker cage containing a quantity of tame birds, lets out one at a time, which alluring the passers-by within gun-shot, five or six may be sometimes killed at one shot. They are also taken by baited hooks, which the birds swallow while swimming on the water. The most curious mode, however, of taking wild-ducks is in India, and frequently practised on the river Ganges, where these birds are very numerous :—A person wades into the water up to his chin ; and, having his head covered with an empty calabash, approaches the place where the ducks are swim-ming ; the latter, not at all suspicious of an object of this kind, suffer the man freely to mix with the flock, when he seizes them by the legs, and pulls them under the water, one after another, till he has secured as many as he can attach to his belt ; and returns as unsuspected by the remainder as when he first came amongst them. The number of calabashes which are constantly floating down the river render the ducks perfectly familiar to the sight of them—hence the reason why the duck taker is ena-bled so easily to approach them ; but the method just described is not practicable either in very shallow or very deep water.

Wild-geese breed in the extensive fens of Lincolnshire and Cambridgeshire : the greater part, however, which are seen in this country retire to more northerly situations for the purpose of propagation. They may be frequently seen in large flocks, flying at a very great height ; and their cry is sometimes heard, while the birds themselves are imperceptible from their distance above. They are extremely difficult of approach. When on the ground, they appear to station a sort of sentinel, which, on the least suspicion, sounds a long loud note of alarm, on which the whole instantly take wing. Their flight appears to be con-ducted with great regularity ; which not only excites the curi-osity of the country people, but calls into action their inventive powers, and they thus make the geese, in their flight, describe all the letters of the alphabet, as well as all the figures used in the common rules of arithmetic. Their track is generally so high, that it is almost impossible to reach them with a fowling-piece: in long and severe frosts, however, they fly much lower, and, at such times, afford good diversion to the sportsman. The common grey wild-goose forms an excellent dish for the table; but there is a larger kind that sometimes attracts the attention of the sportsman, but possesses a very strong and oily flavour.

Wild-geese are found in great numbers in Canada, where the English settlers send out their own servants, as well as employ the Indians, to shoot them. The arrival of the geese in Canada is impatiently expected—it is the harbinger of spring; and the month is named by the Indians the *goose-moon*. In shooting these birds, they never attempt to pursue them, for that would be vain; but a row of huts, formed of boughs, at musket-shot distance from each other, is placed in a line across the vast marshes of that country. Each hut is occupied by one person only. These observe the flight of the geese, which no sooner approach within hearing, than they mimic their cackle so well, that the birds will answer, wheel, and come near the hut, or stand. When the geese are completely within gun shot, the sportsman fires, and immediately seizes another gun, ready cocked for the purpose, and discharges that also. The game that he has killed, he sets up on sticks, as if alive, to decoy others: he also makes artificial birds for the same purpose. In a good day (for they fly in very uncertain and unequal numbers) a single Indian will kill upwards of a hundred. There are several species of geese; and, though each has a different call, the Indians imitate them all with admirable accuracy.

Game Laws Amendment Bill.

PROCEEDINGS OF THE HOUSE OF COMMONS, AND REPORT
OF A SELECT COMMITTEE THEREON.

Lord Cranbourne having presented a petition to the House, complaining of the present state of the laws respecting the preservation of game, and deprecating the harsh, inefficacious penalties of those laws—involving alike life, liberty, and character, and *praying* the House to take into consideration the propriety of permitting of the sale of game, under certain restrictions; the same was referred to the consideration of a select committee to report thereon, with the usual powers to call before them and examine any persons whose evidence might elucidate their inquiries: they sat accordingly, and, after several days' investigation, reported as follows:—

> The select committee of this honourable House appointed to take into consideration the laws relating to game, and to report their observations thereon to the House, and who were empowered to report the minutes of evidence taken before them, have, pursuant to the orders of the House, examined the matters referred to them, and report to the House as follows:—

Your committee, in considering the subject referred to them, have turned their attention principally to those laws which relate to the purchase and sale of game, conceiving that the morals of the lower classes of the community were most materially affected by their operation; and they have ascertained, by evidence, points which appeared to them essential to be inquired into, with a view of showing how far the enactments at present existing, respecting the purchase and sale of game, effect the purposes for which they were made.

The evidence which has been taken, and which refers, for the most part, to the supply of the metropolis with game, establishes, in the opinion of the committee, the following facts :—

1st, That the laws which prohibit the sale of game are constantly and systematically evaded or set at defiance.*

2d, That the trade in game is carried on to a great extent, by respectable salesmen, who receive a commission upon the game sold by them, amounting, on account of the risk, to double that which they receive upon the sale of poultry.

3d, That this trade is also carried on by other persons, such as higglers, waggoners, coachmen, guards, and porters, at the several inns, where coaches and waggons, &c. put up.

* The following extract from the examination of one of the witnesses is illustrative of this position :—

Question. Some years ago an act of parliament passed, to make it illegal to buy game; you were in the trade at that time?

Answer. Yes.

Q. Did you immediately after that find the sale of game diminished at all?

A. Not the least; indeed I consider it a particular advantage, in some respects; I know a person, individually, who has found it so.

Q. Will you state of what advantage it is?

A. There is one particular clause in that act which says, that if I go and inform against any person, and convict him, so that he is fined, I shall be cleared from all pains and penalties up to that moment, to which I have become liable: suppose I had a threat of having a whole bench of country magistrates upon me, and a person comes into my shop, and buys a certain article of game, I lay an information against him, he pays the £5; I procure the record of the conviction, and I am immediately informed against, and the penalties, perhaps, come to 2 or £300; I produce the record of this conviction, and I am cleared; it is in my favour, and I could produce evidence that it has been acted upon.

4th, That the game is, in some instances, delivered by the poachers principally to this latter description of dealers, by absolute sale, or upon commission; in others, it is collected by persons who send it up together with poultry; and lastly, is sometimes received from owners of manors and landed proprietors, who are in the habit of sending their game, either to salesmen or others, for the purpose of sale.

5th, That the markets, by these means, appear to be constantly and abundantly supplied; and that, in consequence of the illegal mode in which it is obtained, it is impossible to regulate the supply by the demand; that large quantities of game are therefore sometimes wasted, and even thrown away.

6th, That the demand, during the season, is constant; and that the practice of purchasing game is not confined to any one class of the community, but is habitual to persons of every class who have not the means of being sufficiently supplied with that article from their own manors or land: and, in consequence, a breach of these particular laws appears not to be considered as any moral offence whatever.

These facts being established, it becomes quite clear that these laws have entirely failed in preventing the purchase and sale of game; and that, although in some instances persons legally in possession of game, dispose of it by sale, yet that the great supply of the market is in the hands of the poachers, who are, by this nearly exclusive trade, encouraged in the greatest degree to the continuance of their depredations.

Your committee, therefore, cannot but recommend the repeal of the laws relative to the purchase and sale of game; and that an act should be passed, permitting persons qualified to kill game in virtue of real property, and who may, therefore, be supposed to be in a situation to have a legal means of obtaining it, to sell it to such persons as shall be duly licensed to retail game, for the use of the public, under certain regulations and restrictions,

This, the committee imagine, would have the effect of inducing the retailers to purchase only from such persons as are so qualified; and, for their own interest, they would assist in putting a stop to an illegal sale of game by the poacher.

In case the House should agree with your committee in the propriety of making the proposed alteration, it is evident that game, becoming thereby an article which may be legally sold, will acquire a real value; and that those who have the means, should be encouraged to supply the market with it, and have a fair claim to any additional protection which it may be capable of receiving, and which may be compatible with other considerations.

In considering this part of the subject, it appears to your committee, that the present laws do not afford a sufficient summary remedy against the depredations of persons who are in the habit of trespassing upon the lands of others, in the pursuit of game; they therefore recommend, in addition to the alteration proposed in the laws as to the purchase and sale of game, that the present laws relating to the latter species of offence should be rendered more summary.

Your committee do not hold out to the House, that poaching can by this or any other mode be suddenly and entirely put an end to: it being evident that many of those now engaged in it are of a description not likely to be deterred from it by any thing but an absolute impossibility of carrying it on, which the most sanguinary laws would not create; but your committee must state to the House their conviction, that the purchase and sale of game, under regulations, will have the effect of decreasing the number of those who are at present concerned, or who might henceforward engage in that practice, which greatly conduces to demoralize the lower orders of society; and that those persons, whose residence upon their property in the country is in all points of view so eminently beneficial, will find in these measures

great additional facilities in the preservation of that which affords,
them the amusement and recreation to which they are fairly
entitled.

Your committee have, in conformity to the opinions here
submitted to the House, directed their chairman to move for
leave to bring in a bill or bills, for effecting the several objects
herein recommended for the consideration and adoption of the
House.

April 18, 1823.

In conformity with the above report, a bill has been brought
into the House of Commons to make the selling of game legal;
and the following are its chief provisions :—

Two or more magistrates at any petty sessions may grant
licenses for one year to any householder (not being an innkeeper
or victualler, or stage-coach owner, or waggoner) to buy game
of a qualified person, and to sell the same.—Persons on taking
a game certificate are to state to the clerks of the commissioners
or surveyors of the district, whether they are qualified to kill
game by virtue of having a real estate ; and every such statement is to be published by the commissioners for the affairs of
taxes, in the lists of certificates directed to be advertised by them;
and any person may inspect the entries of such statements in a
book to be kept by such clerks or surveyors, on payment of one
shilling to such clerk or surveyor.—Qualified persons taking out
game certificates are to be exonerated from the penalty for selling
game, as well as licensed persons for buying it; but licensed
persons are to be prohibited from buying, except of qualified
persons. Power is given, on information, to search a licensed
person and his family, for game, unlawfully purchased or procured ; and also to search an unqualified person and his premises,
for game suspected to have been illegally procured. Innkeepers
not to be liable to penalties for game sold in their inns for con-

sumption; provided such game shall have been purchased by such innkeeper from licensed persons.—Game sent by public conveyances is to be entered in the way-bills, stating the names and places of abode of the persons by whom, and to whom, such game is sent.—Power is also given to search public conveyances for unentered parcels of game.—The act is not to affect the rights now possessed by lords and ladies of manors, nor to extend to Scotland or Ireland.

The agitation of this momentous question in parliament stirred up some of the most humane hearts in the kingdom in support of the intended measure; some of whom were actuated by the purest moral motives, as regards the *prevention of crime*, which they thought this measure was likely to effect, by legalizing the sale of an article that was in constant demand; and thus, by supplying the market according to act, the trade therein might be taken out of the hands of those who would contravene the law—for the radix of this species of *crime* is mooted in the consumers—and the certainty of sale.

The bill now (June 4) pending in parliament, which I have just recited, will probably undergo some trifling alterations; but there is little or no doubt as to its passing:—it will merely authorize the sale of game by persons legally appointed, and in all probability will have no further retrospective influence on those statutes already passed relative to game, and which have been stated, and copiously illustrated, in the preceding pages of this volume.

TECHNICAL TERMS.

A brace of black game.

A leash of black game.

A pack of black game.

To raise a black cock or pack.

A brace of grouse.

A leash of grouse.

A brood or pack of grouse.

To raise grouse.

A brace and a half of partridges.

A brace of partridges.

A covey of partridges.

To spring partridges.

A brace of quail.

A brace and a half of quail.

A bevey of quail.

To raise quails.

A brace of pheasants.

A leash of pheasants.

A ni (or nid) or brood of pheasants.

To push or spring a pheasant.

A couple of woodcocks.

A couple and a half of woodcocks.

A flight of woodcocks.

To flush a woodcock.

A couple of snipes.

A couple and a half of snipes.

A wisp of snipe.

To spring a snipe.

A team of wild ducks.

A gaggle or flock of geese.

A wing of plover.

A trip of dottrell.

A couple of pointers or setters.

A leash of pointers or setters.

A couple of spaniels.

A couple and a half of spaniels.

A brace of hares.

A leash of hares.

To start or move a hare.

A pair—A couple—A brace.—A pair is two united by nature *(par)*; a couple by an occasional chain *(copula)*; and a brace, by a noose or tie. A pair of swans. A couple of hounds. A brace of partridges—a pair is male and female; a couple, two accidental companions; a brace, tied together by the sportsman. He keeps a pair of pheasants in the hen roost. We saw a couple of pheasants feeding on the bank. You shot a brace of partridges.

FORM OF A SPORTSMAN'S JOURNAL.

Where killed.	When.	Black Game.	Grouse.	Partridge.	Pheasant.	Woodcock.	Snipe.	Ducks or Wildfowl.	Hare.	Rabbit.	Total each Day.	Shots missed.	Remarks on each Day.
	Monday..												
	Tuesday..												
	Wednesd.												
	Thursday												
	Friday …												
	Saturday.												
	Total each Week.												

GENERAL OBSERVATIONS.

Receipts for making Shoes resist Water.

One pint of linseed oil, half a pound of mutton suet, eight ounces of bees' wax, and one pennyworth of rosin: the whole to be boiled together, and warmed before using.

Another.—If the shoes are new, take half a pound of bees' wax, a quarter of a pound of rosin, and one pound of tallow: to be boiled well together, and warmed before using.

N. B. It is hardly necessary to mention that the shoes should be cleaned well from the dirt, and perfectly dry, before the application of either of these receipts.

Shoe-soles can have a layer of cork or waxed canvas introduced between.—This will be found a very excellent precaution.

DUTY ON DOGS.

For every greyhound, kept by any person, whether his property or not, £1.—For every hound, pointer, setting dog, spaniel, lurcher, or terrier, the annual sum of 14*s.*—For every dog not being such as aforesaid, kept by any person, whether the same be kept for his own use, or the use of any other person, the annual sum of 8*s.*

But this duty is not to extend to dogs not six months old the proof of which to lie on the owner.

Persons compounding for their hounds, to be charged £36.

SHOTS IN AN OUNCE.

Of B. B. One ounce contains 59 pellets.
B.	Do.	67
No. 1	Do.	85
2	Do.	112
3	Do.	135
4	Do.	187
5	Do.	228
6	Do.	261
7	Do. - -	304
8	Do.	640
9	Do.	930

ADDENDA.

Barren Pairs.—When the nest of a partridge happens to be destroyed late in the season, the old birds remain together, and are called a *barren pair*. However, it sometimes happens, that what are called a barren pair prove to be both cocks—the following appears to be the reason :—when, after pairing time, two cock birds happen to be left in the same district, after the animosity which accompanies genial desire has subsided, the two male birds associate and remain together, if undisturbed, until the following spring.— But barren pairs, whether male and female or otherwise never lie well, or in other words, are much more difficult to approach than a covey.

A dog's skin is not porous, and for that reason he never perspires : the excretions, whether from sickness or otherwise, make their way through the eyes, nose, and mouth. The dog's skin will not easily absorb mercurial nor any other ointment, though it will become sore from external application.

THE END.

𝕎orks

ON

DOMESTIC ECONOMY, AGRICULTURE, AND RURAL AFFAIRS.

1.

JENNINGS'S DOMESTIC CYCLOPÆDIA, be-
ing a complete Code of Family Information. Just completed in 13
Parts, (which may be had by one or more at a time,) price 2s. 6d
each, forming 2 large Volumes, Octavo, price 1l. 14s. boards, an
Original Work, entitled the FAMILY CYCLOPÆDIA, being a
Manual of useful and necessary knowledge, alphabetically arranged;
comprising all the recent Inventions, Discoveries, and Improvements
in Domestic Economy, Agriculture, and Chemistry; the most approved methods of curing Diseases, with the mode of Treatment
in cases of Drowning, other Accidents, and Poisons; observations
on Diet and Regimen; a comprehensive account of the most
striking objects in Natural History, Animate and Inanimate; and
a detail of various processes in the Arts and Manufactures: also,
a concise View of the Human Mind and the Passions, with their
particular application to our Improvement in Education and
Morals. By J. JENNINGS. This Original and Valuable Work
is printed in double Columns, on good Paper, and contains
upwards of *Fifteen Hundred* Pages of Information, immediately
connected with the pursuits of Domestic Life. By means of
close printing and a large page, it comprehends as much matter
as is usually found in *six* Volumes of an ordinary size, and cannot
fail, it is presumed, of being considered a most valuable addition to
a FAMILY LIBRARY.

*** *The Family Cyclopædia,* by JAMES JENNINGS, contains a large mass of information, on subjects connected with
the domestic economy of life. In matters of science and art,
the author has made his selections from sources of the best
authority. The original materials supplied by himself are credit-
able to his observation, good sense, and benevolence. Almost
every topic of general interest will be found in this comprehensive and judicious compilation, treated in a clear and familiar
manner. As a book of daily reference in the common concerns
of life, it will be found to afford important assistance, and its
great practical utility will, we have no doubt, ensure it a ready
introduction, and a favourable reception, in every intelligent
family. In addition to the great heads of domestic economy,

agriculture, and chemistry,. this work points out the best modes of curing diseases, and obviating the effects of sudden accidents; and presents also an outline of the mind and passions, with a view to the improvement of morals and education.—*Monthly Magazine, July*, 1821.

2.

A COMPLETE SYSTEM OF PRACTICAL

AGRICULTURE; including all the Modern Improvements and Discoveries, and the Result of all the Attention and Inquiry which have been bestowed on this important Science during the last Fifty Years; the whole combining and explaining, fully and completely, the PRINCIPLES AND PRACTICE OF MODERN HUSBANDRY, in all its Branches and Relations. With an Appendix of the Laws relating to Agriculture, particularly of the Relative Rights of Landlord and Tenant, Forms of Leases, Setting out Tithes, &c. &c. By R. W. DICKSON, M. D. HONORARY MEMBER OF THE BOARD OF AGRICULTURE, &c. &c. In two large Volumes, in Quarto, illustrated with upwards of *One Hundred Engravings*, (Thirty of which are coloured from Nature,) representing improved Implements, the various Grasses, and the principal Breeds of Sheep and Cattle, from Original Drawings. Originally published at six guineas; but the stock having passed into the hands of the present Proprietors, they have reduced its price to four guineas, thus rendering it the cheapest as well as most comprehensive work on the subject extant.

This Work includes *every* Branch of the important Art to which it relates, particularly the best Methods of Planting Timber of every Description, and the improved Management of Live Stock, with a Description of Implements and Buildings; the Theory of Soils and Manures, the best Methods of Inclosing, Embanking, Road-making, Draining, Fallowing, Irrigating, Paring and Burning; the improved Cultivation of Arable Lands, and of all Kinds of Grain, Artificial Grasses, &c; presenting the most useful and comprehensive Body of Practical Information ever offered to the Public on the interesting Science of Agriculture; a Science which is so intimately connected with the Welfare and Happiness of the BRITISH EMPIRE

Reliance is placed on the Support of *Noblemen, Clergymen, Country Gentlemen,* and intelligent *Farmers,* in this Undertaking, which is calculated to remove the Obstacles that have hitherto presented themselves to the Introduction of Agricultural Improvements.

3.

The FARMER'S COMPANION, being a complete system of Modern Husbandry; including the latest Improvements and Discoveries, in Theory and Practice. Extracted and Abridged from the above Work, by the same Author. In two Volumes, royal 8vo. Second Edition, Price two Guineas, in boards. The leading feature of excellence by which this work is distinguished, is that minuteness of Practical Detail, which renders it singularly adapted to the purposes of Agriculture. The whole scope of its contents has a constant and immediate connexion with the daily pursuits of the Farmer, the Implements of Husbandry he employs, the Modes of Agriculture he adopts, and the system of Pasture and Feeding he pursues. These multifarious topics are all treated with simplicity and clearness; so that the Work presents an ample, but distinct display of every subject connected with the practical objects of a Farm. It is illustrated with upwards of *One Hundred Engravings*, representing improved Implements for Farming, various Breeds of Cattle, Sheep, &c.

4.

AGRICULTURAL REPORTS OF GREAT BRI-
TAIN, drawn up under the immediate Sanction of Parliament, and published by Authority of the Board of Agriculture.

SHERWOOD and Co. beg leave most respectfully to submit to the Notice of the Nobility, Clergy, Gentry, and Farmers of the United Kingdom, the following truly National and most important Work. It consists of New and Improved Editions of the County Surveys and unites every Species of Information relative to the *Statistical Economical, Agricultural,* and *Commercial* State of each County Sixty Volumes, uniformly printed in Octavo, and illustrated with Maps and Plates, are already published, viz.

ENGLISH AND WELCH REPORTS.

Bedfordshire, by Mr. Batchelor ... 15 0	Lincoln by A. Young, Esq 2d Edition	12
Berkshire, by Dr. Mavor 18 0	Middlesex, by J Midleton, Esq. 2d Ed.	15
Buckingham by the Rev. St. John Priest 12 0	Monmouthshire, by Mr. Hassell, of East	
Cambridgeshire, by the Rev. Mr. Gooch 9 0	Wood, Pembrokeshire	7
Cornwall, by Mr. Worgan 12 0	NORTH WALES, by Walter Davies, A.M.	12
Cheshire, by H. Holland, Esq. ... 10 6	Norfolk, by A. Young, Esq.	12
Derbyshire, Vol. I. by Mr. Farey, sen. ... 21 0	————, by Mr. Kent	6
————, Vol. II ditto 15 0	Northamptonshire, by W. Pitt, Esq. ...	8
————, Vol. III. ditto 18 0	Northumberland, Cumberland, and West-	
Devonshire, by C Vancouver, Esq. 18 0	moreland, by Messrs. Bailey, Culley,	
Dorsetshire, by Mr. Stevenson 12 0	and Pringle	9
Durham, by Mr. Bailey ... 10 6	Nottinghamshire, by Robert Lowe, Esq. ...	5
Essex, 2 vols by A. Young, Esq 24 0	Oxfordshire, by A. Young, Esq. ...	12
Gloucestershire, by T. Rudge, B D. 0	Shropshire, by the Rev. J Plymley, A M.	9
Hampshire, by C. Vancouver, Esq. ... 16 0	SOUTH WALES, by Walter Davies, A.M.	
Herefordshire, by J. Duncombe, A. M. ... 7 0	2 vols.	24
Hertfordshire, by A. Young, Esq. 8 0	Staffordshire, by Mr. Pitt ...	9
Huntingdonshire, by Mr. Parkinson ... 9 0	Suffolk, by A. Young, Esq. ...	10
Jersey and Guernsey, by T. Quayle, Esq. 10 6	Surrey, by Mr. Stevenson	15
Kent, by Mr. Boys 8 0	Sussex, by the Rev. A. Young ...	15
Leic. and Rutland, by Pitt and Parkinson 15 0	Warwickshire, by Mr. Murray ...	8
Lancashire, by Dr. Dickson, revised and	Worcestershire, by Mr. Pitt ...	10
prepared for the press by Mr. Stevenson,	Wiltshire, by Mr Davis ...	
author of the Surrey Report ... 14 0	Yorkshire, (East Riding), by Mr. Strickland	12

SCOTCH REPORTS.

Argyleshire, by Dr. J. Smith 9 0	Nairn and Moray, by the Rev. Wm. Leslie	14
Berwickshire, by Mr. Kerr 14 0	Peebles, by the Rev C Findlater ...	10
Caithness, by Capt. Henderson ... 15 0	Ross and Cromarty, by Sir G S. Mackenzie	9
Clydesdale, by Mr. Naismith ... 7 0	Roxburgh and Selkirk, by the Rev. Dr.	
Dumfries, by Dr Singer 18 0	Douglas	
East Lothian, by Mr. Somerville ... 6 0	Sutherland, by Capt Henderson ...	12
Galloway, by the Rev S Smith ... 9 0	West Lothian, by Mr. Trotter	
Hebrides, by J Macdonald, A. M. ... 21 0	Report of the Committee of the Board of	
Inverness, by the Rev. Dr Robertson ... 14 0	Agriculture, concerning the culture and	
Kincardineshire, by Mr. Robertson ... 12 0	use of potatoes ...	7

Any of the Reports may be had *separately;* and, it is presumed every Nobleman, Clergyman, Gentleman, and Farmer, should be in possession of the Survey of his own County, and of the adjoining Counties, as also of any other, which may contain that Species of Information most conducive to his own Local Interests.

₊ *Complete Sets* of the *Reports* are recommended to the various AGRICULTURAL SOCIETIES and BOOK CLUBS, as forming an aggregate of General Information, and point of Reference on all occasions.

5.

The NEW FARMER'S CALENDAR, or, Monthly Remembrancer of all Kinds of Country Business. By JOHN LAWRENCE. Fifth Edition; with large Additions; in One Volume. Price 12s. boards.

Also, by the same Author,

A GENERAL TREATISE on CATTLE, the Ox, the Sheep, and the Swine, in One Volume. Second Edition; with large Additions. Price 12s. boards.

A PHILOSOPHICAL and PRACTICAL TREATISE on HORSES, and on the Moral Duties of Man towards the Brute Creation; in Two Volumes. Third Edition; with large Additions. Price 1l. 1s. boards.

" Mr. Lawrence writes with spirit, good sense, and humanity; and we recommend his Work to the notice of our Readers."—*Monthly Review.*

The MODERN LAND STEWARD, in which the Duties and Functions of Stewardship are considered and explained, with its several Relations to the Interests of the Landlord, Tenant, and the Public; in One Volume. Price 10s. 6d. boards.

" If the Author had not already recommended himself to the Public by his " New Farmer's Calendar," and other Works, the judicious observations and useful hints here offered would place him in the list of those Rural Counsellors who are *capable* of giving advice. His sentiments on general subjects, expand beyond the narrow boundaries of vulgar prejudice; and his good sense is forcibly recommended to us, by its acting in concert with a humane disposition." *Monthly Review.*

** The above Works comprehend a body of useful practical knowledge, relative to the CULTURE OF THE SOIL, POLITICAL ECONOMY, VETERINARY MEDICINE, and the MANAGEMENT OF LIVE STOCK. Complete in Five large Volumes, 8vo. Price 2l. 15s. 6d. in boards.

6.

PRACTICAL OBSERVATIONS on the BRITISH GRASSES, especially such as are best adapted to the laying down or improving of Meadows and Pastures; likewise an enumeration of the British Grasses. By WILLIAM CURTIS, Author of the Flora Londinensis, Botanical Magazine, Lectures on Botany, &c. &c. Sixth Edition; with considerable Additions. By JOHN LAWRENCE, Author of the New Farmer's Calendar, &c. &c. To which is subjoined, a short Account of the Causes of the Diseases in Corn, called by Farmers the Blight, the Mildew, and the Rust. By Sir JOSEPH BANKS, Bart. In 8vo. illustrated with coloured Plates. Price 9s. in boards.

7.

The CODE OF AGRICULTURE; including Observations on GARDENS, ORCHARDS, WOODS, and PLANTATIONS. By the Right Hon. Sir JOHN SINCLAIR, Bart. Third Edition in one Large Volume, 8vo. Price £1 4s. in boards.

This *Third Edition* is considerably improved by a number of Valuable Remarks, communicated to the Author by some of the most intelligent Farmers in England and Scotland.

The Subjects particularly considered, are

1. The Preliminary Points which a Farmer ought to ascertain, before he undertakes to occupy any extent of Land.

2. The Means of Cultivation which are essential to ensure its success.

3. The various Modes of improving Land.

4. The various Modes of occupying Land.

5. The Means of improving a Country.

" Sir John Sinclair's ' Code of Agriculture' is one of the most valuable books of the year. In point of fact, it concentrates the knowledge amassed during the experience of a long life, passed amidst the best opportunities of collecting information; and exhibits the results in a form condensed with great logical acumen, of all the Labours and Publications of modern writers on Agriculture. It merits, therefore, a place in the library of every Gentleman and Farmer in the Country, and of every individual who has any turn for Agricultural pursuits."—*Monthly Magazine.*

8.

A SYSTEM of SHEEP GRAZING and MANAGEMENT, as practised in Romney Marsh. By DANIEL PRICE, of Appledore, Kent. In 4to. Illustrated with Plates, price 2l. 2s. in boards.

9.

A PRACTICAL TREATISE on the Parturition of the COW, or the extraction of the Calf, and on the Diseases of Neat Cattle in general; with the most approved Methods of Treatment, and best Forms of Prescription, adapted to Veterinary Practice. By EDWARD SKELLETT, Professor of that part of the Veterinary Art. In one large Volume, Octavo, price 18s. plain, or 1l. 7s. with the Plates accurately coloured. Illustrated with thirteen highly-finished Engravings.

10.

The GRAZIER'S READY RECKONER, or a useful Guide for Buying and Selling Cattle; being a complete set of Tables, distinctly pointing out the Weight of Black Cattle, Sheep, and Swine, from three to one hundred and thirty Stones, by *measurement;* with Directions, showing the particular parts where the Cattle are to be measured. By GEORGE RENTON, Farmer. A new Edition, corrected. Price 2s. 6d. sewed.

11.

The HORTICULTURAL REPOSITORY, containing Delineations of the best Varieties of the different Species of ENGLISH FRUIT; to which are added, the BLOSSOMS and LEAVES, in those instances in which they are considered necessary:—accompanied with full Descriptions of their various Properties, Time of Ripening, and Directions for Planting them, so as to produce a longer Succession of Fruit; such being pointed out, as are particularly calculated for open Walls, and for Forcing. By G. BROOKSHAW, Author of the " *Pomona Britannica.*"

Illustrated by beautiful Coloured Plates, on which the Fruit is represented in its natural size : the whole Work comprehending nearly Two Hundred Specimens of the choicest Species. In two Volumes, royal 8vo. price 6l 10s. in boards, or may be had in Twenty-six Monthly Parts, by one or more at a time, at the original price of 5s. each.

*** This Work is the result of several years' practical observation. Its obvious utility and general interest, will instantly occur to the reader; it being a curious fact, that while an enlarged taste for Botany has been directed, both scientifically and popularly, to every branch of its extensive province, this particular department has been most neglected, the proper selection of Fruit Trees being generally very imperfectly understood; a deficiency which it is the object of the present work to supply.

12.

A TREATISE on the Improved Culture of the STRAWBERRY, RASPBERRY, GOOSEBERRY, and CURRANT, in which are pointed out the best Methods of obtaining ample Crops of those Fruits. To which are prefixed, Descriptions of the most esteemed Varieties. Illustrated by four coloured Plates, representing the choicest Specimens of the Fruit, drawn in its natural size. By THOMAS HAYNES. In 8vo. price 10s. in boards.

13.

A PRACTICAL TREATISE on Brewing the various sorts of Malt Liquor; with Examples of each Species, and the mode of using the Thermometer and Sacchaiometer : the whole forming a complete Guide in Brewing every Description of Ale and Beer. To which aie added, General Instructions for making Malt, and Tables of the Net Duties of Excise on Strong and Table Beer, payable by Common Brewers in Town and Country. By ALEXANDER MORRICE, Common Brewer. Sixth Edition; with the Laws, (now first added,) relating to Brewers and Maltsters. By JOHN WILLIAMS, Esq. Price 10s. 6d. boards.

14.

The FAMILY DYER AND SCOURER, being a complete treatise on the Arts of Dying and Cleaning every article of Dress, Bed and Window Furniture, Silks, Bonnets, Feathers, &c., whether made of Flax, Silk, Cotton, Wool, or Hair : also Carpets, Counterpanes, and Hearth Rugs. Ensuring a saving of Eighty per cent. By WILLIAM TUCKER, late Dyer and Scourer in the Metropolis. Second Edition, price 4s. 6d. boards.

𝔉𝔦𝔢𝔩𝔡 𝔖𝔭𝔬𝔯𝔱𝔰.

1.

BRITISH FIELD SPORTS; embracing Practical Instructions in Shooting, Hunting, Coursing, Racing, Fishing, &c.; with Observations on the Breaking and Training of Dogs and Horses; also, on the Management of Fowling Pieces, and all other Sporting Implements. By WILLIAM HENRY SCOTT, Author of the " Sportsman's Repository." In One large Volume, 8vo. Price 1l. 18s. in boards; or on Royal Paper, with proof Impressions of the Plates, 3l. 3s.

*** This Work is beautifully printed on fine wove Paper, hot-pressed, and illustrated with upwards of Fifty highly-finished Engravings;—Thirty-Four on Copper, executed in the most characteristic Style of Excellence, by those eminent Artists, Scott, Warren, Greig, Tookey, Davenport, Ranson, and Webb; from Paintings by Reinagle, Clennell, Elmer, and Barrenger; the remainder are cut on Wood, by Clennell, Thompson, Austin, and Bewick.

That we have had several good and elaborate Treatises upon *particular* divisions of FIELD SPORTS is readily acknowledged; but we have had no Work of a portable nature, comprehending the *whole* of them. This inconvenience, however, is removed by the present Publication. The ' BRITISH FIELD SPORTS' is divided into Sections, each forming a Subject which is treated separately and systematically, with all the necessary Legal Information appertaining to it. The Author's object has been to present, in as compressed a form as real utility would admit, Instructions in all the various Field Sports in Modern Practice; thereby forming a Book of general Reference on the Subject, and including, in One Volume, what could not otherwise be obtained without purchasing many expensive ones. The means he has possessed for accomplishing so desirable a purpose, he trusts, have enabled him to produce such a Work on the Subject of Field Sports, as, in point of Paper, Printing, Illustration, and Embellishment, is not to be equalled in the English Language.

" It gives us pleasure to observe the respectability of the Work, entitled " BRITISH FIELD SPORTS." In this kingdom, the Sports of the Field are highly characteristic and interesting. As gentlemanly diversions, they have been pursued with an avidity as keen, and a taste as universal, as the relish of Nature's beauties A corresponding value is set on them, and an appropriate polish is added by time and practice; the various minutiæ in the knowledge of which, and the technical distribution of this knowledge, together with Facts, Instructions, and Anecdotes form the basis of this valuable publication."—*Farmer's Journal.*

2.

The SPORTSMAN'S REPOSITORY; com-
prising a Series of highly-finished Engravings, representing the
HORSE and the DOG in all their varieties; executed in the Line
Manner, by JOHN SCOTT, from original Paintings by Marshall,
Reinagle, Gilpin, Stubbs, and Cooper: accompanied with a com-
prehensive, historical, and systematic description of the different
Species of each, their appropriate Uses, Management, and Im-
provement; interspersed with Anecdotes of the most celebrated
Horses and Dogs, and their Proprietors; also, a Variety of prac-
tical Information on Training, and the Amusements of the Field.
By the Author of " BRITISH FIELD SPORTS." Beautifully
printed in Quarto, and embellished with *Forty* highly-finished
Copper-plate Engravings, and numerous Wood Cuts. Price 3l. 3s.
in boards. It may also be had in Six Parts. Price 10s 6d. each.

3.

THOUGHTS on FOX and HARE HUNTING;
in a Series of Letters to a Friend. By PETER BECKFORD, Esq.
With numerous illustrative Notes by the Author. A new and
elegant Edition, in One Volume, 8vo. Price 14s. boards.

₊ The Publishers beg leave respectfully to recommend the *present* Edition of Mr. Beckford's
valuable Work, to the notice of Sporting Gentlemen. It will be found to surpass all preceding
Editions, in elegance of paper, printing, and illustration. The Author's Notes, also, which
have long been omitted, are here introduced, and render this Edition peculiarly desirable.

4.

An ESSAY on HUNTING; comprising Hunting,
Lawfulness, Benefits, Pleasure, Pastime, Game, Scent, Hounds,
The Horse, Huntsman, Sagacity, &c. &c. &c. Copied *verbatim*
from the Original Edition, printed in the year 1733, and elegantly
printed in 8vo. Price 7s. boards; or, in 4to. 12s.

We consider the Sporting World much indebted to those who have caused the re-printing of this
Work; the style is excellent. Some of the Author's ideas may, since its first publication (1733),
have been controverted, or become obsolete, through the benefits of modern experience; but
good sense, combined with practical knowledge and a playful fancy, are apparent in every subject which the Author touches on; and we candidly express our belief, that few modern Volumes
will afford the reader more pleasure.—*Sporting Magazine.*

5.

SPORTING ANECDOTES, original and selected,
(many of them concerning our late King); including numerous
Characteristic Portraits of Persons in every Walk of Life, who
have acquired notoriety from their Achievements on the Turf, at

the Table, and in the Diversions of the Field : the whole forming *a complete Delineation of the Sporting World.* By PIERCE EGAN. Embellished with a characteristic Frontispiece, representing Eight Varieties of Sporting Amusements. Price 9s. boards, or 12s. elegantly bound.

6.

SCOTT'S SPORTSMAN'S POCKET-BOOK; THE SPORTSMAN'S CALENDAR; or, Monthly Remembrancer of Field Diversions. By W. H. SCOTT, Author of " British Field Sports." Elegantly printed in a neat pocket size, and hot-pressed. Price 5s. in boards.

7.

SOMERVILLE'S celebrated Poem of the CHASE; to which is annexed, his Poem of FIELD SPORTS ; with Memoirs of the Author, and an Essay on the Chase. By EDWARD TOP-HAM, Esq. Illustrated with Engravings, by Mr. SCOTT. Price 6s. in boards.

8.

SONGS of THE CHASE; including some also, on RACING, SHOOTING, ANGLING, HAWKING, AR-CHERY, &c. Handsomely printed in foolscap 8vo. with appropriate Embellishments. Second Edition. Price 9s. boards.

9.

The SHOOTER'S COMPANION; or, Directions for the Breeding and Management of Setters and Pointers, and for the Treatment and Cure of Diseases, to which all Dogs are liable, with an Historical description of Winged Game. The Fowling-Piece, considered particularly as it relates to the Use of Percussion Powder. The various methods of making Percussion Powder, and the best pointed out. Of Scent :—the Olfactory Organs anatomically explained; with the Reason why one Dog's Sense of Smell is superior to another's. Shooting illustrated; and the Art of Shooting Flying exemplified, and clearly laid down. The Game Laws, and every information connected with the Use of the Fowling-Piece. By T. B. JOHNSON. New and Improved Edition. Price 9s. in boards, with Plates.

" This is a well written and well arranged production ; containing much interesting information, not only to the professed Sportsman, but to those who may occasionally seek this fascinating recreation. We may add, that it is not the production of any ordinary Sportsman, but of one who can enjoy the pleasures of the Library as well as those of the Field, and can wield a Pen as well as a Fowling-Piece."—*Literary Chronicle.*

10.

KUNOPÆDIA; being a Practical Essay on the Breaking and Training the ENGLISH SPANIEL or POINTER. To which are added, Instructions for attaining the Art of SHOOT-· ING FLYING; more immediately addressed to *young* Sportsmen, but designed also to supply the best means of correcting the errors of some *older* ones. By the late W. DOBSON, Esq. of Eden Hall, Cumberland. In One Volume, 8vo. Price 10s. 6d. boards.

11.

The ANGLER'S GUIDE; being a New Complete Practical TREATISE on ANGLING, for Sea, River, and Pond Fish. By T. F. SALTER, Gent. Fifth Edition, corrected, revised, and improved. To which is now first added, the Author's celebrated Treatise on Trolling, or Fishing for JACK and PIKE: the whole illustrated with numerous Engravings and Cuts of Fish, Flies, &c. In a neat Pocket Volume. Price 7s. in boards.

"I write from practice, not from book compile."

" This little book is quite studded with well-executed Engravings on wood, exhibiting faithful Portraits of every object of the Angler's pursuit, as well as explanatory representations of all the Implements employed in Fishing, with full and clear Instructions for using them. We were much pleased to find some ample Instructions for Trolling, which we have hunted for in vain in Walton and Cotton "—*Annals of Sporting*, Nos. 22, 23.

Also, by the same Author,

The YOUNG ANGLER'S GUIDE; abridged from the above Work. Price 1s. 6d.; and the TROLLER'S GUIDE. Price 3s.

12.

The ANGLER; a Poem, in Ten Cantos; comprising proper Instructions in the Art, with Rules to choose Fishing-Rods, Lines, Hooks, Floats, Baits, and to make artificial Flies; Receipts for Pastes, &c. By T. P. LATHY, Esq. With upwards of Twenty Wood Cuts. Price 10s. 6d. boards.

13.

The SPORTSMAN'S PROGRESS; a Poem, descriptive of the Pleasures derived from Field Sports: with Thirteen Wood Cuts. Price 1s. sewed.

14.

TAPLIN IMPROVED; a COMPENDIUM of FARRIERY; wherein is fully explained the Nature and Structure of the Horse. By an EXPERIENCED FARRIER. Price 2s. boards.

15.

TEN MINUTES' ADVICE, to every Person going to purchase a Horse. Price 1s.

16.

BOXIANA, brought down to the present time.
The Fourth Volume of BOXIANA ; containing all the Transactions of Note connected with the Prize Ring during the years 1821, 1822, and 1823, in which are developed the fighting capabilities of the men, and short Dissertations on Pugilism, together with many characteristic Traits and Anecdotes never before published The whole preceded by a practical Treatise on Training for pugilistic encounters, including the whole of Captain Barclay's method, after which he trained Tom Cribb and himself; the whole tending to promote the utility of the Art of SELF-DEFENCE in a national point of view.   Illustrated with highly finished whole-length Portraits, in attitude, of G. HEAD, BILL NEAT, CY. DAVIS, JACK MARTIN, JACK COOPER, JOSH. HUDSON, PETER CRAWLEY, and DICK CURTIS, drawn from life, and Engraved in a superior style of excellence. By PERCY ROBERTS. Price 18s. in boards.

Also,

BOXIANA, Vol. I. Containing every Battle and Anecdote, connected with scientific Pugilism, from Figg and Broughton to the period of Cribb's Championship. Price 12s.
BOXIANA, Vol. II. From Cribb's Championship to the first Battle of Painter and Spring. Price 14s.
BOXIANA, Vol. III. During the Championship of Cribb to Spring's challenge to all England. Price 18s. The three Volumes contain Fifty Portraits of celebrated Pugilists.

17.

A VISIT to the FIVES' COURT. By ROBERT CRUIKSHANK. Being a faithful Picture of that celebrated place of Amusement, for displaying manful Sports. Price 2s. accurately coloured ; or may be had, framed and varnished. Price 6s.

⁎⁎ The Artist has been very successful in delineating, not only *Portraits,* but the *Costume* and *Mannerism* of all the Professors and Amateurs of the Prize Ring; amongst which stand prominently, Spring, Neat, Randall, Martin, Gregson, Cribb, Cy. Davis, Isaac Bitton, Belcher, Burn, Jack Cooper, Richmond, Mr. Jackson, Mr. Soames, Mr. Watson, the Marquis of Worcester, Lord Fife, Captain Hugh Seymour, &c. &c.

18.

The ROAD TO A FIGHT. A Picture of the FANCY GOING to a FIGHT at Moulsey Hurst, (measuring in length 14 feet,) containing numerous Original Characters, many of them Portraits; in which all the FROLIC, FUN, LARK, GIG, LIFE, GAMMON, and TRYING-IT-ON, are depicted, incident to the pursuit of a PRIZE MILL: dedicated, by permission, to Mr. Jackson, and the *Noblemen* and *Gentlemen* composing the Pugilistic Club. A copious

and characteristic Key accompanies the Picture, written by
PIERCE EGAN. " For I am nothing, if not CHARACTER !" Price
of the Picture and Key, 14s. plain, or 1l. coloured, neatly done
up in a box, for the pocket. Also, framed in black and gold, and
varnished, in which way it will be found a very interesting piece
of furniture for the GENTLEMAN or SPORTSMAN, (measuring in
(length 43 inches, by 15 wide,) price 1l. 12s. plain, or 1l. 18s.
coloured.

19.

The ANNALS of SPORTING, and FANCY GA-

ZETTE; a Magazine entirely appropriated to Sporting Subjects
and Fancy Pursuits; containing every thing worthy of Remark,
on Hunting, Shooting, Coursing, Racing, Fishing, Cocking, Pugilism, Wrestling, Single Stick, Pedestrianism, Cricket, Billiards,
Rowing, Sailing, &c. &c. Accompanied with Striking Representations of the various Subjects, Drawn and Engraved by Eminent
Artists. The Work is elegantly printed on a fine Paper; the
Drawings made from *life* by the most esteemed Artists; and the
representations of Field Sports, either engraved in the first style
of excellence, or beautifully *coloured after Nature*. It is further
illustrated with numerous Engravings on *Wood;* the Subjects
including the best breeds of Horses and Dogs, as well as every
species of Game. Every Six Numbers form a Volume, price 17s.
each, handsomely half-bound. The Fifth Volume, just completed,
is embellished with the following spirited Engravings.

1. Brutus, a Bull Terrier, by Landseer.
2. Topthorn, a celebrated Hunter.
3. A folding Plate of Gymnastic Exercises.
4. Terriers and Polecat.
5. Foxes, by Landseer.   .
6. Neptune, a Newfoundland Dog, by Ditto.
7. Nelson, a Setter.
8. Barefoot, from a painting by Herring.
9. Buonaparte's White Charger, Marengs.
10. A fine Portrait of Tom Cribb.
11. A celebrated Hackney.
12. Stag and Hind.
13. Five Fox Hounds, of the Hatfield Hunt, engraved in a
masterly manner, by Landseer.

20.

An Engraved Plan and Survey of Epsom RACE

COURSE, on a Scale of six chains to an inch, or thirteen inches
and a third to a mile; with an Appendix of Distances, constitu-
ting a most useful auxiliary of information to all Gentlemen
interested in the business of the Turf. By WILLIAM KEMP,
Land Surveyor. On a large sheet, price 6s. neatly coloured.

9 781332 034604